MONEY AND LIBERTY

MONEY AND LIBERTY

IN THE PURSUIT OF HAPPINESS
&
THE THEORY OF NATURAL MONEY

James Turk

Published by
Wood Lane Books
London, England

woodlanebooks.co.uk

Paperback ISBN: 978-1739851118
eBook ISBN: 978-1739851101

For my two sons,

Charles and Geoffrey.

Table of Contents

List of Charts & Tables

The Importance of Happiness

Happiness is the meaning and purpose of life, the whole aim and end of human existence.

Aristotle

Aristotle is described as one of the 'pioneers of happiness' by Mark Setton, founder of the not-for-profit Pursuit of Happiness Project. He explains:

> According to Aristotle, happiness consists in achieving, through the course of a whole lifetime, all the goods - health, wealth, knowledge, friends, etc. - that lead to the perfection of human nature and to the enrichment of human life.[1]

That is a good definition of happiness and one with which most people would agree.

Every individual makes countless decisions throughout the day to improve their situation in life. Yet everyone defines happiness for themselves, and society flourishes when the pursuit of it follows the first principle of natural law - do no harm.

The fundamental premise of this book is that happiness is achievable with a basic knowledge of natural MONEY while living life ethically within natural law with unimpeded LIBERTY.

Author's Preface

Believe nothing you hear, and only
one half that you see.

Edgar Allan Poe

With this book I hope to disprove Poe's time-honoured adage. My aim is that you will believe all of what you see herein. To accomplish this objective, I use the same tool used to deduce that the earth is not flat - reason. Even though the earth appears flat when gazing at the horizon from a beach, logical deduction proves that it is not.

The application of logic to testing and examining the merits of conventional wisdom is not new. For example, logic was used to conclude that the earth is indeed round long before Magellan circumnavigated the globe.

Around 250-BCE, an inquisitive Egyptian named Eratosthenes questioned the conventional wisdom of his day that the earth was flat. He set out to analyse the matter, using logic and some basic mathematics. He placed a vertical pole in the ground in Aswan and another in Alexandria at noon and used the shadow to measure the angle of the sun. To his amazement, but perhaps not to his surprise, the angles of the sun were different, proving to himself at least if not the rest of the world, that the earth was indeed round. By using the difference in these measurements of the sun's angle at two locations, which he then related to the distance between Aswan and Alexandria, he calculated that the earth's circumference was 24,662 miles, understating the true polar circumference by a mere 198 miles. No computers, no round the world cruises, no satellite photos or even a telescope — just pure logic with the help of some basic maths.

Regrettably, some economic and political beliefs are formed from mere glances that lead to spurious conclusions. Others are based on outdated or flawed theories rather than a sound and methodical analysis of human action. By relying herein on reason and my own experiences in banking and international finance, I overthrow faulty conventional wisdoms as well as many popular tenets about money that will surprise some readers but may be rebuffed by others choosing to obsessively cling to unfounded beliefs.

To be best prepared for what awaits you, be open-minded. Many ideas that may seem new here in the present day are in fact well-established principles upon which the best elements of our civilisation are built. They have lifted countless millions from poverty and made possible the comfortable standard of living that we enjoy today. Unfortunately, many of these vital principles have been forgotten or ignored, the most important of which is the inextricable link between liberty and sound, politically honest money.

Money and Liberty provides me with the opportunity to bring together a lifetime of countless, varied experiences and a wide-ranging knowledge acquired over more than six decades. I am pleased to share with you this personal journey of learning about money in my pursuit of happiness.

As an American, I write from the perspective of one who has come to understand the country's unique position within the history of civilisation and humankind's quest for liberty, which is the freedom of an individual restrained only by natural law to act in their pursuit of happiness. Yet I also bring a broader perspective, having lived in seven countries and travelled to dozens of others in a unique business and entrepreneurial career comprised of international banking, economics, and investments.

Taking material from my earlier writings to bring them up to date in a unified work, I use logic and insight to explain the essential role of money in attaining liberty. The result is what I call the Theory of Natural Money. Its central element is that money is gold, and throughout this work I use these two words synonymously. It asserts that natural law governs money, whereas currency is a human construct with the sole purpose of enhancing the circulation of money.

Money is a tool that simply holds wealth in the form of purchasing power that is conveyed in a transaction from the payer to the payee. We work to acquire purchasing power, which we then exchange into money that we hold until we are ready to spend or save our purchasing power or place it at risk by investing it.

Producing anything requires our time. It is important to realise that work, whether manual or mental, creates purchasing power, and work only occurs because people devote to it their most precious asset, which is each individual's time on earth. Therefore, it is useful to think and make economic decisions in terms of the time and effort that go into acquiring purchasing power and the result to be achieved from it, rather than focusing on the money or currency used to make the decision. This thoughtful insight by Ralph Waldo Emerson on the useful outcome of one's time spent working is revealing: 'The desire of gold is not for gold. It is for the means of freedom and benefit.'

As inflation began to climb in the 1960s and gold rose above the $35 per ounce rate prevailing since 1934, I soon realised that critical thinking outside of what I had learned in earning my university degree in international economics was necessary to understand money. My natural curiosity and penchant to learn new things coupled with the motivation to continually seek opportunities for improving my knowledge, and more generally, my situation – along with an unending eagerness to spend the concomitant amount of time on the demanding work needed to achieve the goals I had set for myself – put me on a course that began with good fortune when I joined a major Wall Street bank. I received extensive training and invaluable knowledge from experienced bankers who had lived and worked through the Great Depression. Their guidance enabled me to build upon the fundamental insights I had learned from my parents about money, savings, and debt. It marked the beginning of my quest to learn and then develop a deep understanding of money and how the world of finance and investments really works.

These accomplished bankers understood and conveyed to me the traditional role of banks as sound financial enterprises that serve principled businesses and individuals within the community. Upon this base I then built a solid understanding of money through my international work experiences and an extensive reading of history and monetary theory. This perspective has enabled me to critically observe, both from within a major bank and from the outside after resigning from it in 1980, the on-going descent of politically honest money that is occurring in conjunction with the insidious degeneration of institutions,[2] particularly, the large financial centre banks.

Central banks 'have been turning to new and riskier investments'[3] while financial centre mega-banks have become high-risk hedge funds with mountains of questionable assets and entangling derivatives that pose incalculable risks to the global economy. More worryingly, they now first serve the State, rather than the community. Government and politicians feed off a machine called the banking system that creates currency by printing banknotes and entering keystrokes to spawn bank deposits. I agree with Thomas Jefferson's assertion that 'banking establishments are more dangerous than standing armies'.[4] What in Jefferson's day was just a threat posed by banks has become a real and present danger that has upended for

Americans what their forebears achieved by winning a War for Independence nearly 250 years ago.

Put another way, banks and the flawed currency system they perpetuate have become a threat to our liberty because the managers of the country's largest banks work hand-in-hand with misguided and/or self-serving politicians who have lost sight of essential American principles. The delicate balance between individual liberty and the power of government, and particularly the U.S. federal government, so thoughtfully crafted by the framers of the American Constitution was disrupted and worn away throughout the twentieth century by the corruption of the monetary system they established.

I will explain why liberty needs sound, politically honest money. Liberty cannot survive – let alone thrive – if banks serve the State instead of society. To achieve this essential and laudable goal, banking and currency must be separated from government intervention and removed from control by the State.

It is not my intention to write a comprehensive history of money and banking. History is like being on the crow's nest of the *Titanic* but watching where the ship has been, rather than where it is heading. Rather, my aim is to simply describe how our monetary system ended up on the wrong course. It began three centuries ago by the British government taking the easy – but dishonest – alternative to get the currency needed to fight the Nine Year's War. It opened Pandora's box by accepting the fraudulent practice of fractional reserve banking.

Famed economic historian John Kenneth Galbraith observed: 'A constant in the history of money is that every remedy is reliably a source of new abuse.' In other words, attempts to make fractional reserve banking work, even though it is unworkable, are not only unsuccessful, they result in a worse outcome. Today, fractional reserve banking has become the harsh wedge being relentlessly used by the State in its attempts to gain greater power by breaking the inextricable link between money and liberty.

Given the time-honoured maxim that money is power, fractional reserve banking enables the State to gain power by creating purchasing power out of nothing, masquerading this empty currency with no substance as a money substitute, and then enforcing through legal tender laws the circulation of this pseudo-money. It is therefore unfortunate that when the term 'money' is generally used, people too often neglect the time an individual spends to honestly earn purchasing power, the value of which can be eroded by schemes devised by the State. Banking and currency as they have come to be practiced robs individuals of their time spent to earn purchasing power and increases the power of the State to the detriment of individual liberty.

Recognising this potential for abuse, principled political leaders created rules to contain the excesses possible by this fractional reserve banking system, including those written into the American Constitution, but over time those safeguards became misinterpreted, ignored, or completely forgotten. After more than a century of total war and growing authoritarian control by governments, the excesses of this currency and banking system and the resulting erosion of liberty have been laid bare.

We individuals are unable to control the excesses of the State and have been placed in an inferior position. The solution is simple. Take away from government the power to create currency and allow the free, unfettered use of our planet's natural money, gold.

Acknowledgements

What I have learned about money, investments and banking has helped me to make many good decisions in my pursuit of happiness, which is the foremost quest of every sentient being. I am pleased to share in this book much of my acquired knowledge as well as my perspective on money and liberty with the hope that readers will find it as useful as it has been to me.

I am a first generation American, the son of immigrants who left Europe a century ago in the pursuit of happiness by seeking an opportunity to improve their lives. Fortunately, they achieved their goal through their wisdom and hard work. I have benefitted immensely from them, including an innate need to understand the world around me, for which I am forever thankful.

I adhere to the basic principles of the Austrian school of economics, named after the country where several brilliant luminaries became its first proponents and whose insights have been invaluable. I have learned much from their body of work, which is derived from perceptive observations of human action and economic thought built on natural law principles and logical deduction. It is the same approach that I apply to the ideas and new concepts in this book.

I owe my sincere gratitude to countless people from whom I have learned so much, including those who have passed down their knowledge over the ages through their writings. It is my good fortune to have learned from the books of giants like Ludwig von Mises, Murray Rothbard, Milton Friedman, Ayn Rand, and many, many others.

I would particularly like to thank John Rubino, with whom I had the pleasure and privilege to co-author *The Coming Collapse of the Dollar*, *The Collapse of the Dollar*, and *The Money Bubble, What To Do Before It Pops*. His expert eye helped make sure that my contribution to those books was well written, which I have this time endeavoured to do on my own. I am also indebted to my colleague Alasdair Macleod for his feedback after reviewing my first draft. My numerous references to his articles posted online at Goldmoney Insights is a testament to how much I admire his work. I am most grateful to Howard Buffett and the organisations that published his magnificent 1948 speech to make his insight and knowledge available for future generations of Americans who share his love of liberty.

My most heartfelt thanks are for my darling wife, Margaret, for her unbounded thoughtfulness throughout the countless disappearances into my home office to write this book.

Finally, I have written *Money and Liberty* for educational purposes, so it does not set out any financial or investment advice. And of course, the analyses, opinions and viewpoints expressed herein are entirely mine.

James Turk
31 July 2021

Definition of Key Words

The beginning of wisdom is to call
things by their right name.

Confucius

Words are powerful tools that unfortunately can be used maliciously. A propagandist twists the meaning of words to achieve a desired end, which is particularly effective when repeated over time.

In describing the changes brought about by oligarchs attempting in 427-BCE to seize control of a democracy at Corcyra sponsored by Athens, Thucydides wrote that 'words had to change their ordinary meaning and to take that which was now given them'. An example today is *inflation*. People now see it to mean rising prices, rather than the debasement of a currency causing a decline in its purchasing power. By disconnecting from its true meaning, people are tricked into believing that inflation is a permanent feature, obscuring that government and central bank mismanagement of the currency is its source.

Another example is how the mainstream media, serving political interests, changed the 'U.S. unemployment report' to become the 'U.S. employment (sic) report'. The key to good reporting is accurately placing the focus where it best highlights the matter at hand, which traditionally has not been those gainfully employed, but rather, the number of workers unemployed but seeking work.

To adhere to the Confucian maxim above, it is necessary to define some key words relating to money. These may differ from how they are generally used today. When properly defined, national currencies such as U.S. dollars, euros and British pounds are not money because none of them are a tangible asset.[5] They are currencies, a word created in seventeenth century London by the nascent banking industry to explain something that circulated current but was not money itself.[6] Gold is money, but unlike national currencies, gold's circulation as currency at present is limited.

The following definitions become clear as they are explained and used throughout this book.

Banknotes	Promissory notes of banks that circulate as paper currency
Cryptocurrency or crypto	A virtual currency that uses encryption to control the issuance of units and verify the transfer of those units
Debasement	The insidious theft of people's time they expend to earn purchasing power, orchestrated furtively by the State though its degrading of the currency, which until the emergence of the socialist State in the twentieth century was regarded as a crime against humanity and a felony punishable by death
Deposit currency	A deposit in a bank that circulates within the banking network by cheque, plastic card, wire transfer and digitally through the internet
Digital currency	Any type of currency that circulates electronically through digital computer systems over the internet or through private networks
Economic calculation	The process by which an individual uses units of money to subjectively judge value to make decisions about prices to spend, save or invest their purchasing power
Economic value	The value expressed in units of money of an item arising from its marketability
Fiat currency	Ledger currency not redeemable in precious metal coin; it circulates by force of law imposed by government, not because of the quality of the currency
Fractional reserve banking (FRB)	The fraudulent banking practice that creates phantom purchasing power and results in a bank's inherent insolvency because its liquid assets are not sufficient to pay the liabilities due to depositors,

	which eventually leads to a crisis manifest by a run-on-the-bank and its possible collapse
Gold price	A misnomer because gold is money, so it has a rate of exchange, not a price
Inflation	A decline in a currency's purchasing power over time that manifests as rising prices of goods and services, but is in essence a tax that robs people of their time spent on work to earn purchasing power
Inherent value	A feature existing within an item that makes it useful, as determined subjectively by each individual
Ledger currency	Two types of currency, banknotes and deposits, that are liabilities recorded on bank ledgers and have value because they are backed by bank assets
Marketability	An item's usefulness in exchange for other items
Money	Any tangible asset that can be used to efficiently store, measure, and express units of purchasing power across space and time, but gold, a unique natural element, best meets the four requirements of money
Money substitute	Any currency circulating in place of money
Numeraire	An unalterable defined weight of gold that is the unit of account used to measure value in economic calculation
Payment	The amount of money needed to extinguish an obligation
Price	The amount of money to which a buyer and seller willingly agree for the purchase and sale of a good or service
Product	Any good or service with economic value, namely, a thing that individuals need or want
Purchasing power	An abstract concept consisting of measurable units of value that are conceived in two radically different ways and conveyed in commerce as money or alternatively by money-substitutes to provide their

owner the financial means to buy, save, or invest:

- Earned purchasing power (EPP) is created by a labourer's time and effort expended on the production of a tangible asset or service that has measurable units of economic value and/or inherent value
- Phantom purchasing power (PPP) is contrived by accounting in banks that results in the unnatural, artificial spawning of units of account with no inherent value that dishonestly masquerade as earned purchasing power even though labour is not expended in their creation and their economic value is solely dependent on promises

State	When capitalised, an organised political body that claims the presumed absolutist authority for the compulsory use of force over an individual and the community within a defined territory to retain unimpeded control to perpetuate its existence, without the express consent of the governed and often at the expense of individual rights
Unfettered market	Unrestricted human interactions not limited, controlled, or influenced by government intervention
Value	An item's usefulness, which determines the demand for it that together with its available supply determine its marketability and its price
Virtual currency	A type of digital currency that is decentralised and circulates through designated software within a virtual community
Wealth	Real property, money, tangible products, capital, and financial assets that are measured in units of purchasing power, and as used herein, excludes intangible assets like knowledge, experience, and other similar qualities of understanding because they are immeasurable

1. Introduction

It is well enough that people of the nation do not understand our banking and monetary system, for if they did, I believe there would be a revolution before tomorrow morning.

attributed to Henry Ford[7]

America does not need a revolution to establish a proper monetary system. That outcome was already achieved after its War for Independence as evidenced by key monetary principles enshrined in the Constitution, which its framers and those elected officials who understood the framers' intent implemented into law with the Mint Act of 1792. Unfortunately, these building blocks central to America's prosperity and its citizens' liberty were allowed to wither away until they were eventually cast aside. So if the uprising speculated in the above quote were to occur, it would be to re-establish what has been lost.

We do need to return to the monetary system that enabled America to achieve the good it once achieved by allowing liberty to flourish, which occurs when individuals are not hindered in their pursuit of happiness. A monetary system that treats everyone equitably is needed, and the journey to achieve that goal begins with a keen understanding of money. Providing this knowledge is the overriding objective of this book, which focuses upon the unique, inimitable usefulness of gold as money and its inextricable link to liberty. Freedom needs sound, politically honest money that only gold makes possible, which explains gold's importance to each and every one of us who cherish the inalienable right to act, speak, or think as one wants within the bounds of natural law, which is the building block upon which American jurisprudence is based.

One's outlook on money and currency fundamentally changes when gold is properly viewed in this way. It is a view that correctly identifies gold's vital importance to society, and stands in stark contrast to today's popular, but incorrect characterisation of gold as an 'investment', which is the first of several misconceptions that need correction in this introduction to the Theory of Natural Money.

Gold is Not an Investment; It is Money

In Congressional testimony in 1912, John Pierpont Morgan, then and now considered to be America's leading financier of that time, uttered one of the most memorable and widely quoted – and often misquoted – lines about money ever spoken: 'Money is gold, and nothing else.'[8]

Mr Morgan's definition of money was not doubted or even questioned by the Congressional representatives and journalists in attendance. But he defined money in a way that is unfamiliar and therefore baffling to the modern mind. So to make his quote understandable today, it is frequently altered, whether wittingly or not, to 'gold is money'.

No doubt further confusing and also somewhat shocking to the modern mind, Mr Morgan – who a century later remains a pre-eminent historical figure – did not say that 'money is the dollar'. It is only gold and nothing else.

Nor was Mr Morgan defining gold. His statement simply highlighted how gold is used, not what it is, which can be defined as a natural element ranking number 79 on the periodic table. Gold is natural money.

An essential argument of this book is that dollars, euros, pounds, and cryptos are currencies, not money. Each is a money substitute. On the other hand, 'money is gold, and nothing else', which means that everything else being used in payment as the means to complete a transaction is a money substitute circulating in place of gold.

There are critically significant differences between money and a money substitute, which derive from their origin in Anglo-Saxon law. In addition, currency circulating as a money substitute is subjective, while money is objective. These distinctions apply to all national currencies, none of which are money in the true legal and accounting sense of that word.

Currency and language are the means by which we communicate; the use of money in economic calculation and intelligible speech are the mental tools that impart understanding. As language is to speech, then currency is to money. In other words, all the languages of the world are means of speech, just like all the currencies of the world attempt to fulfil money's role in society by communicating value in the market process. Though my analysis is applicable to all national currencies, I focus on two: the British pound and the U.S. dollar.

I begin with an analysis of the British pound because of its formative role in the development of currency. The British currency and banking system emerged as the most influential alternative because of the global sway of the British Empire. Few today understand or appreciate the significant contribution by Sir Isaac Newton that helped Britain and its Empire become the most formidable force in global commerce for three centuries. Then being on the winning side of two world wars, Britain ensured the dominance of the system it created, which continues to this day.

The detailed analysis herein reveals the fatal flaws upon which the British currency and banking system was built that continue to plague economic activity and undermine individual liberty. This analysis leads to a review of an alternative solution to redirect currency and banking back to the correct path.

In the twentieth century, the U.S. dollar succeeded the British pound and became the world's pre-eminent national currency, a position it still holds. But the dollar's longstanding role is changing, and not for the better as the country continues to stray even further from the essential monetary principles of the American Constitution.

I focus on this venerable document and the American Declaration of Independence to explain the link between money and liberty. Both documents articulate bold proclamations of fundamental principles and truths on money and liberty that should not be constrained by any geographic, political, or ideological boundary.

Capitalism

> Capitalism is what people do when you leave them alone.
>
> Professor Kenneth R Minogue

When left alone, what people do is pursue happiness, or contentment when viewed broadly. The pursuit of happiness is the natural result of human behaviour. It is the logical and obvious conclusion that people act to improve their situation by satisfying their needs and wants. If they are hungry, they eat. If tired, they sleep. If they need new clothes, they work to earn purchasing power and then shop by interacting with other people. This interaction is a voluntary process as each individual makes countless decisions by participating to some extent in our market economy to satisfy their needs and wants to improve their situation in their pursuit of happiness.

Kenneth Minogue taught at the London School of Economics until his retirement in 1995 and was a prominent spokesperson for British conservatism. His definition of capitalism quoted above is my favourite, but I would add to it an ancient Greek proverb that further explains capitalism and the vision of all experienced, sagacious capitalists: 'Great civilisations are built by old people who plant trees knowing they will never sit in their shade.' True capitalism is all about the long-term and how we in the present leave the planet for our progeny.

The foundation of capitalism is ethical human interaction based on private property and natural money, gold. Capitalism is not about short-term profits, environmental degradation, survival of the fittest, or any of the other misstatements as it is often portrayed. Nor is capitalism about fiat currency, central banks, and government intervention.

The correct view of capitalism contrasts with a statement by the Fabian socialist John Maynard Keynes: 'In the long run we are all dead.' These words, which are frequently quoted, are among the most grossly irresponsible statements ever spoken by an economist. Actions have consequences and planning for the next generation is an essential element of economic activity. What is important to society and indeed our civilisation is not just how we live, but what we leave for future generations. That the planet's environment has become so scarred is an indication of how much we have accepted the ills of progressivism, socialism, and authoritarian control by the State and moved away from capitalism, private property, and individual liberty. The State today rarely leaves people alone.

Keynes's comment is typical of socialists and progressives who focus on satisfying their innate yet perverse need to control others rather than where their attention should be directed, which is the consequences of their actions. For example, they proclaim their vision that forces the world to drive electric cars so that we do not inhale the emissions from exhaust pipes, yet they are blind to the number of the plants needed to generate the electricity to power all those new cars. Decisions cannot be made on emotion. In our world of limited resources, they must be made and based on sound economics and that requires trustworthy money spent and invested at a true cost of capital. These are requirements that only gold can provide. Further, to achieve the best possible outcome decisions need to be unfettered by government involvement and their market interventions.

For Keynes the long run has arrived, and he wrote his own fitting epitaph:

> Practical men, who believe themselves to be quite exempt from any intellectual influences, are usually the slaves of some defunct economist. Madmen in authority, who hear voices in the air are distilling their frenzy from some academic scribbler of a few years back.

It is time to bury Keynes, Keynesianism, and socialism. We need to instead focus on reality to correctly identify the practice that made possible humankind's progress throughout the millennia, which is capitalism.

Economic Calculation and the Market Process

Economic calculation is central to capitalism. It is the process by which individuals participate in an economy based on free markets and freedom of choice.

We are driven by our needs - food, clothing, shelter - and our wants - that shiny new car. We act in our self-interest to improve our situation, but we have limited resources, which is the purchasing power we have earned and accumulated as a producer of economic goods, whether directly, for example, as a farmer or an artist, or indirectly by contributing to the production of a marketable good, say, as a labourer in a manufacturing plant or as an office worker. With our purchasing power we then make decisions about what we choose to purchase for immediate use by interacting with others, which is the market process, or save our purchasing power for use in the future. Economic calculation is the process by which an individual makes decisions to spend, save or invest their purchasing power held as money and currency.

Economic calculation is a cognitive act in which preferences are evaluated, sorted, and then chosen. We make countless decisions throughout our lifetime to buy or sell now, later, or not at all, which highlights the essential role of money. Money makes this calculation possible. It is the measuring stick used in one's decision-making process, which highlights money's critical importance to each individual and to society. But money does more than that. It has a dual role.

We rely on money every time we buy or sell any product, whether a good or service, by using it as currency. Thus, money not only makes economic calculation possible, it is also the product used as the means of exchange. In this role, money enables an unequivocally completed payment for the purchase of goods or services that extinguishes the exchange.

The unhampered exchange of product is essential to a free market economy. We act voluntarily and peacefully as producers and consumers to meet our individual goals, and each person's action provides the basis for exchange with other participants in the market process. Each person improves their situation by completing the exchange, assuming no force or fraud. This process is the formative foundation upon which our society is built and develops. Through this market process, we cooperate to raise our standard of living, which is the cumulative result of each individual living their life in pursuit of their unique view of happiness, namely, making choices given the alternatives on hand and their own resources.

Ludwig von Mises, Friedrich von Hayek, and other economists of the Austrian School have clearly explained that the market process is central to capitalism and our civilisation's prosperity because they efficiently allocate our limited resources to their most effective use. The Mises Institute's profile of its namesake explains this viewpoint as follows:

> Mises concluded that the only viable economic policy for the human race was a policy of unrestricted laissez-faire, of free markets and the unhampered exercise of the right of private property, with government strictly limited to the defence of person and property within its territorial area.

While the free market may not be perfect - and nothing is in our imperfect world - experience has proven that it is by far the best and most equitable method to allocate resources. We have seen that the only other way, which is activity directed by government in a socialistic, centrally planned, command economy, leads to catastrophic results.

Central planning led to the failure of the Soviet Union and disastrous economic consequences for the people of Cuba, Venezuela, and all other countries where government planning was believed to be superior to individuals exercising the free will that leads to the spontaneity of free markets. Although central planning has been discredited because of its manifest failures, people still believe in and practise central planning. For example, it is practised by the U.S. government's central bank, the Federal Reserve, in its control of interest rates that are set by a committee rather than the free market and the natural forces of supply and demand.

It is indisputable that economic calculation is the essential building block of our society because it differentiates humans from other life on earth. Each of us has the innate ability to calculate, the outcome of which is relative values. If some product is in high demand and its supply is constrained, as may occur for example with wheat in a time of drought, its relative value will normally result in a higher price. If we need it, we buy it or seek a suitable alternative.

Prices are expressed in units of account, typically as an amount of national currency. We use dollars and other national currencies to calculate whether in our own subjective judgement a product is worth the price at which it is being offered, but prices alone are insufficient to make an informed decision when spending purchasing power. The price of a bottle of Coca-Cola was five cents in 1886, and it remained that price until 1959, when it began rising in response to the U.S. federal government's debasement of the dollar. This example makes clear the need to understand what is happening to prices and purchasing power to enable accurate economic calculation that results in good decisions.

Purchasing power is usually measured and expressed in terms of national currency but can also be viewed in terms of a weight of gold. Though not commonly used today, an ounce or a gram of gold, or simply a 'goldgram' as I prefer to call it, is a unit of account that is useful in economic calculation and for measuring purchasing power.

For example, Figure 1 presents the price of a barrel of West Texas Intermediate crude oil indexed to a base of 100. It measures monthly the oil price in three national currencies and goldgrams, so the chart illustrates the change in their purchasing power since 1950. Given the importance of energy in our everyday life to maintain the standard of living that our society has achieved, I deliberately chose crude oil as a proxy for all sources of energy, but the message conveyed by the chart in Figure 1, to which I frequently refer throughout this book, also works well when assessing the price of other commodities.

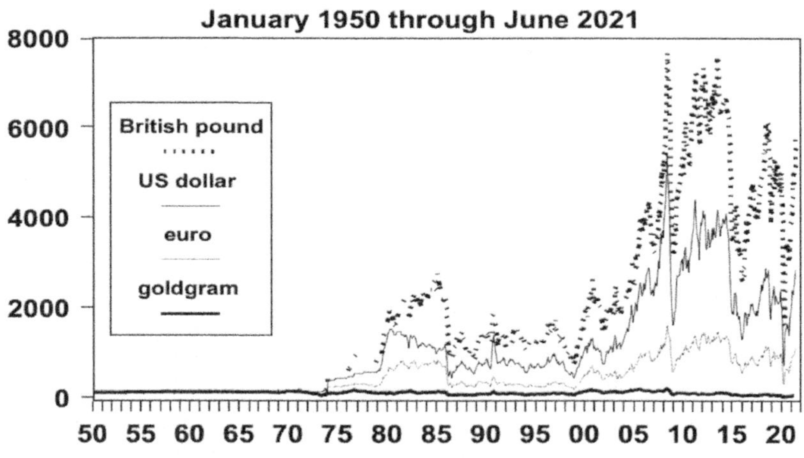

Figure 1 – Crude Oil Prices (Base of 100)

One barrel of West Texas Intermediate crude oil is the same today as it was in 1950. It is an unchanged unit of the same commodity. One goldgram is also an unchanged unit throughout this period, but the dollar and the other national currencies are different because they have lost purchasing power. Only their name remains the same over these seven decades.

The dollar and other national currencies are not useful as a measuring tool because each is an elastic unit of account whose purchasing power can stretch or shrink depending on actions by a country's government and its banking system, including its central bank. These changes to a unit of purchasing power are the equivalent to changing the length of an inch or the weight of a tonne, both of which would cease to be useful measures if they were stretched or shrunk by governments or banks.

These changes in the measuring unit of national currencies inevitably end up diminishing – not enhancing – their purchasing power. This ebbing is not usually noticed because it occurs like small knife-cuts repeating over long periods of time, which cumulatively make them harmful.

For example, gold exchanged for $20.67 per ounce in 1913, the year the Federal Reserve was established, and is nearly $1800 per ounce today. An ounce like other measures – the inch, metre, gallon, etc. – and gold are the same today as they were in 1913, but the dollar has endured over a century of debasement. The purchasing power of national currencies shrinks like a melting ice cube. They are flawed tools because an unvarying yardstick is needed to measure value, which Figure 1 makes clear.

In contrast to a dollar and other national currencies, a goldgram is always the same unchanging unit over time. A goldgram today is identical to a goldgram in 1950 or any other point in time throughout history. Further, gold does not change from natural causes because unique among the known universe, gold does not suffer from entropy.

We must take care not to confuse the name of the unit of account with the measurement function the unit is intended to accomplish. If the name remains unchanged, it is easy to ignore a unit's change in purchasing power inadvertently but mistakenly, like the erosion of purchasing power that is occurring with the dollar and other national currencies. But some changes even apply to gold.

While gold's purchasing power is consistent over lengthy periods of time, as evidenced by Figure 1, its purchasing power can increase or decrease in the short-term. This outcome results from ephemeral changes in the supply of and demand for gold as well as the ever-changing supply and demand of crude oil. Consequently, the goldgram price of crude oil may fluctuate daily and even minute-by-minute, as is typical for market prices, but as the chart in Figure 1 illustrates, a goldgram maintains its purchasing power over time.

Fluctuations also occur in gold's exchange rate to national currencies in what is called a 'floating rate' regime. Gold's purchasing power may therefore appear to be volatile in relation to that of national currencies and for those commodities whose price in a national currency remains unchanged during the period gold's purchasing power is being evaluated. The reality is that, while currencies may be floating in relation to each other, when their purchasing power is compared to that of gold, they are sinking.

Most currency today is created by government and circulates under its control, which is a relatively recent phenomenon. Government involvement and regulation of national currency has increased throughout the twentieth century to the present, but more to the point, national currencies are not money. The differences between money and currency will become clear from Chapter 4, which explains the four functions of money.

Purchasing Power and Wealth

Purchasing power is the financial means to buy goods and services or make an investment. It is an abstract concept but can be visualised by applying it to any product available for purchase. In our world of limited resources, you either have or do not have the purchasing power needed to buy what you need or want.

When national currencies were delinked from gold in 1971, their purchasing power began eroding as illustrated in Figure 1. The barrel of crude oil that cost $2.57 in 1950 now takes $73.47 to purchase. In contrast, a gram of gold over the past seven decades purchases broadly the same quantity of crude oil, from we which we can draw two important but distinct conclusions.

First, it is widely believed that oil is becoming more valuable because its price over time has generally been rising when measured in terms of national currency. A different picture emerges when using a weight of gold to calculate and express the oil price, from which we can conclude that oil is no more valuable today than any time over the past seven decades. Its usefulness as measured in BTUs is unchanged as is its price, but only when measured in terms of gold, except for inconsequential price fluctuations in the short-term that result from transitory factors causing changes in oil's supply and/or its demand.

Housing prices offer another example. The result is eye-opening when prices are calculated using gold.[9] Like the price of oil, house prices rise and fall slightly but when measured in terms of goldgrams, remain largely unchanged over long periods of time. From that observation we can conclude that houses are shelter, not an investment, which corrects another misconception that is widely held today. Rising house prices result from the debasement of the currency used to measure the price.

Second, Figure 1 reinforces the point that gold is not an investment. An investment is made in the expectation of increasing one's wealth over time. Gold did not achieve that goal. A goldgram bought roughly the same quantity of crude oil at any moment over this seven-decade period. Gold did not increase one's wealth; it only preserved it by maintaining the same level of purchasing power, which is what money is supposed to do.

Wall Street legend Warren Buffett has often said that he would rather own a productive asset in preference to gold, and Figure 1 illustrates his point. A productive asset like farmland, a manufacturing company paying dividends to shareholders, or a building generating rent from tenants can be expected to increase wealth over time, but gold does not. Gold may not be a productive asset, but it is a useful asset. It is money that preserves purchasing power and can be used to buy, sell, and through economic calculation measure the value of assets.

This observation confirms the point that gold is not an investment, nor does one *invest* in gold. Money is not an investment, nor it is expected to generate a return. You should expect a return only if you use money to make an investment, thereby putting your money at risk.

As money, gold is simply bought, held, and then sold or spent, and is no more an investment than Swiss francs bought by someone before travelling to Zurich. One holds gold for the same reason that one keeps national currencies on deposit in a bank account. National currencies and gold are liquidity ready for spending, saving or or investing but are not investments themselves.

One can change the purpose of national currencies and the gold that one holds. Instead of using them for their liquidity, currencies can earn interest income when loaned to others or placed with a bank in a time deposit. The same is true for gold, which can be loaned or deposited in a bullion bank, though the minimum account size these banks require is beyond the reach of everyone but the wealthiest individuals. This change of purpose places the asset in a different category of wealth, a financial asset, which also changes the risks in relation to owning it.

Financial assets are not true wealth in and of themselves. Financial assets are only claims to wealth because they are not consumable goods and services. They can buy goods and services to satisfy one's needs and wants only after they have been converted into money or currency acceptable to the payee.

When categorised by their essential nature and excluding immeasurable assets like knowledge and will, there are two fundamentally different classes of wealth: tangible assets and intangible financial assets. These two asset classes are then cut across by a unique type of wealth, purchasing power, which represents one's liquidity and their potential to purchase any of the different assets, whether for need (e.g., commodities for food or a house for shelter), investment (e.g., equities and debt instruments), or pleasure (e.g., personal effects and travel). These various categories of wealth are illustrated in Figure 2 along with the type of risk incurred when owning these two different classes of wealth.

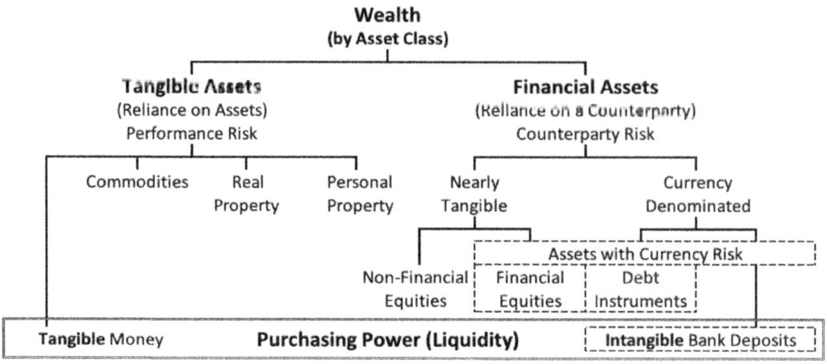

Figure 2 - Categories of Wealth

The line between these two assets classes can be blurred by nearly tangible financial assets. These are equities in companies that mainly own tangible assets. Examples are agribusiness companies with substantial land and equipment holdings, mining companies and other commodity producers, transportation companies like railroads, and other companies with similar characteristics.

The counterparty risk inherent in financial assets is fundamentally different from the performance risk that exists with tangible assets. For example, the benefit that you expect to receive from a tangible asset is inherent in the asset itself and can be stated as whether the asset will perform as expected. Will the farmland produce the same amount of crops this year as last? Is the rental income of the office building you own reliable? Will gold continue to preserve your purchasing power? The same question about performance holds true for a house that provides you with shelter.

Tangible assets are real things that exist in the physical world. Real property includes land and anything fixed to it, like buildings. Personal property includes all movable assets.

I have purposefully distinguished between gold and commodities. Gold in its true historical, social and legal sense is a unique form of wealth. As explained in Chapter 3, gold is not a commodity. It is a tangible asset, but with attributes unlike anything else that differentiate it from commodities. Its unique attributes make gold money.

The other major category of wealth is the myriad financial assets that are available. The anticipated benefit of a financial asset depends on a counterparty. Financial assets have performance risk as well in the sense that an investment might not achieve the expected return, but the value of these assets is always dependent to some degree on a counterparty, which introduces two other risks.

The first is credit risk. The debt instruments you own are dependent on the person, company, or government to whom you loaned purchasing power. A bond is only as good as the financial capacity and willingness of the debtor to repay its debt. The counterparty of national currencies is the central bank that issued the banknotes you hold, or the bank where the currency is deposited and the creditworthiness of the government insuring those deposits, which introduces the second risk of financial assets: currency risk. The government may force its central bank to debase the currency to erode its purchasing power over time from inflation.

Debasement is a hidden tax and the unethical subversion of the quality of the circulating currency. The preservation of purchasing power throughout history has always been the purpose of money, but as has happened countless times by government actions and is today occurring throughout the world, currency is being purposely debased so that prices are targeted to rise by 2 per cent per annum or more because of central bank stated policy.

Equities in companies are a financial asset, but some are nearly tangible. A company's assets are owned indirectly through the ownership of shares. An example of a nearly tangible equity is a commodity producer owning land and other tangible assets needed for production, with relatively few currency denominated assets. In contrast, a bank's assets consist primarily of assets denominated in a national currency, and banks typically own relatively few tangible assets. This difference in the composition of assets is important when considering currency risk, which cannot be ignored because of the dozens of currencies that have collapsed to worthlessness since the end of the Second World War.

Money and investments are assets, but they are distinguished by distinct concepts and owned for different reasons. Both are held in one's portfolio, leading to the frequent question on whether to hold 'cash or stocks', which can be more precisely expressed as whether to hold liquidity or investments. Portfolios require both but for entirely different uses and goals.

Warren Buffett also once famously declared that gold 'has no utility',[10] but I disagree. If gold had no utility and was not useful, it would be worthless and without any price. Yet gold's rate of exchange to the dollar is not far from a record high and roughly six times higher than when Mr Buffett stated his view. So gold does in fact have utility, and its usefulness is clearly illustrated in Figure 1.

Gold's utility arises from its usefulness in economic calculation. In other words, gold has value because it is useful as money, but gold is a sterile asset. As such and in contrast to investments, gold does not generate cash flow. In fact, money and currency do not produce wealth. They are useful tools that store your purchasing power and can be productively employed in commerce and make investments, and for those reasons have value, but money and currency are not in and of themselves wealth producing instruments.

Consequently, an increase in gold's rate of exchange to any national currency does not, nor can it, increase wealth in a macro sense. Its rising exchange rate increases the purchasing power of the person holding gold, but there is no new wealth being created for society when gold's rate of exchange rises in terms of the currency in which gold is being measured. Using the dollar as an example, when gold's exchange rate rises, the purchasing power embodied within the existing quantity of dollars declines relative to that of gold but is not lost. This purchasing power, which has already been created, simply moves from the holders of dollars to the holders of gold.

As is clear from the chart in Figure 1, accurate economic calculation using national currency is fundamentally fraught with problems and near impossible. It is comparable to measuring a length of cloth with an elastic tape measure.

When we ignore the elastic measurer and use a yardstick that cannot be stretched, an entirely different picture emerges. Even when not using gold as currency, we can still rely on gold as the reliable measuring stick that makes rational calculation possible in an irrational national currency regime. It is a timeless principal as evidenced by this quote from *An Enquiry into the Paper Credit of Great Britain* by London banker Henry Thornton in 1802:

> We assume that the currency which is in all our hands is fixed, and that the price of bullion moves; whereas in truth, it is the currency of each nation that moves, and it is bullion which is the more fixed.

In contrast to our pre-First World War ancestors, we have learned to calculate in terms of national currency, rather than grams or ounces of gold. Thoughtful, prudent economic calculation is not possible with the ever-changing measuring stick that national currencies have become.

Comparing Value and Price

Value and price are the two key elements of economic calculation. Price is the objective result of an exchange. Value is the subjective judgement each person exercises before agreeing to the exchange.

Price is a label attached to a marketable good or service. It is a quantification of value placed on goods and services by the seller, and a transaction occurs if the buyer and seller reach an agreement on value, which is a market price. So price is the measurement used in an exchange with someone else in the marketplace. It is an outcome of economic calculation and a measure of how the buyer and seller each view the value of the item in their transaction.

Value comes from what someone considers to be useful in meeting their immediate needs or wants. Value is what something is truly worth, which is determined by its usefulness to the individual who needs or wants the item being valued, but a time-honoured adage applies: 'One person's junk may be another person's treasure.' For this reason, an item's marketability will vary, as will its price.

The market process enables the essential price discovery needed for two different people with different wants and needs to bid on an object and agree to the price. Without this label communicating value judgements needed to facilitate the exchange of goods and services, buyers and sellers would not be able to transact. So prices are essential to the market process that is the fundamental base upon which our society is built, grows, and develops. Value is determined and expressed by each individual's subjective judgement and communicated in terms of prices.

Because value is subjective, it is therefore fleeting and not certain. Anything that has value today may not have value tomorrow because people's perceptions change, which affects demand for a good or service. Also, the availability of the good or service changes because supply is not static.

It is commonly believed that gold and other assets have intrinsic value because labour is expended in their production. While labour and other costs spent in mining gold or in the creation of any good or service are factors that need to be considered before spending the time to produce an item, they do not determine whether that good or service has value.

Because value is a subjective concept, it is the consumer who determines whether anything has value, which also explains why governments cannot stop something from having value. For example, the Volstead Act's prohibition of alcohol in the United States from 1919 to 1933 was unsuccessful, despite the resources expended to enforce this man-made law. The prohibition of narcotics in recent decades has met a similar result.

The Problematic Fragility of Banks

In 2008, the world's banking system teetered on the edge of calamity, as it has many times before. Companies and banks with household names collapsed or were kept afloat by the injection of countless billions from taxpayers and newly borrowed government debt. The very real threat of an economic catastrophe was narrowly averted. Or was it instead just diverted and postponed to the present?

As I write, the world is now engulfed by the aftermath of the 'corona shock', which led to the biggest collapse in economic activity since the 1930s. Such a profound surprise to an unprepared and inherently fragile banking system is again causing many banks to force a reappraisal of their real worth and solvency, with untold consequences. There is no better time than the present to ask whether the financial cornerstone upon which capitalist economies are operating - namely, the system of money, currency, and banking - has a flaw at its very heart that leads to recurring crises.

It may appear that the blame for recurring crises should be laid at the door of banks and corporations and particularly the obscenely reckless and foolhardy - and in some cases criminal[11] - behaviour of those individuals who mismanage them. Corporations eagerly assumed responsibility for countless entangling derivatives arranged by banks and mountains of debt loaned on relaxed conditions by the banks, particularly in the current era of financial repression in which central banks have forced interest rates to artificially low levels. But to blame them is to blame human nature.

We know from history that human frailties can and do lead to excesses, and the managers of these enterprises were merely operating within - and taking advantages made possible by - the currency system upon which the economy operates. And for that we need to look to the Bank of England.

The Unwelcome Legacy of the Bank of England

Three things cannot be long hidden:
the sun, the moon, and the truth.

Buddha

Two pernicious ideas about public debt and banking underpinned the founding of the Bank of England in 1694. Both are harmful to the society of natural liberty that was emerging in Britain after the Glorious Revolution of 1688.

That era is appropriately named the Age of Enlightenment, as John Locke, Voltaire , and other writers were re-thinking humanity's social contract by questioning the authority of the State over the individual. When William and Mary ascended to the throne and agreed to govern according to the laws of Parliament, not the will of the monarchy, it was confirmation that Britain had rejected the concept of the divine right of kings. This bloodless revolution led to the removal of the Stuart dynasty and its claim to absolute monarchical power, thereby enabling Britain to peacefully adopt a parliamentary system of government.

Yet, after much debate, the Bank of England was formed even though both ideas central to its operation are antithetical to a society of natural liberty. Short-term expediency prevailed. The British government needed funds to continue fighting the Nine Years' War, and the promoters of the Bank of England promised to provide those funds upon receiving royal ascent to their new venture, which was quickly given.

Over the centuries, these two pernicious ideas that underpin the Bank of England and indeed all banking systems built on the same model, have morphed. While initially controlled, they are now uncontrolled and have reached the stage where they do not just threaten but are overthrowing our society of natural liberty. It is therefore not surprising that people are reacting. Evidence for this statement is the rise in populism in the political sphere and, in financial matters, the emergence and growing sway of cryptocurrencies.

The Bank of England promoted the idea that public debt incurred by the government is a good and socially moral undertaking, even though the proceeds of the debt are used on current spending and the burden of the debt falls on future generations. Not everyone agreed that a public debt was ethical, both in Britain and its newly freed former colonies across the Atlantic.

For example, the inequity of a public debt is the substance of a letter by Thomas Jefferson sent to James Madison on September 6, 1789[12] as the thirteen sovereign American states were ratifying and beginning to plan for the implementation of their new Constitution. According to Jefferson, the iniquity of a public debt arises from borrowing so 'that we may eat, drink, & be merry in our day'. He goes on to say: 'We seem not to have perceived that, by the law of nature, one generation is to another as one independent nation to another.' He calculates that a generation extends for nineteen years and recommends:

> But with respect to future debt; would it not be wise and just for that nation to declare in the constitution they are forming that neither the legislature, nor the nation itself can validly contract more debt, than they may pay within their own age, or within the term of 19 years.

While gently reprimanding Madison, he recommends that they use 'reason for our guide, instead of English precedent, the habit of which fetters us with all the political heresies of a nation equally remarkeable (sic) for its early excitement from some errors, and long slumbering under others.'

The British public debt made possible through the Bank of England had already existed for far too long to be moral and equitable in the view of Jefferson, one of the brightest legal minds of his day. The idea of a perpetual growing debt binding future generations that was believed to be a national strength to seventeenth century mercantilists was repugnant to him and other leaders in the Age of Enlightenment.

The second pernicious idea from the promoters of the Bank of England is their embrace and the subsequent institutionalisation of fractional reserve banking, which also was mistakenly deemed to be a beneficial and morally acceptable practice. It is not. Murray Rothbard puts it succinctly;

> Fractional reserve banks...create money out of thin air. Essentially they do it in the same way as counterfeiters. Counterfeiters, too, create money out of thin air by printing something masquerading as money or as a warehouse receipt for money. In this way, they fraudulently extract resources from the public, from the people who have genuinely earned their money.[18]

There exists in fractional reserve banking (FRB) an inexorable instability, and recurring attempts to make this practice viable have proven that it is incurable, which is to be expected from any fraudulent activity. As Ralph Waldo Emerson cogently penned in 'Nature', his 1836 transcendentalist essay: 'A paper currency is employed, when there is no bullion in the vaults. In due time, the fraud is manifest.' The consequence is bank failures, which in turn have led to increasing government intervention in the market process aimed to perpetuate this fraudulent activity that benefits a small group even though it adversely affects the economy and individual liberty.

FRB was implemented by the promoters of the Bank of England, and it became the norm in national banking and currency systems throughout the globe as the British Empire grew to encompass more land and people. Even in those locations where the Empire's influence declined, for example after the American War for Independence, FRB remained. It had been firmly planted in American and other currency and banking systems, making its institutionalisation global.

FRB rests upon a fundamental flaw in monetary theory and thinking that has plagued economic activity since its adoption by the Bank of England. It is the practice by which a bank falsely claims that its liquid assets are equal to or greater than its liabilities to its customers, which is the currency the bank issues.

This deception to a bank's customers is obvious. The Bank of England held less gold in reserve in its vault than the total of its promises to pay gold on demand by its customers, hence the term 'fractional reserves'. This inherently unstable financial position was put to a test in 1696, which resulted in a financial panic and the near bankruptcy of the Bank of England.

Responding to this insolvency, occurring only two years after the Bank of England's formation, Sir Isaac Newton devised and implemented a policy to control the worst excesses of FRB. Unfortunately, over time, unprincipled bankers, acting with the consent of unprincipled politicians in government, periodically tweaked Newton's Rule to weaken it, debasing the British pound much like Henry VIII debased it by mixing copper into silver coin, which were then unethically spent as if the full metal weight of the coin was intact.

The control on the expansion of credit provided by Newton's Rule was steadily reduced in the nineteenth and twentieth centuries and then completely abandoned in 1971 when the remaining formal link of national currencies to natural money, gold, was ended, but that did not end FRB. Banks continue to falsely claim that their liquid assets are equal to or greater than their liabilities, even though a bank makes multi-year loans funded by customer deposits payable on demand. There is an asset/liability mismatch between loan and deposit maturities, an inherently unstable practice.

FRB has been portrayed by bankers and other beneficiaries over time as useful to society, leading to the misguided belief that it is an ethical process. It is not because FRB is based on deception that results in financial gain at the expense of others.

This financial gain was first identified by Spanish theologians and jurists of the Salamanca School writing soon after Columbus's discovery of the Americas. Watching the impact of precious metals flowing into Spain from the new lands, they noted the rise in prices resulting from the increase in the quantity of currency, which for them was gold and silver coin, but this result they observed is a fundamental monetary principle that also holds for money substitutes. In other words, when new money or currency is added to the total quantity already in circulation, the people who spend it first receive greater purchasing power than those who subsequently receive and spend it. Prices rise from the injection, but only over time as the market adjusts to the greater level of money and/or currency in circulation.

This phenomenon is usually now referred to as the Cantillon Effect, named after an insightful banker living in Paris during the 1710s and early 1720s. Richard Cantillon witnessed first-hand and wrote about the expansion of the French currency that led to the speculative bubble and collapse of John Law's Mississippi Company, which along with the contemporaneous South Sea Bubble in Great Britain stand out as quintessential examples of financial folly and mania.

The Cantillon Effect applies to all increases in the quantity of currency, whether gold brought to Spain by the conquistadors or central bank currency dropped by helicopter, as former Federal Reserve chairman Ben Bernanke once observed without highlighting the pernicious side effects. Prices rise whether the increase of currency is sudden or occurs slowly over time, provided the newly added supply is greater than the demand for it. The financial scheming made possible by FRB gives an unfair advantage to those who are able to borrow and spend the loan proceeds before the currency is debased from the artificial expansion in the quantity of currency resulting from the loan.

The resulting insidious effects have led to disruptions that threaten our society of natural liberty, which is the most unfortunate result beyond the currency debasement and the economic instability resulting from FRB. It does this by feeding currency to the State, which expands its power to the detriment of individuals in our market society. FRB is incompatible with a society based on natural liberty. Nevertheless, though neither moral nor equitable, this unscrupulous practice remains public policy.

We need to reassess how we arrived at the present situation, from which we can then plot a path forward. We need to take things back to basics. Throughout history, money has served one purpose. It meets humankind's need to safely store earned purchasing power, which is the result of human labour. Currency is different.

Because of advances in technology, currency evolves and becomes more efficient by lowering the costs of transactions, increasing speed of payment, enhancing convenience, reinforcing security, etc. These improvements to currency reduce impediments to commerce, which is a good thing. We raise our standard of living through our interaction with others, so a more efficient and trustworthy currency reduces friction in transactions, creating greater opportunities for commerce and so providing more opportunities for individuals in their pursuit of happiness.

An accurate reassessment of our present system of money, currency and banking requires an analysis isolated from FRB. Nearly all monetary theories or other propositions about money and currency since the formation of the Bank of England are flawed, because they are built upon an FRB framework. That framework needs to be dismantled to properly understand money and its inextricable link to liberty. Only then can we today fully appreciate what writers in the Age of Enlightenment understood intuitively and explained in their works.

Freedom of choice is an essential and central requirement of a just and viable system of social order. To live in a world of natural liberty, a natural money is essential, which I propose herein as the Theory of Natural Money. It is based on logic and supported by my observations and extensive reading.

It is also supported by an undeniable fact of history succinctly stated by Murray Rothbard: 'The State is, and always has been, the great single enemy of the human race, its liberty, happiness, and progress.' To mitigate this unfortunate result, the State's power over money and currency must be controlled by a vigilant, knowledgeable, and moral electorate that values individual freedom.

2. The Pursuit of Happiness

Action may not bring happiness, but there is no happiness without action.

William James

Everyone has 'certain unalienable Rights, that among these are Life, Liberty and the pursuit of Happiness'. These few words penned nearly 250 years ago by Thomas Jefferson have left an indelible mark on the progress of civilisation and are as stirring today as the moment the Declaration of Independence was presented to the American public.

Jefferson has been called a hypocrite because his eloquence about liberty is marred by being a slave owner. Yet I quote him often in this book because according to historians at the Thomas Jefferson Foundation: 'Throughout his entire life, Thomas Jefferson was publicly a consistent opponent of slavery. Calling it a "moral depravity" and a "hideous blot", he believed that slavery presented the greatest threat to the survival of the new American nation. Jefferson also thought that slavery was contrary to the laws of nature, which decreed that everyone had a right to personal liberty.'

Each of us is individually unique, but we all seek and are engaged in the pursuit of happiness. It is a common goal. We make decisions and work to achieve this goal to improve our situation. One does not work just for the sake of having a task to occupy their time.

There have been various analyses explaining the pursuit of happiness that are broad and diverse. In my interpretation, a society is best served when there is minimal State intervention in the lives of individuals and the markets that result from our interaction with other individuals.

Linked as it is with life and liberty, happiness is achieved within an environment that enables every individual to flourish by working toward those goals set by that individual. The most fundamental among these are the will to survive and the desire to improve one's situation in life.

One of the most equivocal concepts of economic activity is money. Like political opinions, there are many different viewpoints. Money, as properly defined and not in its modern meaning, is an essential tool for everyone in our society because money makes possible for each individual – excluding the self-sufficient hermit – their chosen pursuit of happiness.

In life we learn from parents, through education, and experience that there are limits to everything, and there is no free lunch. We also learn that there are immutable natural laws that each and every one of us follow. They form the most basic, prudent rules that we live by:

- to live, we work to meet our needs and those wants that we can afford, but wants always exceed needs
- to prepare for an uncertain and unpredictable future, we save our surplus, which we achieve by consuming less than we produce, which is the basis of wealth accumulation
- as our savings grow to a level with which we feel comfortable, we begin investing our surplus
- debt is a burden best avoided

We strive to achieve personal goals that are singularly unique to each individual, as are each person's efforts to achieve their goals. The most basic question is that only each individual can decide what is best for them. People are not homogeneous, but they do share the same trait as they work to satisfy their needs and wants. Their motivation is self-interested behaviour. In 1776, Adam Smith, a Scottish scholar deemed to be the pioneer of political economy, named it the 'invisible hand' in his monumental treatise on economic theory, *An Inquiry into the Nature and Causes of the Wealth of Nations*, which helped shape British policy as its empire expanded throughout the globe.

Guiding the Invisible Hand

This motivation inherent in each individual to improve their situation in the pursuit of happiness can be seen from two distinct and opposing points of view, with palpable consequences. One seeks to channel the activities of all individuals, and the other to control them.

Some believe, like Smith, that the immeasurable power of self-interested behaviour can be purposefully channelled for the betterment of society. To achieve the best possible socially desirable ends, society must not hinder individuals working toward their goals, regardless of whether an individual's actions are spontaneous or purposefully planned.

When pursued in an economy of free markets governed by natural law consistently and equitably applied, this serendipitous human action maximises the creation of wealth, which is a beneficial outcome because standards of living are raised as commerce expands. This outcome rests upon a fundamental principle, namely, that without fraud, coercion or other antisocial factors, people benefit from their interaction with other people.

For example, even a simple conversation leads to increased knowledge among the participants. When viewed in the context of commerce, both parties using free will in a market transaction end up better off from their exchange, the importance of which cannot be overstated.

To complete an exchange, we trust others, even strangers. We trust companies, which highlights the importance of their brand. Without exchange there would be no economic activity. If we view the things we own and buy, we can fully appreciate the importance of exchange. Consider how many things we rely on others to produce which we cannot produce ourselves or, when we try, cannot achieve the quality attained by others.

Because the seller receives value from the buyer in an exchange, each improves their situation, though some strive more often or work harder than others to achieve this end. As a consequence, wealth has not been divided by fate or providence into equal portions among the population, which leads to the opposing view, namely, controlling an individual's actions rather than channelling them.

Those who take an unenlightened opinion of humankind and a society based on free markets question Smith's invisible hand and take a cynical view of individual integrity and motivations. They believe that society only progresses when using the power of the State to impose controls on individual behaviour.

Politically motivated controls impede the invisible hand and obstruct an individual's pursuit of happiness. Yet its proponents typically claim the moral high ground by seeking socialistic cradle-to-grave objectives purportedly aimed to 'improve' society. Advocates of control range widely from social democrats in many countries to self-aggrandising authoritarian central planners, like the socialists in the restrictive command economy of the former Soviet Union or Venezuela today. In the words of former U.S. Congressman Ron Paul:

> Socialism and fascism are two sides of the same totalitarian coin, with the latter being an offshoot of the former. While socialism preaches the State being the sole owner of the means of production, fascism preaches a partnership of State (power) and corporations (money). Socialism leads to rapid ruin, while fascism leads to a longer and

drawn out ruin. The destination is the same regardless of the speed in getting there. Freedom and free markets are the only escape from this totalitarian vice.

There is perhaps no better example of the consequences of this control than the two German states prior to the country's re-unification in 1990. 'Economic conditions in West Germany and East Germany diverged dramatically because one had economic freedom and one suffered from socialism.'[14] The dismantling of the Berlin Wall marked the collapse of a socialist state that rigidly controlled individual behaviour in the East, in marked contrast to a relatively pleasant standard of living available in the comparatively free market economy of West Germany. We can learn from this real-life example.

When individuals are allowed to flourish, a vibrant, robust society ensues to everyone's benefit. 'It is actually the poor, those who have been historically disenfranchised, people with disabilities, and lower-skilled workers who benefit the most from rising economic tides.'[15] A rising standard of living and improved quality of life result from voluntary, peaceful interaction among individuals.

In contrast, interference of any sort that impedes the invisible hand adversely impacts society as a whole and the individuals living within it, regardless of whether the intrusion is from cataclysmic events of nature or intervention in the market process by central planners.[16] Humanity needs a free market and not government intervention, which just distorts normal market forces and gives an unfair advantage to those who front-run the interventions.

Given these two alternatives, the outcome from channelling the self-interested behaviour of the invisible hand is preferential to controlling it. This conclusion rests solidly upon a foundation of logic and real-life examples, as does the need for maximal liberty, which can only be provided by natural money, namely, gold.

The foundational underpinnings of this book rest upon three basic concepts:

- Money is gold, notwithstanding prevailing conventional wisdom that states otherwise and regardless of what governments, academics, and others may pronounce.
- Liberty is attained when gold circulates as currency in a polity operating with consent of the governed and rigorously adheres to a rule of law purposefully aimed at creating a level playing field for everyone by protecting their natural right to life, liberty, and the pursuit of happiness.

- To achieve maximal liberty, government must be precluded from intervening in economic activity.

The above concepts provide the basis for achieving what James Truslow Adams named the 'American dream' in his 1931 book, *The Epic of America.* It is the possibility 'of being able to grow to fullest development as man and woman, unhampered by the barriers which had slowly been erected in the older civilizations, unrepressed by social orders which had developed for the benefit of classes rather than for the simple human being of any and every class.' He further explains that it is a 'social order in which each man and each woman shall be able to attain to the fullest stature of which they are innately capable, and be recognized by others for what they are, regardless of the fortuitous circumstances of birth or position.' The American dream is the motivation empowering an independent people to spur ingenuity and work ethic in their pursuit of happiness.

Money and Society

Economic activity is based on trust, which is a very fragile thing. We trust another person only if we believe that person will honour his or her obligations. We expect the person to keep a promise. If an exact knowledge of that person's financial circumstances or code of morality is not known or available to review, it is necessary to proceed on blind faith by trusting one's own judgement.

Trust is an action taken based on knowledge, intuition, and subjective judgement, but trust can only be verified by action. Therefore, watch what governments and central banks do and do not rely on what they say. Central banks run today's flawed currency system behind closed doors, without accountability to the electorate. In the words of Patrick Henry, 'The liberties of a people never were, nor ever will be, secure when the transactions of their rulers may be concealed from them.' When they emerge from their secret meetings, they only tell us what they want us to hear, much of which is propaganda in an attempt to buy the public's trust.

A person cannot purchase our trust because trust is not for sale. Indeed, the attempt to obtain trust through purchase or bribery is futile and self-defeating. These misguided efforts undermine the very nature of trust, thus putting it further out of the reach of those who so vainly seek it. Yet central bank propaganda aimed at perpetuating their flawed system that is broadcast by a complicit mainstream media is widely accepted by an unquestioning and docile public, even though it is damaging society.

The need for sound, reliable money is succinctly explained by this quote from John Maynard Keynes: 'Lenin was certainly right. There is no subtler, no surer means of overturning the existing basis of society than to debauch the currency.'[17] Once the currency is corrupted, very little in a society will remain just and moral, which then disrupts the trust that is the foundation upon which human interaction is based. That in turn disrupts the pursuit of happiness.

We act to pursue happiness by fulfilling our needs and wants, and our work is an essential part of that process. We exchange our labour by accepting payment in a national currency, but it is the underlying nature of this transaction that is of importance, as explained in 1803 by Jean-Baptiste Say.

Say was a French journalist and businessman who lived during the French revolution, so he witnessed first-hand the currency and economic collapse that followed. From this event and his business experience, he wrote about economic activity, arguing in favour of competition and free trade.

Having lived through hyperinflationary collapse of the French assignat, Say observed that, even in an economy with no viable currency, life though distressed went on, much like it does today in Venezuela without any reliable currency. Say concluded that people work to purchase the work of other people, or in other words, products are paid for with products. Say understood that only assets can extinguish an exchange. In his words, 'Money performs but a momentary function in this double exchange; and when the transaction is finally closed, it will always be found, that one kind of commodity has been exchanged for another.'[18]

Say contributed an economic observation summarised as 'supply creates its own demand'. Being intuitive, it is not a revolutionary concept and Say's Law remained a basic tenet of economics up to the twentieth century when 'modern' thinking took economic thought in a different direction. Keynes questioned Say's Law during the depths of the Great Depression.[19] The result was Keynes' published works provided the basis for government intervention and a command economy driven by a central authority, rather than individual free will guided by the invisible hand.

So while money to Say served as a facilitator for commerce, to Keynes money was a means to give government the control over the economy in an attempt to stimulate demand in the hope of increasing economic activity. Whether Keynes intended or even recognised it, his thinking was used as the basis for increasing the power of the State.

It is not an exaggeration to say that by turning classical economics on its head, what is now referred to as Keynesianism moved society down a different path away from free markets that as a consequence imperils liberty. Central banks are at the centre of that threat because they control the currency and are debasing it, which is subverting our capitalist society as Lenin warned.

3. Gold Essentials

Gold is durable, not like wheat, divisible, not like diamonds, convenient, not like lead, constant, not like real estate, and as jewellery, it has inherent value.

Aristotle

Understanding gold is a prerequisite to gaining the correct perception of money and recognising gold's link to liberty. The key to understanding gold arises from focusing on its utility, which are the unique attributes that make it useful as money. Yet it is likely that gold is the most fundamentally misunderstood asset in the world today. For this reason, it is necessary to overthrow much conventional wisdom about this precious metal.

Gold is not a Commodity

To begin this process of rediscovering and understanding gold, consider that gold is not a commodity, which might have you pondering. That reaction is understandable given that each of us has been programmed through schooling and the media to reach the same - albeit misguided - perception about gold's essential nature. Gold and commodities are tangible assets, but that is where their similarity ends.

1) Different essential nature

Commodities are grown or mined. They are tangible products that come from the natural abundance of the earth and are produced because they are useful. Gold is mined as are lead, zinc, copper, and many other commodities, but what happens to them after mining is generally ignored.

Whether it is grown or mined, a commodity is consumed, after which more of the commodity needs to be produced. So commodities get consumed and disappear, which is the first distinguishing feature that sets gold apart and establishes that it is something different from commodities.

Gold does not get consumed, nor does it disappear. Gold is accumulated. So commodities and gold have different aboveground stocks.

2) Different aboveground stocks

Because each commodity is produced for consumption, none has a large aboveground stock. Gold is different. Because it is accumulated, its aboveground stock is all the gold mined throughout history. Storing unused commodities can be costly, and agricultural produce deteriorates and eventually rots. The cost of storing gold is inconsequential relative to the value of the volume of material being stored.[20]

Gold's aboveground stock is continually growing. New mine production each year is a net increase to the existing aboveground stock of gold. Presently, gold's aboveground stock weighs about 182,200 tonnes, which if fabricated into one large cube would slide under the arches of the Eiffel Tower.

Because their aboveground stocks are different, the available supply of gold is fundamentally different from that of commodities.

3) Annual or accumulated supply

All commodities are produced in anticipation of what will be consumed in the near future, which generally is not further ahead than several months, or in the case of agricultural commodities, one growing season. Anything not consumed is discarded, unless in certain cases it can be stored, which might then cause producers to reduce anticipated production if there is a significant carryover of stock from the previous growing season.

The supply of gold is not only what is produced each year, but also its existing aboveground stock. Gold mined historically is perfectly substitutable for gold being mined today. But not only do gold and commodities have different supply characteristics, demand is different too.

4) Elastic and inelastic demand

Commodities are produced based on estimates of potential demand made by the growers and miners of those commodities. Overproduction is wasteful but output above or below actual demand is possible and occurs often. When too much of a commodity is produced, resulting in a glut, the excess might be discarded because the cost of shipping it to a market exceeds the revenue that would be received.

Gold is different. The demand for gold is inelastic. In other words, notwithstanding gold's large, existing aboveground stock, people always want more of it and willingly acquire all that is mined. Gold never goes begging for a buyer.

No commodity has this feature, all of which have elastic demand that is sensitive to price. The result is that the price of a commodity depends on its new supply and its relationship to ever changing demand for the consumption of that commodity so that little residual supply remains unused in an aboveground stock.

While gold like any commodity is subject to the interaction of its supply and demand, gold's result is measured in purchasing power, not a 'price'.

5) Commodities have a price; gold has a rate of exchange

Gold, like every economic product, has value. In the case of commodities, that value is expressed as a price. Given that gold is money, it is does not have a 'price'; instead, it has rate of exchange that both expresses and results from gold's purchasing power. The widespread use of the term 'gold price' today is a reflection of its mischaracterisation as a commodity.

Gold's exchange rate is determined in the same way as the exchange rate of any currency. They are exchanged at a mutually agreed rate established by the buyer and seller, which determines the purchasing power of one compared to the other.

6) Gold's interest rate

Gold has an interest rate, which is a feature attributable only to money and currency. Gold for delivery in the future has a higher price than physical gold one owns. This structure is called contango, and this difference in spot and futures, or between two different futures, arises from gold's interest rate. No commodity has an interest rate.

While sometimes commodities trade in contango, they also can trade in backwardation, where the future price is lower than the current price. Commodity backwardation can occur for several reasons, one of which is that commodities have significant storage costs and/or are perishable, so they have a limited aboveground stock readily available for sale. These features contrast with gold and its large aboveground stock accumulated for its use as money.

Backwardation in gold, like negative interest rates in national currencies, can only occur in a market fettered by government intervention. After all, who would expect to have less purchasing power in the future after forgoing its usefulness today?

7) Other reasons why gold is not a commodity

There are more distinguishing features that set gold apart from commodities. For example, commodities have grades to determine quality, but gold does not. Not only does gold mined 2,000 years ago by the Romans still exist in the aboveground stock, it is exactly the same as gold being mined today.

Gold does not deteriorate over time, nor corrode, rust or spoil. Gold is the only thing on earth that is not subject to entropy. Gold is eternal, as money should be, to facilitate consistent, reliable economic calculation and the comparison of prices over time.

Gold is also distinguished by its scarcity. There is 106 times more coal produced every day than the weight of gold mined throughout history. But gold is not valuable because it is scarce. Gold's value, like every product, comes from its usefulness. Gold's scarcity just makes it costly to mine and then protect from theft. Like any valuable item, once mined gold needs to be safely stored.

Another reason gold is different from commodities is that it will not go to zero, or even turn negative like crude oil did in May 2020. Commodities can turn into liabilities in an economic collapse because of their storage costs.

The only feature that gold and commodities have in common is their tangible nature, but gold is the sole tangible asset in a class of its own. Its unique features and attributes set it apart from commodities and make gold special. Gold therefore is not a commodity, nor should it be labelled as such. Gold is a tangible asset called money, which is how it is categorised in Figure 2.

Calling gold anything other than money is a disservice to the entire gold industry. Mislabelling gold causes harmful confusion about the usefulness of this marvellous element that is unique throughout nature and the only thing on earth that is eternal. That feature alone makes clear that gold is truly special.

Gold Mining

Given that people always want more gold and willingly acquire all that is mined, then why has not more gold been mined?

Gold production is limited in a way that commodity production is not. The production of gold, more than other minerals, is constrained by how it is disseminated in the earth's crust. Gold is dispersed in small quantities that require sufficient capital, exceptional technology, and expertise to mine it to mitigate risk to human life because mining can be a dangerous activity.

Throughout history, most gold was discovered by sight. It was visible in rock outcroppings or nuggets found in streambeds or occasionally on the surface of a dried-up watercourse. As this easy to extract gold became exhausted, new factors were introduced that added to the cost of gold production. Primitive mechanised mining was applied to placer techniques to extract gold from alluvial sediment in streambeds. Underground mining began by following into the earth the veins visible in rock outcrops. Today, miners can profitably extract a tonne of rock bearing just a gram of gold, a quantity so small and thoroughly dispersed in the rock that it typically is not visible to the miner.

Gold is becoming harder to find and mine but fortunately, as civilisation progresses, so does technology. The importance of technological advances to exploration and mining cannot be overstated. Gold is being mined today from deposits that would never have been discovered using the methods available in the past. Gold is also being mined from deposits that would have been considered uneconomic or impossible to extract the gold from, based on the technology known at the time.

Also of importance are the ever-present risks. Turning dirt into a gold mine is not an easy undertaking, and there are many failures for each success. The prospect of attaining sufficient profitability is therefore needed to meet the expected return on invested capital that is spent to take the risk of discovering and then mining gold.

So gold is only mined if entrepreneurs, after assessing the risks, can expect to receive a reasonable rate of return on their capital, which in turn depends upon the available technology and appropriate legal system protecting property rights to secure the expected result. Encouraging entrepreneurship through dependable property rights explains why mining is presently flourishing in some countries, while in contrast, gold mining has reached a near standstill in Venezuela, even though it ranks high among countries with abundant gold resources yet to be mined.

The interrelationship of these factors of production determines how much gold is mined. Together, they interact to create a natural governor that limits new mine production. Of particular importance to the Theory of Natural Money is the relationship between annual mine production and the aboveground stock of gold.

The Aboveground Stock of Gold

To ascertain the weight of the aboveground gold stock, in 2012 I completed a study to measure the quantity of historical gold production including all the gold discovered and mined throughout history.[21] It is based on my estimate of gold accumulated in prehistory along with by a detailed analysis of annual mine production based on the generally reliable record keeping that began in 1492.

The weight of gold lost in shipwrecks, by attrition of circulating coinage, etc., is unknowable. Because of the care given to gold in view of its high value, the aggregate amount lost over the ages is small and inconsequential when viewed in relation to the existing aboveground stock.

The aboveground stock includes gold held in all its various forms, including two types of jewellery, adornment and monetary. Gold sold in Asia and the Middle East is fabricated into jewellery that is viewed as a means of saving money, for example, as a dowry and other traditional and cultural reasons. When viewed by weight, gold purchased in that part of the world represents nearly all the gold purchased as jewellery, so the adornment role of gold is a relatively small part of the aboveground gold stock and overall demand for gold.

Most of gold's aboveground stock is fabricated into bars, coins, and high-carat jewellery, but even gold in a Rolex watch is money. The owner of that watch may not see it that way, but a thief might because the gold content, which can be melted down, may be more useful to the thief than the watch. The same logic applies to any item of gold, whether a beautiful nugget in a museum, jewellery, or an historical artefact. Ancient treasures were looted for their gold, changing the purpose for which that gold had been fabricated from art or religion to money. The uses to which gold is applied can change, but the aboveground stock of gold only changes by increases arising from new mine production.

I have updated my 2012 report and learned that there are now about 182,200 tonnes of gold in its aboveground stock. Annual production and the accumulated total weight from 1900 to the present are provided in Appendix B. This weight is gold's M3, namely, the quantity of gold money.

Central banks use 'M' designations to quantify the amount of national currency in circulation, with M3 being a broad measure of the total quantity. It includes currency available for immediate spending and currency being saved and held in bank deposits. These M categories can be applied to gold too, with M3 being its entire aboveground stock.

Similarly, M3 of the dollar, the total quantity of dollars in existence, can be viewed as its aboveground stock. But there is a stark difference between gold M3 and that of any national currency.

The M3 of any national currency can easily be increased by using a printing press or entering keystrokes into a computer. There are no natural limitations to these processes that control how much national currency can be created. In contrast, I noted how gold mining is dependent upon the way gold is dispersed in the earth's crust in relation to the interaction of capital and technology. These factors of production naturally limit the weight of gold that can be mined, which in turn determines the rate at which gold is accumulated in its aboveground stock.

Capital accumulates and technology advances as civilisation progresses. Over time, the world becomes richer and more developed, essential factors needed to offset the difficulty of discovering and extracting gold. In other words, more capital and science are necessary as gold becomes harder to discover and mine.

As it happens, these factors of gold production increase more or less in line with world population growth. Consequently, the aboveground gold stock grows fairly consistently by about 1.8% per annum. Actual annual increases since 1492 range between 1.4% and 2.2% per annum, even during nine gold-rush years which saw anomalous growth rates above 2%.

Can this consistent rate of growth in gold M3 continue?

Doubts have been raised. For example, in 2015, MarketWatch described a research note by a metals and mining analyst at Goldman Sachs claiming that the world would run out of mineable gold in twenty years.[22]

Despite the scepticism, gold's growth rate continues to this day, now into its sixth century of measurement. It is a lengthy and well-established track record, but things do change. Those changes result mainly from politics and technology.

Politics determines where and whether gold is mined and stored for safekeeping. Capital will not be invested in countries where it is not welcome, but politics also impacts accumulated capital. An excessive tax burden hinders capital accumulation and can be a major factor in determining where capital will be deployed by its owners. Excessive regulatory requirements can also be an insurmountable barrier to mining.

Further, gold mines, like gold bullion itself, have been confiscated by some governments. Such drastic actions highlight the real political risks that exist, which need to be reasonably assessed and quantified. These risks alter the financial criteria by raising the expected return that mining companies need to achieve before deploying their capital. The higher the risk, the higher the expected compensation, assuming of course that any company chooses to invest at all.

Regarding mining technology, new applications have enabled a consistent growth rate for hundreds of years, which itself is reason to suspect it will continue. Looking at recent history, for example, in the 1980s a mining process call 'heap leaching' was developed. It made mining profitable from land that fifty years ago would be considered as nothing but dirt. Similar important advancements in exploration are also being made.

So, given its multi-century track record, it appears safe to assume that for the foreseeable future, gold M3 will continue to grow around 1.8% per annum, notwithstanding the political risks and difficulty to discover and mine gold. This fortuitous outcome is a key element to the Theory of Natural Money explained in Chapter 11.

Debunking the Myths Levied at Gold

Many myths and criticisms are often levied against gold. Typically, they can be easily dismissed by those with a good understanding of gold or anyone willing to logically analyse the comment to expose its flaw. Here are some of the more common sophisms.

1) Gold has been demonetised

This sophism implies that gold is no longer money, which is not correct. It is hubristic to claim that a 5,000-year track record has ended or does not matter simply because of some government or central bank pronouncement. Even though gold no longer circulates as currency, Figure 1 illustrates that it has not been demonetised because gold is still useful in economic calculation, a key function of money.

One reason I purposefully distinguish between money and currency is to provide an obvious rebuttal to this sophism. Governments can make a currency become worthless, and throughout history many currencies have been debased or collapsed. Governments can affect this outcome because they issue currency, so they are in control of it. They cannot affect the same outcome for gold, whose value is determined by millions - probably billions - of market participants who want to acquire and hold gold because it is useful to them. By now I expect it is becoming clear to readers that gold is natural money, but there are more insights to come that reinforce this key principle underlying the Theory of Natural Money.

2) Gold does not generate any interest income

Gold is a tangible asset, so it does not generate cash flow, unless you put it at risk to earn interest income. Just like the dollar or any other currency, gold can earn interest income if you choose to take the risk of lending it or depositing it in a gold-denominated interest-bearing bank account. Keep in mind that gold is not an investment, so it is not expected to generate any return. The interest income earned arises as compensation for deferring spending to the future and the risks related to the reliability of the expected interest income and whether your gold will be returned to you at the end of the deposit period.

3) The dollar is no longer on a gold standard

The U.S. dollar's formal link of $35 to one ounce of gold ended in August 1971 when President Nixon decided, in his own words, to 'suspend temporarily' the definition of a dollar that established the fixed link. In other words, since then the dollar is no longer being defined as a weight of gold, and five decades later the 'temporary' suspension continues. Nevertheless, gold remains the standard by which value can be accurately measured as evidenced by Figure 1. For this reason, the value of fiat currencies, namely those that circulate because of the force of law, and indeed all economic activity, should be measured by a weight of gold, whether an ounce or a gram.

While it can be said that the dollar and other national currencies remain on a gold standard, it is not the one that existed in 1971. Today, their rate of exchange is not defined at a fixed and unchanging level, it fluctuates from minute to minute in markets around the world. Further, national currencies cannot be redeemed for gold by turning them in to a central bank, but they can be used to purchase gold, which remains the standard. In the words of Charles De Gaulle, 'In truth, one does not see how one could really have any standard criterion other than gold.'

4) Newly mined gold determines the gold 'price'

This sophism is based on the misguided thinking that gold is a commodity. The error continues by claiming that gold has a price instead of a rate of exchange. New mine production of less than nine tonnes per day adds inconsequential supply when compared to the 182,200 tonnes existing in gold M3, most of which is extremely liquid and can be sold at a moment's notice. Therefore, new mine production is unimportant to gold's rate of exchange to national currencies. What is important to gold's rate of exchange is the amount of newly created currency. If the M3 of a national currency grows more rapidly than gold M3, which as noted above is historically and currently is about 1.8% per annum, the national currency is being debased in terms of gold. Assuming demand for gold and the currency remain constant, the debasement from the different M3 growth rates will result in more units of the national currency being needed to exchange for the same weight of gold.

5) Gold will decline if the U.S. government sells any of its gold stock

This sophism is a variant of the one above and again reveals the prevalent misguided thinking that gold is a commodity. Any government – just like any company or individual – can become worse off when an asset is sold. To make this point clear, assume that the U.S. government decides to sell all the national parks and other land it owns and then spends those proceeds. Its financial condition would deteriorate, and doubts would arise about its creditworthiness and the outlook for the dollar. Demand for dollars would fall, and demand for gold would rise. There is a real example to demonstrate this point.

As its obligations for the Vietnam War escalated, the U.S. government dishoarded from January 1960 to March 1968 about 7,700 tonnes of gold, approximately 68% of the total weight of new production during that period. Yet despite foisting this relatively huge weight of gold on the market, their exchange rate never fell below $35 per ounce.

The key element to understanding this counterintuitive result and to answering this sophism is to determine whether gold is overvalued or undervalued at the time it is dishoarded. The dollar was overvalued for much of the 1960s when this dishoarding occurred, meaning that gold was undervalued in terms of dollars. Consequently, buyers who recognised that fact eagerly scooped up at $35 per ounce all the gold offered during the dishoarding.

6) Central bank buying benefits the gold market

Central bank gold buying is frequently cheered by gold advocates, but it is not a good thing when central banks buy gold. Gold is earned purchasing power because it is mined with time, labour, and capital. Central banks buy it with phantom purchasing power conjured 'from thin air' and conveyed with newly issued currency given to the seller of gold. It is not an equitable exchange because of the difference in purchasing powers and risks used in the transaction. What is worse, it puts physical gold in the hands of central bankers, which they can use to help manipulate and control gold's rate of exchange to national currencies. Gold is money, and money is power, which should always be in the hands of the people, not the government. The aim is to have gold in private hands and private vaults.

7) At $1,900 gold is expensive

The word *expensive* is misleading in two ways. First, it shows that the person is using dollars for their economic calculation. So relative to recent history, gold may appear expensive given that it is near a record high. A more accurate statement would be that the dollar is losing purchasing power, which is clear from Figure 1.

Second, the term *expensive* is subjective and misses the key point. Like any asset, gold can become overvalued or undervalued relative to dollars or any other national currency. My methodology for measuring relative value is explained in Chapter 8.

8) There is not enough gold to use it as money

This sophism does not only apply to gold. It also applies to any national currency and is often the lament of central bankers who believe that they have no alternative, particularly in times of economic turmoil, but to turn on the printing press and issue more currency. Rudolph Havenstein was a central banker who followed this strategy during 1922-23. The result was the hyperinflation of the German mark that obliterated the country's middle class, which some scholars argue helped create the conditions for the fascism that followed.

In a free market, any weight of gold is sufficient to use as money because prices of goods and services adjust as a result of supply and demand. Prices adjust to reflect prevailing conditions, including the quantity of money or currency. If M3 is relatively low, the price of the product being purchased will also tend to be low, assuming normal supply availability and demand for that product. Conversely, as occurred in the German Weimar Republic, a rapid increase in the mark's M3 resulted in its hyperinflation.

In 1933 President Roosevelt claimed that there was not enough gold in the U.S. gold reserve, which was backing the dollar under the prevailing gold standard. Actually, there was sufficient gold, but the dollar had been debased and was therefore overvalued at the $20.67 exchange rate at which the dollar was defined. So to bring the dollar's relationship back into balance with gold, he devalued the dollar to $35 per ounce. With the stroke of a pen, he increased the dollar value of the U.S. gold reserve by 69% without changing its weight.[23]

9) Owning gold is risky

In reality, the risk actually occurs when holding national currency, as is clear from Figure 1. Your purchasing power is eroded over time when holding dollars, particularly in the current environment of financial repression which has forced interest rates to artificially low levels, but there is another risk.

Dollars are a liability of some bank, so anyone holding dollars has counterparty risk, which is that the bank will have the financial capacity to return those dollars to you when you need to spend or invest them. Even paper currency has counterparty risk because circulating notes are a liability of a central bank. To explain this risk, many central banks without any announcement or warning have changed overnight the notes they have issued. So, for example, a $100 bill could become a $10 bill because the Federal Reserve chooses to reduce the quantity of its liabilities to make it appear more solvent relative to its assets, particularly the U.S. Treasury gold certificates it owns.

Some readers may take exception to my comment that owning gold is less risky than owning any national currency. I understand their point when viewed from a short-term perspective. For example, if you purchase an ounce of gold today for $1,900, you might find that tomorrow the exchange rate is $1,890, indicating that there is a fluctuation risk to owning gold. From the moment governments abandoned the gold standard, economic calculation and commerce have taken place in a world of so-called 'floating' exchange rates. Everything fluctuates, but the chart in Figure No. 1 shows that only gold floats and national currencies sink. In contrast to gold, they are losing purchasing power.

Gold is not riskless, nor is anything else, including so-called 'risk free' U.S. government debt instruments. Gold has unique factors of supply and demand, and its supply changes relatively consistently. In theory, supply could change relatively quickly if, for example, a huge solid gold asteroid were to land on earth, which of course is highly unlikely because it has not happened in the four billion year history of the planet.

It is difficult envisaging a collapse in demand for gold. One would think that a gold confiscation or outlawing its use would cause demand to drop, but experience shows the opposite. When the U.S. government confiscated privately owned gold in 1933 and made it illegal to own, demand for gold did not drop.

Gold Markets

There are two gold markets, and they are fundamentally different, each with its own supply and demand. One is for physical gold, a tangible asset, and the other is for so-called 'paper-gold,' which is a financial asset.

The paper-gold market encompasses all gold derivatives, the more popular of which are futures, forwards, options, Exchange Traded Funds (ETFs), and certificates. These financial products, some of which use leverage, are priced in national currency. They give you exposure to gold's rate of exchange to the national currency in which the product is denominated, but you do not actually own any gold. Being derivatives, they have counterparty risk because a promise to deliver a tangible asset is never as good as owning the tangible asset itself. A paper promise is not a substitute for a tangible asset.

Gold in its various physical forms trades in a market that encompasses all tangible gold products. These include doré bars that mining companies send to refiners, which may contain 75% gold or even less, to countless bars and coins of varying gold content with a fineness ranging typically from 91% up to 99.99%, commonly referred to as '4-nines'.

These two gold markets, with paper-gold by far the larger in terms of trading volume, interact to a great extent. Picture them as a dog for which the tail is the market for physical gold, and its body is the market for paper-gold. Sometimes the tail wags the dog. This odd result occurs because there are times when possession of physical metal outweighs any advantages of owning paper-gold.

Because paper-gold can be expanded without limit, the quantity issued far exceeds gold M3, making it difficult if not impossible for the obligor of the derivative to fulfil their promise to deliver physical gold. During these periods of imbalance, the degree of counterparty risk is heightened, meaning that market participants are alerted to the possibility of a default, which is a failure of the obligor of the paper-gold product to deliver as promised. A default is like being left standing in a game of musical chairs when the music stops because there are not enough chairs (gold) to go around. The consequence of a default is an increased awareness of counterparty risk that reduces the demand for derivative products that simultaneously results in increased demand for physical metal.

In recent years there has been a concerted effort to change the nature of many of these paper-gold products. For example, instead of settling the derivative with physical gold, the obligor settles the transaction with dollars, further distancing the product from physical metal. This change also makes it easier for central banks to manipulate the gold market, which is a topic I delve into later, but the principle on which the manipulation is based is clear. There exists a limited amount of physical gold, but the ability to create dollars by a bank's bookkeeping entries is limited only by the willingness of the general population to continue accepting dollars. It is easier for the obligor to deliver newly created dollars than physical metal, significantly reducing the possibility of default and undermining confidence in the fiat currency system.

Another factor impacting both gold markets is interest rates, which is the difference between owning gold in the present and deferring its possession into the future. Interest rates are a natural result of time preference and risk. There is a sacrifice to foregoing today the use of your purchasing power until some future date. Put another way, possessing something in the future is less valuable than possessing it today. So it is reasonable to expect and receive income as compensation while waiting for the future date to arrive, but many things can happen during this interval because time introduces risk.

Currencies are at risk from inflation and other forms of debasement that devalue the currency (the 'debasement risk'). There is also the risk of default by the obligor to pay interest or fulfil the promise made in the derivative (the 'counterparty risk'). The higher these risks and the longer the period the use of one's purchasing power is deferred, the higher is the interest rate in a market unfettered by government intervention.

Interest rates vary among different currencies because they tend to have different degrees of risk. For example, interest rates in the Brazilian real are higher than those of most currencies because of the real's higher debasement risk. Similarly, interest rates are higher for a borrower or for an issuer of derivatives that has a higher credit risk rating. The greater the perceived risk, the higher the interest rate is needed to induce a counterparty to accept that risk.

In a market unfettered by government intervention, gold always has the lowest interest rate because it has the lowest risk. Physical gold cannot be printed like paper currency or created by a bank's bookkeeping entry. National currencies can be inflated, and ledger currencies have counterparty risk, which are not risks found in gold. So gold's interest rate – what today is erroneously called a 'lease' rate – is an approximation of the natural rate of interest, which I define as the interest rate that would prevail for borrowing/lending money in a market unfettered by government and central bank intervention.

My experience has been that this natural interest rate is more or less about 0.5% per annum for a 1-year loan to a triple-A credit. Rates can vary because time preference is unique to the subjective judgement of each of the two parties of a transaction, as is the lender's view about the creditworthiness of the borrower. Gold's contango is the natural interest rate in an unfettered market.

Interest rates at present are not market-driven; they are artificial. For many years, interest rates have been and still remain distorted by government intervention. Nevertheless, interest rates are one of the areas in which the markets for physical gold and paper-gold intersect. To control and manipulate dollar interest rates, central banks need to manipulate gold interest rates. The interaction of the two gold markets is visible from a comparison of the spot market to the price of a derivative obligated to deliver gold in the future.

The spot market is the rate at which physical gold is exchanged for a national currency. The price of derivatives results from transactions in the forward market that as its name implies are 'derived' from the spot market. Derivatives trade in an over-the-counter market of banks and other gold dealers, and in the futures market, for which there are several regulated exchanges. For reasons that relate to risk and time preferences, the price of a derivative contract to deliver gold in the future is always higher than gold's exchange rate in the spot market.

When the future price of a commodity is below its spot price, the market is in backwardation. In a market unfettered by government intervention, gold is always in contango for two reasons. Gold is money, not a commodity. Because current possession of money today is always less risky and therefore more valuable than possession in the future, interest rates on money must always be positive. Negative interest rates on national currencies is a result of government intervention distorting normal market processes. Second, because gold has the least risk compared to national currencies, it has the lowest interest rate. So contango in gold is a mathematical certainty.[24]

The forward market in normal times is very liquid. That is because the forward market is more an interest rate market, rather than a gold market. Banks quote the spread between gold's spot and a future date, making the forward market a pure interest rate play in which traders, investors and corporate treasurers can go long or short the contango.

The volume of debt in today's global economy makes interest rates a major factor in economic activity generally, whether as a hedge or to speculate. So gold's forward market has grown along with the increasing debt load, and the volume of transactions has become a key factor in the bottom-line profitability of banks.

Bullion banks try to earn the contango, but generally own little gold. If they receive gold deposits or borrow gold, typically they sell this gold in the spot market and lend the proceeds or use them to buy national currency debt instruments. If the interest income and savings on storage fees together are greater than the cost of the forward position, the bank earns a profit.

Some central banks sell the gold they own in the spot market, using the proceeds to buy debt instruments and earn interest income, and then immediately buy back in the forward market. The riskier alternative is to leave their short position unhedged hoping to buy back gold in the future at a lower rate than that at which they sold. They win if their income exceeds any increase in gold's exchange rate.

Another alternative is that the central bank simply lends its gold to a bullion bank to earn interest income, but there is a risk. For example, several central banks were exposed in this way when Drexel Burnham collapsed in 1990.[25]

The interests of central banks and bullion banks are aligned, and they work together to achieve their mutual objectives. In particular, neither of them wants gold's exchange rate to rise. That would signal inflation and/or debasement, which in turn would erode the privileged position they hold in keeping the fiat currency system together, which earns profits for the banks and gives power to the government. Also, the bullion banks that act as agents for governments profit from their short positions in gold, and a rising exchange rate if it climbs high enough would expose these banks to losses. Therefore, bullion banks and central banks work together to keep gold's exchange rate as low as practically possible. Importantly, it is now becoming more difficult for the bullion banks and central banks to keep gold's exchange rate low, given the increasing speed at which fiat currency is being debased.

Earning the contango is tempting. It has always been tempting, which is understandable because everybody desires interest income, but it comes with risks, as do all paper-gold products. Those risks provide an incentive to manipulate gold to make sure the market outcome is what governments and their central bank agents want. It is the reason governments intervene in any market. If they do not like the verdict of the market, they use force trying to subvert the market's judgement so that it reaches a different conclusion about values, namely, one that is closer to what the government is seeking from their policies, regardless of whether those policies are practical and achievable. Consequently, true price discovery becomes difficult, leading to a harmful misallocation of resources.

Under the gold standard, it was the responsibility of central banks to manage the national currency to make its purchasing power consistent with that of gold. They did this by maintaining a large enough gold reserve to accommodate redemptions of currency into precious metal and raising or lowering interest rates, but governments bent the rules. Instead of managing the national currency, by the nineteenth century, governments instead began managing gold. Their aim was to keep its exchange rate to national currency low hoping that people would not notice the ever-diminishing purchasing power of the currency being inflated away.

Manipulation in the Gold Market

> There are no markets anymore, just interventions.
>
> Chris Powell, Secretary & Treasurer, www.gata.org

Since 1998, the Gold Anti-Trust Action Committee (GATA), a not-for-profit educational and civil rights organisation, has actively exposed and litigated against collusion aimed at controlling gold and related financial instruments. GATA's efforts comprise the work of many analysts whose reports, including several of mine written in the early 2000s, have detailed the manipulation. The extensive body of work GATA has compiled is available for review and download at its website: www.gata.org

Broadening the awareness that the gold market is manipulated is the first step to achieving a free market in gold unfettered by government intervention, which is GATA's goal. Because of the breadth and quality of the work that it has compiled, along with the numerous donations made to GATA by contributors helping to publicise the manipulation to bring it to light, GATA has successfully exposed the manipulation in the gold market, resulting in fines for banks engaged in this illegal activity.[26]

Nevertheless, the manipulation continues because suppressing a free market in gold with surreptitious intervention is U.S. government policy condoned by the Gold Reserve Act of 1934. The intent of the law is explained in an article published by the Independent Institute: 'Although a gold standard was still on the books, it was nothing more than a facade for Fed-Treasury manipulations.'[27]

The following cable from the U.S. embassy in Beijing released by Wikileaks states in clear and simple terms one of the reasons the gold market is manipulated. It quotes an April 28, 2009 article in *World News Journal*, a sponsored newspaper of China Radio International. Both are state-owned media outlets of the Chinese government.

> The U.S. and Europe have always suppressed the rising price of gold. They intend to weaken gold's function as an international reserve currency. They don't want to see other countries turning to gold reserves instead of the U.S. dollar or euro. Therefore, suppressing the price of gold is very beneficial for the U.S. in maintaining the U.S. dollar's role as the international reserve currency.
>
> U.S. Embassy, Beijing[28]

Governments have deliberately dismantled gold's role as currency. Internationally, the International Monetary Fund, under forceful guidance by the United States, in the 1970s changed its founding statutes to prevent member countries from tying their national currency to gold. Domestically, governments have accomplished this outcome by imposing restrictions, like taxes[29], that impede gold's circulation as currency.

The motivation for governments intervening in the gold market is twofold. They want control over it to protect their power to create currency. As Chris Powell has observed, 'Gold is the most serious threat to government power and the strongest protector of individual liberty.' Second, gold is a messenger; it becomes more expensive as national currencies are debased. So governments seek control of the messenger to disguise the dire consequences arising from their control of the national currency. As Ludwig von Mises unambiguously observed, 'It is precisely when a free gold market is needed that most modern governments seek to suppress it.'

Central banks, acting as agents for governments, intervene to marginalise gold and keep its rate of exchange to the U.S. dollar as low as possible. They employ four tools to do this of which propaganda is the most obvious. For example, the U.S. government disparages gold through disinformation and touts 'a strong dollar' policy yet actively pursues perennial inflation, which is the antithesis of a strong dollar. As Robert Bleiberg, then the Managing Editor of *Barron's* wrote in June 1979, 'To serve as a central banker, as Barron's again reminded its readers early last year when G. William Miller took over at the Fed, one needn't be a flim-flam man, but it helps.'

Second, central banks occasionally dishoard gold from their vaults, but only reluctantly because, once it is sold, it can be difficult to buy back, particularly when large volumes are involved. They learned that lesson in the 1960s when their cartel, the London Gold Pool, eventually collapsed in March 1968 after the U.S. federal government dishoarded over 10,000 tonnes from its Fort Knox vault in a vain attempt to maintain the fiction that gold was worth only $35 per ounce. Despite their rhetoric, central bankers understand that gold is valuable, so these days they only dishoard, and then only sparingly, when forced into it to maintain the illusion that gold is not in short supply.

The third tool is paper-gold in the form of various derivatives. Because of the large trading volume in derivatives and the fact that most gold is held by people and institutions who see it as the bedrock of their portfolio, they have no intention of selling it, particularly when it is undervalued as it is at present. Therefore, paper-gold sold by central banks through their bullion bank agents can be exceptionally effective in manipulating the market for physical gold to keep gold's exchange rate subdued.

The fourth tool is that central banks make decisions behind closed doors impervious to the outside world except for redacted minutes of their meetings disclosed weeks later. Further, they operate in secret by employing certain bullion banks to act for them, thereby enabling central banks to hide their interventions. As further proof of this point, their reporting to the International Monetary Fund is unreliable. 'Central banks often accumulate gold for a long time before reporting it, if they report it at all.'[30]

Another example of central bank secrecy is financial statement disinformation. Many report 'Gold & Gold Receivables' on their balance sheet as one line item, as if they were the same thing. This breach of accounting principles is recommended by the International Monetary Fund. Defying accounting principles enables central banks to operate in secret by cloaking their interventions in the gold market by not accurately reporting whether the country's gold is actually being stored in the central bank's vault.

In the present system of fiat currencies, gold acts as the messenger that governments want to shoot because, in the words of economist Joseph Schumpeter, gold 'blurts out unpleasant truths'. Those truths are inflation, debasement, and all the other afflictions imposed on individuals and economic activity by fiat currency under government control, which are exposed for all to see when gold's exchange rate rises in terms of the U.S. dollar and other national currencies. Gold's rising exchange rate highlights the bad consequences that arise from government control over the issue of currency, and mismanagement of the currency raises questions that logically should lead to restrictions on government and central bank power, given their poor track record.

Gold is the major competitor to government issued fiat currency, and governments do not want demand for their fiat currency to decline. A decline in demand would weaken the currency's exchange rate to gold, and gold's rising exchange rate may alert people to inflation or other currency ills. Gold acts as a warning device, like a canary in a coal mine. The suppression of its rate of exchange to the dollar offers an example of the consequences of government intervention. Asset bubbles persist longer than they otherwise would if gold was not being suppressed. When gold is allowed to rise from natural forces of supply and demand, it provides an early warning that: (1) there is too much credit extension, (2) financial asset prices are too high, and (3) the national currency is overvalued.

In contrast to national currencies, gold does not need law to force its circulation, nor propaganda to encourage people to buy and hold it. To overcome this reality, the U.S. government and those governments under its influence intervene in the gold market to suppress gold's exchange rate. An example is Canada, which had one of the highest per capita holdings of gold from the formation of its central bank in 1935 up to the 1980s, when it began dishoarding over several years nearly its entire stock of gold reportedly on a recommendation from the U.S. government.

Governments outside the influence of the U.S. government use these periods in which gold becomes exceptionally undervalued as a result of the intervention to accumulate gold. China and Russia are two examples that have in recent years benefitted by actively building their gold reserve.

Gold is an inimitable asset. It can be influenced by government manipulation and anti-gold propaganda, but unlike national currencies, its rate of exchange cannot be forever suppressed and controlled by governments seeking to achieve their aims, be it creating more currency to supposedly rescue the economy or bribe the voters by spending newly created currency on new programmes before an upcoming election. Notwithstanding government manipulation efforts, gold is a messenger of national currency debasement because governments cannot create physical gold out of thin air. The importance of this unique attribute of money that is a tangible asset whose supply is limited by natural constraints cannot be overstated. Barring the total destruction of the free market process, as occurred in the former Soviet Union or as exists today in Cuba and Venezuela, gold's exchange rate will inevitably rise when governments produce fiat currency by turning on the so-called 'printing press' because doing so always erodes the national currency's purchasing power.

Governments have been effective in distancing gold from the mainstream population and impeding its usefulness as currency. They have also relied on the mainstream media and those economists who are trained to believe in market outcomes and therefore ignore – whether wilfully or not

– government interventions that distort the outcome that otherwise would have occurred without the intervention.

The aboveground stock of gold is limited, but the supply of dollars and dollar-denominated government paper is not. That means the only explanation for a market anomaly in which gold remains undervalued for an exceptionally long period is surreptitious government intervention, particularly when there is logic to expect them to intervene. The motivation to do so is to retain their existing power. Their intervention carried out through central banks is aimed at preventing gold's rate of exchange from rising so that it does not attract attention and more buyers, which would lessen the demand for dollars as wealth flowed away from it into gold.

Nevertheless, Figure 1 provides empirical evidence that governments have not stopped, nor can they stop, gold from being money, even when they impede its role as currency. The net result of this government intervention, however, has been to create a system that favours banks and works against individual liberty. It is only when gold is restored as a currency in an unfettered free market that a level playing field will again exist.

The Role of Silver

Silver circulated in commerce before gold and has therefore played a key role in the history of money. For this reason, both precious metals are normally mentioned in the same breath. An example is this quote from Thomas Paine, an English-born political activist in America during and after its War for Independence: 'Nature has provided the proper materials for money: gold and silver, and any attempt of ours to rival her is ridiculous.'

Bimetallism is a monetary system that operates with coins of both precious metals used as tender in payment. It is a system that developed naturally with the advancement of civilisation, with the rarer gold used in high value transactions and silver as subsidiary coinage. Because of its high relative value, even the smallest gold coin is too large for use in everyday transactions, making smaller denomination silver coins a necessity.

So that the payee would be indifferent to receiving either metal, governments sought consistency in the measurement and transfer of value regardless of the metal being used in payment. They therefore would fix the ratio at which the two metals would be exchanged, typically around 16-to-1, namely, sixteen ounces of silver to one ounce of gold, which explains why bimetallism is flawed. It is in effect price fixing by government dictate, which never works. Exchange rates cannot be predicted because changes in the relative supply and demand of the two precious metals are unpredictable.

The ratio between gold and silver fluctuates from market forces, namely, the interaction of the supply and demand for gold with the supply and demand for silver. These fluctuations create the opportunity for arbitrage, with the undervalued metal exported to those countries where it is valued more highly. To ensure that there were always sufficient quantities of both metals on hand, governments would occasionally need to adjust the gold/silver ratio. These adjustments were rare until the advancement of communication in the nineteenth century highlighted the differences in the relative value of the two precious metals that could occur among different countries, increasing the cost to government to maintain a fixed bimetallic ratio.

To address the shortcomings inherent to government price fixing, various steps were taken to minimise the role of silver. For example, in Britain, then the dominant global power with the largest economy, silver was made legal tender up to £2, above which a payee could legally demand payment in gold. The net effect decreased the demand for silver, which occurred at a time that bonanza grade silver deposits were being discovered, increasing the available supply.

Silver was also being buffeted by other changes. Like base metals after the Industrial Revolution, silver became useful in the manufacturing advancements then occurring and thereafter in electronics, health, and a variety of other areas. While the demand for gold is almost entirely monetary, the demand for silver comes from both monetary and other areas. These new non-monetary demands for silver and changes in supply began impacting the historical 16-to-1 ratio, with increasing volatility in the relative market value of the two metals. At the same time, governments were reducing the role of gold, as explained in Chapter 6, so silver also felt these pressures reducing, if not completely supplanting, the monetary role of the precious metals.

The monetary demand for silver diminished significantly in the twentieth century with government efforts to remove precious metals from the monetary system. Silver's role in coinage ended in the 1960s. President Lyndon Johnson signed the Coinage Act in July 1965 because the dollar had become too debased relative to the face value of silver coins, which were being hoarded instead of circulating in commerce.

Although silver's official monetary role has ended, as it has for gold, silver offers the same thing that gold offers. They are money outside the banking system, with silver evolving to become a gold substitute. By following the gold/silver ratio, which in March 2020 reached a record 120-to-1, one can measure silver's value relative to gold, and with this knowledge decide whether to hold a portion of their precious metal portfolio in silver.

The Unique Attributes of Gold

Gold is truly unique. There is nothing else in nature comprising all the physical characteristics of gold. What is more, gold is the only substance in our known universe that is eternal. It is unchanged throughout time and fungible, meaning that gold mined thousands of years ago by the Romans is identical to gold being mined today in Nevada or anywhere else. Together these factors make gold useful as money, which explains why it has been money for thousands of years. From this formidable track record, we can reasonably deduce two points important to the Theory of Natural Money.

Its lengthy use as money makes clear that gold is money upon which one can rely because of its unique attributes. Second, gold will continue to be money for the foreseeable future simply because gold is useful today for the same reasons it has been useful throughout history.

With its truly unique attributes that set gold apart from everything else, gold's existence leads to many profound questions that are beyond the scope of this book, but some readers may find them interesting to ponder. Here are some thought provoking examples.

- Is it an immutable law of nature that the supply and demand of gold remain closely balanced to preserve purchasing power over long periods of time in a world that is not static?
- What would life on earth be like today if gold did not exist to contribute to humankind's progress after emerging from the primordial swamp millions of years ago?
- How would civilisation without gold have advanced, assuming of course that human interaction as we experience today could have even developed at all without money?
- And, perhaps most profound of all, is gold, with all of its unique features, a serendipitous occurrence of nature or the purposeful creation of intelligent design – by a creator – in a complex and seemingly limitless universe, the essence of which the human mind still struggles to grasp?

I make no attempt to answer any philosophical or anthropological questions, but I share herein my personal knowledge of gold in the possibility that readers will find it helpful. Understanding the role of gold as money has been useful to me. Even more useful has been owning some of it to benefit from the security it offers as timeless money willingly accepted around the globe. The deep knowledge about gold that I have accumulated from extensive reading and experience have contributed immeasurably to my pursuit of happiness.

4. Money Essentials

Money is money, and paper [currency] is paper. All the invention of man cannot make them otherwise.

Thomas Paine

To restate an essential point critical to understanding a key premise of this book, money and currency are different. Currency is the medium used by us as we participate in the market process buying and selling products to fulfil our needs and wants. Currency facilitates the exchange of goods and services between participants in the market process. Currency is the tactile - or perceptible, in the case of digital currency - agent in the process of buying or selling. Money may also circulate as currency, but not all currencies are money.

We often use the words 'money' and 'currency' interchangeably, and this intermingling can cause confusion. As a result, their contrasting essential nature and other differences are ignored or overlooked, leading to a misunderstanding of money and ultimately its critical importance to a free society.

Money is always and has always been a tangible asset. I explain why this is so by exploring the many facets unique to money, starting with its origin in prehistory.

The Origin of Money

The discovery of money marks the beginning of commerce, which is the process by which society and standards of living advance over time because of human interaction. Given the central role of money in the development of humankind, this book is based on the view that the discovery of money also led to the beginning of capitalism, which is a natural result of human behaviour.

Money emerged from the process of exchanging assets arising from the so-called 'double coincidence of wants'. Anyone acting with rational self-interest in the pursuit of happiness could improve their situation in life by voluntarily exchanging with another person something of value for something he or she valued more highly.

By letting go of the asset they possessed for the asset they wanted more, both parties benefitted from their exchange. This resulting benefit provided each of them with the incentive to find more valuable items or to create more useful products to be able to enter into more exchanges. With this purposeful effort directed to these tasks, they were working to create purchasing power, which was conveyed by the asset they found, grew, or made.

By helping themselves while also helping others through these exchanges, individuals eventually formed the tribes that emerged from these earliest moments of human cooperation. Then, as communities grew, so did the opportunities for exchange, but the 'double coincidence of wants' was a limiting factor. Exchanges would occur only when by fortuitous circumstance two people would meet at the same moment in time and be willing to exchange the asset he or she held for a preferred asset held by the other person.

Eventually, an intermediate good emerged. It facilitated this process of exchange by eliminating the need to wait for another person with the preferred asset. The intermediate good of course is money. It is the asset that people were willing to accept because it was either consumable or something easily marketable, unlike their own product created to attain purchasing power, which was reliant upon the limitations of the double coincidence of wants. Further, they held this easily marketable asset received in the exchange until it was needed to complete their own exchange because it stored their purchasing power, which had moved from their product to the money.

This process of exchanging assets reflects the preferences of the individuals completing the exchange. The expression of preferences manifested through the exchange would naturally encourage thought and economic calculation from which, I suspect, speech emerged. It is probable that even before our prehistoric ancestors were able to speak intelligibly, they discovered money – the valuable item used to facilitate the exchange of assets from which the mental process of economic calculation developed.

In fact, there are similarities between money and articulate speech, not the least of which is their obscure origin in prehistory. Money is not only an intermediate good; like speech it is also a means of communication. The buyer and seller can communicate their own subjective view on the value of an asset by completing a transaction without speaking a word, for example, as travellers to a foreign country who do not speak the local language may need to do when making a purchase.

Both money and speech lead to and require understanding, but money has a distinguishing feature. Money is a tangible good, as it was in humankind's first exchange of assets, and as it is to this day.

As an aside, there are many theories about the origins of intelligible speech, which is not surprising given the absence of contemporaneous observation or direct evidence. Interestingly, the process of exchange and the cerebral activity arising from thought about preferences and economic calculation is not, based on my cursory analysis, generally considered to be a factor. It should be added to the mix of theories to explain how verbal communication developed.

The countless exchanges of assets that occur through the market process are the base upon which our society is built. Money is the tangible asset that made possible the economic calculation that has enabled this process of exchange to evolve over millennia to achieve the standards of living enjoyed today. But there is more to understanding the true nature of money and its vital role in the advancement of civilisation.

Inherent Value and Economic Value

Money, like all tangible assets, has an inherent value and a possible economic value. Inherent value arises from a tangible asset's usefulness. An asset you possess has economic value if others attach importance to its inherent value.

In some locations, tobacco, cattle, salt, grain, and many other things were occasionally put into service as money. In these instances, the economic value of these assets as a marketable item was more useful to their owner than their inherent value. So instead of consuming these items, they were used in commerce along with gold and silver, the inherent value of which is adornment, but have a higher economic value when used in commerce and circulated in the form of coins. But regardless of what good serves as money, they all share one characteristic; they are a tangible asset.

Consequently, money had value in transactions because the asset being used as money had some inherent usefulness and was therefore valuable. What is more, payment for an item being exchanged was instantaneous because it was a tangible asset that facilitated the exchange. Though money often took different forms, with coins of precious metals being the most common, the asset serving as money passed from hand-to-hand. The exchange was extinguished at the moment the money moved to the hand of the seller and the buyer simultaneously received the product being purchased.

When tangible assets are used in an exchange, there is no lingering obligation. The exchange is extinguished the moment the assets being exchanged in the transaction change hands. Namely, the buyer receives the product from the seller who receives the tangible asset from the buyer.

In contrast, payment risk arises when anything other than a tangible asset is used as currency. This absence of payment risk, to which I will return, is a key element central to my definition of money that rests on the fundamental principle of human interaction that goods and services pay for goods and services.

The Specialisation of Labour

As humankind passed from the Stone Age into the Bronze Age, communities emerged as individuals realised that there were mutual benefits to be gained by working together with other individuals, for example, in providing for their common defence. Once a community formed, individuals began devoting their time to specific occupations: making tools, farming, building shelters, providing defence and so forth.

Preferences and skills became factors in determining who would complete essential tasks, and the community developed as individuals became increasingly specialised in completing the tasks needed by members of the community. For example, by relying on a toolmaker instead of making their own tools, farmers could devote greater time, care, and attention to their fields and animals, with everyone in the community benefiting from better products.

With this specialisation of labour, individuals were producing more than the bare essentials they needed for their own subsistence. Specialists were producing food, pottery, tools, domesticated animals, and providing services like defence. The resulting efficiencies in production from specialisation created more products, which provided the impetus for more interactions with others both within and outside the community with the result that commerce expanded. Individuals could use the products they produced in an exchange for the products of others because the principal motivation and result of the exchange continued to be met. Each party was pursuing happiness (contentment) with both parties to the exchange improving their situation.

The result of this specialisation of labour was twofold. First, commerce developed by advancing beyond the double coincidence of wants. People motivated to improve their situation worked in anticipation of their individual output being exchanged for the production from others. For example, builders no longer needed to provide for their own food. They could rely on the food produced by farmers.

Money facilitated this human interaction resulting from the specialisation of labour, with gold and silver emerging over time as the preferred form of money. Individuals willingly accepted this intermediate step to the exchange because using money was beneficial. The goods and services workers produced were sold in exchange for money, which they then held until deciding to make a purchase to fulfil a need or want. Thus, as a result of specialisation, workers exchanged their labour for purchasing power that was stored in money until they chose to spend some or all of the purchasing power they accumulated.

The foremost measurable result of this exchange of purchasing power through the use of money is the advancement of civilisation. Money played the essential role by increasing opportunities for commerce, thereby facilitating the accumulation of capital and raising standards of living. Money is central to this process of exchange that has enabled civilisation to develop, advance and flourish.

Second, the community as a whole benefitted from the specialisation of labour that resulted in better products, whether tools, food, homes, or security. Through a process of selection, individuals who exhibited skills in producing a certain product better than others demonstrated to the community that competition is a beneficial force. Food from the better farmers or higher quality tools from the more skilled toolmaker were preferred over inferior products. Those who could not farm or make tools sought other activities to use their abilities by working so they too could fill their needs and wants by participating in the market process. The key point is that by pursuing their own goals, each individual was contributing to the development of society that advanced as it gained accumulated knowledge, experience, and wealth.

Specialisation of labour has continued to this day. Farmers produce food, a builder a house, a manufacturer a car, and so forth. Similarly, a barber cutting hair, a waiter serving food, a programmer writing code, etc., provide services that we consume. All of these items are useful products, which is a generic term that can be applied to all things produced that have some economic value to someone, meaning that it can be exchanged. Gold explorers and miners expend labour and capital over time to find, retrieve and supply a useful product we call money.

The key point is that money comes into existence in the same way as any other marketable product. They all result from labour and capital diligently applied to a task completed over time to produce a useful outcome. Money is not created out of thin air nor does it fall off a moneytree. In this sense money is no different from any other product.

If any product is deemed by market participants to have usefulness, it has value, which makes it marketable and can be exchanged for something else that is preferred by the owner of that product. In effect money is the most marketable product.

There remains one other point of note regarding the origin of money. Government had no role to play; money was not created by law or force. Money arose from the spontaneous, capitalistic interaction of individuals seeking to improve their situation in life, or stated another way, in their pursuit of happiness.

Money and Purchasing Power

Purchasing power and money are used interchangeably, but they are not synonymous. Purchasing power transcends money. Purchasing power comprises time and effort, the output of which is merely conveyed by money. It was the existence of purchasing power – the labour that someone in prehistory expended to produce a product desired by someone else – that led to voluntary exchange and then to the invention of money as the product people chose to hold as their most marketable asset. Introducing this intermediate step of holding money improved the market process by facilitating these voluntary exchanges. A labourer earned purchasing power and then exchanged his or her product for money, which was eventually exchanged for another product the labourer needed or wanted and was able to afford.

Purchasing power is received as compensation for one's labour expended on a product for a person or entity willing and prepared to pay for the labourer's time and effort. Usually expressed in terms of money or currency, the underlying nature of a transaction is the movement of purchasing power from one party to the other, namely, from the buyer to the seller. In other words, existing purchasing power is needed to pay for the new goods or services being created by one's labour unless, according to the Theory of Natural Money as explained in Chapter 11, the good that labour is producing is money, namely, mining gold.

Earned or Phantom Purchasing Power

In the present currency and banking system, purchasing power comes into existence in two ways. In the proper and equitable way, purchasing power is a consequence of work performed in the present. In the inequitable way, purchasing power is simply an accounting record based on promises to be fulfilled in the future.

Obviously completed work today is different from a promise and, consequently, earned purchasing power (EPP) is fundamentally different from promised, or phantom, purchasing power (PPP). It is a critical deficiency of the present currency and banking system that the essential difference between these two types of purchasing power is not clearly identified, which is an important point explored in this book because the conjuring of PPP by governments and banks is a fraudulent accounting practice that has become abusive. It robs people of their time spent working to acquire EPP, and it erodes individual liberty by conveying abnormal power to the State with its control of the currency creation process to conjure up new currency 'out of thin air', as the saying goes.

Not everyone is comfortable with accounting. Therefore, the concept of creating something 'out of thin air' can be difficult to grasp, and banking uses this circumstance to help perpetuate their sleight of hand to create PPP. There is a practice in the stock market, now illegal, called naked short selling that can help explain what it means to create something 'out of thin air'.

Short selling deals with shares of a company that exist as certificates or records in a share depository. For this example, assume a company has issued 1,000,000 shares. Hedge funds and speculators often sell short shares in the expectation of earning a profit if a company's share price declines, after which the shares are purchased to complete the transaction.

To sell short a company's shares, existing shares must first be borrowed by the short seller from an investor who owns them and is willing to lend them for a fee. Let us further assume that a hedge fund borrows 5,000 shares owned by an investor, which the hedge fund sells in the market. The borrowed shares are eventually bought back and returned to the investor who loaned them along with the borrowing fee. Throughout this process, the quantity of shares remained at 1,000,000. This process is legal and conforms to the rules of major stock exchanges. This legitimate short sale is fundamentally different from a naked short sale.

Naked short selling is an infamous stock price manipulation tool used in so-called 'bear raids' by the notorious stock market speculators of the nineteenth century, and today it is illegal in countries reliant upon a respectable rule of law. It occurs if the shares are not borrowed but are still sold. The result is that a company will have more shares nominally outstanding than it has shares legally issued.

In the example above, the hedge fund would have completed a naked short sale if did not borrow any shares but still sold 5,000 shares. There would now be 1,005,000 shares of the company nominally outstanding. The hedge fund is selling something it does not have, which is illegal.

An example occurred in 2017 when Dole Foods had more shares owned by shareholders than it had issued,[31] so some shareholders did not realise that they were buying phantom shares. The difference between the number of shares issued and those nominally outstanding equalled the amount of naked short selling. The phantom Dole Foods shares sold short were created by spurious bookkeeping and existed only in 'thin air', namely, an accounting record.

This process of naked short selling that creates phantom shares is identical to what happens in fractional reserve banking that creates PPP. They both arise from spurious bookkeeping.

A phantom share of a company is created by a broker with accounting entries and then loaned to the hedge fund, which then sells the shares. Similarly, PPP is created by a bank with bookkeeping and loaned to its customer, which now has currency units for its use to purchase goods and services.

The outcome of selling naked shares is different from lending PPP. The naked shares are eventually bought back, and the broker's bookkeeping entries are reversed. When units of PPP are loaned by banks, they remain outstanding, and in fact continue to grow from new loans until a financial crisis forces banks to recall loans to improve their liquidity by reducing the quantity of their assets. Regardless of these different outcomes, the principle in law is the same. It does not matter one whit whether one sells or lends anything that they do not possess. It is fraud. Yet while naked short selling has been made illegal in civilised countries around the world because of the obvious fraud that it is, fractional reserve banking and the creation of PPP has not been made illegal, even though it too is fraudulent.

The share price of Dole Foods was negatively impacted by the naked short selling, just like happened with the naked short selling in the nineteenth century bear raids of stock market manipulators. By artificially increasing the number of units through bank alchemy that transformed debt into currency, as explained in the next chapter, the units of EPP created legitimately through the application of labour, capital, and time are debased by the bookkeeping that creates and records the lending of PPP. The shares of a company and a unit of EPP incur the same result when their quantity is expanded by naked short selling and naked lending. They are being debased and cheapened.

The Four Functions of Money

Aristotle propounded that money is a medium of exchange, unit of account, and store of value. This classic definition of money remains widely accepted to this day, but it is no longer adequate. It needs updating to explain money and currency in our modern economy.

In ancient Greece, only silver coin circulated as currency. There were none of the currencies - paper, bank ledger entries, and virtual - that are in circulation today. So Aristotle's three functions of money were perceived differently during his time and during subsequent centuries when precious metal coin circulated as currency. Few economists acknowledge this difference and therefore overlook the fourth function of money, which is the final payment for a transaction.

Because precious metal coin does not circulate today, many people are unaware of this fourth function. What is more, they are taught misconceptions from which they are led to believe that national currencies are money.

Beliefs can be difficult to overcome, discard, and then replace with a new way of thinking, complicating both the historical comparison and a correct explanation of the functions of money. But they must be overcome to achieve a correct understanding of what truly is money, and more to the point, why currency is different, even though currency seemingly performs the functions one usually expects of money.

Two nineteenth-century British economists recognised that Aristotle's definition needed updating. Walter Bagehot in *Lombard Street: A Description of the Money Market* (1873) and William Stanley Jevons in *Money and the Mechanism of Exchange* (1875) both understood that currency was evolving into new forms and went to great lengths to explain them. Current accounts and chequebooks were becoming increasingly popular, supplanting but not replacing gold and silver coin and the paper banknotes the Bank of England had been issuing since its formation in 1694.

In addition to some useful insights about economic theory, Jevons even identified a fourth function of money. It is the function that the ancient Greeks intuitively understood when using their silver coin, but both he and Bagehot failed to pursue the key point that the new forms of currency coming into circulation were not money in the true meaning of that word because these currencies were not tangible assets. They therefore did not and could not immediately extinguish an exchange.

Paper banknotes and current accounts, despite their deficiencies which I will explain later, seemed to meet all the needs one required of money, so it is understandable that few recognised that the real meaning of money was being lost over the generations as these money substitutes circulated in place of gold. Further, new forms of currency like banknotes that could circulate efficiently in place of money itself were seen to be a worthwhile development and were proving to be successful. Not only were these new currencies more convenient, they saved the loss of valuable precious metal that occurred from wear and tear when used as coins.

Jevons's fourth function of money never gained wide acceptance and subsequent writers mostly relied on Aristotle's definition. Consequently, it is time to rethink the functions of money.

To do this, keep in mind that from prehistory to the mid-twentieth century, money to Aristotle and everyone else was precious metal coin. So the fourth function - money as a means to complete a payment - was intuitive to almost everyone until precious metal coins stopped circulating.

Payment is a critical task that in today's economy with the use of various types of currency has been widely misunderstood or just simply ignored. A detailed analysis of modern currency is needed, as is an enquiry into the true meaning of *payment* and how it is achieved.

As the fourth function of money, the means of payment is an essential component of the Theory of Natural Money. It recognises that *payment* is not a process. It is an instantaneous event that cannot be attained with today's currencies, all of which introduce risks not found when gold is used in payment. From a practical point of view, money as a means of payment is becoming more important than ever in today's world because the many risks arising from the use of national currencies are growing. These are risks that exist when a money substitute is used in an exchange instead of money itself, i.e., gold, and they are risks that cannot be avoided.

1) Medium of exchange

As a medium of exchange, money is the asset through which an exchange is completed. By serving as an intermediate good, money overcomes the hurdles posed by the double coincidence of wants. Because of money, two people no longer need to wait for the fortuitous circumstance of meeting at the same moment and in the same place to exchange the asset held by one person for the preferred asset held by the other person. As the intermediate asset, money facilitates the exchange in which an item of production is turned into an item for consumption.

Note that the double coincidence of wants has not disappeared with the use of money. Its nature has simply changed. Instead of goods and services being exchanged directly for other goods and services, they are exchanged for money, which has become one side of the double coincidence of wants. The seller willingly accepts the money received for the product being sold because they believe that the money can be used to purchase a product needed or wanted.

Money as the medium enabling an exchange also facilitates commerce in another way. Money provides the means by which we communicate economic value with others. With money we express our subjective preference for the money we possess relative to products we need or want, or alternatively, for the product we want to sell in exchange for money. So in regard to the double coincidence of wants, the seller's preference is for the money, whereas the buyer's preference is for the product being purchased with money.

As the intermediate asset in the exchange, money is, by definition, marketable, meaning that it moves from buyer to seller on the willingness of both parties. The more widely accepted, the better it is for money to serve as a medium. There are few, if any, assets more widely accepted around the world than gold.

Given that money's first function is a medium of exchange, a unit of account must enjoy widespread acceptance to be effective as a communication tool. The logic of this point is straightforward and can be compared to language. It is a good thing when one language is widely accepted because it facilitates communication which in turn leads to greater interaction between people and more commercial opportunities. For example, global business has benefitted from English becoming the predominant language in cross-border finance and trade.

To be effective as a reliable means of communicating value, money must be a known unit that can be trusted and easily understood. To achieve these essential characteristics, units of money must be produced to a consistent and unvarying standard, and gold achieves this objective when expressed in units of weight, either grams or ounces.

2) Unit of account

A unit of account is a measurement tool. National currencies fail to meet this requirement of being money because they are not consistent in measuring value.

To provide an accurate measurement, a unit of account must be an unchanging standard. An inch, litre, gram, and all other units identifying size – whether length, volume, or weight – each have a specific definition that does not change. They became standards of measurement by general consent, and their definition is known and accepted.

A money unit of account presents a unique situation. Confusion arises when a money substitute appears to fulfil this money function but does not. For example, the term 'ten dollars' is understood by both parties of the exchange. The word 'dollar' is used simply from force of habit and convenience to have a common term to communicate the contemplated transaction, but it is a vacuous label because it no longer has a fixed, unchanging definition.

Apologists for fiat currency contend that the dollar is defined by 'what it can buy', which is a tautology, not a definition. It is like saying that an inch is whatever it measures, but unless you know what an inch is, it is a meaningless concept, particularly when viewed over time if the length of an inch changes, as is happening to the dollar from inflation. To be effective as a measuring unit, an inch cannot be an undefined concept. It needs to have today the same definition as it did yesterday or any other time in the past, and for that matter, as it will have in the future.

A unit of account applied to money is no different from any other unit of account used for measurement; the unit of account must be defined, as was the case under the gold standard. For example, from 1792 until 1900, the U.S. dollar was defined as 371.25 grains (24.1 grams) of pure silver, at which time the dollar was moved to the gold standard. The Gold Standard Act defined the dollar as 23.222 grains of fine gold ($20.67 per troy ounce).

By 1934, the dollar had become debased and was devalued when its definition was changed to 13.714 grains of fine gold ($35.00 per troy ounce). It was devalued again in 1971 to 12.632 grains of fine gold ($38.00 per troy ounce), but the dollar continued to be debased. So it was devalued again in 1973 to 11.368 grains of fine gold ($42.22 per troy ounce), which the federal government announced would remain its 'official price' and that the dollar from that point would not be defined as a weight of gold.

That announcement marks the beginning of the fiat currency era, in which the dollar began circulating solely because of force of law. Since then, the dollar has not been defined by gold or anything else. If a currency is meant to be effective at measuring anything, it must be defined as a fixed standard of measurement.

Everyone knows that the purchasing power of a dollar today is different from that of a dollar in 1913 when the Federal Reserve was created. But few actually adjust their economic calculation to account for this change, which adversely impacts decisions to allocate capital and to measure a true rate of return on that capital.

With regard to a unit of account as a communication tool, the dollar is more widely used than gold. That is not a consequence of any problem with gold. Rather, it is a function of government influence through legal tender laws forcing the circulation of national currencies to supplant gold from circulation. In the nineteenth century, during the period of the gold standard, the terms 'British pound' and 'gold' were considered synonymous. Even though the formal link to gold has now been abandoned, the names of national currency continue to be used leading to confusion about money and its function as a unit of account.

To ensure the widespread acceptance of money as a unit of account, there is a need for a numeraire. The numeraire of the British pound was the sovereign, a gold coin containing .2354 of a troy ounce. The American numeraire was the eagle containing 232.22 grains of fine gold and equal to ten dollars, which along with the double-eagle equal to twenty dollars were popular American gold coins.

Gold is often quoted in the anachronistic troy ounce, whereas grams have emerged as the most widely used measurement of weight around the world. Therefore, a more practical numeraire is one gram of gold, or a goldgram.

Whether measured in grams, troy or avoirdupois ounces, or grains, weights of gold have been an effective unit of account for millennia. The results illustrated in Figure 1 confirm that a goldgram is just as useful as money today as it was in 1950 or any time since then. This usefulness as a unit of account is one of the reasons gold became money.

3) Store of value

As previously explained, gold is not an investment. It is money, and Figure 1 proves this point.

It is reasonable to expect that an investment will increase your wealth, which is why you take the risk that comes with making the investment. Gold, however, does not increase one's wealth. When viewed over a lengthy period of time, gold simply preserves wealth in the form of purchasing power. A goldgram purchases basically the same amount of crude oil today that it did anytime over the past seven decades shown in Figure 1. No one wants an investment like that because their purchasing power held in the gold they owned did not increase over seven decades, but everyone wants money like that. Gold did one of the things that money is supposed to do, which is preserve purchasing power. Stated another way, money needs to be a store of value.

To be a store of value, money must also achieve one other objective. It must provide absolute liquidity, which is another concept widely misunderstood today. Liquidity means more than being able to find a buyer for your asset. True liquidity must be unconditional. In other words, whether in good times or troubled economic times, money must be marketable without any contingencies being imposed on it, particularly any reliance on a counterparty.

Gold meets this test because it is a tangible asset. In contrast, all money substitutes, namely, national currencies, are dependent upon the third party that issued them, regardless of whether it is a central bank, commercial bank, or government treasury. I explain this crucial point below. For now, we can simply note that gold provides absolute liquidity because it is money you own, in contrast to money substitutes issued by the financial institution to whom you loaned your purchasing power, which they now owe to you.

4) Means of payment

An exchange is a transaction in which assets move between buyer and seller, the payer and payee. When properly defined, payment occurs when the payee receives a tangible asset.

I use the word *tangible* purposefully because not all assets have substance. Try to hold in your hands the substance of a bank deposit or putting your hands around any other financial asset. This fundamental difference in the essential nature of tangible assets in contrast to financial assets is important in understanding how payments are made.

Payment is not a process. It is an instantaneous event occurring the moment a tangible asset changes hands from the payer to the payee. The exchange is extinguished the moment the buyer receives the product being purchased, and the seller receives the money, a tangible asset, used to make the purchase. There is no lingering, unfilled obligation, and both parties to the exchange they completed are satisfied.

For example, assume you are in a store and purchase a good with a gold coin. The exchange is extinguished the moment the coin passes from your hand to that of the seller. There is no lingering obligation. You have the good that was purchased, and the seller has the money paid for the purchase.

Now consider the differences if a national currency is used for the purchase. The seller receives a promise of some bank, not money. The promise is evidenced by a banknote, if the purchase is made with cash. Otherwise, if a cheque or plastic card is used, a deposit is added to the seller's bank account, and the bank promises to make that deposit available when the seller chooses to spend it. The transaction is not extinguished until the seller takes the currency and purchases a product to satisfy their needs or wants.

Because national currencies are not a tangible precious metal, we can reasonably surmise that Aristotle would not consider the dollar, euro, and all the others to be money. Nor would anyone else until the twentieth century. In ancient Greece and until gold and silver coin stopped circulating in the 1960s, a farmer sold food and in effect bought an asset called money.

That is how exchanges used to be viewed; assets exchanged for assets. This view was also true for international trade. Gold was the settlement asset that moved between countries to pay for goods and services.

In recent decades we have generally lost sight of this essential nature of transactions that tangible assets pay for tangible assets, both domestically and internationally. These days, the United States has been successful in exporting dollars instead of gold to purchase and import assets.

This axiom that goods and services pay for goods and services is a key element of the economic principles described by Jean-Baptiste Say and has been an underlying common-sense principle of commerce since the first transaction by a primitive man or woman in prehistory. Something of wealth is needed to purchase something else of wealth. This process explains how new wealth is created and civilisation advances because tangible assets used in payment arise from earned purchasing power (EPP), not the phantom purchasing power (PPP) arising out of thin air from fractional reserve banking. PPP does not and cannot extinguish an exchange. In fact, any ledger currency cannot extinguish an exchange, which is the essential ingredient to complete a payment.

If the seller accepts a ledger currency, the exchange becomes troublesome because there is a third party in the exchange, namely, the bank(s) that process the transaction. This third party introduces an element of time that in turn injects risks into the transaction not found with instantaneous payments using gold. A transaction with national currency instead of a tangible asset has payment risks arising in three ways.

First, the use of ledger currency involves three or more parties to the transaction. These are the buyer, seller, and one or more banks. Reliance on the banking system is necessary to process the transaction, which is not instantaneous. An element of time is introduced, regardless of whether it is seconds, minutes, or the two days typically required by banks to complete wire transfers. When ledger currency is accepted in payment, you do not have immediate access to your purchasing power, and that may mean you miss an opportunity to make a timely purchase or an investment.

The second risk also relates to the passage of time that delays completion of the transaction. The risk is that the purchasing power of the ledger currency may erode from debasement. It may even disappear completely, which has happened throughout the history of ledger currency in different ways. If a bank fails or if the government issuing that currency were to declare that it no longer has the same value, the holder of the ledger currency will lose their purchasing power. This risk exists until the amount of the purchasing power the national currency conveys is realised by purchasing a product.

By this definition, even gold has some currency risk, but it is minimal. While in the short-term its purchasing power can be diminished from the moment you accept it in exchange until you spend it to purchase a good or service because gold's rate of exchange to goods priced in national currencies fluctuates, in the long-term this currency risk is inconsequential because gold's purchasing power is consistent.

Third, there is counterparty risk. The seller is now dependent upon the creditworthiness of a financial institution as the third party in the transaction. There is a risk of diminishment and at times even the total loss of purchasing power a payee incurs from the moment they accept ledger currency in exchange for a good or service, until the payee uses the currency received to purchase a good or service. The risk is that the financial institution is unable or unwilling to process the transfer of currency from the buyer's account to the account of the seller even though it is obligated to do so. The key point is that banks go bankrupt or declare *force majeure*, and it matters not one whit to the seller that these events are typically done with government consent. The seller has given up a tangible product but did not have the opportunity to benefit from the sale of goods by using the ledger currency received. This intermediate step necessitated by accepting a national currency introduces counterparty risk, which can only be avoided when tangible assets are used in payment.

In our modern economy, nearly all transactions are completed with ledger currency, and the biggest banks process the largest portion of these. They are therefore declared to be 'too big to fail' because their collapse would severely impact the economy by disrupting the processing and settling of the ledger currency that circulates within the banking system. I will return to this matter when I look at banking and how it is currently practised. For now, suffice it to say that each transaction using a money substitute is dependent upon the financial institution processing the movement of currency from the buyer to the seller. Consequently, the exchange is not extinguished at the moment the seller releases their product. Payment, in the true meaning of that word, has not been made because a product has not been exchanged for product, and payment will not be completed until the seller uses the national currency to acquire a product.

If a seller accepts a currency for the product being sold, the seller needs reasonable certainty that the currency can be used to purchase a product the seller needs or wants. In other words, the payment risks related to the currency need to be low for the currency to be trusted, but better yet is to avoid these risks altogether. Gold fulfils this role perfectly, and as some will argue, so do cryptocurrencies, which I will discuss later. As a hint, they are called cryptocurrencies for a reason; they are not cryptomoney.

What is Money?

Having established this background information, what is money?

Money has the four basic functions described above. It makes economic calculation possible and enables people to communicate their own subjective view of value to transact with others. In the broadest sense, it is any tangible product that facilitates human interaction in the market process. In the narrowest sense, it is the most marketable tangible product that best fulfils all four requirements of money, which is gold.

As a means of economic calculation, we use money countless times throughout our life because we must make decisions about how we live. What do we need? What do we want? How much can we afford? And because we cannot afford everything we want, what do we buy, and what do we forgo? How much do we save to afford what we want to buy?

As economic beings, we need to make decisions like these every day. We live in a world ruled by scarcity, and in our pursuit of happiness, we therefore decide our preference of the different alternatives and then choose. If money did not exist, society as we know it would not exist, just like our society needs language to exist.

To be effective in communication, money like language must be clear, easily understood, and consistent. The components of a language are words, and the components of money are units of account. To be useful as a means of communication, the components must be consistent. If one day we call the structure in which we live a *house* and the next day we call it a *hose*, we would not be able to communicate. Each new day would require everyone to redefine the terms to be used when speaking to one another. The same logic applies to any unit of measure, whether inches, litres, tonnes or goldgrams.

It is essential that society has available for its use a money through which everyone can communicate using an identical unit of account established by a clear definition. Those people who are good at understanding the changing definition of the dollar – currency speculators, for example – can make a fortune if they guess right, but it differs from the fortune earned by tech entrepreneurs, whose wealth was created by the delivery of goods and services that helped people in their pursuit of happiness. Those benefitting from currency turmoil arising from today's unsound currencies make their fortune at the expense of others who do not understand what is happening to currency and who as a consequence are left at a disadvantage, which is the vast majority of the population.

Currency today creates an unfair advantage where there should be none. Gold in contrast levels the playing field, making the completely honest economic interaction between individuals that is the foundation of a free society. So the logical conclusion is clear and unmistakeable. To have a just and fair society, money must be gold.

Gold fulfils all the requirements of money better than any other asset. Because a stated weight of gold is a consistent and unchanging unit of account over time, it is a reliable measure of value throughout time, as illustrated in Figure 1. A gram of gold as a unit of account and means of communicating value is not confined by any country border.

The term 'sound money' is used to describe money that maintains its purchasing power, but 'sound money' is a tautology. Money is gold, which is always sound. What can be unsound is currency when the circulating medium is anything but gold coin. Even silver coins can be unsound in the very limited sense that the ratio of gold and silver fluctuates, causing variations in their relative purchasing power.

One of the essential requirements of money is to make and receive payment with any risks mitigated, which only tangible assets can achieve. This requirement is based on a fundamental economic principle that is the basis of human interaction, namely, that we are producers and consumers, and that product pays for product. Money therefore is any tangible asset chosen voluntarily without force or edict by the payer and the payee.

By this definition, all money is 'sound' because payment is achieved the moment assets are exchanged between the buyer and seller. The payee can rely on the inherent use of the tangible asset accepted as money if after accepting payment the payee discovers that it does not have economic value because no one else is willing to accept the tangible asset as money. Today's currencies do not have this feature because they have no inherent value.

Money is an outcome of human action. It is not an item based on financial institutions or their creditworthiness. Nor is money an intangible tool created for us by the State, though governments like to think they possess that power. The spurious theory that governments create money had its origin only a century ago.[32] Just as spurious is the notion that governments can demonetise gold. As Figure 1 clearly illustrates, gold still is money despite government pronouncements to the contrary and even though these days it rarely circulates as currency.

Money has one distinguishing feature that sets it apart from money substitutes purporting to be money. At the moment the buyer and seller complete their transaction, the exchange is extinguished. In short, products pay for products. The money used by the buyer, which is tangible, pays for the product offered by the seller. With money there are no lingering obligations to the payment process. No national currency has this feature, which is one of their critical deficiencies.

5. Currency, Banking and Accounting

What advantages does [one] derive from the
system of book-keeping by double entry? It is
among the finest inventions of the human mind.

Johann von Goethe

Accounting is one of the finest inventions of the human mind, but like any other tool, it is only valuable when applied honestly and put to a useful purpose. Unfortunately, history shows that accounting has been used fraudulently to deceive the human mind, as is the case with fractional reserve banking (FRB).

A detailed analysis of FRB is essential to understand why money substitutes circulating as currency have become a disruptive force that is fracturing the link between money and liberty. This analysis requires some knowledge of accounting and law and the use of logic. Some background information is also necessary, beginning with Gresham's Law, as well as a principal tenet of the Theory of Natural Money. Namely, the nature of currency is that it conveys purchasing power in commerce through the unit of account that we use for economic calculation, but unless the currency is moving gold, it is not moving money. Instead, it is moving units of account denominated in a money substitute.

Gresham's Law

Sir Thomas Gresham was a financial advisor to Elizabeth I, who ascended the throne of England in 1558 with the nation's currency in disarray. Her father, Henry VIII, removed silver content from coins, replacing it with cheap base metal during the last several years of his reign and that policy was followed by his son and immediate successor, Edward VI. In this way, coins were debased and lost about three quarters of their value over a period of about fifteen years before Elizabeth ascended the throne.

This debasement harmed economic activity, both within England and in relation to the country's trading partners. More importantly, it undermined trust in the monarchy, which concerned Elizabeth and her advisers. The new monarch's position was not secure given the tensions arising from religious conflict at that time and, more to the point, the claim to the English throne made by Mary, Queen of Scots.

By tradition, an image of the ruling monarch was placed on coins to attest to the integrity of the coin's metal content. As the silver veneer of Henry VIII's debased coins began to wear down, his nose on his image on the coin revealed the coin's copper interior, making 'Old Coppernose' – and by implication, the monarchy – a subject of derision. Trust in the currency would mean trust in the monarchy, so Elizabeth turned to Gresham.

Probably building upon the insights that Copernicus advised the Royal Prussian Assembly on the reform of Prussian coinage three decades before, Gresham advised her that 'bad money drives out good', which is the essence of the timeless law that bears his name. People spend the bad money, the debased coins, and to protect their purchasing power hold/save the good money, which are those coins with a metal content whose value in exchange is limited to the face value of the coin. For example, when silver was removed from dimes, quarters and half-dollar coins in the United States in the 1960s, the silver content of existing coins became higher than their face value, so they were hoarded and quickly disappeared from circulation. It is a natural reaction by holders of coins to protect the purchasing power conveyed by their coins.

Further, Gresham understood that underweight coins disrupt economic activity. So he recommended a recoinage to the new monarch.

In 1560, under Gresham's guidance, Elizabeth instructed the Royal Mint to remove all debased coinage from circulation. These were then melted down and replaced with newly minted coins with the correct metal content so that the face value minted on the coin equalled the market value of its metal content.

There is a corollary to Gresham's Law. The word 'currency' had not yet come into usage; it would only appear a century later.[33] The principle that Gresham recognised also applies to currency, so as people act to protect their purchasing power, 'bad currency drives out good', which as we will see is as important today as it was in Gresham's time.

The Three Types of Currency: Coin, Ledger and Virtual

The history of currency can be divided into three categories that reflect the substance and appearance of the currency: coin, ledger, and virtual. Each fundamentally transformed the essential nature of currency.

Coin composed principally of precious metal was the only circulating medium until the seventeenth century.[34] At that time, ledger currency in the form of banknotes developed within the new banking industry emerging in London. After 1844, ledger currency in the form of bank deposits enabling payment by cheque began to grow rapidly, largely supplanting banknotes and coin. Breakthrough technologies like wire transfers and then in the twentieth century, plastic cards, provided new means for deposit currency to circulate more efficiently and at lower cost.

The development of the internet in the twenty-first century has enabled ledger currency to circulate digitally, which has become widely accepted, but the internet has contributed in another way. It has made possible the innovations that resulted in the third transformation in the nature of currency. Virtual currency, which is fundamentally different from all predecessor currencies and still evolving, is now circulating digitally through the internet.

A closer look at each of these three forms of currencies will highlight the one achievement they all share. Each innovation made currency circulate more efficiently, which is a beneficial outcome. By reducing the impediments to commerce, of which cost of making a payment is just one, the threshold to conducting commerce is lowered. It is also lowered as efficiency of the currency improves. Taking these steps and introducing the innovations that reduce the impediments of conducting commerce is an important achievement. A lower cost and more efficient currency creates more opportunity for individuals to interact to meet their needs and wants in their own pursuit of happiness.

Weights of gold and silver in natural or fabricated form have been circulating in commerce since prehistory, with rudimentary coins appearing circa 600-BCE. The occasional and fleeting experiments with money substitutes are only significant for their single shared trait; they all eventually failed. The quality of coins improved over time with better refining and minting techniques, making coins more reliable, and precious metal fabricated into coin became the preferred medium for use in commerce over other tangible assets.

Advancements in printing and the manufacturing of paper that lowered their costs and improved their quality inspired new innovations of money substitutes. The most significant development occurred in seventeenth century London with the creation of ledger currency.

Ledger currency, as its name implies, is simply an accounting entry. It is a record of the units of account owed by a bank to its customers, and these units of account are a liability on the balance sheet of the bank issuing the ledger currency. The bank's liability has value because the assets backing the liability are believed to have value, so the ledger currency is accepted and used in place of the asset itself. Allowing liabilities to circulate as currency is a monopolistic privilege given exclusively to banks. The liabilities of Apple, Microsoft and every other non-bank corporation are not permitted to circulate as currency.

There are two types of ledger currency, and the first to develop was a paper banknote, which circulated as a money substitute because it was redeemable into gold coin. In the past, each bank issued its own banknotes. I experienced this practice myself when first arriving in Hong Kong in 1971 and used Hong Kong dollar banknotes issued by Hong Kong & Shanghai Bank and Chartered Bank. The issuance of this paper currency in most countries has now been arrogated by central banks, which issue banknotes that are not redeemable in precious metal. They are fiat currency that circulate by the force of law.

The second type of ledger currency is the deposit account, which in theory are redeemable into banknotes. It was developed by commercial banks in the eighteenth century, but used infrequently, and mainly just between banks to settle their respective balances. After the power to issue banknotes was taken away from them, commercial banks rapidly expanded the use of deposit currency. These deposit currency units initially circulated only by cheque, but that changed as communications technology advanced. The units of account on bank ledgers began to circulate by wire transfer, and more recently, by plastic cards through private networks.

Bank created ledger currency now also circulates by means of the internet, which has proven to be yet another major advancement in communication technology. The digital circulation of ledger currency has already become well established even though the commercial aspects of the internet are barely two decades old.

The internet continues to spark innovation, changing the status quo in many areas including currency. The bank cartel is being challenged by these new technologies from which virtual currency has emerged and the speed of its development opens up untold possibilities.

Virtual currency also circulates digitally through the internet but is fundamentally different from ledger currency and coins. Virtual currency is not a tangible asset, nor is it a liability on a balance sheet. For example, cryptocurrency, which is one type of virtual currency and to which I will return later, is based on a complex mathematical formula, not tangible assets like gold and silver nor assets on a bank balance sheet giving value to the bank's liabilities circulating as ledger currency.

Virtual currency is fundamentally changing the nature of currency just like ledger currency did when it was first introduced. There is another similarity. Ledger currency was so new and radically different from the coins then circulating that it eventually supplanted, it took a while for people to embrace ledger currency. So too with virtual currencies.

The use of virtual currencies in online gaming goes back to the earliest years of the internet, and they are therefore familiar to Millennials and even more so with subsequent generations. As reliance on the internet has increased over time, and the problems of ledger currency have become increasingly apparent, virtual currencies are becoming familiar to older generations and more widely used. As new tech applications develop, currency will become even more efficient, but gold never changes, which is an essential requirement for money.

Alchemy at the Bank of England

Alchemy is the medieval pseudoscience based on the misguided belief that the transmutation of matter was possible. More specifically, deluded time wasters conducted experiments trying to prove that a base metal like lead could be turned into gold, despite the countless futile attempts to do so and bare logic saying it was an impossible task.

Nevertheless, the Bank of England (or simply as it is often called, 'the Bank') in a way achieved with sleight of hand what the alchemists could only dream. The Bank transmuted paper by getting people to believe it was 'as good as gold', which is probably the world's biggest-ever con given the countless number of people who have swallowed that lie promoted by the Bank as it cunningly travelled through three centuries since the Bank's founding.

A piece of paper can never be as good as gold. A promise can never be as good as the real thing.

The transmutation is deceptively simple. Here is an example describing how it worked when the Bank first opened its doors but using gold's recent exchange rate. Assume the Bank receives ten gold Britannia coins from the Royal Mint, each of which weighs one ounce and is valued at £1280, or £12,800 in total. The Bank then issues 12,800 of newly created £1 banknotes that it gives to the Royal Mint, which are then used by the government to pay for its expenses. The gold coins have been transformed into currency. The coins remain in the Bank, but the banknotes it issued circulate current because they are redeemable into the coins held by the Bank. Here is where the alchemy comes in.

Let us assume the Bank prints £1 million of new banknotes, without receiving any gold coins from the Royal Mint, and then lends the banknotes to the government. These new banknotes are spent by the government and thereby become intermingled with previously issued banknotes. The new banknotes are no different in appearance from the banknotes the Bank previously issued, but all of them are now only partially backed by gold. This deception is called fractional reserve banking.

The Bank is said to 'monetise' the government's debt, but that term is a misnomer. A better word would be 'currencise' because banks engaged in the deception are creating currency, not money. This term 'monetise' is misleading and deceptive but used regardless of whether the assets being turned into currency are tangible like gold or intangible, like a promissory note. So its use accomplishes what the alchemist aimed to achieve. The Bank alchemises the government's debt by transforming it into banknotes denominated in British pounds that are misleadingly portrayed by the Bank's apologists to be as good as gold.

Only select, government approved agents can alchemise their assets into currency. They are a country's central bank and its commercial banks. Two examples may be useful here to describe this unique privilege granted to banks.

Assume that a bank lends 1,000 units of account to a borrower by buying the borrower's promissory note and crediting 1,000 units of account to the borrower's current account. By this action, the bank has created 1,000 units of ledger currency. The borrower's debt has been alchemised because it results in the creation of new currency.

In another example, assume a finance company lends to a borrower 1,000 units of account. The finance company buys the borrower's promissory note and either gives the borrower banknotes or a cheque. In either case, the currency being borrowed already exists, having been created by either the central bank (if banknotes are disbursed to the borrower) or a bank (if the borrower receives a cheque drawn on the finance company's currency in its account at a bank). A new debt is created when the finance company lends 1,000 units of account, but the debt is not alchemised. A finance company cannot create currency because it is not part of the banking cartel.

In theory, central banks can create currency by alchemising any asset of value, but in practice this power is limited. Only assets thought to be liquid and readily saleable are typically used in this process. At the time of the Bank of England's creation, only gold and silver met these criteria while real estate and other tangible assets did not, but it was not long before these other assets and even just mere promises were tried.

In 1716, John Law formed the Banque Générale in France, which two years later became that country's central bank and renamed as the Banque Royale. It issued irredeemable paper currency that led to the ill-famed Mississippi Bubble and its financial and economic collapse in 1720. Several decades later and not long after the collapse of the American continental and the French assignat used as currency during those countries' revolutions, Law's financial folly was immortalised by Johann Wolfgang von Goethe in his most famous allegory, *Faust,* in which paper currency is the invention of the devil. Although it may be the most damning criticism of fractional reserve banking, it was not the last.

Not too long thereafter famed nineteenth century British economist David Ricardo observed, 'Neither a state nor a bank ever have had unrestricted power of issuing paper [currency] without abusing that power.' In the twentieth century, the outcome of these paper currency follies is forcefully captured by Ayn Rand: 'Oceans of tears, all the guns in the world can't transform those pieces of paper in your wallet into the bread you'll need to survive tomorrow.' In the words of Professor Hans F. Sennholz, who experienced the post-Second World War inflation in Germany, 'The history of fiat money is little more than a register of monetary follies and inflations. Our present age merely affords another entry in this dismal register.' What was true in Ricardo's day is still true, but the present 'Money Bubble'[35] has not yet popped.

Regardless of the lessons of the past, these days central banks with self-assured hubris continue to alchemise assets of inferior quality. These institutions have assets on their balance sheets that are presumed to have value, but are simply promises of questionable value, which is a point to which I will return in Chapter 8 by examining the factors affecting the quality of currency.

Fractional Reserve Banking Explained

Banking and currency have been built upon fractional reserves. It is therefore necessary to take an in-depth look at how this process works. Doing so will help explain why it has stirred so much controversy since first introduced by the Bank of England over three centuries ago, and the origins of banking in seventeenth century London is the logical place to begin.

In Figure 3, I use the British sovereign, the gold coin of the realm equal to £1. Five coins are placed in a hypothetical bank by its customers, and their coins are recorded in the financial records of this bank.

This hypothetical bank has assets consisting of premises, a vault, and coins that it owns and uses for its own working capital. It has no liabilities, so the capital invested by the bank's owners equals the bank's assets. The coins placed with it by its customers for safekeeping are recorded in a memorandum account, which is off-balance sheet data. That means the customers' coins are not an asset of the bank, and therefore not available to the bank for use in its operation. The customers' coins are stored in the bank's vault but kept separate from the bank's own coins.

Figure 3 – Hypothetical Bank, Custody Services Only

Bank owned coins	£	5	Liabilities		0
Bank premises & vault	£	10	Bank capital	£	15
Total Assets	**£**	**15**	**Total Capital & Debt**	**£**	**15**
			Memorandum Account:		
			Customer coins in custody	£	100

In the custody agreement establishing the arrangement between the bank and its customers, the customers' coins always remain in the vault for safekeeping, and the owner of the coins pays a fee to the bank for this safekeeping service. The bank is bound by the terms of their contract with each customer to return the same coins to their customer on demand by the customer. Even though the owner of the coins does not have possession of them while they are in safekeeping, the owner keeps title to them with unencumbered ownership during the safekeeping process, except to the extent as provided in the custody agreement that the bank can take some of the coins in payment of the contracted storage fee if the coins' owner is late in paying this fee.

There are two types of custody receipts used when placing coins with a banker for custody storage. A bearer receipt meant that whoever presented the receipt could remove the coins from the bank's custody. The other receipt was issued in the name of the registered owner, meaning that only the owner could remove the coins from the vault. That limitation made this type of receipt less popular. If the owner died, there could be a long legal battle to allow the heirs to retrieve the coins in storage.

Placing coins with a banker for custody storage is fundamentally different from lending coins to a bank. Instead of receiving a custody receipt, the lender of coins receives the bank's promissory note (colloquially shortened to 'banknote', which is the correct term for paper currency) detailing the terms and conditions of the loan. The banknotes issued by the Bank of England stated that the bearer of a banknote could redeem it for either gold or silver coin on demand.

Lending coins to the bank exposes the owner of those coins to the bank's balance sheet, which introduces counterparty risk. Exposure to a bank's balance sheet is not a risk to the owners of coins placed in a bank's custody for safekeeping, but they do have performance risk, namely, that the bank will perform as promised and keep the coins safely stored and not lend or spend them. Nothing in life is risk-free, particularly when it comes to banks. These different risks can be explained with some basic accounting.

This process of lending coin to a bank is illustrated in the following balance sheet of the same hypothetical bank. Like Figure 3, the bank's capital is invested in its premises and vault, with £5 still in coins as its own working capital. In this example I assume that customers have removed £75 from custody to lend these coins to the bank. These customers were inclined to make these loans to avoid the storage fee that would otherwise be incurred had their £75 of coins remained in custody storage.

Figure 4 – Hypothetical Bank, 100% Reserved

Customer & bank owned coins	£	80	Owed to depositors (banknotes)	£	75
Bank premises & vault	£	10	Bank capital	£	15
Total Assets	**£**	**90**	**Total Capital & Debt**	**£**	**90**
			Memorandum Account:		
			Customer coins in custody	£	25

Note the comingling of coins recorded as an asset of the bank. Customer money has moved from the memorandum account onto the bank's balance sheet. The customer no longer owns these coins; they are now owned by the bank and owed to the customer, which poses a risk to the owner of the coins. Because the bank owns the coins, its managers can do with them whatever they choose. Normal practice of course is to lend those coins, as we will see in a moment, but for now the coins are owned by this non-lending bank that does not have any loans as assets.

The bank has borrowed coins that in the aggregate are valued at five times the amount of its capital. While this amount of capital is nominal compared to the amount of money owed by the bank to its customers, there is negligible risk of default by the bank because its liabilities - its banknotes issued to its customers who loaned their coins to the bank - are fully reserved by the coins held by the bank in its vault.

To entice its customers to accept the risk of lending their coins to the bank, the bank waived the storage fee. Avoiding this fee is a financial incentive to those people who choose to lend their gold or silver coin to the bank. Customers gain from this arrangement, but there is a problem with this non-lending bank model. It cannot earn a profit to generate a return on its invested capital.

The customer coins are being stored, but the bank is not charging any storage fee on them, which identifies the problem of this business model. The bank is not generating any income from the £75 it is storing, yet expenses to operate the bank need to be paid. It is therefore clear that this model is not workable, so let us look at the balance sheet of a bank that makes loans.

Figure 5 introduces the concept of fractional reserve banking. It occurs when the bank has liabilities greater than the amount of assets available to repay its liabilities.

Figure 5 – Hypothetical Bank, Fractional Reserves

Bank owned coins	£	35	Owed to depositors (banknotes)	£	75
Coin loans to borrowers	£	45			
Bank premises & vault	£	10	Bank capital	£	15
Total Assets	**£**	**90**	**Total Capital & Debt**	**£**	**90**
			Memorandum Account:		
			Customer coins in custody	£	25

The right side of this hypothetical bank's balance sheet not changed. It still records the same level of bank debt and capital, which balances with the £90 of total assets.

The composition of the assets has changed significantly, with £45 of coins removed from the vault and loaned to the bank's borrowing customers. As a result of lending, the bank now has more banknotes in the aggregate outstanding and circulating as currency than coins held in reserve in the vault. Holders of banknotes are now at risk. The bank only holds £35 of coins but is liable to pay £75 of coins on demand by the holders of its banknotes.

This example illustrates fractional reserve banking, which is derisively but accurately described as creating currency 'out of thin air'. There are more banknotes circulating than there is gold in the vault, which reveals the alchemy - the bank has turned paper into purchasing power purportedly as good as gold. It is a deceptive process and fraudulent because the bank gains financially from the deception. The alchemy persists as long as the holders of the banknotes believe them to be as good as gold.

The bank is technically insolvent because it does not have enough coin on hand to pay its liabilities on demand. Nevertheless, bankers consider this 60% loan to banknote ratio (£45 divided by £75) to be manageable because it is unlikely that all banknote holders will demand repayment of their coins at the same time. Of course, sometimes they do, and bank runs are the result, particularly in those banks that apply a high degree of leverage to their fractional reserves, as shown in the following example where the coins to banknote ratio is only 3%.

In Figure 6 all the customers' coins have been loaned. The bank also printed £100 of newly created banknotes and loaned those, increasing its total assets to £190. The bank owes to its customers £175 of banknotes redeemable into coin but only holds £5 of coins in its vault. If just 3% of its customers ask to redeem for coin the banknotes they are holding, the bank will be unable to meet their request, proving that the bank is insolvent.

Figure 6 – Hypothetical Bank, Leveraged Fractional Reserves

Bank owned coins	£	5	Owed to depositors (banknotes)	£	175
Coin loans to borrowers	£	75			
Banknote loans to borrowers	£	100			
Bank premises & vault	£	10	Bank capital	£	15
Total Assets	**£**	**190**	**Total Capital & Debt**	**£**	**190**
			Memorandum Account:		
			Customer coins in custody	£	25

There are real risks to the customers who hold its banknotes, demonstrating the truth of the time-honoured adage that there is no free lunch. The higher the leverage used by the bank, the higher the risk to the customer.

In these hypothetical bank examples, the liability is labelled a banknote, and these are issued nowadays by central banks. The liabilities on the balance sheet of a commercial bank are deposits. That means depositors are in effect lending their currency - or if they deposit gold, their money - to a bank, which from an accounting point of view have essentially the same risk as banknotes. Fundamentally, a deposit by a customer is no different than if the customer loaned currency to the bank. In both instances, the customer is exposed to the bank's balance sheet, which introduces counterparty risk.

In seventeenth century London, it was difficult to discern the significant differences between coins placed with a banker for storage in safe custody in contrast to the coins the customer deposited or lent to the bank. It can be confusing because banks perform two disparate functions: safe custody and deposit taking. Customers often did not realise that storage began taking on a different meaning as the nascent banks began expanding their activities by lending money placed with them, nor did banks fully disclose the risks to their customers.

Consequently, not only were the terms money and currency being conflated, the lack of awareness or the confusion over the differences gave the banks the cover they needed to begin creating banknotes to circulate as currency for which they did not hold precious metal in reserve. It meant that a bank could now leverage its balance sheet as illustrated in Figure 6 and increase bank profits by increasing their lending, adding to the aggregate number of banknotes circulating as currency.

Some dishonest bankers simply loaned the new banknotes to themselves. Their spending and newfound 'wealth' led to questions about the safety of banks, and being built on an inherently insolvent business model, banks did fail. In other words, the introduction of fractional reserve banking had consequences as banks began to expand their operation when moving away from custody into this new area of lending.

The Risks of Fractional Reserve Banking (FRB)

The history of banking is littered with countless bank failures. These early banks were no longer just in the business of providing safe custody. They were lending money too, creating risks for its customers and impeding economic activity when a bank failed. Even today, the larger the bank, the bigger the negative impact from its failure directly on its customers and indirectly on the geographic area in which it operates.

When customers began asking to redeem their banknotes for gold coin and the bank did not have enough gold coin in reserve to meet its obligations, the bank was therefore forced to begin calling in loans, demanding its borrowers repay in gold coin. The loans were then either repaid or defaulted. If repaid, the bank's balance sheet shrinks. If multiple banks are in the same position, an economic contraction begins.

The bank's balance sheet also shrinks if the loan is defaulted, but the consequences are even more dire. Not only does the request for repayment of the loan contribute to an economic contraction, but the bank may also be declared bankrupt if the defaulted loans are greater than the bank's capital.

In bankruptcy the bank is put into liquidation, which negatively impacts its customers. They soon discover that the banknotes they are holding are no longer being accepted for payment in commerce because the bankruptcy of the bank issuing those banknotes has become public knowledge. As the bank's creditors, its customers need to wait for the bank to be liquidated, which could take months or even years. The proceeds of the liquidation are then paid to them by the court appointed administrator, the amount of which depends on the quality of the bank's assets. For example, they may only receive 75% of the face value of the banknotes they are holding, or even less if the bank made a large number of bad loans that were not repayable.

Not only did FRB increase the risk for its customers, but everyone - rich or poor - where the bank operated was adversely affected. When loans were made, the quantity of currency began to exceed the quantity of money, which negatively impacted economic activity in three ways.

First, the currency was now partially backed by credit, an intangible asset, rather than being wholly backed by precious metal, a tangible asset. Credit by nature introduces a degree of uncertainty because one never knows whether the person or firm that owes precious metal to the bank will have the financial capacity to repay that loan. When the amount of outstanding credit is large enough, losses by banks can have a destabilising effect on the currency, which in turn will impede commerce because trust in the currency is diminished.

Second, the increase in the quantity of currency is artificial and essentially the same as occurs with the debasement of coins. Dishonest monarchs cheated the populace by adding base metal to precious metal coins. That meant the same aggregate weight of metal would result in more coins, which increased the quantity of currency. The debased currency resulted in higher prices, which hurt everyone, but higher prices did not occur overnight, which highlights another pernicious effect from creating currency out of thin air. The debased coins and new banknotes have a greater purchasing power if spent at once after minting or printing because the market has not yet adjusted to the debasement or to the additional currency, which is an example of the Cantillon Effect.

Third, the creation of currency based on credit heightens payment risk. Payment would be disrupted if banknotes are accepted, and the bank declares bankruptcy before the banknotes are spent. The two functions of banks - making loans and handling payments - blend as poorly as oil and water. They are fundamentally different activities. Lending is a risky business but facilitating the circulation of money is not. Attempts to combine these two disparate activities into one entity exposes those looking simply for payments exposed to the risks the bank takes from its lending, threatening the trust that is essential for any currency to circulate successfully. Further, currency backed by credit runs counter to the principle that product pays for product, which is a moral imperative.

Notwithstanding these issues and the risks, bank customers in seventeenth and eighteenth century London, whether wittingly or not, were prepared to accept the risks of FRB. They considered the arrangement to be attractive. By depositing their precious metal in these newly formed banks, customers not only avoided paying a fee for the storage of their money, but they could also earn interest income on certain deposits offered by banks. The nascent banking industry began to grow.

The arrangement seemed too good to be true, which, as it turned out, was right. It was too good because the bankers had overissued the notes and created too much deposit currency, making the system vulnerable to disruption and collapse. Like the children's game of musical chairs, there were not enough chairs/gold to go around when the music – or more to the point, the good times – stopped. Without calling in loans, the bankers did not have enough metal in the vault to repay their liabilities by returning coins to their customers who were demanding them, and which the bank was contractually obligated to return. Because of the relative illiquidity of loans, some of which were made for months or even years, it typically is never possible for a bank to satisfy the immediate demand to pay depositors by calling in loans.

Fractional Reserve Trickery

Fractional reserve banking has been a controversial practice since its inception over three centuries ago. Given its longevity, one would think that it is beneficial to society, but it is not.

The natural constraints on mining that prevent a rapid increase in the quantity of physical gold have historically been seen as an impediment, rather than one of the strengths that makes gold so useful and successful as money. FRB was viewed as a way to overcome this limitation. The added currency it made possible does not make a nation wealthier, nor does more currency create wealth; all it does is raise prices. This principle even applies to money.

For example, Spain experienced rising prices from the huge influx of gold and silver arriving from its conquests in the newly discovered Americas. This monetary phenomenon was not yet widely recognised by the seventeenth century. It was only in the twentieth century that Milton Friedman proposed an insightful axiom according with reality that has now been widely accepted as an incontrovertible truth: 'Inflation is always and everywhere a monetary phenomenon in the sense that it is and can be produced only by a more rapid increase in the quantity of money than in output.' In other words, prices rise when the quantity of money and/or money substitutes circulating in commerce increase by more than economic output. Excess money does not create more wealth, nor does excess currency.

FRB has been correctly called a fraud, and its beginnings were indeed deceitful.[36] The new banknotes issued were identical in appearance and circulated interchangeably with those already in circulation, but without any increase in the weight of gold in the vault. That is deceptive and dishonest, yet the British government condoned it. Encouraged by banks, English legislators and jurists moved in a new direction away from common law principles safeguarding property rights. To accommodate banks, a deposit of money became an asset owned by the bank and owed to the depositor, exposing the depositor to the risks of a bank's balance sheet. What is worse, the deceitful nature of issuing banknotes more than the weight of gold in reserve became accepted practice.

Paper currency was a useful innovation. However, FRB radically altered the essential nature of currency. In contrast to precious metal coins that circulate as currency, banknotes do not have any inherent use. Their value as currency is derived from the assets backing them, thus making it clear that currency had become an item of balance sheet accounting and double-entry bookkeeping. To the extent that the circulating currency was not backed by a tangible asset like gold or silver, the purchasing power of individuals using banknotes and the banking system itself was placed at risk.

The acceptance of FRB when first introduced is a failure of seventeenth century thinking, but it is to some extent understandable. It became standard practice because it fits within the rigid mercantilist thinking prevailing at the time that placed the wishes of the monarchy and the State above the individual.

Unfortunately, avid mercantilists of the time put monetary thinking and practice on the wrong road headed in a direction unfavourable to individual rights and liberty. Humanity has ever since been dealing with the consequences.

Nevertheless, it is human nature to progress, and history shows that innovation and technology together are a powerful force. Modern technology and new advancements are continually making currency more efficient. Human innovation being forever present, entrepreneurs and inventors are always looking for ways to improve the status quo. We will soon see that while efficiency is an important goal, the key to achieving a successful currency is trust.

6. Currency and the State

'I am of the opinion that the main and final cause why the prince pretends to the power of altering the coinage is the profit or gain which he can get from it...the amount of the prince's profit is necessarily that of the communities' loss but whatever loss the prince inflicts on the community is injustice and the act of a tyrant.

Nicolas Oresme, fourteenth century French scholar[37]

Governments became involved with currency as a practical matter to improve the level of trust. Ironically, that trust was often broken, and the deterioration in trust made the currency less efficient. Governments throughout history often used their involvement with currency to exploit the populace rather than ensure the integrity of the currency.

Back when the Deutschemark was still circulating as currency before the introduction of the euro, it was common to speak of hard currencies and soft currencies. The Dmark was a relatively trusted hard currency because it preserved purchasing power better than the soft currencies, like the U.S. dollar. We do not hear this term used these days because all national currencies are soft currencies.

Currency works well when it is trusted. Currency works even better when it is both trusted and efficient.

These twin goals are essential because together they interrelatedly improve the currency. The better the currency, then the better it facilitates commerce, which is the key objective. Removing impediments to commerce - lowering transaction costs, ending barriers - and improving trust result in more opportunities to complete transactions in which individuals interact to improve their situation as each person strives to achieve their own unique pursuit of happiness.

I begin by focusing on the role of the British government, given that the currency and banking system it adopted spread throughout the world as its empire grew.

The Evolution of Currency

From the first barter transactions in prehistory, there have been several important transformations in the nature of currency to make it more efficient. Ancient texts note the use of gold and silver, which initially circulated as measures of weight being the unit of account.

Eventually coins composed of precious metals began circulating as currency, with the weight becoming the name of the currency, like the British pound, the origin of which dates to circa 755-CE. At that time, trade between the seven Anglo-Saxon kingdoms in Britain and continental Europe was expanding during Charlemagne's rule. King Offa of Mercia, that era's most influential Anglo-Saxon king, found it expedient to introduce within his domain the French denier, a silver coin. The purpose was to increase commerce by creating a common currency among a wider trading bloc that encompassed the British Isles, France, and areas of French influence around the Mediterranean Sea that used the denier, which raises an illustrative point. Offa did this some 1,200 years before the introduction of the euro.

This historical example provides unmistakable evidence of a logical economic principle that a common currency is beneficial to commerce. This principle applies best when the currency is gold or silver and not a money substitute. The gold or silver coin is voluntarily accepted in commerce not only because of its economic value from use as currency but also because of its latent, underlying value – its inherent value – arising from its potential use as an item of adornment.

When Offa eventually minted replicas of the denier that added his name to the coin to attest to the integrity of its metal content, it became the silver penny. There were 20 pennies in a shilling, and the weight of 240 pennies equalled one pound, leading to its £-s-d appellation. The coin's use spread rapidly to encompass other Anglo-Saxon kingdoms and remained the British unit of account until decimalisation in 1971, throughout which the letter 'd' was the abbreviation for pence. Coins became synonymous with silver, hence the term 'pound sterling' which is still heard today even though the concept that money is a weight of precious metal is rarely understood.

This transformation from the denier to the silver penny points to one distinguishing feature in the history of currency – it evolves, which is beneficial. Its evolution has made currency more efficient, which is a principal objective. An efficient currency lowers the cost of transactions and mitigates other impediments, such as completing a transaction where the two parties are not in the same location.

This evolution of currency is another reason for distinguishing it from money. While currency evolves over time, money does not. Money, as I have defined it, remains unchanged. Money is the same today as it was thousands of years ago. It is a tangible asset used by the buyer in exchange for the tangible product offered by the seller. A variety of tangible assets have been used as money in various places over time under a multitude of unique circumstances, but for 5,000 years gold and silver have been chosen by market participants to be the preferred money.

The introduction of coins in prehistory was a major step in the evolution of currency, as was their ongoing improvement over time with newly developed minting techniques. Government stepped in to ensure fairness, namely, that the coins contained the gold and silver weights they were said to contain, whether franc, mark, pound or other measures of weight, fineness, geographic location, or other factors that gave currencies their name.

Tangible assets serving as money, however beneficial in completing a transaction by extinguishing the exchange, could be inconvenient. Even when ignoring some of the more unusual or esoteric forms of currency, the most prevalent currency, precious metal coins, could be awkward. They are bulky and can be unwieldy when a substantial number is required to complete a high value transaction.

Even worse, coins can easily be nicked or scratched in use and worn down from constant handling, dissipating the precious metal content that gave them their value. There was also the constant battle with thieves who clipped or shaved the edges of a coin to remove a small weight of the precious metal. The pilfered metal accumulated over time could be substantial and therefore quite lucrative for a dishonest person who had access to numerous coins, whether a merchant, jeweller or operator of a vault who accepted coins for safekeeping.

Therefore, gold and silver were considered to be too valuable to circulate as currency even when great care was given to their handling, a reality that acted as an incentive to develop alternatives. Eventually the limitations of coin were overcome by an important technological innovation - paper currency. It developed within the banking industry, which itself was set to begin a new cartelised role that placed banks at the centre of commerce.

The Introduction of Paper Currency and Banking

The new innovations of paper currency and banking made currency more efficient, and their impact was profound. They did more than just enhance and thereby expand the opportunities for commerce. Their introduction in London in the seventeenth century took the world in a new direction. They became a world encompassing convention because the globe-spanning British Empire was built on the pound and its banking system. We are today dealing with their consequences because the policies and procedures that guided their use has morphed into practices that are unrecognisable from those that prevailed from their origin until the height of the Empire in the nineteenth century.

The global commerce that the British Empire engendered and which contributed to its growth was built around the Empire's financial structure. Paper currency and banking were introduced to the four corners of the globe, and their use grew along with the expansion of the Empire. Even in those areas where the Empire withdrew, for example, America after its War for Independence, the seeds of the British financial model had been firmly planted. Paper currency and banking had taken root.

This British model has had a direct, perceptible impact on the evolution of currency, mainly for the good but also with some harmful consequences. For example, its introduction marks the beginning of the conflation of the terms, 'money' and 'currency'.

This misperception of their different meanings and their distinct functions is understandable because paper currency and other derivative instruments serving as money substitutes appear to perform in commerce like money itself. Appearance though is different from reality, which today when it relates to money is rarely questioned, even in academia. As a result, the core meaning of these two terms, money and currency, as well as their differences, have been largely forgotten or ignored over the generations, so that few today are aware of their unequivocal distinctiveness.

Before the introduction of paper currency, money and currency were the same thing. Gold and silver coin circulated current. It is interesting to note that the word 'currency' itself only came into being in seventeenth century London.[38] Its appearance was a natural response by market participants to create a term for use in commerce to distinguish this new paper currency invention from what they knew to be money, such was the intuitive understanding from ancient Sumer up to that time that a piece of paper circulating current was not money.

This foray into paper currency in England was not the first attempt to use paper in place of metal. The Chinese are usually credited with the invention of paper currency in the ninth century. It did not end well for the Tang dynasty for the same reason other money substitutes inevitably fail. When the creation of currency is not curbed by unbreakable natural constraints, the currency is inevitably overissued.

Self-imposed man-made constraints rarely last, human nature being what it is. An insightful French adage says, 'The more things change, the more they stay the same.' One could paraphrase it by saying that humans progress but remain human. In other words, human nature does not change.

History has repeatedly shown that the temptation to create money out of nothing is simply too great. Many of London's new bankers learned this fateful lesson. So did the founders of the Bank of England, after which this renowned institution was set on the right course with the help of Sir Isaac Newton. It is an interesting story that needs telling because the Parliamentary debate at the time illustrates the inextricable link between money and liberty. Resistance by freedom loving individuals to political leaders who try to gain control of money and the creation of currency is a battle that has been fought for centuries.

Paper Currency and Banking Begin Serving the State

With the end of the English Civil War and the Protectorate of Oliver Cromwell in 1660, Charles II ended his exile in Holland and returned to the British throne, thereby re-establishing the Stuart dynasty. No doubt mindful of his autocratic father's beheading, Charles was respectful of the changing mood that sought to end the absolute power of the monarchy seemingly granted through the generally accepted practice of the divine right of kings. Nevertheless, the relationship between the king and Parliament was strained as both sought supremacy that meant, among other things, control of the public purse.

Despite these ongoing political tensions, banking became an established trade in London. Like all new businesses that succeed, these early bankers provided a useful service, the storage of gold and silver coin.

The typical practice back then was to keep money stored at home, which obviously came with risk. So people with excess cash not needed for immediate spending, namely, their savings, recognised the advantages of storing their coin in commercial vaults for safekeeping.

As commerce and the British Empire were expanding, a growing wealthy merchant class needed to store their money and began placing their coins in vaults for safekeeping. Most of these vaults were privately owned and operated by goldsmiths, as they needed a vault for protecting the precious metal being used in their trade of making jewellery. Some precious metal was also stored for safekeeping in the Tower of London, where British coins of the realm were minted.

The owner of the gold and silver coins received a receipt, typically handwritten by the goldsmith, recording the amount of money handed over and placed in safe custody. The owner of the coins paid a fee for the safe custody service being provided and expected the exact same coins to be returned when so demanded. It was a pure safekeeping transaction, but ledger currency emerged with the second step. It was an entirely new form of currency that relied on accounting ledgers.

Some goldsmiths eventually noticed that their custody receipts began to circulate in commercial transactions. It was an evolutionary step in the development of currency. Paper representations of the gold and silver coin in storage were being used by buyers of goods and services and accepted by the sellers of those products. Paper currency in the form of goldsmith notes began circulating because market participants began to accept the notion that the coins represented by the paper remained safely stored in the goldsmith's vault. This new paper currency was a spontaneous development by market participants.

The gold and silver contained within the coins were too valuable to be moved around from person to person because abrasion from handling reduced the metal content. It was also more convenient for transactions for the coins to be represented on slips of paper. The gold and silver coins remained locked up in a vault, thereby ensuring the quality of the paper currency that was circulating as currency in place of the valuable and inconvenient coins.

Viewed from a seventeenth century perspective, this new currency was a technological development. Paper currency circulated more efficiently than money, and when there was confidence in the system, all was well. Lord Macaulay described the effects of this new paper currency in his epical *The History of England from the Accession of James II* published in 1848:

> The new system, it was said, saved both labour and money. Two clerks, seated in one counting house, did what, under the old system, must have been done by twenty clerks in twenty different establishments. A goldsmith's note might be transferred ten times in a morning; and thus a hundred guineas [a £1 coin in gold equal to 21 shillings in pre-decimal currency], locked in his safe close to the Exchange, did what would formerly have required a thousand guineas, dispersed through many tills.[39]

This new paper currency in the form of goldsmiths' custody receipts was not money itself. It was a money substitute because the paper did not have any inherent value once it was scribbled on and used by the goldsmith as a receipt, but it did have economic value that derived from its redemption feature by which the paper on demand of the holder could be exchanged for the weight of physical metal stated thereon.

This feature offering quick access to one's metal provided holders of these receipts some certainty that their money would be returned to them, but it also introduced a risk, namely that the goldsmith would default on its obligation. A default seemed unlikely though because the coins were stored in the vault, and the threat of prosecution for theft acted as a deterrent to ensure that the goldsmith did not start taking or even just using customer coins for their own purposes. So, for a time, the advantages of paper currency were seen to outweigh the risks. However, beliefs soon changed.

Despite the increasing number of various privately owned vaults that became available over time, the Tower of London was deemed to be the safest vault because it was protected by the king and presumably the military. That line of thinking changed abruptly in 1672 when Charles II, perennially in need of money, seized the gold stored there. He did offer to pay interest to the owners, but that brought little comfort to them because they no longer had access to their money.

The king's actions further heightened tensions with Parliament, particularly with those members who had placed their savings in the Tower. It introduced them and other victims of this confiscation to counterparty risk, a term that became well understood because of the loss of property rights they incurred.

Nevertheless, the perceived benefits offered by this new currency were in the main still believed to outweigh the risks. Although the Tower no longer was viewed to be safe, gold and silver coins could still be stored in private vaults considered to be trustworthy. Further, the paper currency in circulation was convenient and lowered the cost of transactions, which encouraged commerce and thereby helped the economy.

Eventually some goldsmiths went from being a custodian to become a banker. Instead of just storing coins, they began lending them.

To increase the quantity of coins placed with them to make more loans and earn greater profit, some of these new goldsmith-cum-bankers began borrowing coins. By lending their coins to the goldsmith, the coin owner avoided the storage fee and even earned interest income on the loan. According to Henry Dunning Macleod in his *On the Mechanism of Banking*, these new bankers paid 6% on deposited money. The depositors were fully aware that their money had to be loaned by the bank for it to pay deposit interest to them, with the bank earning the margin between the interest received and paid. The coin owner received the banker's promissory note to repay the amount of British pounds in the face value of the coins loaned to it, but there was some deception.

Recognising how well their custody receipts were being used, these new bankers wanted their promissory notes to be given the same level of trust, even though a bank's obligations for its custody receipts and its promissory notes involved an entirely different degree of risk to the holder of the bank's paper. The deception occurred when the appearance of custody receipts and promissory notes was made indistinguishable, which would make them interchangeable in commerce on par with each other. In other words, the riskier promissory note would not trade at a discount to the less risky custody receipt, but this was not the only deception.

These early banks were no longer just in the business of providing safe custody. They began creating currency without gold and silver coins being placed with them for safekeeping. It was the introduction of fractional reserve banking.

People storing their coins in banks were not oblivious to the sudden extravagant living of the occasional unscrupulous banker using others' coins for his own purposes. Nor did they overlook the problems of well-intentioned bankers who loaned money to borrowers who could not repay their debt. Trouble soon followed, whether from fraud or a bank's unsuccessful lending activity did not much matter to the bank customers whose coins were at risk and who accepted the risks of banknotes.

People began to lose faith in the paper currency and to withdraw their coins from storage to protect their wealth. Eventually, as this demand for their coins grew, the point was reached that broke many fractional reserve banks. These bank runs made clear the insolvency of those banks that began defaulting on their obligation to return coins when the rightful owner asked for them.

Consequently, trust in the currency, which is one of the key pillars that makes a currency circulate in commerce, was periodically eroded, and there was an unfortunate knock-on effect. When these disruptions to the currency occurred, there was an adverse impact on the economy. The currency was no longer trustworthy, which made commercial transactions harder to complete. That made them less frequent, and the economy slowed.

The bank runs left the nascent seventeenth century banking industry in disarray, with commerce disrupted and people fearful of the new paper currency. Yet the advantages of paper currency to bring efficiency to commerce were well recognised. To solve this quandary on how to make paper currency work, a variety of ideas were floated, including one that led to the creation of the Bank of England. It was a bit of a ruse, but nonetheless, the proponents of this new scheme to form this new bank devised a clever stratagem.

By this time Charles II had died and was followed by his younger brother, James II. His autocratic tendencies heightened tensions with Parliament, but they were resolved in 1688. The so-called Glorious Revolution established the supremacy of Parliament by creating the British constitutional monarchy. James II abdicated and was succeeded by co-monarchs William and Mary.

Their ascension to the throne brought England into the Nine Years'

War, which was a European alliance to stop French expansionism. From Parliament's and the co-monarchs' point of view, the war was essential to end French support of the deposed James II, who King Louis XIV aspired to return to the British throne.

To raise money for carrying on the war, a bill presented to Parliament in 1694 proposed a new duty on shipping tonnage. Known as the Tonnage Bill, it included a provision to create the Bank of England.

Money and the Battle for Liberty

The presentation of this bill quickly set off a howl of strident protests because the controversial measure of creating a bank to issue paper currency was tied to a bill deemed essential to raise money for the ongoing war. Opponents of what they derisively called the Tonnage Bank recognised the potential for abuse. Having fought long and hard to secure the supremacy of Parliament, and by implication the rights of the people, few wanted to transfer from the House of Commons to the directors of the proposed bank, and by implication to the monarch, the control over the public purse.

This power to control government spending is dependent upon the power to tax and borrow to raise the money needed to fund the government's spending plans. The Parliamentarians were fearful that uncontrolled spending by the monarch would lead to uncontrolled taxation and borrowing facilitated through the Tonnage Bank to fund the public purse. Their fears directly relate to the rallying cry of the American colonists just several decades later: 'no taxation without representation'.

Lord Macaulay, who was a staunch advocate of Parliament and the rights of the people, describes control of the public purse to be 'the one great security for all the rights of Englishmen', such was the clear recognition at the time of the inextricable link between money and liberty. Supporters of the supremacy of Parliament, according to Macauley:

> ...predicted ruin to our liberties...[because of uncontrolled power over the public purse that]...is an instrument of tyranny more formidable than the High Commission, than the Star Chamber, than even the fifty thousand soldiers of Oliver [Cromwell]. The whole wealth of the nation will be in the hands of the Tonnage Bank...and the Tonnage Bank will be in the hands of the Sovereign.

In the end, the Bank of England was set up for one reason. The monarchy and the government did not have money, and money was needed because Britain was seven years into what became the Nine Years' War. The founding of the Bank of England is a prime example of government and politicians pursuing expediency over principle. Again referring to Macaulay, 'Money [purchasing power] must be had, and could in no other way be had so easily.'

This scornful excuse has been used by countless governments throughout history to justify its actions seeking the purchasing power they do not have but want to spend. The critical point is whether the necessity the government identified to cause its immediate need for money was principled and justified, which is a matter for historians to debate, but the lesson to be learned from this event is clear.

There is but a thin reed upon which government control rests, namely, that money is power and without it, government is powerless. Thus, to control government and to ensure that the rights of each individual to life, liberty, and the pursuit of happiness are protected, the people must ultimately control the money that flows to a government.

Achieving this goal requires several interrelated measures. The money of a nation must be gold, not a money substitute. There must be a total separation of banks from the State so that banks are not controlled by the State. Fractional reserve banking must be prohibited because it is a fraudulent practice. Control of the public purse must rest with the body of government that represents the people, not the executive, be it a monarch or president. Last and most important, the people themselves must be knowledgeable about money and its inextricable link to liberty, and they must elect to their representative body in government those individuals whose principal aim is to protect individual liberty by controlling the power of the State.

The message from the founding of the Bank of England was well understood in America, which issued its Declaration of Independence not too many years later and achieved its freedom from colonial rule after its revolutionary War for Independence. As we will see in Chapter 9, the means to attain the ultimate prize of liberty by protecting individual rights was enshrined in the American Constitution.

The 'Tonnage Bank' is Founded

The Bank of England was formed because expediency won the day, to which those in opposition agreed, but only after a concession was extracted from the proponents of the Tonnage Bill. Banknotes would only be advanced from the Bank to the monarch under authority from Parliament. Further, if there was an infraction of this restriction, a penalty of three times the advance would be paid, with the important proviso that the monarch did not have the authority to cancel the penalty.

Thus, Parliament retained control over the public purse, but as it turned out, lost control over the creation of this newly invented paper currency. What is worse, it legitimatised fractional reserve banking, which over time has led to increasing government control over the currency and banking system and made possible its potential abuse by government authorities when that power is misused.

Fractional reserve banking became the tool of imperialism, or its modern equivalent, statism. The adoption of this policy set the currency and banking system on a course that has repercussions to this day.

The power to create currency 'out of thin air' in the hands of the State is even more detrimental to liberty than its absolute control of the public purse. Currency creation is a power largely unseen and whose impact on economic activity was not well understood at the time. Nor is it well understood today, even though it is self-evident that creating currency out of nothing through fractional reserve banking is a harmful process that destroys wealth when abused, impairs the market process, and erodes liberty.

What Parliament had done with the creation of the Bank of England and allowing the iniquitous practice of fractional reserve banking was to hand to the government the ability to create an ever-increasing amount of currency. This power elevated the status of the Bank making it and the government interdependent.

Though privately owned, the Bank became a quasi-government institution. Its multifaceted role raised questions on whether the Bank was serving its shareholders, the government, or the interests of the nation. Quoting from Macauley with some inserts to make the point clear:

> So closely was [the Bank's shareholders] interest bound up with the interest of the government that the greater the public danger the more ready were they to come to the rescue [by printing currency]. In old times, when the Treasury was empty, when the taxes came in slowly, and when the pay of the soldiers and sailors was in arrear, it had been necessary for the Chancellor of the Exchequer to go, hat in hand, [to borrow money and supplies]. Those times were over. The government, instead of laboriously scooping up supplies from numerous petty sources, could now draw whatever it required from an immense reservoir.

The reservoir of course is the Bank's ability to print its banknotes pretending to be 'as good as gold' without a full complement of gold or silver in reserve. Though devious and iniquitous, this alchemy was a godsend to a cash-strapped British government, but the ability to create an ever-increasing amount of currency made it inevitable that one day this power would be abused. As we will see, it did not take long for that to happen.

Once approved by Parliament and royal assent was given, the Bank offered its banknotes to the public in the form of a promissory note that paid interest. Each note was a promise by the Bank to pay on demand the weight of gold or silver loaned to the Bank and 8% interest. The 8% yield proved to be attractive, as was the implied backing of the government. This offering of 'banknotes', namely, the promissory notes of the Bank, was quickly filled. The monarch received the gold and silver coin loaned to the Bank by private investors, and these coins were then sent to the Continent to pay the army's bills.

The excitement about the newly formed Bank of England turned out to be premature. The folly of holding only fractional reserves against the Bank's liabilities to pay coins on demand became clear in May 1696. Just two years after its formation, there was a run on the Bank of England. The Bank could not meet its obligations to redeem its promises to pay in coin as it was legally bound to do. Trust in the Bank and its new paper currency broke, and a crisis ensued.

The Bank was overextended. It had issued more banknotes than it had gold and silver in storage, regardless of whether that metal was fabricated as coins or as bars. The problem the Bank faced was not a shortage of coin or precious metal, but the overissue of liabilities, namely, its banknotes.

The Bank of England was insolvent, but it did not collapse. It sidestepped that fate because it was – to state it in modern terms – 'too big to fail'. The government engineered a bail-out. The Bank's hand-in-glove working relationship with the government meant the Bank had become indispensable. The government wanted ever-increasing amounts of currency and turned to the Bank to open the spigots. It complied by increasing the quantity of banknotes it put into circulation.

Recalling Macaulay's pithy observation, printing banknotes was the easiest way for the government to get its hands on the purchasing power it needed to meet its spending plans. It is a pernicious refrain regrettably repeated countless times throughout history by innumerable governments desperately seeking purchasing power and willing to obtain it fraudulently through fractional reserve banking regardless of the adverse consequences.

Sir Isaac Newton and the Royal Mint

The run on the Bank of England was only a small part of the various financial and economic problems in 1696 faced by Parliament and William III. The king was now a widower alone on the throne, which made his position even weaker because the direct hereditary line passed through his wife, and they did not have children. Not only did he need to assert his authority and quell the disturbances of the Jacobites that posed a continuing threat to his title, money was needed to fight the ongoing Nine Years' War. Additionally, the economy was in terrible distress, and both the government's and the king's purses were empty.

Fortunately, the king wisely turned to one of the brightest minds of that time. He appointed Sir Isaac Newton as Warden of the Royal Mint, and then later to the position with the highest authority, Master of the Royal Mint. Newton does not need an introduction, but oddly, he is not widely recognised as an important historical figure outside of his role in science. Yet the monetary guidance he provided at this critical moment in time helped secure the foundation that enabled the growth and expansion of the nascent British Empire.

Traditionally appointments to these posts in the Royal Mint were a sinecure for past service to the crown, but Newton did not accept the position to rest on his laurels. As a first task, he set about tackling the most pressing problem plaguing the economy, which was the state of the country's coins. Once that problem was solved, he turned to the Bank of England to address its insolvency.

The country's coins were underweight as a result of abrasion from many decades of usage and the illegal but widespread activity of clipping or shaving the edges of a coin to remove precious metal. As a result of this debasement, the market value of the coin's metal content was far less than the nominal value stated on the face of the coin. Commerce slowed because farmers, merchants and other vendors of marketable products understandably were unwilling to accept in payment the debased coins at their face value.

To solve this problem, the Royal Mint under Newton's guidance and following the remedy employed by Gresham over a century earlier, minted new coins so that the face value of the coin was again equal to the market value of the weight of precious metal contained in the coin. Trust in the coins was re-established, an event recorded in history as the Great Recoinage of 1696, the significance of which is reflected in its superlative title.

To ensure the success of the recoinage, Newton implemented another fundamental change. He recognised that the ratio at which gold and silver were trading in the market was out of line with the face value of coins. A balance between the market value of the two precious metals and a gold or silver coin's content is important. When the metal content within a coin is inconsistent with its face value, the coin that is more highly valued in other countries will be exported to them (bad money drives good money out of circulation), thereby leaving a shortage of that coin in the domestic economy that would be disruptive to commerce.

To accept the reality of the market, Newton adjusted the ratio at which gold and silver coins were valued by changing the weight of precious metal within them. The result was that he moved the British pound from a silver standard to a de facto gold standard.

Turning to the Bank of England, Newton recognised that banknotes were more efficient than coin. To ensure this new currency was trustworthy, he tirelessly entreated the Bank to battle counterfeiters as doggedly as he did with coin-clippers.

More importantly, he created a rule designed to temper the inherent fragility of fractional reserve banking. The Bank would thereafter keep in its vault a weight of gold equal to at least 40% of its gold liabilities, which were its banknotes. Although the Bank was still technically insolvent by its mismatch of assets and liabilities, he believed a 40% reserve would prove sufficient to allow for redemptions of paper into gold under normal circumstances. It was a safety ratio of sorts, that would enable the Bank to operate even though technically it was insolvent.

The Nine Years War ended in 1697, followed thereafter by the War of Spanish Succession which began in 1701 and lasted until 1714. The second front of this war, fought in North America, is known as Queen Anne's War, named after the reigning monarch and successor to William III.

The Bank of England served the government during these conflicts. Though privately owned, the Bank worked with the government to rebuild the depleted treasury, further tightening the increasingly interdependent relationship between the State and the fractionally reserved Bank of England. There were several factors contributing to the Bank's success.

Perhaps foremost was the widespread hope that the Bank would succeed, not only because of its advancement that made currency more efficient but also for the political gains that might result by helping to fund the government. Newton and other luminaries of that time understood that the banknotes issued by the Bank of England provided the means by which the government could borrow funds the monarchy needed to secure its position and win the wars that were raging. It was commonly expected that achieving these goals would bring about the much-desired political stability that was of paramount importance to most people. That stability did arrive in 1714 with the ascension of George I.

Another factor in the Bank's success was effective propaganda. One example is Joseph Addison's allegory of public credit published in 1711. Its widespread adulation helped the Bank, its proponents, and its apologists to convince a sceptical public, even though the Bank's failure in 1696 was still fresh in mind. According to Macauley, it also revealed the connectivity of the Bank to the government. 'The truth which this parable was meant to convey was constantly present to the minds of the rulers of the Bank.'

The principal reason for the Bank's success was the governance

Newton implemented, principally his minimum reserve ratio requiring four gold ounces in the Bank's vault for every ten ounces in its banknote liabilities. Newton's Rule prevented an excessive overissue of banknotes. The government recognised the rule's 40% limit and did not force the Bank to break it, perhaps because Newton lived to 1727 and was thus able to reinforce its importance. Over time, the pound and gold became synonymous, which facilitated Britain's commercial success throughout the globe.

The run on the Bank of England in 1696 had been a wake-up call both for the Bank and the British government, but the alarm pointing to the inherent instability of fractional reserves was subdued. The Bank continued to operate because Newton's Rule brought a meaningful level of control to the quantity of banknotes being used as currency. Nevertheless, expediency was the driving force, which displaced the needed thoughtful analysis of the changes being brought about by the introduction of paper currency and fractional reserves. These changes uprooted longstanding principles and practices and gave birth to misconceptions about money and its link to liberty that have persisted to this day.

We will see how the Bank's directors ultimately were not able to cope with the shaky ground upon which the Bank was built. Because of their close connection to the government, over time the government and the Bank to their mutual benefit dismantled Newton's Rule to expand beyond his guideline the Bank's issuance of currency. But for a time, his guidance provided the means for the Bank to play a vital role in the commercial expansion of the British Empire. The wealth from expanding commerce helped provide through taxes and borrowing - and not the overissue of banknotes - the money the government needed when military conflicts arose.

Newtonian Mechanics Applied to Currency

Before continuing with this overview of the development of currency, an explanation of the gold standard is needed because of its importance in history as well as to appreciate the brilliance of Newton's accomplishment. Even today, the acclaim in which the gold standard is held can be seen in its dictionary definition: 'a thing of superior quality that serves as a point of reference against which other things of its type may be compared.'

I contend that the gold standard is one of Newton's greatest achievements. His monetary system lasted for more than three centuries and became the backbone of the British Empire.

Newton brought a scientific method to money and currency with systematic observations, throughout which he showed a clear-cut understanding that money is a measurement tool. By making a specifically stated and unchanging weight of gold as the standard of measurement, he defined the British pound, which through centuries of government debasement no longer contained the weight of silver from the time of King Offa. Then simultaneously fixing the ratio at which gold and silver could be exchanged for each other, Newton formalised bimetallism so that both precious metals would be accepted as tender in payment. The British pound was the unit of account and remained nominally on a silver standard, but the pound was now de facto an unchanging weight of gold, with one gold guinea of twenty-one shillings in a pound.

Bank of England banknotes continued to be denominated in British pounds. Its banknotes served as money substitutes circulating current, and on demand of the bearer could be redeemed for gold coin. Silver was relegated to a subsidiary role, basically to provide small coinage used in daily transactions, but when accumulated in sufficient weight could be exchanged for gold coin or banknotes.

Newton established a modern monetary system for Britain and indeed the world as the empire expanded. This foundation he crafted provided the basis for the tremendous expansion of harmonious global trade and commerce that raised the standards of living for countless people throughout the world. This achievement was made possible by the precepts he formulated to control the harmful excesses possible from fractional reserve banking. The government then introduced these precepts to the Bank of England, which were implemented and followed by the Bank's managers to avoid a repeat of the run on the Bank that occurred in 1696.

The pound became the world's common currency because of its uncommon attributes, which were a defined unit of account stated as a weight of gold that was consistently adhered to by the Bank and British government. It was the measuring stick adopted throughout the globe for the same reason King Offa adopted the denier; a common currency is as useful as a common language in encouraging interaction between people anywhere in the four corners of the globe. Human interaction expands commerce, increases wealth, and raises the standard of living to the greatest extent with money and a reliable currency.

In a Newtonian monetary universe, currency is seen as a fluid that acts and reacts to external forces in much the same way that fluid moves in the physical world in response to his laws of motion and gravity. The gold standard is in effect Newtonian mechanics applied to money and money-substitutes in a global system that allowed fractional reserve banking. Joseph Schumpeter describes this linked global network in his *History of Economic Analysis*:

> An 'automatic' gold currency is part and parcel of a laissez-faire and free trade economy. It links every nation's money rates and price levels with the money-rates and price levels of all the other nations that are 'on gold'. It is extremely sensitive to government expenditure and even to attitudes or policies that do not involve expenditure directly, for example, to foreign policy.

The principal force within the monetary network is the expansion of credit and currency and their subsequent contraction. Their ebb and flow are a natural result that arises when tying a country's stock of gold to the quantity of national currency.

These expansions and contractions of credit and currency manifest as a boom-and-bust cycle, generally called the Austrian business cycle in recognition of the detailed analysis of it by several prominent economists from that country. Economic booms are damaging if allowed to become excessive, which explains why the gold standard is important to attaining relative stability. It limits the extent of credit expansion by banks, and thus acts as a governor to prevent a damaging boom from occurring.

During good times, the banks lend and then lend some more. In the process they create currency 'out of thin air'. This ephemeral currency conveying phantom purchasing power is not the result of new gold entering the system and held as reserves; it is an accounting entry recorded in bank ledgers. Its creation expands a bank's balance sheet because its assets and liabilities rise simultaneously. Each new loan is an asset on a bank's balance sheet, and the offsetting bank liability is created by a ledger entry recording the currency being created 'out of thin air, which are the banknotes advanced to the borrower.

The impact of this newly created currency means that during the boom, the ratio of gold held by a bank as an asset (said to be 'held in reserve', hence the term fractional reserve) falls relative to the bank's liabilities. As that happens, the bank, which is already insolvent because of its fractional reserves, is moving toward collapse because it is not holding sufficient gold to pay the total amount due to its customers. FRB places the deposits of bank customers at increasing risk as a bank's loan portfolio grows during the boom.

Customers watch these events to guard that portion of their wealth placed in a bank. It is therefore understandable that they respond when the boom becomes overextended, at which point customers consider the risk they are taking to be excessive. They withdraw their gold coin, and the bank's assets and liquidity are directly affected. This outflow of gold forces banks to begin calling in loans to remain liquid and lessen the risk of collapse. When the loan is repaid, there also is a reduction in the quantity of currency recorded in the bank's ledgers. This simultaneous reduction of loans and liabilities increases the quantity of coin on the bank's balance sheet relative to its banknotes still outstanding, improving its solvency. By demanding repayment of loans and reducing their banknote liabilities, banks end their credit expansion, meaning the height of the boom has been reached.

A contraction of available credit inevitably causes defaults by those borrowers who borrowed too much or used the proceeds of the loan for an inferior purpose that did not generate sufficient cash flow to repay their debt when demanded by the bank. The resulting impact is economic distress, or to put it bluntly, the contraction of credit leads to the 'bust' that inevitably follows the 'boom' that occurred from too many bank loans being made to too many unworthy purposes including, for example, stock market speculation. If the defaults by borrowers in the aggregate cause a bank to take losses greater than its capital, the bank is bankrupt, which undermines the trust needed for a successful currency. It may also lead to a liquidity crisis throughout the economic area served by the collapsed bank.

These crises are a scramble for unconditional liquidity and highlight the fragility of a bank issuing banknotes based on loans rather than gold held in its reserves. Debts are paid, either by the borrower or through the loss incurred by the lender holding an unrepayable debt. As the crises deepens, more loans are called, and more debts are paid or defaulted. The point is that the liquidity comes from the reduction of outstanding loans, not from pumping more debt into the system (as an aside, which central banks are worryingly now doing today).

The boom-bust cycle also needs to be viewed from a global perspective. If banks in one country begin lending too much and create a boom, the currency of that country is cheapened relative to the gold reserve within its banks because the quantity of ledger currency is growing faster than the total gold reserve. Consequently, the gold flows out of the country to other countries where it is valued more highly, that is, where there is less bank lending and currency creation. This outflow of gold causes a currency contraction as banks demand that loans be repaid. to enable them to maintain a reasonable level of liquidity, namely, gold coin on hand relative to the bank's liabilities.

In addition to demanding repayment of loans in a liquidity crisis, banks raised interest rates. Rather than incurring the cost of a higher interest rate, borrowers might then choose to repay their loan before it is due, reducing the bank's loan portfolio.

Regardless of whether bank loans are repaid by force or voluntarily, the resulting reduction of loans and the simultaneous reduction in the quantity of the bank's ledger currency causes the relationship of the bank's liabilities to gold to move back toward a prudent balance. The return toward a prudent level of gold reserves typically occurred over months, but as the bust took hold, it could speed up to weeks or even days in a banking panic, which could be quite destructive.

To control the excesses of fractional reserve banking, Newton's gold standard system proved invaluable. The key element was the restrictive policy that he developed to be followed by the Bank of England's management and accepted by the government. It was purposefully designed to govern the inherent fragility of fractional reserves and to ensure financially prudent behaviour.

Recognising that the 1696 run on the Bank could recur in the future, his policy was designed to prevent the over issuance of currency. Newton concluded that prudent management required at least 40% of the banknotes in circulation had to be backed by gold coin held in the Bank's vaults. In this way he was limiting the extent to which fractional reserve banking could be employed by mathematically controlling the amount of credit that could be extended by the Bank. By controlling the amplitude of the boom-to-bust cycle, his system minimised the size of the boom, which mitigated the negative impact resulting from the bust that inevitably followed. This rule achieved two interrelated goals.

First, the Bank had what it considered to be sufficient gold on hand to allow for the redemption of banknotes into gold coin that occurred in normal day-to-day commerce. It would function because it appeared to be solvent. Second, by continuing to meet its commitments to redeem its banknotes for gold coin, the Bank would be seen as trustworthy, even though it was insolvent because it had less gold in reserve than it owed.

Newton lessened but did not eliminate the possibility of bank runs. Over time other steps were also introduced to justify fractional reserve banking. These were said to be taken to 'defend the gold standard', but this rallying cry is simply a diversion from what really was being defended, fractional reserve banking.

Foremost among these steps was the Bank raising the rate of interest on loans to prevent excessive credit expansion. Making credit more expensive caused borrowers to forgo new loans and repay existing loans, which in turn reduced the quantity of currency that had been created out of thin air in the boom.

Another measure was to better match the tenor of loans to the liabilities. To maximise their margin and profitability with a higher level of risk, banks tend to borrow short-term money, paying the lowest possible interest rate, and make long-term loans, earning a higher interest. By matching liabilities payable on demand with loans extended on demand, a bank would achieve a balance that made insolvency less likely.

Not all of the policies the Bank of England developed to defend the gold standard were transparent. The appearance of being solvent was critically important. It was a time of limited financial disclosure, and little was disclosed by the owners and managers of the Bank. To prevent the occurrence of bank runs in an inherently fragile system, the Bank acted in secret. By not disclosing the actual percent of gold in reserve in relation to its liabilities, and letting the unwitting public believe that the Bank's reserves were adequate, the Bank believed that it was lessening the risk of realising its inherent insolvency.

The Bank's shareholders considered this privilege to be justified by the fact that the Bank was privately owned and should enjoy the confidentiality of any non-governmental business, but its private status was dubious. In addition to aiding the funding of government, the Bank worked with the government to establish fractional reserve banking into English commercial law, thereby defying common law precedent regarding the custody of precious metal placed in safekeeping. Banking law developed as a separate body of law, outside of Anglo-Saxon common law principles applicable to tangible assets.

When a tangible asset is placed in the custody of another, the custodian is compelled by law and moral principle to return the same gold bars or coins back to its owner. Putting gold into a bank was no longer an act of storage. Instead, the gold was being 'deposited' into the bank, which was a new term to describe the bank's relationship its customers. With a deposit, title and all rights of ownership of the metal are transferred to the bank, meaning the gold owner now became a creditor and was in effect lending metal to the bank. Even though placing money with the bank was called a 'deposit', a depositor's position was no different than that of a lender to the bank.

The evidence of the bank's indebtedness to the depositor, namely, the former owner of gold, took different forms depending on the arrangement requested. If the former gold owner wanted immediate access to spend the gold, the bank issued a banknote. If there was no immediate need to spend the gold and interest income was desired, the bank issued – to put it in modern terms – a savings booklet or a certificate of deposit. Regardless of the evidence of its debt, the pounds being recorded on bank ledgers were set to become an increasingly important currency, even though the general public was not aware of the weight of gold in reserve nor the number and total value of banknotes in circulation and therefore unable to assess the risks of holding banknotes not fully backed by gold coin.

The extent of these risks is illustrated by the Exter Inverted Pyramid in Figure 7. It is named after John Exter, a former central banker who created it in the 1960s to help explain the post-Second World War monetary system as it disintegrated from the overissue of currency.

The inverted pyramid illustrates the expansion in the circulating currency made possible by fractional reserve banking. It also clearly shows the inherent fragility of a system in which the quantity of currency redeemable into gold is greater than the quantity of gold.

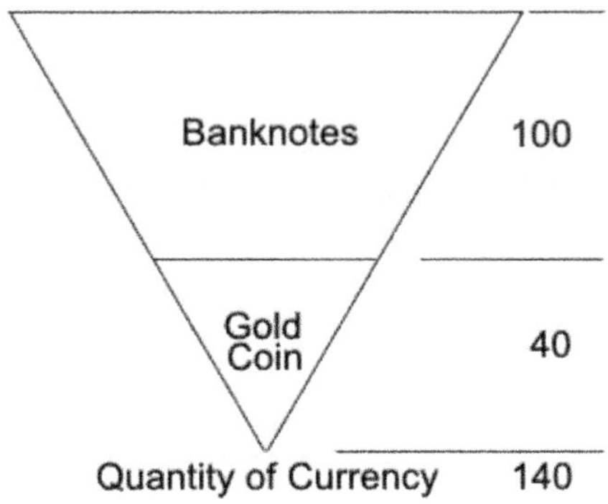

Figure 7 – The Exter Inverted Pyramid

At the base of the pyramid is gold, a tangible asset. Everything above it is a money substitute circulating in place of gold, whether as a convenience or for other reasons. While there are potentially numerous money substitutes, as we will see as we follow this path on the development of new currencies, this pyramid in Figure 7 lists only one type. It is all the banknotes issued by the Bank of England.

For illustrative purposes I have not used the £ designation. The pyramid and its principles apply to all national currencies.

I have assumed that the total quantity of currency in this pyramid is 140, with 40 in gold coin and 100 in banknotes. So with a 40% gold reserve the Bank of England was able to issue a total quantity of banknotes that was 2.5 times greater than the gold in reserve (100/40).

This leverage clearly shows why fractional reserves are inherently risky. The Bank's inherent insolvency rested on the hope that all the Bank's liabilities would not come due at once, even though its liabilities were payable on demand.

However, normal commerce did not always prevail, and there were other factors too. Given that the Bank was a privately owned entity, the Bank's shareholders might not want restrictions on the size of the Bank's loan portfolio, which was its main profit-making function. The 40% reserve limits the amount of credit that could be extended and directly throttles the Bank's profitability. Also, in time, new directors who had not lived through the 1696 bank run would be appointed. Not having lived through this experience, they may let standards and prudence slip.

Newton's recommended ratio always rested upon the fundamental flaw on which fractional reserve banking is built, namely, the hope that every holder of every banknote would not ask for their gold or silver coin at once. The Bank would not have sufficient liquidity to pay its liabilities if too many banknote holders asked to redeem their banknotes, as actually occurred in 1696, an event it was hoped would not recur. But that unrealistic outcome was not to be.

France Breaks the Bank of England

With political stability re-established with the accession of George I to the British throne in 1714, the Bank of England was well positioned to benefit from the Industrial Revolution that was just beginning in Britain. As the British economy and the Empire expanded, Newton's gold standard was put to the test. It survived throughout the century, even during the American War for Independence from 1775 to 1783 and the loss of the Empire's thirteen American colonies. But not long after, problems arose from the inherent instability of fractional reserve banking.

The French Revolutionary Wars began in 1792 when France declared war on Prussia and Austria. Britain joined militarily with several other countries to contain French expansionism and contain the radicalism and anti-monarchical forces of the French revolution.

The war was costly, and the army had to be paid, with the result that by 1795 gold began flowing out of Britain. Initially, the Bank of England was able to cope. To maintain Newton's ratio, credit was contracted. Banknote 'circulation was steadily diminished, as the supply of gold became smaller and smaller. But this policy of contraction was seriously hampered by the necessities of Mr. Pitt, then Prime Minister, who insisted upon advances...'[40] that were invariably provided by the Bank. Banknotes were used by the government to pay its domestic expenses, and gold coin was exported to pay expenses being incurred by the army in Europe.

This contraction meant that government borrowing from the Bank was crowding out private credit. The financial and economic situation was becoming precarious.

The tipping point was reached in 1797. A planned invasion of Britain by France went awry except for a small force that landed in South Wales. The French were quickly overcome by the local militia, but the psychological damage had been done. The news of the invasion sent shockwaves throughout the country and raised fears about what many believed was to come. The turmoil of the French Revolution and beheading of Louis XVI just four years earlier was still fresh in everyone's mind. The response was predictable.

To protect their wealth, people throughout the country began redeeming their banknotes for gold coin. Money in hand was safer than any bank's paper promise to pay them money on demand. The Bank of England was overwhelmed by the demand for gold coin, an event that its directors and shareholders had hoped would never occur. Even though the Bank was still adhering to Newton's guidelines, the fraud of fractional reserve banking was fully exposed. It now became clear that anything less than a 100% gold reserve backing the Bank's liabilities was wrongful deception.

The government's response was predictable; it bailed out the Bank. It passed into law the Bank Restriction Act, by which the banknotes of the Bank of England became irredeemable. They could no longer be converted into gold.

At the time, English law made the directors of a company personally responsible for the failure of their company. Consequently, the governor of the Bank and its directors would be held personally responsible for any failure to convert the Bank's banknotes into gold coin. They could be sued for damages to the extent of their personal net worth. So the government bailed them out too. They were indemnified for all legal actions that might be brought against them.

In modern terms it could be said that the directors of the Bank were trading recklessly by knowing full well that even when following Newton's guidelines, the Bank's liabilities arising from its banknotes to pay gold on demand exceeded its liquidity of gold coins on hand. The Bank defaulted, but no one went to jail for committing fraud.

The French wars intensified after Napoleon assumed power in 1799. The drain of bullion continued, and the resulting monetary disruption led to economic distress, which became particularly severe by 1808. The cause was similar to that which resulted in the economic distress in 1696. Farmers, merchants, and other vendors of marketable products were unwilling to accept in payment the debased currency at face value, though now the currency in question was banknotes and not underweight coin. Parliament formed the Bullion Committee in 1810 to study the situation with a view to making recommendations.

The Committee's report, led by famed economist David Ricardo, provided an accurate analysis explaining that too many banknotes had been issued relative to the Bank's stock of coin, causing the debased banknotes to trade at a discount to coin. A gold coin in hand is always worth more than a promise evidenced by a banknote to pay a gold coin on demand, even if there were 100% reserves. Nevertheless, Parliament voted to conclude, in effect, that the irredeemable banknotes were as good as gold, even though the proponent of that bill was ridiculed for making such an outrageous proposition.[41] Expediency again prevailed, though there is also a subtle, yet more important message.

The obvious fatuity of the legislation was a departure from accepted norms. It signalled that Parliament was defining a new relationship with the voters, namely that Parliament could dictate what was or was not money. More to the point, Parliament in effect was claiming, albeit immorally, that it had the power to force whatever it declared to be money for use among the public.

By legislating that irredeemable banknotes were as good as gold, Parliament turned millennia of convention on its head and planted the seeds for what became known as the State theory of money, namely, that the State and not individuals participating in the market process would determine what is or is not money. As we will see, those seeds took hold to the detriment of individual liberty. They eventually grew to become the fiat currency used today throughout the globe. Fiat currency circulates because of laws that force its circulation as tender in payment, not because the currency has any inherent usefulness. In other words, the currency is given artificial economic value by force of law. Parliament's foray into this new legislative territory triggered a fierce debate that rages to this day as governments continue to increasingly usurp control of money, currency, and the economy.

Before long, as fortune would have it, the war was turning in favour of Britain and its allies. Nelson's victory at Trafalgar had secured British control of the seas, thereby preventing Napoleon's planned invasion of Britain. As peace returned after Wellington's victory at Waterloo in 1815, Newton's precepts were reinstated and formalised by Parliament.

The Coinage Act of 1816

To make a clean break from the turmoil of the Napoleonic Wars and to address the 1797 Bank Restriction Act that was still in effect, Parliament passed the Coinage Act of 1816. It sought a return to normalcy.

The Act's key provision defined the British pound in law as a weight of gold equal to 7.3224 grams of pure gold, or 0.2354 of one troy ounce, the same pre-suspension rate prevailing from Newton's time of £46 14s 6d for one troy pound of standard (22 carat) gold. The pound was redenominated as a 20-shilling gold coin that replaced the 21-shilling guinea. The coin was styled the gold sovereign, using the name of a coin first struck during the reign of Henry VII, even though it was half the weight and size of the earlier coin. By this Act, the gold sovereign became the coin of the realm, which the Royal Mint continues to produce to this day.

It is interesting to note that in contrast to the coins of other countries, the gold sovereign did not have a face value minted into it. In other words, the coin did not say one pound nor was there any other designation. Nor did it specify the gold weight, which is a practice that continues. These labels are not needed. Being the coin of the realm, the gold sovereign is the numeraire.

By law, the gold sovereign was one pound, which was a known and accepted measure of value. The Bank issued £1 banknotes that continued to circulate as a money substitute. When redeemability was finally restored in 1821, banknotes were redeemable at one gold sovereign per £1.

The Act relegated silver to a secondary role, with silver coins minted in small denominations to complement the sovereign. Weighing nearly one-quarter of a troy ounce, the sovereign had too large a value for use in small transactions, for which silver was used. The ratio at which silver could be exchanged for gold was adjusted to ensure that silver was not exported, which could have led to a shortage of small denomination coins.

Introducing a new term that continued to expand Parliament's role in monetary matters, silver coins were declared 'legal tender' for sums up to £2, thereby forcing their acceptance in payment up to the £2 limit. The purpose was to resolve the issue of bimetallism, namely, to ensure that both gold and silver coin circulated current. This provision in the law prevented a large number of silver coins being used in payment where gold sovereigns would be more appropriate.

Though introducing the concept of legal tender was well intentioned, it was another step in expanding Parliament's control over currency, thereby lessening the control of it by the populace. The meaning of legal tender and its application to currency would unfortunately continue to change over time, so its use in this Act is noteworthy as a first step.

Legal tender laws opened the door to abuse of individual rights because they allow the government, rather than the buyer and seller contemplating a transaction, to determine the means of payment. Though insignificant relative to what the term 'legal tender' would over time come to mean and how it would be used, this Act was another small step that increased the power of government to the detriment of individuals in continuation of the ongoing process of monetary powers being usurped by the State.

The other significance of this Coinage Act is the recognition by the government that its Bank Restriction Act in 1797 that stopped the redemption of banknotes into gold violated Britain's long tradition of protecting property rights. It was also a tacit but clear acknowledgement that the turmoil irredeemable banknotes caused was disruptive to the economy. So, while expediency won the day during the French and Napoleonic Wars, the government reversed direction by eventually choosing the honourable course and returned the British pound to the same definition in gold weight that Newton had given it.

Although more than a century had passed since the Glorious Revolution, the government operated with a noteworthy degree of morality. The post-war return to normality meant adhering to the social structure that evolved from the Age of Enlightenment, which recognised individual property and contract rights and limited government as the foundation of a lawful society. The government believed that those foundation stones could only be disrupted by a war that threatened the country's survival, which would also justify intervention in the currency creation process of the Bank of England. Its actions therefore contrasted to the dictatorial regimes of the Stuarts and their claim to absolute power to rule under the divine right of kings. It also highlights the Tonnage Bank debate described by Macauley. There remained a widespread understanding that the government could use the currency creation process to enhance its power, which would abuse individual rights. By returning to the pre-war definition of the pound, the Act indicated that the government recognised the limits of its power to rule and the need to act morally, but that was to change by the end of the nineteenth century.

This Coinage Act is also significant for yet another reason. The British pound had reached its zenith, which more or less occurred in tandem with the zenith of its Empire as the supreme world power. Subsequent actions by the government were harmful to the pound. The resulting debasement contributed to the decline of the Empire, repeating the process occurring in many empires before it and proving Keynes and Lenin were right, namely, that there is no surer means of overturning the existing structure of society than to debase the currency.

Bank of England Charter Act of 1833

As the British economy expanded during the Industrial Revolution and after the Napoleonic Wars, so too did the number of private banks. They were set up throughout the country, particularly in those areas where manufacturing and international trade were becoming important economic contributors. Most of these private banks focused on a particular trade and a limited geographic area; for example, a bank's customers might only be companies and individuals involved in cloth manufacturing in Manchester.

These private banks typically operated from one office and were established as partnerships. Although joint-stock investment companies did exist, joint-stock banks that limited the liability of its owners to the amount of capital they invested were not yet well established. The reason is that bank customers preferred to place their gold with those banks where its owners and managers had their personal wealth tied up in their bank. It was an important point because these private banks followed the Bank of England practice of fractional reserves. Bank customers had learned the risks of paper currency from reading history or having family experiences passed down to them about the run on the Bank of England in 1696 or its insolvency in 1797.

The partnerships operating private banks were limited to six members. Larger partnerships were legally restricted from issuing banknotes. When a bank made a loan, the borrower received banknotes. So the issuing of banknotes facilitated lending, which typically was the bank's main area of profitability.

The banknotes issued by these private banks were redeemable either in Bank of England banknotes or directly into gold coin. Some private banks operated with a reserve of gold coin stored in their own vault.

The Bank of England was the banker to the government, the only joint-stock bank by law within 65 miles of London, and the only joint-stock bank allowed to issue banknotes. Because of this privileged position, its charter was subject to a periodic review by Parliament, which decided whether the charter would be renewed for another limited period.

The monetary turmoil experienced during the Napoleonic Wars was still fresh in the minds of many both inside and outside of government as the 1833 charter review date approached. Nevertheless, the pressure by banks to expand credit by making more loans remained ever present as were the arguments by private banks to break up the Bank of England's monopoly position.

The constraints of Newton's Rule became a hotly debated topic. The Bank's governor at the time proposed the eponymous Palmer Rule, which recommended a ratio of 33%, the 67% balance of which could be held in interest bearing debt instruments. Though not formally adopted into law, the debate about the ratio signalled the intent of the Bank to increase its profitability by generating more interest income and reducing the ratio of gold to its liabilities, regardless of the risks.

In the end, the Bank's charter was renewed, and its monopoly position was protected, but the Act went further. The 1833 Act expanded the concept of legal tender.

The term legal tender today has been twisted from its original meaning, but these two words are incongruous. What the buyer and seller decide for payment is a private matter between themselves, not involving the government. As Thomas Paine correctly observed several decades before the 1833 Act:

> If anything had or could have a value equal to gold and silver, it would require no tender law; and if it had not that value it ought not to have such a law; and, therefore, all tender laws are tyrannical and unjust and

calculated to support fraud and oppression.

The Bank of England Charter Act of 1833 was another step taken by the government and the profit seeking owners of the Bank of England to erode Newton's governance. It is likely that the first step in this direction, the 1797 Bank Restriction Act, made the government realise that there was no limit to its power over money other than the prudent and moral application of its own self-restraint. This latest Act was another step in the process of debasing the quality of the currency and separating it from gold.

These steps by the British government and the Bank did not go unnoticed. American banks had suspended the redemption of banknotes in the War of 1812. The United States was also learning that adherence to Newton's Rule was voluntary and could be diluted to increase government power by gaining more control over the process of creating currency.

The Banking Act of 1844

The growth of the banking industry after the Napoleonic Wars and the distancing from Newton's governance resulted in an increase in loans and an expansion of the quantity of banknotes in circulation. This newly created currency in turn put upward pressure on prices. People became fearful that the Bank of England would stop redemption into gold coin and the inflation that had occurred during the period of irredeemable banknotes would recur.

Although the charter of the Bank of England was not due for review until 1855, a break clause in the 1833 Act allowed a review in 1844. Following a crisis in 1839 in which the Bank of England was forced to borrow £2 million of gold from the Bank of France to maintain redeemability of its banknotes[42], the prime minister Robert Peel seized the opportunity to conduct a review.

There had been a growing debate in the preceding decades that crystallised into two disparate schools of thought known as the Banking School and the Currency School. The former believed that currency should be infinitely flexible, with banks allowed to print as many banknotes as bankers believed necessary to meet the needs of customers who wished to borrow. The latter group was appalled by that idea. To control the flaw inherent in fractional reserve banking that allowed the creation of phantom purchasing power, the Currency School believed a bank should not be able to issue more banknotes than could be backed by the gold coin in its vault. In their view, the issuing of banknotes in a fractionally reserved system debased the currency, which causes prices to rise and that hurt workers and the growing middle class.

The debate came to a head in the 1844 review of the Bank of

England's charter led by Peel, who favoured the arguments of the Currency School. Its proponents won the debate but lost the battle.

The Bank of England, as required by the Banking Act, began reporting its financial statements for these two schools of thought and two activities separately as the Issue and Banking departments. The Currency School achieved its goal because the Act restricted the total value of banknotes that could be issued, but the Act had a fatal flaw that ironically led to precisely the opposite outcome of what it was meant to achieve. It did not restrict the use or quantity of deposit currency and that omission undermined the intent of the Act's proponents, which was to control the total quantity of currency in circulation.

Because the Banking Act bounded bank lending and therefore bank profitability by limiting the use of banknotes to make loans, bankers were quick to exploit the deposit currency loophole. Looking at what happened in practical terms, if you borrowed £100 from a bank before 1844, you were given one or more banknotes totalling £100. After 1844, you walked out of the bank with a chequebook and £100 of deposit currency recorded in your current account.

The limit on banknotes mandated by the Act forced banks to begin using deposit currency to make loans, the quantity of which soon surpassed all the banknotes in circulation. The Act also in effect awarded to the Bank of England a monopoly for banknote issuance, which further incentivised its cooperation with the government to achieve mutual goals that heightened their interdependence. The bankers would not be stopped.

The Banking Act was intended to ensure financially prudent behaviour. Lord Overstone, one of the foremost authorities on banking at the time, declared, 'Never again will one great public body [namely, the Bank of England] be entrusted with the dangerous power of creating [currency] at its own discretion and extending or contracting the amount of circulation uncontrolled by any fixed rule.'[43] Others had similar comments. These strong words about the 'dangerous power' of controlling the creation of currency echoed those of Macauley, whose *History of England* was soon to be published. As noted above, Macauley described the uproar caused by the proposed creation of the Bank of England because of the threat it posed to 'the rights of Englishmen'.

Even though it was 150 years after Newton had devised his rule to control the Bank of England's power to issue currency, there was still a clear understanding by many that the creation of currency needs discipline. It was also intuitively understood that gold as natural money was the foundation on which the monetary system should be based because gold cannot be created 'out of thin air' like ledger currency, which was the dangerous power feared by advocates of liberty and individual rights.

From Banknotes to Deposit Currency

The next evolutionary step in currency was the growth of deposit currency. These are British pounds circulating as currency that exist only as accounting entries on bank ledgers and move within the banking system from the payer to the payee.

Banks were increasingly relying on cheques, a product that had been around since Newton's time but infrequently used. This change occurred because one of the key advancements of the Industrial Revolution was to speed up the means of communication.

Moving a document by rail was much faster than horseback, horse driven carriage, or by barge in the canals built in the eighteenth century to cater to the growing needs of Britain's manufacturing industry. Banks took advantage of this revolution in communication by focusing on different products and services, one of which was a current account in which the customer's currency is recorded on a bank's ledger and could be spent or withdrawn by cheque.

Like a banknote, deposit currency is a bank liability, but it is evidenced by a statement of account. Further, and in contrast to banknotes, the customers' account statement does not circulate as currency. Rather, the deposit currency recorded on bank ledgers only circulates when the bank customer writes a cheque. The recipient of the cheque deposits it to their own current account. If both parties use the same bank, the bank simply updates its ledgers, in effect moving the deposit currency from the account of the cheque writer to that of the cheque depositor.

This process requires extra steps when two banks are involved. When a cheque drawn on a different bank is deposited, an obligation arises. The bank receiving the cheque also needs to receive deposit currency from the bank on which the cheque is drawn. The complexity of this process is compounded by the flow of numerous cheques between banks during the course of a day. It was simplified by the introduction of a clearing process in which cheques from its participating banks are properly accounted and reconciled, typically daily at 3 p.m., at which time banks calculate and then close their balance sheet for the day, even though commerce may continue with the continuous flow of cheques.

Through this daily clearing process, in which the Bank of England continues to this day to play a central role – hence the term 'central bank' – banks settle among themselves the flow of deposit currency. Banks have deposit accounts with other banks, and debit or credit these accounts with the net results from the clearing process, meaning that banks are financially exposed to other banks.

This achievement in efficiency for clearing cheques resulted in the introduction of a new risk. Banks became interconnected and reliant upon the financial strength of other banks.

What is more, the daily clearing process only works if banks are willing to accept the risks of lending to other banks, and this interconnectivity makes the entire network of banks vulnerable to a failed bank. One failed bank could lead to a cascade of bank failures. So the clearing system that is essential to make deposit currency circulate is only as strong as the weakest link in the chain.

The clearing of cheques introduced a new risk, adding to the fragility of the banking system and its inherent insolvency. This risk increased as the number of private banks grew, each of which began extending credit and creating new ledger currency.

To illustrate the excessive expansion in the circulating currency that is possible through fractional reserve banking, these new private banks added two levels of currency to the Exter Inverted Pyramid, as shown in Figure 8. They are banknotes issued by private banks that are redeemable into Bank of England banknotes. The other category is the deposit currency. The amounts are presented solely for illustrative purposes.

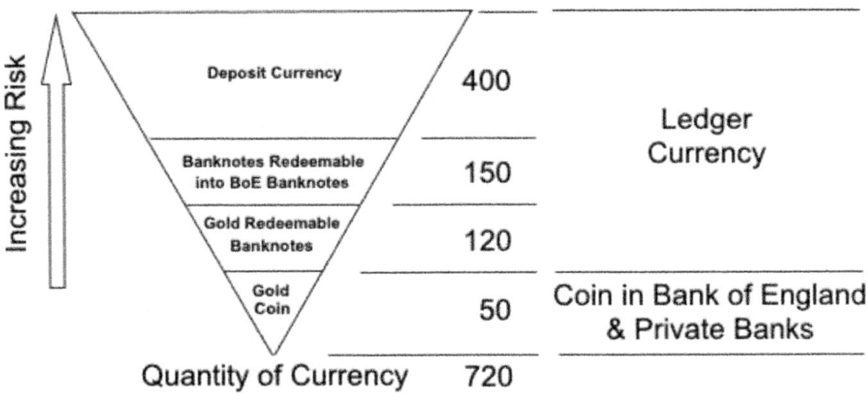

Figure 8 – The Exter Inverted Pyramid with Private Bank Currency

The pyramid also highlights the greater risk of these new private bank currencies and the daisy-chain relationship arising from their interdependence. The higher up the pyramid, the greater the risk because of the conversions needed to get gold in one's hands. Deposit currency is at the top of the pyramid and furthest away from the gold coin within the system because it was redeemable into the banknotes of the private bank where it was recorded. These banknotes then had to be redeemed for gold in the private bank's vault or the banknotes of the Bank of England, which in turn had to be presented to the Bank to get the requested gold coin obligated by the banknote. Being furthest away from direct redemption into gold meant that deposit currency carries a higher level of risk than banknotes.

There is a stark, fundamental difference between gold coin in hand that is money you own and gold at the base of the pyramid that is owned by banks. The difference becomes even more stark when comparing the gold in the base to everything above it. Bank created ledger currency, whether as banknotes or on deposit, is money owed to you by the bank.

This pyramid also illustrates the exponential growth of credit that is possible with increased leverage. From Newton's 40% ratio that restricts total money substitutes to 2.5 times the stock of gold, the money substitutes in Figure 7 are 13 times greater than gold on hand, and their ratio to gold drops to 6.9%. Exponential growth of the quantity of currency is possible with fractional reserves when an increasing rate of leverage is applied, which banks aim to do to increase their profitability.

The most significant effect of higher leverage and the currency creation resulting from it is to intensify the boom-bust cycle. There are always consequences from the greater amount of debt arising from higher leverage. It creates more risk and a bigger economic boom, which then inevitably leads to a bigger bust. If the bust is severe, a banking crisis and bank failures are unavoidable because banks with fractional reserves are by their very nature insolvent, which was a point well understood by the partnerships operating private banks.

The partners managing their bank understood that if the bank failed, they were liable to the extent of their total net worth to recompense their depositors. The risk of losing potentially all their wealth if their bank failed encouraged caution. That understandable restraint on the expansion of credit in a fractional reserve system was lost with the growth of joint-stock banks, which limited the liability of the bank's owners to what they had invested. That change in ownership structure added even greater risk to banks when profit motivation exceeded caution, which occurred often and contributed to bank failures.

Deposit currency was an advancement that improved the efficiency of currency. It offered advantages over banknotes, particularly convenience. Nevertheless, the uptake of deposit currency in the eighteenth century was slow, given the technology of the time and the antiquated means of communication available, so its total quantity was insignificant compared to banknotes in circulation. That changed after the Napoleonic Wars because of technological developments and government legislation. As we shall see, deposit currency became more important to commerce than all other money substitutes.

The Decline of the British Empire

It is not a coincidence that the British Empire reached its zenith in the nineteenth century, after which the quantity of newly created British pounds began to grow beyond the weight of the gold reserves in the Bank of England and private banks. It suffered the same fate and shared the same outcome as other empires before it. An empire of different lands and their peoples is only as strong as the money that binds them, and British monetary history is a tapestry of short-term gain over long-term consequences, of expediency over principle, and mendaciousness over plain fact. Debase the currency and loyalty to an empire disappears along with the erosion of the currency's purchasing power.

The pound - a term synonymous with gold and used interchangeably with it - was being debased. The British Empire began its decline with the pound. The debasement was slow and subtle, but nonetheless, its purchasing power was being eroded for several reasons.

Banks and their customers took advantage of the Banking Act's failure to restrict deposit currency, resulting in tremendous growth in the volume of loans made and the number of cheques written. The quantity of deposit currency increased from £1 million in 1844 to nearly £35 million by the end of the nineteenth century to represent 18% of the total currency in circulation, reflecting the significant growth in the use of deposit currency and the diminishing role of coins and banknotes.

Deposit currency was supplanting banknotes just like banknotes had supplanted coins. This change was driven in part by government legislation but in the main was accepted because cheques enabled currency to circulate more efficiently, which leads to another factor that contributed to the growth of deposit currency - improved communication technology.

By the late nineteenth century, banks were using the telegraph to transfer deposit currency. Moving currency by wiring the accounting entries banks needed to be entered into their respective ledgers to keep their accounts in balance was a major advancement over the circulation of deposit currency by cheque. Macauley's remarks above comparing the efficiency of banknotes to coin, namely, new to earlier currencies applies here as well.

The higher the degree of efficiency of a currency, the less currency is needed to achieve the same level of economic activity, which is an observation beyond the scope of this book but deserves further study. This efficiency is measured by the speed at which a transaction to purchase goods and services is completed. The key element is the speed at which two parties can communicate and agree to the value involved and then complete the transaction to their mutual satisfaction, namely, delivery of product and payment.

There was another downside to the 1844 legislation that added to those forces causing the currency to become less trustworthy. It forced two distinct and incongruous functions into a bank: making loans and clearing payments. If a bank failed because of bad loans it made, its clearing function would be disrupted, negatively affecting the economic activity in the geographic area where the bank operated and potentially causing other banks to fail. There were failures of systemically important British banks in the second half of the nineteenth century.

The growing use of money substitutes resulted from credit extended by banks to businesses as well as to accommodate the growing spending plans of the government. Government spending is rarely productive because it is mainly used for consumption, not investment.

Bank loans have the opposite result when they are directed to businesses and wealth producing undertakings that are successful. There are of course exceptions, namely, when bank loans are used for non-productive speculation or extended to uneconomic ventures. Bank failures will often result during the contraction of a boom-bust cycle.

Although gold coins continued to circulate, their use declined further as money substitutes gained an ever-growing share of commerce. As the everyday use of gold coins declined, so did perceptions and beliefs about the essential nature of money and the importance of gold. People were also losing sight of the payment risk that is unavoidable with all money substitutes, which led to one other important change.

Risks in the currency and banking system were rising. The growth in credit increased the fragility of a system built on fractional reserve banking because the quantity of currency grew faster than the gold reserve.

In the 55-year period from the Banking Act to 1899, the total quantity of currency grew by 1.71% per annum, compared to the 1.36% per annum growth in the Bank's gold reserve, which was less than the 2.0% per annum growth in the aboveground gold stock. This mismatch occurred even though there were great gold rushes taking place in Australia and the Yukon, which at the time were part of the British Empire, and South Africa, over which Britain claimed suzerainty.

This disjunction raises the possibility there may have been a growing preference to hold gold coin instead of banknotes. As credit expanded relative to available gold, a decline in trust in pound currency reflected growing fear about the safety of purchasing power being conveyed by the pound. See the discussion of the Fear Index in Chapter 8.

Throughout this period, Newton's Rule remained relevant because deposit currency could be converted into banknotes that were then redeemable into gold coin. In 1844, the ratio of gold coin in the Bank of

England relative to its banknotes in circulation – the key measure highlighting the inherent insolvency of fractional reserves – was 31%, already less than Newton's recommendation. Thereafter, the ratio of redeemable currency to gold continued to decline to 17% in 1899, putting the Bank of England in an increasingly precarious position. It further distanced its banknotes from gold while increasing the inherent insolvency of the Bank's position, having only £17 of gold on hand for every £100 of banknotes redeemable into gold, not to mention the quantity of deposits in other banks in theory redeemable into the Bank's banknotes. It is understandable that trust in the currency was declining.

Contributing to the fall in the trust in the currency were the periodic banking crises. The British government and others around the globe used these upheavals as an opportunity to increase through central banks their involvement to manage gold and money substitutes. This trend was well underway as the nineteenth century ended. Government intervention in commerce by legislation, management of the currency, and other means accelerated with the outbreak of the First World War.

From today's perspective, the decline of the British Empire can be seen as predictable. The pound tied it together, but the pound was built on the fraudulent practice of fractional reserve banking, which was exposed by the suspension of convertibility during the Napoleonic Wars. Newton's Rule enabled the currency and banking system to work for a time. There was relatively mild volatility from the periodic excesses that arose from too many loans. The boom in economic activity induced by easy credit was always followed by the inevitable, but contained, bust, just as night follows day.

Rather than abandon fractional reserve banking then and there, political leaders simply sought to re-establish what had previously existed before the war. The loopholes in the Banking Act in 1844 then unleashed a flurry of experimentation that led to greater control of the currency creation process by the British government. Human nature being what it is, rules were broken, and Newton's Rule soon became ignored or simply dismissed as an anachronism dispensable in what was then being viewed as a 'modern monetary' system.

What is worse, as this tinkering to currency and banking system was occurring, there was little challenge coming from great minds of that era questioning the changes evolving in the social contract. Absent were the likes of John Locke, the writers in the Age of Enlightenment, and firebrands like Thomas Paine and William Cobbett among others. Libertarian capitalists of the day like Herbert Spencer were popular and widely read but exerted limited influence.

Even though the Empire continued a while longer, the commercial benefits upon which it began and were the incentives to expand had been eroded by the end of the nineteenth century. Relentlessly disappearing was the proper balance between government and the governed, intellectual honesty, and a moral code with a rule of law that created a level playing field. The decline accelerated and became apparent at the turn of the twentieth century in the Boer War. To subdue a guerrilla force of 88,000, some 400,000 troops, then the largest military force ever gathered, were sent to southern Africa. As occurred with the American colonies, no longer was the Empire being held together by consent of the governed.

The End of the Gold Standard

> The gold standard makes the money's purchasing power independent of the changing ambitions and doctrines of political parties and pressure groups. This is not a defect of the gold standard; it is its main excellence.
>
> Ludwig von Mises

With the outbreak of war in August 1914, the British government took steps to remove gold sovereigns and gold half sovereigns from circulation. It stopped short of completely abandoning the gold standard. As it did during the Napoleonic Wars, the government pursued the fiction that the pound remained linked to gold, even though it was not possible to redeem banknotes for gold coin, distancing the Bank of England from the gold standard.

Newly issued paper currency in the form of Treasury notes was made legal tender, which meant that they could not be refused in payment. This new paper currency circulated along with the banknotes of the Bank of England.

To meet the growth in government spending during the war, both the Bank and the Treasury printed paper currency and commercial banks created deposit currency by buying government debt instruments. Because paper currency could not be redeemed for gold coin, currency creation became excessive. It was the natural result of abrogating key law, impeding market forces, and abolishing Newton's Rule that kept the quantity of currency in check. Even though the British government falsely claimed that it remained on the gold standard, the natural balancing of gold flows that is a central element of Newton's monetary system was thwarted by the inability to redeem banknotes. Consequently, the quantity of currency surged, just as it did during the Napoleonic Wars, the previous episode in which the redemption of banknotes into gold was prohibited by the government due to the Bank of England's inherent insolvency from fractional reserves.

In 1925, Winston Churchill, then Chancellor of the Exchequer, declared:

> A return to an effective gold standard has long been the settled and declared policy of this country. Every expert conference since the War – Brussels, Genoa – every expert committee in this country, has urged the principle of a return to the gold standard. No responsible authority has advocated any other policy.

Yet his proposal to return to gold was half-hearted. It was not Newton's system but something newly designed to keep gold out of circulation. The Gold Standard Act 1925 allowed redemption only in 400 ounce bars (today equivalent to about £500,000), thereby denying redeemability to the mass of the population.

The scheme failed owing to its flawed design and the reality of prevailing circumstances, namely, the pound was a debased currency. Too much currency had been created during the war and remained in circulation, so the pound had significantly less purchasing power compared to the weight of gold that defined its pre-war value.

In the decade prior to the war, the quantity of circulating currency averaged £217 million per annum. At the war's end the total quantity of currency was £737 million, more than trebling the pre-war average. It had dropped to £580 million by the 1925 attempt was made to return to gold. This contraction resulted in a deflation that increased the vociferousness of the trade unions and soon thereafter led to the 1926 general strike that paralysed the British economy. This economic downturn was blamed on the gold standard, not fractional reserve banking or the uncurbed, exorbitant costs of the war. The British government finally abandoned all pretence in its relation to the gold standard in 1931. The United States followed in 1933, as did most other countries.

There was a confluence of factors that brought the gold standard to an end. First among them was expediency, which had plagued the currency and banking system from the moment the Bank of England was created. Short-term goals and the ease of foisting newly created currency on an unsuspecting public were given priority over long-term moral principles. Politicians put their interpretation of the best interests of the State – and perhaps their own personal interests – ahead of the best interests of each individual and his or her welfare, which highlights another factor.

Government became too involved in control of the currency. It and the Bank of England were inextricably interlinked from the moment of the Bank's creation, and their interrelationship only grew tighter as time progressed. The Bank served the interests of the State, and there was little political will to change that relationship. Where political will was turned into action, the result was unsuccessful, for example, the Banking Act of 1844. The government's dependence on the Bank as a funding source continued to grow and was enhanced by the Bank's central role as a cheque clearing mechanism within the banking network.

Newton's gold standard stood the test of time when it was properly managed by adhering to his design, even though it was built upon the flaw of fractional reserve banking. In fact, his system was designed to mitigate those flaws and worked well enough to enable Britain to build its Empire. His monetary system lasted for more than two centuries and by 1900 was used throughout the globe when the United States that year moved from a silver to a gold standard, the last major country to do so.

The pound was the British Empire's currency and the Bank of England its agent at the centre of the successful expansion of commerce that occurred throughout the globe. They were the backbone of the Empire, which in contrast to other countries with global sway that came before it was built on commerce, not war. The Royal Navy did not win the Empire; it simply protected along with the military the rule of law in a commonwealth that was built upon commerce in which the British pound and gold were thought to be synonymous, despite the fractional gold reserves of the Bank of England.

Because of the global expansion of commerce that was the major achievement of the British Empire in the eighteenth and nineteenth centuries and the accompanying economic success and wealth creation, the British currency and banking system were adopted throughout the world. By the late nineteenth century, however, governments began using central banks and their control of the currency creation process to bend Newton's Rule and eventually abandon it altogether.

There was a shared motivation by governments and banks to act in concert to force the end of the gold standard. Governments wanted ever-increasing amounts of purchasing power to meet their growing spending aspirations to increase their power. The so-called progressives seeking socialist political agendas had become increasingly more vocal and powerful since the publication of Karl Marx's radical tracts. That trend continues to this day as evidenced by their stultifying political correctness[44] and promulgation of laws to prohibit what the anti-freedom forces define as hate speech[45], defying a self-evident truth expressed by George Orwell that freedom of expression is the distinctive feature of free societies: 'If liberty means anything at all, it means the right to tell people things they do not want to hear.' The extreme left-wing's clamour is manifest by their emphatic embracing of authoritarianism and their adoption of anti-capitalist ideas, dishonestly ignoring or purposely oblivious to the many failures of socialist experiments. In their view the gold standard had to be removed because it was a restraint on the ability to create money substitutes, thwarting the progressive's plans to spread their harmful tax and spend ideas that give increasing power to the State.

It was a new direction that commercial banks were happy to accommodate because a lower gold reserve enabled them to generate even greater profits in the fractional reserve system within which they operated. What is more, shareholders of the privately owned Bank of England were protected from any loss on their investment because the Bank was backstopped from collapse by the British government. Its reliance on the Bank to create phantom purchasing power for the government to spend was too great to forgo.

The gold standard was a voluntary system that worked as long as governments and central banks operated with morality by following the governance that Newton established to manage the inherent instability of fractional reserve banking. His rule did not end the boom/bust cycle, but it did control its amplitude to make it manageable and without excessive misallocation of capital and resulting economic distress during the inevitable bust. The rule achieved this outcome by imposing meaningful discipline on the creation of phantom purchasing power, preventing excessive debasement of the currency that arises when it is overissued in a monetary system that allows fractional reserve banking.

Just like Newtonian physics explains fluids in the visible universe, the gold standard accurately explains the flow of money and currency in global commerce. Gold moving around the world in commerce is like water sloshing around in a bathtub until a natural balance is reached, which describes the genius of Newton's invention. It is a self-correcting mechanism that responds to natural market forces, rather than the dictates of central bankers serving government interests, which explains why the gold standard was killed by governments and the vested interests who rely upon the State.

The gold standard did not die a natural death. Autocrats in government want control but do not want to be disciplined or have their powers limited. Alan Greenspan, former chairman of the Federal Reserve, confirms this point: 'It wasn't the gold standard that failed; it was politics.'[46]

During periods of stress, steps were taken to defend the gold standard, but other factors caused it to unravel, mainly the lack of political will to correct the situation. By the turn of the twentieth century, it became conventional wisdom to blame the gold standard instead of fractional reserve banking for every currency crisis. They are indeed interrelated, but neither did the gold standard nor gold itself fail. The failure came from those political leaders with an agenda that aggrandised the role of the State and disparaged the role of gold to the detriment of individual liberty.

Even to this day, gold meets the four tests needed to be money. Further, the crude oil prices in Figure 1 clearly illustrates the usefulness of gold in economic calculation and its ability to maintain purchasing power over long periods of time, which are essential components of a good money.

In the end, the gold standard itself did not fail. It was fractional reserve banking that failed. Newton's monetary system worked well enough to address the inherent fragility of fractional reserve banking, but his system was broken by politicians, bankers, and the people in Britain and other countries using the gold standard that allowed it to happen. The United States government also recognised that Newton's Rule was voluntary and could be diluted, thereby increasing its power by gaining control over the process of creating currency.

From the time Sir Isaac Newton created the gold standard circa 1696 until the dismantling of his system began in the nineteenth century and the remnants of it came to an end in 1914, the world had never before, nor has it since, experienced the same degree of real economic growth seen in the British Empire and the other countries that adhered to his monetary rule. The resulting global advancement in living standards is a crucial point that today's revisionists ignore, whether wittingly or not, about this admirable accomplishment achieved with the gold standard.

7. Currency After the Gold Standard

With the exception only of the period of the gold standard, practically all governments of history have used their exclusive power to issue [currency] to defraud and plunder the people.

Nobel Laureate Friedrich Hayek

Friedrich Hayek was one of the great economists of the twentieth century. He was 93 when he passed away in 1992, so he had a long lifetime of experiences. Imagine what he would be saying now given all the currency destruction, inflation, and the resulting human suffering that has been caused by governments and their central banks over the past three decades. Given their horrendous track record, it is distressing that currency after the gold standard has evolved into a near total reliance on central banks and their government handlers.

The Evolution of Central Banks

Lending and borrowing go back to prehistory, and lending institutions have existed for hundreds of years. When viewed over the millennia, the concept of a central bank is a relatively new phenomenon. As Paul Volcker observed in 1994, 'central banking, as we know it today, is, in fact, largely an invention of the past hundred years or so.'[47]

Central banking began with the development of ledger currency and fractional reserve banking in seventeenth century. Once the Bank of England was formed and operating, other countries caught on to the scheme, and their central banks began to emerge. Banco de España was created in 1782 to aid the State under the guise of stabilising government finances. Napoleon established the Banque de France in 1803 to ensure he controlled the finances for his military campaigns.

No doubt a student of history as well as understanding that money translates into power, Bismarck formed the Reichsbank in 1876 after the Franco Prussian War. It brought under central authority the issuing of banknotes, replacing the thirty-one note-issuing banks within each of the German states. The Reichsbank issued a single currency defined as a weight of gold, the mark. This centralised control of the creation of banknotes helped Bismarck cement the unification of the sovereign German states into the German Empire that became the dominant power in continental Europe.

Apart from the short-lived Bank of the United States at the beginning of the nineteenth century, the United States did not have a central bank until the creation of the Federal Reserve in 1913. Americans recognised that Europe's central banks were established to make loans to their country's monarch and create a national debt, with the funds then being utilised to fight wars. Borrowing for that purpose was not consistent with the prevailing American thought at the time.

Also, central banks existed to rescue those banks that became insolvent by printing too much paper currency without adequate gold backing. Living as they did in a capitalist country, Americans believed the best outcome was to let the badly managed banks fail. From unfettered competition, the best banks would emerge. That point of view changed completely by the end of the twentieth century with several larger banks receiving U.S. government support.

Once they were established, central bank powers started expanding. To enhance their power, governments in the nineteenth century began distancing national currencies from Newton's Rule. Interestingly, to help sell the concept of a central bank to a sceptical American public, Newton's Rule was made a fundamental part of the Federal Reserve Act enacted into law in 1913. It required the new central bank to have a vaulted gold reserve at least equal to 40% of its issued banknotes. By 1919, the Federal Reserve was working actively with the banking system to remove gold coins from circulation, bending the requirements of the Act.

By removing gold coins from circulation, banks could increase phantom purchasing power by expanding credit while still meeting the 40% requirement. Every $20 double eagle coin removed from circulation could be replaced with $50 of Federal Reserve banknotes, but Gresham's Law was already at work. Gold coins were being hoarded because inflation was taking hold. The U.S. dollar was being debased by the expansion of credit during and after the First World War.

Removing gold coins and subsequent actions validated much of the criticism arising when the bill to create the central bank was being proposed, including one of its most outspoken critics, Congressman Charles Lindbergh, father of famed aviator: 'This Act establishes the most gigantic trust on earth. When the President signs this bill, the invisible government by the Monetary Power will be legalized...The worst legislative crime of the ages is perpetrated by this banking bill.'

The mention of an 'invisible government' may at first blush seem farfetched, but these words come from a congressman who in his time was widely respected. Consider too the following statement by Woodrow Wilson before campaigning for and becoming U.S. President. It is deliberately quoted at length to give credence to the notion that the power to control the nation's currency results in the power to control its economy and supress liberty:

> The great monopoly in this country is the monopoly of big credits. So long as that exists, our old variety and freedom and individual energy of development are out of the question. A great industrial nation is controlled by its system of credit. Our system of credit is privately concentrated. The growth of the nation, therefore, and all our activities are in the hands of a few men who, even if their action be honest and intended for the public interest, are necessarily concentrated upon the great undertakings in which their own money is involved and who necessarily, by very reason of their own limitations, chill and check and destroy genuine economic freedom. This is the greatest question of all, and to this statesmen must address themselves with an earnest determination to serve the long future and the true liberties of men. This money trust, or, as it should be more properly called, this credit trust, of which Congress has begun an investigation, is no myth; it is no imaginary thing...I have seen men squeezed by it; I have seen men who, as they themselves expressed it, were put 'out of business by Wall Street,' because Wall Street found them inconvenient and didn't want their competition.
>
> We are at the parting of the ways. We have, not one or two or three, but many, established and formidable monopolies in the United States. We have, not one or two, but many, fields of endeavour into which it is difficult, if not impossible, for the independent man to enter. We have restricted credit, we have restricted opportunity, we have controlled development, and we have come to be one of the worst ruled, one of the most completely controlled and dominated, governments in the civilized world – no longer a government by free

> opinion, no longer a government by conviction and the vote of the majority, but a government by the opinion and the duress of small groups of dominant men.[48]

In 1989 the *Secrets of the Temple: How the Federal Reserve Runs the Country* was published, which by the publisher's description 'takes us inside the government institution that is in some ways more secretive than the CIA and more powerful than the President or Congress.' It was written by William Greider, who is reported to have made this comment about the political process: 'Money is power in American politics. It always has been.'

Governments and the moneyed interests that control them and the nation's currency have today achieved the culmination of power for which they have been striving since recognising that Newton's Rule was voluntary and could be ignored. Governments also ignored and are apparently oblivious to the harmful consequences of their actions that greater government power leads to less individual freedom.

The Pernicious 'Too-Big-to-Fail' Doctrine

Until the passage of Peel's Banking Act in 1844, there had been two distinct types of banks developing. Commerce banks were used for safely storing gold and silver coin and for savings. Though primarily used for safekeeping of money, customers could complete a payment transaction by instructing their bank to move coin from their account to that of another customer. The business model was based on the bank earning storage fees and if the coin was moved, handling fees. The Hanseatic League was noteworthy for its use of fully reserved banks, and even though it had disbanded by the time Napoleon marched through the German states on his way to Russia, he is said to have been surprised that so many banks were still following that practice.

In credit banks, customers borrowed currency. These loans were funded by customer deposits, which creates a vulnerability for banks because they typically use short-term liabilities to fund longer-term loans. In other words, customers would deposit their currency in the credit bank, and access it with a chequebook, meaning that the bank was required to pay on demand. However, the bank had loaned most of its depositors' currency, some of which the bank may not be repaid for months, depending on the tenor of the loan agreed between the bank and its borrowing customer.

Both business models could achieve profitability, especially when viewed on a risk adjusted basis. The fees earned by banks of commerce were lower, but so was the risk. That meant less capital was needed for investment in the enterprise.

Credit banks could earn wide margins on the loans made to its customers, which typically were a multiple of the storage fees earned by commerce banks. The riskier the credit, the wider the margin earned. However, because of the greater risk arising from these extensions of credit, fractional reserve banking, and the use of leverage, credit banks needed greater amounts of invested capital.

After 1844, the distinction between these two types of banks began to blur in Britain, and the United States followed soon after. It adopted the National Bank Act in 1863 to resolve a financial problem. The Northern states were lacking the funds needed to pursue its war against the Southern states. The National Bank Act created a national banking system that bought federal government war loans, which supplemented the unbacked banknotes – the so-called 'Greenbacks' conveying phantom purchasing power – already circulating as currency.

These legislative acts in Britain and the United States forced the expansion of deposit currency to the detriment of commerce banks. To adjust to their new government-imposed circumstances and to achieve the greater profit margins that credit banks were achieving, commerce banks began to disappear, being merged into or bought by credit banks.

Before the end of the nineteenth century, all banks operated both lending and payment functions. This development has led directly to countless banking crises, which could be avoided. There is no logical reason the high-risk lending function and low-risk payment function should both be lodged within one type of financial institution. In fact, experience proves the opposite, namely, that these two functions should be carried out in separate entities. Their different risks make these two functions incompatible.

Because banks inevitably get into financial difficulty by overextending credit, governments have pursued a 'too big to fail' policy for large banks because they are aware what a bank failure could do to the wider economy. Any bank's failure resulting from the unrepayable loans it made would also cause the bank to fail on its payment function. It is the failure of this function that governments fear because the disruption that arises when the payment process stops functioning has an adverse ripple effect throughout the economy. And what's true for a domestic economy is also true for the global economy, as I will soon explain what occurred in 1974 with the collapse of Bankhaus Herstatt in Germany.

The Politics of Gold

> To prefer paper to gold is to prefer high risk to lower risk, instability to stability, inflation to steady long term values.
>
> Lord Rees-Mogg

The twentieth century is marked by radical ideas overthrowing millennia of precedent that brought a revolution in economic theory and practice. Most notable is the ascendancy of the power of the State and the distancing of national currency from gold.

A habitual chant emerged that the gold standard does not work and was destabilising, notwithstanding the data indicating that while it was properly followed it produced an unrivalled period of economic growth and prosperity. But critics of the gold standard are correct in one respect. The redeemability of national currency into gold has been destabilising, but that is the consequence of fractional reserve banking, not any shortcomings with gold or the gold standard.

The occasional episodes of going off the gold standard did indeed disrupt economic activity and society as a whole. But critics of gold blithely ignore the reason countries periodically stop redeemability, which is that banks extend too much credit and governments spend too much money that together cause central banks to print more currency than they have metal in their vault. This reckless activity is made possible by fractional reserve banking.

The erosion in the nineteenth century of Newton's management principles aimed at keeping currency creation in check accelerated in the 1930s. Rising along with it have been authoritarian governments headed by demagogues, making the decline in unfettered markets and individual liberty all too apparent.

What is worse, gold became the scapegoat for the Great Depression. An example is this statement by Ben Bernanke, former chairman of the Federal Reserve and considered to be a leading expert on the Great Depression: 'The gold standard was one of the main reasons the Great Depression was so bad and so long.'[49] But wet streets do not cause rain. The real culprit is fractional reserve banking. Nevertheless, countless misconceptions have arisen since the end of the gold standard. Whether offered wittingly or not is unclear, but they share a common feature.

Because gold is the most serious threat to government power, criticisms are put forward with the aim of disparaging gold in favour of an agenda that consistently favours the State and those who control it. Central banks hope to marginalise gold by disparaging it through their propaganda, but the more phantom purchasing power they create to feed the State and its controllers, the better value gold becomes.

Some dispute this observation that propaganda is a tool actively used by central banks and governments. Given that the acceptance of fiat currency rests largely on the demand for it, common sense and logic suggest that central banks and their government sponsors need to constantly endorse their product just like any business enterprise speaks favourably of its product. However, in contrast to private enterprise that sells their products on its merits, central banks produce a fraudulent product and have a poor track record. They must 'sell' their product another way, so they rely on propaganda. For example, officials at the U.S. Treasury periodically speak about its policy to maintain a 'strong dollar', even though the Federal Reserve has an inflation policy that erodes the dollar's purchasing power, which is the antithesis of the Treasury's declaration.

Actions are more important than words and given that it is the Federal Reserve that is in control of the dollar, it is clear that the Treasury's pronouncements about a 'strong dollar' are propaganda, which relates back to Congressman Lindbergh's point. He strongly objected to the Federal Reserve Act because it would enable an 'invisible government by the Monetary Power' to assume unconstitutional control. Events after its establishment give credence to his assertion.

Most notable are the unconstitutional confiscation of gold in 1933 and President's Nixon's 1971 declaration ending gold convertibility of the dollar even though the monetary power in the Constitution is delegated to Congress, not the executive branch of the federal government. Control by the monetary power is evident to this day in the market interventions by the Federal Reserve. Events relating to the 2008 financial collapse provide a clear example.

According to a poll by the Los Angeles Times released after the Lehman Brothers bankruptcy during the height of the 2008 financial panic, Americans opposed by nearly two to one the massive taxpayer bailout of the teetering Wall Street banks then being discussed by the federal government. Despite this strong popular opposition, the bailout went ahead, which gives one pause about where the country's ruling power really emanates.

Commenting on the influence of banks in April 2009, Senator Richard Durbin said, 'The banks, hard to believe in a time when we're facing a banking crisis that many of the banks created, are still the most powerful lobby on Capitol Hill. And they frankly own the place.' In an interview the following week on the Public Broadcasting Service when asked to better explain his comment about the banking lobby, he said, 'The people [bankers] who brought this crisis to us are the ones that are dictating policy.'

In his 1928 book, *Propaganda,* Edward Bernays describes how an invisible government can maintain its power in a democracy:

> The conscious and intelligent manipulation of the organized habits and opinions of the masses is an important element in democratic society. Those who manipulate this unseen mechanism of society constitute an invisible government which is the true ruling power of

> our country.[50]

It is interesting to note his use of the term 'invisible government' fifteen years after Congressman Lindbergh used it to describe his concern. Its use also reinforces the link between money and liberty in that the latter is impaired when currency is controlled by the political process, particularly when the currency is backed principally by debt rather than gold.

There is also another factor to consider as John Adams warned in 1765: 'Liberty cannot be preserved without a general knowledge among the people.' Propaganda is more successful when the electorate is not knowledgeable about or are apathetic to the invisible government, even though its actions are very visible. Consequently, it is not surprising that with the power of propaganda behind it, the twentieth century's radical new ideas about money and currency took hold, while gold was disparaged and ostracised by the invisible government seeking to consolidate its power over the people.

A typical criticism during the gold standard period was the oft repeated refrain that there is a shortage in the supply of gold, rather than correctly stating that there is an excess in the amount of bank created currency in circulation arising from the creation of too much debt. Left unasked is why decisions were made at the Bank of England, the Federal Reserve, or any central bank that favoured the creation of more ledger currency aimed at undoing the natural automaticity of Newton's gold standard.

Criticisms of the gold standard overlook or wilfully ignore the monetary excesses of the First World War, the mismanagement of banks, and the implementation of government policies that expand the role of the State with new programmes for which it lacks the purchasing power to put into effect. These criticisms reveal a lack of understanding of what money is and how markets operate. For that reason, the politically motivated criticisms of gold can be debunked and should therefore be ignored. What cannot be ignored is the movement to an anti-gold world that has been gaining momentum since the nineteenth century.

One must marvel at the disinformation about money and gold that mendacious propaganda has accomplished when persistently applied over two or three generations. Ludwig von Mises captures the extent of the government apparatus that has been mobilised to propagandise against gold:

> The gold standard did not collapse. Governments abolished it in order to pave the way for inflation. The whole grim apparatus of oppression and coercion — policemen, customs guards, penal courts, prisons, in some countries even executioners — had to be put into

> action in order to destroy the gold standard. Solemn pledges were broken, retroactive laws were promulgated, provisions of constitutions and bills of rights were openly defied. And hosts of servile writers praised what the governments had done and hailed the dawn of the fiat-money millennium.[51]

We need to remove from government the powers it has usurped to issue currency and more broadly, its interventions in markets. After all, why do they intervene? It is because they do not like the verdict of the market on their policies. They then try to overthrow market forces with their interventions, control of the currency creation process, and other means. These include, if they believe it to be necessary, trampling on individual rights, like the freedom to travel with banknotes without needing to declare whether you are carrying over $10,000.

Many have noted how gold limits central bank power to create currency, as if that was a disadvantage. Restraining central banks is a key result and reason for using gold. This observation highlights the point that the criticisms levied against gold are usually made by those who benefit from the present system. Their interests are served by central bank authorities and government officials proclaimed as monetary maestros and masters of the universe in the mainstream media by what Mises calls 'servile writers'.

Only gold itself can provide the best possible money. The practice of fractional reserve banking should be stopped, and no central bank or government intermediary should be allowed to interfere with the market process.

Restoring the Gold Standard

> I am sure that nostalgia for the relative automaticity of the gold standard will rise among those of us engaged to replace it.
>
> Alan Greenspan

The classical gold standard was 'a period of unprecedented economic growth with relatively free trade in goods, labor, and capital.[52]' For this reason – and gold's ability to preserve purchasing power over long periods – some have argued for the restoration of the gold standard.

The gold standard could be restored, but it is unlikely to happen. Governments are bolstered by the power they receive from their market interventions and control of currency, so they are unfriendly to gold. They will always bend the rules to suit some perceived aim just as they have for decades, whether in the name of national security, their definition of social fairness, or whatever excuse is made up at the moment in an attempt to justify their interventions. From their track record, there is enough reason to reasonably assume that any attempt to return to gold would surely eventually be derailed by government itself. The vested interests controlling government are too powerful.

Perhaps that is the message by President Eisenhower after concluding two terms in office. His farewell address to the people of the United States apply throughout the globe. He warned: 'The potential for the disastrous rise of misplaced power exists and will persist.' He specifically named the 'military-industrial complex', to which I add 'financial'. When he spoke in January 1961, the U.S. dollar was still nominally tethered to gold, and the country had accumulated the largest gold reserve ever known, both of which no longer apply. The financial sector, and specifically the big banks, have become a threat to liberty by facilitating the government's quest for power by its obtaining full control over the country's currency.

What is more, every government seeks to perpetuate itself, and the easiest way to do that is to control the currency. So various theories of money are proposed to enhance the power of the State. Academia has become dishonest along with the government. There are too many PhDs propounding unsound theories that serve the State's interests, rather than acknowledging how the world really works, which also prompted a warning from President Eisenhower. 'The prospect of domination of the nation's scholars by federal employment, project allocations, and the power of money is ever present and is gravely to be regarded.' Expressing concern that scientists tend to agree with whoever funds them, he went on to say it is necessary to be alert to the 'danger that public policy could itself become the captive of a scientific-technological elite'. It is a prescient observation given the current debate about the unprecedented restrictions of liberty being forced by the government in response to the Covid-19 outbreak as well as the growth and expanding role of so-called 'big tech' in areas restricting the freedom of speech.

It is doubtful that government will give up willingly the power politicians have gained by taking control of the creation of currency. Governments today do not have the desire to restore the gold standard. Nor do they have the credibility needed for the gold standard to work as it did when governments saw their mandate simply as a moral imperative to protect the rule of law to ensure a level playing field for everyone, including the government itself.

Gold remains the standard by which to measure value, but I do not recommend restoration of the gold standard. History has clearly demonstrated that government cannot be trusted to follow the voluntary rules needed to make the gold standard mechanism work in a fractional reserve banking system. Those rules will again be bent or completely overlooked to enhance government power at the expense of individual liberty.

Those who advocate the restoration of the gold standard are looking backward, not forward. They ignore the fact that currency evolves. Resurrecting the gold standard is not achievable, practical nor desirable. The technology today makes ledger currency circulating as a substitute for gold unnecessary. Gold can circulate digitally, which is a process I developed and patented in the 1990s and to which I will return later. Digital technology made possible by the internet enables a precious metal to circulate more efficiently and safely than any ledger currency or coin.

History has shown that freedom loving people do not want government or central banks involved in the monetary system. Government does not have the responsibility to deliver currency for residents within its geographic boundaries. Currency – like any other good or service – is a product of the free-market, where there is no role for government to play.

The Bank of England was privately owned until 1946, and the Federal Reserve to this day remains private as it is owned by its member banks, although both central banks are in effect controlled by the government. Sadly, people everywhere have allowed governments to usurp the currency function, in complete disregard of the warnings and the sound advice given by countless advocates of gold and individual liberty since the Bank of England was formed. It is battle raging over three centuries.

The gold standard system that Newton created worked well enough, but fractional reserve banking over time threw up various tests. Beginning in the nineteenth century, governments seeking expediency and practicing short-sightedness used those tests to increase their power, leading to the problems we have today. Because governments created these problems, we cannot expect them to deliver a solution, particularly given their track record of perverting the rule of law. Only the free market can restore the currency needed to right the balance between government power and individual rights that has been lost.

The United States Defaults

> The State was thought to have eternal existence and its promises to pay were accorded unconditional faith. Consequently, government bonds appeared as a means to remove wealth and income from the uncertainties of life into the sphere of eternity. We need not waste any more words on the fallacy of this idea. It is sufficient to point out that even States can fall and that States can repudiate their debts.
>
> Ludwig von Mises, 1932

In the twentieth century, Lenin, Mussolini, Hitler, and Franklin Roosevelt confiscated the gold owned by the citizens of the countries they led and ruled. Why did they do it?

Alan Greenspan answers this question in a 1962 essay appearing in *Capitalism: The Unknown Ideal.*

> Gold and economic freedom are inseparable...In the absence of the gold standard, there is no way to protect savings from confiscation through inflation. There is no safe store of value. If there were, the government would have to make its holding illegal, as was done in the case of gold...The financial policy of the welfare state requires that there be no way for the owners of wealth to protect themselves. This is the shabby secret of the welfare statists' tirades against gold. Deficit spending is simply a scheme for the 'hidden' confiscation of wealth. Gold stands in the way of this insidious process. It stands as a protector of property rights. If one grasps this, one has no difficulty in understanding the statists' antagonism toward the gold standard.

The goal of twentieth century tyrants was to increase their power by increasing the power of the State. They sought to end the principle of limited government, which could only be achieved by absolute control of the currency and banking system and seizing gold from the hands of the populace. Once totalitarian control was achieved, the government could borrow phantom purchasing power to give the politicians more spending power to grow the government and increase the number of people reliant on it. Doing so would give it greater control over people and their pursuit of happiness.

Franklin Roosevelt created the Bureau of Public Debt in 1940. It was another of his schemes that strengthened central government and big government. The creation of permanent bureaus carried out this objective by giving the bureaus a mission that perpetuated their existence. The mission of the Bureau of Public Debt is not to encourage the repayment of the debt, nor even educate the American people about the burden of a national debt. Its Mission Statement[53] is to borrow money, which is an act that only perpetuates this bureau's existence.

The traditional and prudent strategies that had been proven sound over time and prevailed before Roosevelt took office have disappeared. They can be summed up by the words of President Andrew Jackson: 'I am one of those who do not believe a national debt is a national blessing.'[54] He put his belief into action.

It took the first six years of the total eight years he served as president, but he managed to repay the national debt in its entirety by January 1835, the only president to have accomplished this admirable feat. It was the first and only time the country had no debt, a remarkable accomplishment by his administration.

Jackson was the model of fiscal prudence and was emulated, or at least admired, by all subsequent holders of the esteemed office, at least until President Lincoln's war. The nature of the federal government then began to change. No longer would it be an institution that earnestly and sincerely tried to protect the rights of individuals and private property.

The federal government has become ever bigger and more totalitarian. As Orwell pointed out, totalitarian government can rewrite history, even the most important events of history.

What is the single most important event in the history of the national debt of the United States? Without a doubt it was the default of the federal government, passed by Congress and signed into law by President Roosevelt on June 5, 1933. To quote the joint resolution of Congress:

> Every provision contained in or made with respect to any obligation which purports to give the obligee a right to require payment in gold or a particular kind of coin or currency, or in an amount in money of the United States measured thereby, is declared to be against public policy...Any such provision contained in any law authorising obligations to be issued by or under the authority of the United States, is here by repealed.

In other words, even though the U.S. government was obligated to pay in gold the debts its Treasury Department had incurred, it would not do so. The Treasury defaulted, but never declared it a default. What is worse is Roosevelt's sham justification of the default. 'Since there was not enough gold to pay all holders of gold obligations, the Government should in the interest of justice allow none to be paid in gold.'[55]

There was not enough gold because the country was in default and needed to work through a voluntary bankruptcy with its creditors, not a grab for fascist power contending that its needs as it defines them are greater than the sacrosanct right of contract. This basic principle of American law that protected individual rights was jettisoned. To usurp power, the American government was following the same path as the British government to achieve supremacy for the State but with an accelerated and exacerbated decline in honesty and morality.

From Bretton Woods to Fiat Currency

As the Second World War was drawing to a close, the major powers began to focus on those issues that would be important in the post war environment. High on this list was international monetary order. The instability that prevailed during the 1920s and the Great Depression was fresh in everyone's memory, and no one wanted to repeat the unpleasant experiences from those years.

The major Western powers led by the United States and Great Britain convened in Bretton Woods, New Hampshire in 1944 to hammer out the working arrangements for a new monetary order, which further distanced national currencies from gold. The dollar would be redeemable into gold at $35, except U.S. citizens for whom the ownership of gold remained illegal. The currencies of other countries would be tied to the dollar at a fixed rate of exchange. This arrangement required the signatory countries to maintain domestic economic and monetary policies that would keep their respective national currencies at an unchanging rate of exchange to the dollar. The United States agreed to follow policies that would keep the dollar tied to gold.

The Bretton Woods Agreement did not last long. It began to unravel after the war as the United States policies implemented during the Roosevelt administration were debasing the dollar. With the war concluded, gold no longer needed to be stored in the United States for safety. Consequently, countries began to redeem dollars for gold, starting a two-decade trend. During this period, the U.S. gold reserve declined from 707 million ounces to 291 million ounces until the United States unilaterally stopped further redemptions in August 1971 to keep its gold stock from being depleted as the debasement of the dollar was accelerating.

Many economists blame the failure of Bretton Woods on the mechanical aspects of the agreement. They fault the cumbersome and inconvenient facility by which only one currency, the dollar, was directly tied to gold, with all other currencies tied to the dollar. This arrangement no doubt contributed to the failure, but the true reason is easy to explain. The quantity of dollars grew at a rate far greater than any increase in the demand for dollars, meaning that it was being debased. Consequently, countries dumped the overvalued dollar in exchange for undervalued gold.

The fiscal and monetary policies being followed by the United States made it impossible to maintain the fixed $35 rate of exchange to gold and prevent redemptions, which became increasingly obvious over time. By 1971, the dollar's purchasing power had fallen significantly from what it had been in 1944 when the Bretton Woods Agreement was signed.

Responsibility for its failure rests principally with Congress and the president because of their reckless policies of too much spending and borrowing, but the Federal Reserve cannot escape blame. As the saying goes, it never took away the punchbowl and let the good times roll to reach extreme, unsustainable levels. Its interest rate and other policies, like reserve management, facilitated the harmful policies being pursued. A toughminded and principled Board of Governors would have taken those steps necessary to nip in the bud the actions of politicians and banks that debased the dollar. Instead, the Federal Reserve kept the floodgates open until inflation soared and Paul Volcker became its chairman in 1979.

The German Bundesbank and Central Bank Independence

The Second World War ended with Germany occupied by four nations but divided by two political philosophies. The east was under the authoritarian socialist control of the former Soviet Union, while the allied nations of France, Great Britain and the United States re-established democracy in West Germany along with relatively free market capitalist policies.

With the German economy in ruins, the Allies had one aim. Having just ended a second war with Germany, they wanted to ensure that there would not be a third. They accomplished this objective by creating for West Germany a purposefully designed monetary system.

Wars need money. The Allies recognised that wars are fought when a country's central bank is under political control. Because the cost of a war typically exceeds a country's financial capability, warmongers need access to the 'printing press', namely, the currency creation process.

To fight the war, the government issues bonds, which are bought by the central bank. It pays the government with newly printed currency, which the government then spends on its war efforts, thereby putting this new currency and the phantom purchasing power it conveys into circulation. Government control over this currency creation process enables the politicians to fool its citizens about the cost of wars.

To achieve a independent central bank, the Allies understood that the central bank's managers alone would need to determine the quantity of currency in circulation. With that power in the hands of a truly independent central bank, the West German government had to be disciplined in its spending aspirations and live within its means. Balanced budgets would ensure that the government did not receive funding for another war. In other words, an independent central bank could not be forced into purchasing West German government debt that would be paid for by creating additional circulating currency. This restrictive, yet enlightened policy would prevent the government from receiving the 'printing press' currency it needed to fight another war.

The Allies established a process enshrined in West German law that the country's central bank would be truly independent. That required it to be outside the control of politicians. Achieving that objective meant the managers of the country's central bank could act as they thought best, regardless of the financial needs of the government and what politicians might ask them to do.

West Germany's economic rebirth began in 1948 with the introduction of a new currency, the Deutschemark. This new Dmark was initially managed by a central bank controlled by the Allies, the Bank Deutscher Länder. They relinquished their control in 1951. By that time, the Allies were confident that the structure they established would ensure that West Germany's central bank was independent from the country's political process, which is the core feature of the Bundesbank Act passed into law that year. The Bundesbank had no legal obligation to buy government debt instruments. By adhering to the law, principled managers of the Bundesbank could force the government to live within its means, which they did as evidenced by repeated annual government surpluses of revenue greater than expenses.

The Bundesbank became the most respected central bank in the world because of its skilful management. For example, from 1951 to 1999 when it was superseded by the euro, the Dmark appreciated in value from US$ 0.24 to US $0.60, and throughout the world was viewed to be a so-called 'hard currency'. During this period, the Dmark preserved purchasing power better than any national currency, as illustrated in Figure 1.

The famed independence of the Bundesbank is well known. The irony here is biting. The Allies did not impose on themselves the same discipline they imposed on West Germany. Their central banks could continue to create phantom purchasing power.

The Dmark is now gone, and so are the great central bankers of the Bundesbank's illustrious past, most of whom had lived through the Second World War and experienced the currency chaos from the collapse of the Reichsmark. Having that experience in their living memory no doubt contributed to the careful attention and cautious management given by them in exercising their responsibility as stewards of their nation's currency.

The Dmark has been superseded by the euro, the issuance of which is controlled by the European Central Bank (ECB). To the chagrin of thoughtful Germans who are knowledgeable about their country's currency history, mindful of their country's legal requirements, and understanding the harm caused by central banks under political control, the ECB is buying the debt of its member governments with newly created euro currency, putting it on the same road as the failed Reichsmark, the Dmark's predecessor. Today, central bank independence is a myth, and not just in Europe.

President Nixon's Fateful Decision

Gold is out of favour in political circles principally for two reasons. It is the discipline that gold imposes when the creation of currency is tied to the gold standard. The second reason arises when currency is not tied to gold, as is the case at present. A competitive threat to the national currency occurs when gold becomes more expensive. Gold acts as a messenger of currency debasement, which explains the counterintuitive result that the demand for gold increases as it becomes more expensive. Further, and of greater worry to politicians and central bankers, as demand for gold increases, demand for the national currency decreases.

Politicians want to spend money, so they do not like governors on the process by which currency is created because doing so restricts their spending aspirations. Nor do they like gold becoming more expensive in terms of national currency because it highlights the currency's loss of purchasing power, as illustrated in Figure 1. The political elite have therefore taken steps to remove the link between national currencies and gold.

From the abandonment of the gold standard at the outbreak of the First World War to the present, many governments have ostracised gold, led in particular by the U.S. government. There are many examples, but most obvious is President Nixon's executive order in 1971 to 'suspend temporarily', to use his words, the ability to convert dollars into gold at the U.S. Treasury. It was a default by the United States, but masked by a clever wordsmith.

Another example is the U.S. influence - and some would claim control - exerted over the International Monetary Fund. In the 1970s, a U.S. effort resulted in that organisation preventing any member country from linking gold to its national currency, which is a restriction that prevails to this day.

President Nixon's action was unconstitutional because the Constitution's monetary powers were delegated to Congress, not the Executive Branch of the government, which I address in Chapter 9. Nevertheless, his action meant that since then the dollar is no longer defined as a weight of gold, nor can dollars be redeemed for gold at the U.S. Treasury. It is fiat currency. It has no inherent value, so the economic value that enables it to circulate current arises solely from force, which is a combination of legal tender law and police enforcement. There was one other significant consequence inherent in this change.

By breaking the tether to gold, there was no longer any meaningful way in which to measure a currency's value. The fixed exchange rates under Bretton Woods were no longer viable. Currencies began to rise and fall against each other, creating a new risk for banks and businesses from fluctuating foreign exchange rates. National currencies were said to 'float' in relation to each other but, as we know from Figure 1, national currencies began to 'sink' relative to gold because it continued to preserve purchasing power.

Nixon chose his words carefully. By holding out the hope that redemption would resume after the temporary suspension ended, he was able to disguise what actually happened. It was another default by the federal government because the dollar could no longer be redeemed for gold. Instead of devaluing the dollar against gold, as President Roosevelt did in 1933, Nixon broke the dollar's formal link to gold. For the first time in its roughly 470 year history going back to the Habsburg Empire, the dollar was no longer defined as a weight of silver or gold.

Five decades later, the temporary suspension continues, this year being the 50th anniversary of Nixon's shock decision, but gold remains the standard by which value can be accurately measured as made clear by Figure 1. What is more, by allowing banks to create money without prudent limit, governments have built the worst possible currency and banking system. The consequences of 1971 have been dire, which are illustrated by a number of useful charts at: www.wtfhappenedin1971.com

The problems confronting President Nixon have not been solved. For five decades the federal government has been kicking the can down the road, which has encouraged denial of the underlying problems that caused the crisis. The failure to correctly address one crisis begets another crisis, which is typically worse than the first as errors can compound.

The Collapse of Bankhaus Herstatt

Not only was the world adjusting to fiat currency after 1971. Fluctuating foreign exchange rates posed new challenges for which many banks were not prepared.

The risk of using money substitutes in commerce became clear in June 1974, when the West German regulators withdrew the banking licence of Bankhaus Herstatt. Its licence to operate was withdrawn because the losses it incurred in foreign exchange trading meant its assets were not able to cover its liabilities. It was bankrupt. Though just a medium size bank, many banks throughout the world had clearing relationships with Herstatt. Its collapse therefore had global repercussions, and it no doubt worsened the recession and economic turmoil being experienced in many countries at the time.

As the first major banking calamity in the new fiat-currency era with fluctuating exchange rates, the shock waves from this bank's collapse circled the globe. The repercussions eventually led to the too-big-to-fail policy requiring the government to bail out any systemically important bank that fails. Some background on basic banking operations is necessary to explain why Herstatt's collapse had a global impact.

Throughout the day cheques are written and deposited and bank wires are sent and received countless times as ledger currency circulates throughout the economy. Then at the appointed time – usually at 3.00pm – banks begin the settlement process, with each bank calculating the amount of ledger currency it received and paid during the course of the day. The amounts are rarely equal, so there are two outcomes. A bank experienced either an outflow or inflow of currency, meaning that a bank's balance sheet did not balance.

To bring accounts back into balance, banks with a net inflow lend to those with a net outflow, which identifies the risk. A well-managed bank may end up lending to a poorly managed bank. The risk increases when country borders and different time zones are involved, as happened with Herstatt.

Its banking licence was withdrawn at 4.30pm local time in Germany at the end of the business day. Its customers had already deposited Dmarks into the bank in the expectation they would receive U.S. dollars, but they had to be remitted from Chase Manhattan Bank in New York where it was 10.30am. Because Herstatt was now bankrupt, its New York assets were frozen, and no U.S. dollars had yet been paid to those firms expecting to receive them. They in turn then had to scramble to make other arrangements for the dollars they did not receive.

The knock-on effect kept spreading around the world because banks are interconnected. The Bankhaus Herstatt collapse created such chaos that this toxic mix of lending and settlement risks that are unavoidable when using ledger currency is now often referred to in banking circles as Herstatt risk. Banks have tried to cope with this risk using techniques such as real-time settlement, but the risk nevertheless exists because ledger currency is a liability of a bank. Only a currency that is a tangible asset is free of Herstatt risk. Gold and silver, for example, do not have this risk. For example, when you place gold and silver coins on a shop counter and receive a product, the payment is immediate. There is no lingering obligation requiring a clearing and settlement process essential to ledger currency.

To this day, banks are plagued by Herstatt risk. Decades of regulation have been sold to the voters on the premise that they need to be protected and that regulatory oversight will encourage sensible practices by the financial services industry to mitigate risk. Yet the fines and criminal convictions of banks are racking up because there is regulatory capture, not regulatory oversight. It has resulted in the too-big-too-fail doctrine because the failure of a large, systematically important bank would result in a financial calamity that would ripple through the economy. Therefore, failure is not an option, regardless of whether the bank has bad managers or even if it engaged in criminal activity.[56] To avoid failure, the government steps in to bail out the bank, further distancing the economy from free market principles.

What is more, government support introduces the so-called moral hazard. Because of it, bankers are likely to take ever-greater risks in search of greater profits. They need not be cautious in their decision making knowing that they are protected from their own bad mistakes by the government being ready to bail them out. Nor do the regulators get fired for doing a poor job by not preventing a bank's bad decision making and failure.

The Great Financial Crisis

Fractional reserve banking, fiat currency and the modern world's unnatural over-reliance on debt make the global economy unstable even in the best of times, but the instability is most clear during financial crises. The collapse of Bankhaus Herstatt was a wake-up call that alerted another generation to the fragility of banks and the weaknesses of an increasingly interconnected system for the clearing and settlement of payments. Herstatt was just one of many casualties over the following decades leading to the most recent collapse, what is now often called the Great Financial Crisis of 2008.

In early 2007, subprime lenders and homebuilders began defaulting on their debts as a consequence of the popping of the housing market 'bubble'. Another global financial crisis had begun. Complicated financial structures thought to be safe were unravelling quickly after word spread that two highly leveraged hedge funds run by Bear Stearns were in trouble.

The eventual failure of those funds in July 2007, followed a few months later by the collapse of Bear Stearns itself, pointed a dagger right at the heart of over-leveraged banks that had made too many imprudent loans and/or were entangled into complex derivative structures with little opportunity to liquidate at prices close to their book value. When Northern Rock Bank failed in the United Kingdom, there was no longer any doubt that the worsening crisis was global in scope. It reached a climax in September 2008 with the collapse of Lehman Brothers, a U.S.-based investment bank founded in 1847, but the knock-on effect continued to roil the global financial markets for months. Northern Rock Bank and Lehman Brothers had made bad choices and their customers suffered the consequences, including worry, angst and time wasted wondering and then waiting how much of their wealth in those banks was lost and what amount would be returned to them.

A search on Google Scholar reveals dozens of analyses explaining the cause of this crisis, and there is no doubt a multitude of symptoms. There is however just one cause, human nature, which leads to bad outcomes when a financial structure reliant upon promises - whether just one company or an entire economy - becomes tenuous from the burden of excessive credit. It has been that way throughout history, so financial crises are not new. The collapse of two Roman banking houses, Brothers Pettius and Maximus & Vibo, brought about the business panic of 33-CE when loans they extended could not be repaid.[57]

A business panic is different from a currency crisis. The currency in ancient Rome was gold and silver coin, so when credit collapsed, the quality of the currency was not affected. Hardest hit by the fallout were the Romans who deposited their money in the failed banks, but others also suffered. As always occurs when trust in commerce is questioned because of broken promises, there was a jolt to the Roman economy. It was the inevitable knock-on effect resulting from the panic.

The credit collapse in 2008 was more than a business crisis caused by company failures. It became an economic crisis considered to be the worst and most widespread since the Great Depression, but these two calamitous events were different in one key respect.

In the Great Depression trust in the dollar waned as credit collapsed, which was manifest by widespread bank failures. There was a currency crisis as holders of ledger currency rushed into gold and silver coin, just like occurred in the run on the Bank of England in 1696. A currency crisis impacts everyone who holds the ledger currency, and for dollars that is everyone in the United States and a good portion of the rest of the world given the dollar's international role. A currency crisis leads to an economic collapse like the Great Depression when ledger currency is no longer trusted.

The Great Financial Crisis did not become a currency crisis because trust in the dollar itself was not questioned, although that event awaits us in the future. Today, currency is backed by credit, except for the relatively small weight of gold held in central bank vaults. It is credit – and not gold – that principally gives economic value to the ledger currencies circulating in commerce, namely the dollar and other national currencies.

The overextension of credit is almost invariably at the heart of any business or financial panic. The most severe and widespread consequences occur when the currency is based on credit because promises can be broken, thereby eroding and even destroying a ledger currency's usefulness.

It is basic human nature to test the limits of endurance, and not just in obvious ways like sport or exploration. We also test the limits of finance. We are driven by curiosity. Like everything else we do, these tests are endured in the pursuit of happiness, which is manifest in profit, recognition, or other motivations in which we seek to improve our situation by fulfilling needs and wants.

This strength to try new things in the hope of moving forward is also a weakness when applied to finance because we often keep testing until the breaking point is reached. For that reason, discipline is required to mitigate the excesses. This need for essential discipline explains why Newton developed a prudent rule for managing fractional reserve banking, which was completely abandoned in the twentieth century.

So crises occur for the simple reason that excessive credit expansion is made possible by fractional reserve banking. There are recurring periods when banks lend – and borrowers borrow – too much phantom purchasing power, putting both in dire straits. These imprudent extensions of credit inevitably strain the capacity of both the borrower and lender to make good on their promise to meet their financial obligations. The crisis then permeates throughout the economy because the currency derives its value principally from debt rather than gold. This weakness will become clear from the Monetary Balance Sheet in the next chapter.

The overriding problem in the 2008 financial crisis was not housing, but rather, derivatives. It is a problem that has continued to grow with the five largest banks now holding an estimated 95% of the $640 trillion derivative market, as estimated by the Bank of International Settlements. It is reasonable to ask why regulators have allowed banks to abuse prudent principles by taking on these risks and diverting their human and capital resources away from normal banking activities.

We face another bank crisis because banks are stuffed full of the questionable debts owed by over-indebted sovereigns and unprofitable companies. It is a powder keg just waiting to be lit by a collapse in demand for the currency backed by this debt. The Great Financial Crisis was foreseeable and expected by me and others,[58] but do not expect an honest appraisal from central banks. Even after the crisis began, the Federal Reserve was putting out disinformation, like this comment by Ben Bernanke on March 28, 2007: 'The impact on the broader economy and financial markets of the problems in the subprime markets seems likely to be contained.' The next credit-cum-financial crisis is a certainty, but no one can predict when it will happen.

The Impact of the Internet

The welcomed evolutionary improvements that make currency circulate more efficiently are usually gradual, but there have been abrupt changes, each with long-term consequences. The first of these step functions was the invention of coinage. Even though people would continue to use cattle, salt, and other tangible assets as currency, over time coins became the preferred currency.

The second next step function occurred in seventeenth-century London with the invention of ledger currency. Coins did not disappear of course, but they have been largely supplanted by the different forms of ledger currency circulating in commerce.

We are now living through the third step function in the history of currency. Virtual currency promises to be as profound and long-lasting as the two previous abrupt changes in the essential nature of currency.

When a novel technology appears, its full potential is not immediately recognised. For example, the first motor-powered cars looked more like a carriage without a horse than what comes to mind when we now think of a car. Those early inventors were thinking of transportation as it then existed and did not at first realise that the previous limits of horse-drawn transportation could be overcome by their invention. There needs to be some creative thinking and testing by entrepreneurs over time to discover the full potential of the new technology. So too with currency on the internet.

Like those newly invented cars over a century ago, the early entrepreneurs on the internet developed ways for ledger currency to circulate. Mechanisms were built to accept credit and debit cards. Others developed peer-to-peer payment platforms, again using ledger currency, which was designed for hand-to-hand transactions in the seventeenth century. Ledger currency therefore does not circulate efficiently in online commerce, nor does it eliminate the costly, complex and risky clearing and settlement system that ledger currency requires. Further, there are costs when converting one country's currency to another, and perhaps most importantly, with national currencies it is not possible to make instantaneous and non-repudiable 24/7 payments, which are an important requirement to achieve efficiencies and maximise the potential of global online commerce.

I too experimented with the technology, but my approach was different because I came up with the idea of digital gold currency in 1979, long before the internet arrived. The 1974 Herstatt debacle had intrigued me. After a few years of studying what had happened, learning more about gold, and thinking about alternatives, I realised that currency evolves and becomes more efficient because of advances in communications technology. I also concluded that the problems created by the Herstatt collapse and the costs of its fallout were just too significant and would eventually be overcome with a new and better currency.

Understanding the limitations and problems of ledger currency, I then set out to discover a better alternative, focusing on the benefits of gold coin in preference to ledger currency. By 1979 I developed my idea as to what that better currency would be. My idea incubated until I filed a patent application in February 1993, and not long thereafter the technology arrived to make it a reality.

The first of four patents was granted in September 1997, so my invention of digital gold currency was a key element to provide me with the motivation of taking the financial risk to establish Goldmoney the following year and then build it to launch goldmoney.com in February 2001. It enables physical gold to circulate on the internet without the counterparty risk that plagues ledger currency and with even greater benefits than can be achieved when gold coin circulated hand-to-hand.

The payer clicks their ownership of a specified weight of gold in a vault to a payee. Title to the weight of gold transfers immediately, so the gold 'moves' as currency even though it remains safely stored in the vaults, overcoming numerous issues related to coins. It is not ledger currency because title to the gold remains with its owner until used in payment.

Digital gold currency is modern and innovative, but gold and the benefits it offers are as old as time itself. Almost as old is Gresham's Law, which had a direct impact on Goldmoney. Rather than spending the good money and taking advantage of the efficiencies available from digital gold currency, my business colleagues and I soon learned after our launch that customers began to save the gold they were accumulating, preferring instead to spend the bad currency, which of course are the various national currencies. It was a natural reaction of bad currency driving good money out of circulation. The net effect made Goldmoney an efficient vehicle for saving money.

Virtual Currency Sparks the Creation of Cryptocurrency

It was not long after the internet began appealing to a wide audience with the adoption of browsers in the late 1990s that virtual currency appeared in online gaming. The potential of virtual currency opened a world of new possibilities, and it was not long before entrepreneurs acted. Capitalism creates new products to replace those no longer working because they fail to provide for every individual's best interests of life, liberty, and the pursuit of happiness. In 2008, virtual currency was taken to an entirely new level with the publishing of 'Bitcoin: A Peer-to-Peer Electronic Cash System' by Satoshi Nakamoto.

I read this paper soon after it was released and have been following bitcoin, cryptocurrency, and related developments ever since. I remember when the first commercial transaction was made using bitcoins to purchase a slice of pizza, which garnered a lot of publicity at the time in the small circles in which I was involved that wrote about and discussed currency, particularly from the potential impact of the internet.

The currency Satoshi created is built with math, and its design is based on gold, which was purposefully chosen because it is the ideal model to replicate. Gold is the best money because of its attributes, but being a physical asset, gold is subject to confiscation. So Satoshi set out to create a virtual currency that had all the features of gold, but, in contrast to gold, would be a currency that was beyond the reach of authoritarian governments.

Bitcoin in essence is virtual gold that derives from a mathematical model it uses to regulate the creation of new bitcoin units. Encryption techniques enable the security and verification needed for the safe transfer of the value denominated in bitcoin.

Fiat currency derives its value from the faith placed in government declarations. Once that faith is lost, the currency is lost too. Bitcoin is different. Its value rests on people's faith in maths, not politicians.

Relative to currency's two previous step functions, it still is early days for bitcoin. Nevertheless, it has already done well (BTC/USD is about $35,000 as I write) because it clearly has advantages compared to national currencies. Commenting about its recent rapid price acceleration, bitcoin enthusiast Max Keiser stated: 'Bitcoin has no top because fiat currency has no bottom.'

Bitcoin is an open system making available a global currency that anyone can use without asking for permission. The various features of bitcoin, like solving the double-spend problem, limiting the quantity of bitcoins, and achieving pseudonymity, are simply by-products of Satoshi's invention that replicate the numerous features of gold, whether used as physical coin or digital gold currency.

Because it is virtual, bitcoin does not have physical form. So bitcoin offers a means to store accumulated wealth in a decentralized cryptocurrency that is beyond government restriction or confiscation, which is a sweeping statement that is based on current technology. There is no known way at present to break its governing mathematical model.

It is worth noting that Satoshi avoided using in his paper words like 'accounting' and 'ledger' and had the good sense to come up with the word 'blockchain'. Doing so helped make clear that bitcoin was something new and completely different from earlier types of currency and should therefore be meaningfully distinguished as an important advancement, which explains why I describe it as the third step function in the history of currency.

Admittedly, when bitcoin first appeared I was sceptical and said so in a number of interviews at the time. Those generated some negative feedback from early bitcoin enthusiasts, which prodded me to study and ponder bitcoin's potential thoroughly. By the time it reached $100 I was convinced that bitcoin was here to stay.

Both digital gold currency and cryptocurrency operate independently of a central bank, but the similarity ends there. There is a stark difference between the physical and virtual worlds, which helps explain bitcoin's success and leads to one final point about bitcoin and its relation to gold.

They are complementary, not competitive. The disadvantage of gold, that it can be and has been confiscated by governments, is the advantage of bitcoin. The disadvantage of bitcoin, that you cannot hold it in your hand, is the advantage of gold, particularly given its long and successful track record and eternal attributes. Satoshi's decision to choose gold to replicate as virtual currency was purposeful. How do I know that? On what basis can I make any insights into Satoshi's thinking?

It is a speculative guess based on logic. Gold's superior attributes and track record make it the ideal money to replicate, but my guess is also based on observation. Goldmoney was launched in 2001 before the advent of social media, but the demand existed to discuss money and currency in general and digital gold currency in particular. So Goldmoney began an email listserv called DGC Chat in which emails and replies were posted for the participants to read. Anyone could join with their email address. Real names were not required. Some people chose to disclose their name, while many others did not. Nevertheless, from the content of the discussions it was clear that DGC Chat attracted a broad range of thinkers across the spectrum from business people to cypherpunks and probably some government snoops interested in staying informed of the emerging technology.

With such a diverse group, it is not surprising that the topics were varied, but one in particular kept recurring. It was that gold as a physical asset could be confiscated and has been confiscated by various governments throughout history, taking gold from the hands of their citizens and not the country's enemies. The upshot of these exchanges on DGC Chat ended with the same thought. Would it not be a wonderful advancement for individual liberty if there were a currency that had all the attributes of gold but could not be confiscated. I have no proof that Satoshi Nakamoto subscribed to DGC Chat, but what he created was wished for by many of the DGC Chat subscribers cherishing liberty and who recognised the growing tyranny of the State.

Cryptocurrency and the Old Order

> I don't believe we shall ever have a good money again before we take the thing out of the hands of government, that is, we can't take it violently out of the hands of government, all we can do is by some sly roundabout way introduce something they can't stop.
>
> Friedrich Hayek, 1984

As can be expected from any new technology that affects society, the emergence of cryptocurrency has triggered a heated debate. Depending on who you listen to, you will get a different view on cryptocurrencies. Central banks are negative about it, but many individuals are at least curious. Those who are positive about cryptocurrency know that fiat currency is not in their best interests and understand that central bank digital currency, which is gaining increasing attention and discussion, could further expand a government's ability to monitor and shape economic behaviour, with adverse consequences to individual free choice.

We can learn from what the Luddites did not understand and apply it to today's technology. Namely, technology changes everything over time and is a fundamental element of capitalism.

Overseers of the old order, banks and government, are today's Luddites arguing for the status quo because they recognise the threat posed to their current position and power. For example, the *Financial Times* on June 23, 2021, headlined: 'Central banks step up fight against cryptocurrencies', with the sub-headline making clear their intent in this warning from the Bank of International Settlements: 'Battle for control of global monetary system escalates as BIS warns against private innovation'. It is a uniquely statist reaction and not held by those people preferring control over their own money and the freedom to engage in commerce with whomever they choose.

Countless people have enthusiastically embraced cryptocurrencies because they find them useful in their pursuit of happiness. They have rejected fiat currency by voting with their pocketbook. The purchasing power voluntarily placed by those who earned it into cryptocurrencies is a no-confidence vote in fiat currency. These voters see that cryptocurrency serves them better than fiat currency, and that trend will continue if governments and their central banks continue down the same path of currency mismanagement, tightening control, and financial repression.

The old order will continually offer many different excuses – they will call them 'reasons' – to clamp down on cryptocurrencies. High on this list is their concern for financing terrorism, which is understandable. For example, the U.S. government does not want the U.S. dollar to be used against it, but any government's argument against cryptocurrency as a tool of terrorism is misguided.

Cryptocurrency is neutral to geopolitics, recognising that a terrorist seen through the eyes of one person may be viewed as a freedom fighter through the eyes of another. Given its neutral role, cryptocurrency becomes even more important when geopolitics adversely impact free markets and the ability for people to interact without interference from government controls and other forms of intervention.

An oft-repeated government concern is money laundering, which is another expression that has evolved over the years. When I began my banking career over fifty years ago, it meant turning banknotes into deposit currency, which provided more flexibility for spending the ill-gotten gains generated when using banknotes. The definition of money laundering today is much broader and is basically a catch-all phrase for anyone concealing the receipt of currency obtained through an ever-widening range defined by the government as illegal activity.

Recently a few central banks have stated that they need to create their own digital currency. It is well known that governments would like to eliminate banknotes from circulation. So the intent of central banks is to issue digital currency to replace banknotes, but without all the features of banknotes, particularly the privacy that banknotes offer. This step would obviously place yet even more control with central banks, with the removal of privacy further eroding an individual's inalienable right to privacy when contracting with others.

Cryptocurrency is a threat to government control and its dominance of currency creation, and governments recognise the threat. So far, they have not come up with a coherent response because cryptocurrency offers something fiat currencies do not. Recalling a basic feature of currency, it must be trustworthy. This critical factor makes bitcoin, at present the premier cryptocurrency, better than fiat currency. The often capricious, harmful political aims under which central bankers operate adversely impact the national currency they manage, which erodes people's trust.

Many are placing their trust in maths rather than the fiat currency of central bankers and the politicians who control them. The State cannot be trusted with the process of currency creation. Their record of consistent failures throughout the millennia - from Roman debasement of coins through the over-issuance of ledger currency to create phantom purchasing power - provide irrefutable empirical evidence that the State inevitably destroys currency. Just since the end of the Second World War, there have been many dozens of currencies destroyed. They became worthless, causing immeasurable harm to the lives of countless people, so it is to be expected that free market alternatives are being sought.

Another reason currency is evolving is because global online commerce requires it, and so does the high cost of operating the present ledger currency system. According to the Federal Deposit Insurance Corporation, the banking industry in the United States collectively made $233 billion in profits in 2019. There have been estimates that about 40% is related to their payments business that enables the ledger currency they create to circulate current. That is a high cost borne by consumers and businesses, particularly when considering that modern computer and communications technology exists today to significantly lower these costs, which is why currency evolves. Lowering the costs of any currency will lessen that particular impediment and encourage more commerce, which is a good outcome.

Worryingly, national currencies have been turned into a geopolitical weapon.[59] Denying access to clearing systems and freezing assets are warlike provocations. When actions considered to be hostile are imposed, the role of currency changes. It no longer is a neutral tool in commerce. The resulting impact can be broad and harmful because impediments imposed on currency undermine economic activity.

A cryptocurrency like bitcoin does not belong to any government and is not controlled by any bank. Bitcoin is not a company. It is a virtual currency and payment system that shares a published protocol that is available to anyone for review. It is used in a decentralised global network, outside of any central bank or the mandates of government, which therefore makes it empowering for individuals, particularly because it is easy to use. Simply download to your phone or laptop an app called a wallet, and you can then receive and send cryptocurrency.

It would be difficult for any government to ban a cryptocurrency. In theory it is possible by exerting strict control over the internet but enforcing the ban would be even harder. Without rigid enforcement by the government, individuals can download wallet software to complete cryptocurrency transactions. If there is a demand by people to pursue a course of action, entrepreneurs and technologists will find a workaround for any hurdle stopping people in their pursuit of happiness.

Perversely, rather than impede the widespread adoption of cryptocurrency, any attempted ban by a government might cause the demand for it to increase. A number of politicians who have disparaged bitcoin caused its popularity to increase as an unintended consequence from the publicity given to it. That response is similar to gun control proposals in the United States. Attempts by the federal government to interfere with the Constitution's Second Amendment right results in increased sales of firearms and ammunition.

Another consideration that government must take into account before attempting to impose a ban is that cryptocurrency has increasingly made inroads into financial systems, particularly in the United States. Entrepreneurs have profited from it, producing tax revenue for the federal government. That revenue would disappear from a ban and cause billions of dollars in cryptocurrency assets to move outside the United States, such as occurred with the gold trading industry after the federal government confiscated privately owned gold in 1933.

A ban would receive negative publicity because government-imposed prohibitions impede innovation and cause job loss. There are companies employing individuals to meet the demand for cryptocurrency products and services.

The cost of a ban by the old order can be measured in terms of liberty as well as money. Because cryptocurrency is a tool that is re-levelling the balance between government power and individual rights in a post-gold standard world, cryptocurrency is one of the best things that could happen for lovers of liberty.

Cryptocurrency is educating people throughout the globe that fiat currency and government control of currency is harmful. They are a toxic mix that inevitably leads to the debasement of currency, impairing the ability of individuals to save for their future. A fair and just society cannot be achieved without strict, rigid discipline in the currency creation process, like the world had for a time under the gold standard. Money is a creation and product of human activity, and not handed down by government, which highlights another advantage of cryptocurrency.

By avoiding a country's banking system, cryptocurrency can be an escape currency until market forces drive governments out of the currency business. It can help protect purchasing power by transferring it out of a fascist country into one where property rights are respected, which is another factor explaining its rapid and widespread adoption.

People buy cryptocurrency to protect their purchasing power. This usefulness is not available with any national currency because governments have ultimate control of bank payment systems, and it is becoming increasingly difficult to move purchasing power out of national currency confidentially to protect one's right to privacy.

Cryptocurrencies and bitcoin in particular have been wrongly criticised as Ponzi schemes. Ponzis convey no economic benefits and are therefore destined to collapse. But successful cryptocurrencies like bitcoin have value because they are useful and are bought by people who seek that usefulness.

The early adopters of bitcoin have also been wrongly criticised. They did not invent bitcoin, but they are entrepreneurs and entitled to the profits they have earned by buying and then holding bitcoins as their value increased. They took a risk with their purchasing power to buy bitcoins and are being rewarded for their prescience and acumen for using their purchasing power wisely, which is the essence of capitalism.

There was no guarantee that Satoshi's invention would be successful. So the early adopters of bitcoin should be viewed in the same light as those individuals who used their purchasing power to become early shareholders of Apple, Microsoft or any other tech company that offers a useful product for which there is a demand.

As the demand increases from the growing number of people using the product, greater profits result in a greater success for the inventors and early shareholders. The early adopters of bitcoin should be held in high regard because of their foresight and willingness to take a risk with something new with potential, though unproven.

The Disadvantages of Cryptocurrency

There are disadvantages to cryptocurrency, and these need to be considered, beginning with control. In contrast to ledger currency which is owed to you by the bank issuing banknotes or holding the deposit you placed with them, you own cryptocurrency. Nevertheless, you do not possess it, as would be the case with a gold coin that can be held in your hand, so you do not fully control what you own. What is more, you are still reliant on the internet and the ability to use it to communicate.

Cryptocurrency has the same fate as digital gold currency and gold coins, all of which are subject to Gresham's Law. Good currencies will always be driven out of circulation by bad currencies, which explains in part why cryptocurrencies are not often used in payment. People hold the cryptocurrency and spend the fiat currency, just like in Goldmoney people choose to save their gold to protect their purchasing power and spend fiat currency.

Some cryptocurrency, like bitcoin, is a surveillance coin. Each coin has a history, and you become part of that history because bitcoin does not offer the anonymity of banknotes. This link to a coin's history can be troublesome if you own a coin that happened to be previously owned by bad guys being sought by governments. It is possible that a bitcoin you own was used for illegal activities before you received it in a legitimate transaction, just as can occur with banknotes. In contrast to banknotes, reputation as well as value transfers with surveillance coins.

Cryptocurrencies have an environmental impact. Electricity is continually being consumed by the computer systems that operate cryptocurrencies. In contrast, gold is mined and coined only once. Then mine sites are restored to their natural habitat after the gold has been extracted, but the greenhouse gases from the electric generation for cryptocurrencies are continually impacting the earth's atmosphere.

It is incorrect to say that bitcoin is 'mined'. It is a gross misuse of that term, which is apparent to anyone who understands the resources needed, expended and the risks taken in mining gold, which in South Africa for example is done three or more kilometres below the surface of the earth. Cryptocurrency coins are not mined into existence and applying that term to bitcoins does a disservice to the mining industry. It is noteworthy that Nakamoto does not use the term in his 2008 paper to label the process creating bitcoins: 'The steady addition of a constant of amount of new coins is analogous to gold miners expending resources to add gold to circulation. In our case, it is CPU time and electricity that is expended.' Cryptocurrency coins are not mined or minted. They are electrified into an intangible existence recorded in computer memory, so one could say they are 'farmed', with electricity rather than sunlight being the key source needed to create a coin.

Cryptocurrencies, like ledger currencies, do not have an inherent use. Gold accepted in payment can always be used for adornment, if no one will take it in payment. Intangible currency does not have that feature. Like ledger currencies, the payment risk of cryptocurrencies is only eliminated when an exchange is extinguished by spending the intangible currency to buy some tangible good or service, so cryptos do not eliminate payment risk.

Cryptocurrencies do not have counterparty risk. They are not a liability on a balance sheet backed by assets that have value. A cryptocurrency's value arises from people's belief in a mathematical formula, so it has performance risk that manifests itself in several ways beyond its reliance on the internet. For example, it is impossible to predict whether a newly developed technology in the future that rapidly solves complex mathematical models will change the reliability of a cryptocurrency, undermining the way it is intended to perform.

Cryptocurrencies are by their nature fungible, meaning that one bitcoin is identical to another bitcoin. Bitcoin is decentralised but becoming centralised within China, which could potentially impair its fungibility if the computer systems in that country were to be negatively impacted by government controls. The result could be a fork, as already occurred with bitcoin cash, which could affect liquidity of bitcoin or the new cryptocurrency emanating from the fork.

Cryptocurrency can be viewed as one way to meet the basic need for unfettered liquidity. But like all assets, timing is important when it comes to buying and selling, and for money and currency, spending. The newness of cryptocurrency makes it volatile, and these fluctuations in exchange rates and purchasing power may not be acceptable to everyone.

The Outlook for Currency

> Inflation is made in one place and one place only – Washington, D.C. The chief source of it is the Federal Reserve board and a major accomplice sits in the halls of Congress.
>
> Milton Friedman

Currency will continue to evolve. There may even be more step function changes in the future that move society and commerce beyond virtual currency. Consequently, to protect and preserve individual liberty, look for companies that exploit innovative technologies that create a means for natural money and complementary cryptos, and not money substitutes, to circulate current.

Beyond its usefulness as currency, cryptocurrency is an educational tool. It is a real-life example for people to understand that currency today is an abomination that erodes individual liberty by disrupting the balance between the natural, inalienable rights of the people and the power of government. The educational knowledge being spread globally by cryptocurrencies is particularly important for the millennial generation. They have not had the opportunity to transact with silver coins in the 1950s and 1960s like the boomer generation, which learned from the inflation of the 1970s about the destruction of purchasing power that arises when government is in control of the currency creation process.

A fundamental building block of the Austrian School of economics is that value is subjective, and this principle also applies to money and currency. Some people may value a cryptocurrency's advantages more than what they see as its disadvantages. Conversely, other people may view it the opposite way and never use any cryptocurrency, unless its use becomes mainstream and unavoidable.

This observation about the efficacy of cryptocurrency and the ability to choose describes the underlying principle and benefit arising from competition in currencies, as recommended by Nobel Laureate Friedrich Hayek in *Denationalisation of Money*.[60] Let each individual choose the currency they want to hold their purchasing power before they decide to spend or invest it. The cumulative wisdom of the market knows better than any government how best to let each individual pursue happiness. Governments must never impose restrictions or any impediments on the development of new currencies.

The reality though is that governments find cryptocurrency to be frightening, which speaks volumes about their motivation behind the disservice they are already doing by attempting to marginalise cryptocurrency. Their reaction is an indictment of themselves, and not any imputation of wrongdoing by the pioneers who adopted and developed bitcoin and other worthwhile cryptocurrencies like ether.

National currencies need not be replaced by any virtual currency and will not be if national currencies deliver what people want and need to spend and save their purchasing power. If a currency denies an individual's pursuit of happiness, alternatives to national currencies will be sought and eventually invented and implemented. It is how the market process works. Entrepreneurs pursue their ideas to invest their time and capital to offer what they believe is a better product, and the market – humanity – then votes with their pocketbook. For that reason, the timing of cryptocurrencies is propitious and should be seen as the 'better product'.

Inventions always offer a steppingstone to a new world with unimaginable potential for the pursuit of happiness to raise our standard of living. Who knew at the dawn of the internet how many changes would affect how we live our life? While some accurate guesses may have been made by a handful of people, the future is unpredictable. For that reason and given the disastrous track record of government and their captive central banks in managing currency, it is possible that cryptocurrencies will break the present monopoly privilege given by government to banks, which will be of untold benefit to individual liberty and our society.

Satoshi Nakamoto, the anonymous creator of bitcoin, stated in an online forum shortly before he launched bitcoin in 2009, 'The root problem with conventional currency is all the trust that's required to make it work. The central bank must be trusted not to debase the currency, but the history of fiat currencies is full of breaches of that trust.' Nothing has happened since then to change the truth of this statement. Neither central banks nor the politicians who control them can be trusted when given any power to create currency.

Finally, keep in mind that bitcoin and all the other cryptocurrency so-called 'coins' are *units*, not coins. They are not tangible assets which explains why they are called cryptocurrency and not cryptomoney.

8. Source of the Dollar's Value

Gold will be money when the dollar and the euro
and the yuan and the ringgit are mere memories.

Richard Russell, *Dow Theory Letters*

What is a dollar worth? What is a euro worth? What is any national currency worth?

Many economists will say that a dollar is worth whatever a dollar can buy, but that glib response is unsatisfactory. Why can a piece of paper with no value as paper and ink or a bookkeeping entry in a bank account with no tangible value be exchanged for valuable goods and services? There is more to understanding the essential nature of currency than just measuring its purchasing power.

A Monetary Balance Sheet

All national currencies are created with debits and credits, the basic tools of double-entry bookkeeping. Because they are ledger currency, their essential nature and the source of their value can only be explained with a balance sheet. Each national currency can be analysed with what I have named a Monetary Balance Sheet (MBS).

An MBS is not the balance sheet of any one financial institution but is the aggregated balance sheet of a country's agents that issue circulating currency. These agents are a country's central bank and its commercial banks. They are given the monopolistic privilege by the government to issue and manage the country's circulating currency, which is recorded as liabilities on their balance sheet.

The banknotes you hold and the deposit in your bank account

represent units of purchasing power owed to you by a bank. In other words, you became a creditor to a bank the moment that you accepted currency, whether from your employer in exchange for your labour, the sale of one of your possessions, or any other transaction in which you accepted currency instead of money.

Turning to the asset side of the balance sheet, in most countries the currency's MBS has a mix of tangible and intangible assets, namely, gold and debts. It is important to recognise that these two types of assets are fundamentally different. Gold does not default because it is a tangible asset. In contrast, a debt is only as good as the borrower's financial capacity and willingness to repay.

In the United States, the MBS of the dollar combines the monetary assets and liabilities of the nation's banks and the Federal Reserve, which is its central bank. The MBS records all the ledger currency these banks have issued and the assets from which the ledger currency derives its value. An MBS clearly reveals the alchemy originated by the Bank of England that transmutes the assets of banks - their gold and the debts owed to them - into currency.

Figure 9 – Monetary Balance Sheet of the Dollar (Assets at book value)

31 December 2020
(billions of dollars)

Gold: 261.5m oz @ $42.2222 per oz	11	Federal Reserve Banknotes	2,038
Debts	25,175	Deposits in banks	23,148
Total 'monetised' assets	**$25,186**	**M3**[61]	**$25,186**

The assets on the dollar's MBS are the U.S. gold reserve and debts. The Federal Reserve owns U.S. Treasury Gold Certificates, an intangible asset, that give it a claim to gold stored in the U.S. Department of Treasury's vaults. The intangible assets that the Federal Reserve and the nation's commercial banks hold are the debts owed to them in numerous forms and maturities, with each debt of varying quality that is dependent on the financial resources of the borrower.

Banks issue each and every dollar, the total quantity of which is called M3. The total quantity of dollars circulating in the United States and the global economy as of 31 December 2020 was $25,186 billion.

It is clear from the MBS that dollars are liabilities of the banks, and further, there are two distinct types of dollar liabilities circulating as currency.

These are banknotes issued by the Federal Reserve and deposits in bank accounts, which together equal M3.

Types of Dollar Currency

The Federal Reserve has printed $2,038 billion of banknotes, a measure it reports weekly. The nation's banks have created $23,148 billion of deposits, which is calculated by subtracting the amount of banknotes from M3.

Coin is fabricated by the U.S. Mint and issued by the U.S. Treasury. Their quantity and the relatively small value of their base metal composition make them inconsequential. Coin therefore can be ignored and excluded from the MBS.

Banknotes are a liability of the Federal Reserve, which is evidenced by the words 'Federal Reserve Note' printed on all paper currency in circulation. Deposit currency is a liability of banks, with the bank's indebtedness to its deposit customers evidenced by documents issued in the bank's name. The documents provided to its customers are either a statement of account or a deposit certificate. These deposits are each bank's liability for Federal Reserve dollars. Bank deposits can be exchanged into banknotes on demand, although this right of the depositor has been eroded in recent years because the U.S. government has taken steps to discourage the use of banknotes.

It is the government's aim to keep currency locked up within the higher section of the Exter Inverted Pyramid to give them greater control over your currency. Bank deposits can be frozen, and transactions can be traced and monitored, so deposit currency is easier to control than banknotes.

Given that the Federal Reserve is owned by its member banks, which themselves are privately owned institutions, it is important to keep in mind that what we call a U.S. dollar is actually a Federal Reserve dollar. The dollars circulating current are not a liability of the U.S. Treasury.

It matters little to the basic accounting of the MBS that the U.S. federal government has a role in appointing managers to the Federal Reserve's Board of Governors. Nevertheless, it should be recognised that because the federal government created the Federal Reserve, it also holds the power to end it.

Assets on the Monetary Balance Sheet

The left side of the MBS lists the assets that back the dollar, or, stated another way, give the dollar its value. If the assets on the MBS had no value, then the dollar would not have value, at which point it would not circulate as currency. Proponents of the State Theory of Money refute this proposition, arguing that currency circulates because of government fiat, namely, laws that force the currency's circulation. The specious claims of these proponents fail to explain the numerous currencies that have collapsed throughout monetary history despite government attempts to force their circulation.

It is an aim of this book to debunk misguided and pernicious theories proposed by monetary cranks, which relate more to ideological aims than any sensible theory of money. Among the worst are Modern Monetary Theory and the State Theory of Money, which are devoid of logic and common sense. What is worse, they increase the power of the State at the expense of the individual and are therefore harmful to liberty. They are also destructive to capitalism and our market economy by their belief that there is no practical limit to the quantity of currency that can be issued when based on the powers of the State.

We know the assets on the dollar's MBS equal $25,186 billion. It is a basic premise of accounting that a balance sheet must always balance.

The book value of the United States gold reserve equals $11 billion at its 'official' government recognised exchange rate of $42.22 per troy ounce. This rate is used simply for recording the dollar's historical value. It is totally artificial because it does not reflect the decline in the dollar's purchasing power since the $42.22 rate was last seen five decades ago.

This nonsensical $42.22 rate is a good example that governments do not create their own reality, contrary to the belief of an unnamed official in President George W. Bush's administration.[62] Reality is created by natural forces in the physical world and the market, which expresses the cumulative outcome of human action.

The U.S. gold reserve is reported by the Federal Reserve as its asset because what it does not own directly, it owns indirectly through the U.S. Treasury Gold Certificates it holds that give it a claim to the U.S. gold reserve. Even though the Federal Reserve is owned by its member banks, the Federal Reserve and the Treasury are for all practical purposes part of the U.S. government. The precise determination of who really owns the U.S. gold reserve is not critical to the basic principles conveyed by the MBS nor does it detract from its usefulness.

The value of all other assets of the Federal Reserve and the nation's banks are labelled in the MBS as debt that equals $25,175 billion. This amount is calculated by subtracting the book value of gold from total assets. Shareholder capital and long-term debt of the banks are excluded from the MBS. They are assumed to equal other bank assets, such as premises and equipment.

One could argue that the MBS is not a precise accounting treatment of all the assets, liabilities and shareholder's capital of the Federal Reserve and the nation's banks, and that person would be right. However, the purpose of the **MBS** is not to present a precise accounting consolidation. Rather, it is meant to be illustrative of the currency system in use today to highlight the basic principles that make clear the essential nature of the dollar and the source of its value, and further, to provide a methodology for objectively calculating what the dollar - a money substitute - is worth in relation to money, namely, gold.

To reach these goals the **MBS** must be adjusted to market values. Banks do not disclose sufficient data to accurately assess the quality of their loan portfolios and the debt instruments they hold, but it is only of secondary importance what the agents consider the value of their assets to be worth. The market always determines the value of their assets, and prices fluctuate to reflect the market's ever-changing assessment, which explains why the market capitalisation of many banks trade well below the bank's book value.

Figure 10 – Monetary Balance Sheet of the Dollar (Assets at market value)

31 December, 2020
(billions of dollars)

Gold: 261.5m oz @ $1,893.10 per oz	495	Federal Reserve Banknotes	1,759
Debts	25,175	Deposits in banks	18,942
(1.9% Bad debt reserve)	(484)		______
Total monetised assets	**$25,186**	**M3**[63]	**$25,186**

Figure 10 updates Figure 9 with market values. Total assets remain unchanged at $25,186 billion because a balance sheet must always balance, and the quantity of dollar liabilities has not changed. The debts are also unchanged, but note the new line item, a bad debt reserve of 1.9%. It reflects the difference between the book and market value of these debts and is derived from an increase in gold's value.

Figure 10 records gold's market value, which is $484 billion above its $11 billion book value. By rising above its $42.22 official exchange rate, gold has kept the **MBS** in balance. The higher valuation is the market's assessment of what the market believes the debts on the **MBS** are worth. In other words, the market believes that 1.9% of the debts will be defaulted.

There are two types of debt held by the banks that they alchemise into currency. One portion is an amount of U.S. government debt. This debt is both long and short-term and is evidenced by T-bills, T-notes and T-bonds owned by the banks. The other debts on the **MBS** are those owed to banks by countless customers, ranging from loans owed to banks by triple-A creditworthy borrowers at one end of the spectrum to bankrupt companies at the other.

A debt of a bankrupt company or one near bankruptcy has zero or little value. These bad debts therefore cannot give value to a bank's liabilities. To reflect the bad loans that banks inevitably make, a bad debt reserve has been added. It is the market's assessment of the discount to book value that needs to be applied to the debts to accurately reflect their true value. To keep the MBS in balance, gold's exchange rate to the dollar rises, when the market's assessment changes course by sensing that the total bad debts are climbing, or falls when they have declined. The bad loan reserve equals the amount of the gold reserve's market value over its book value.

As interest rates rise, the value of long-term debt with fixed interest rates falls. For example, a U.S. Treasury bond with a 3% coupon will trade below its face value if prevailing interest rates are higher than 3%. So as interest rates rise, the gold's exchange rate to the dollar also rises to keep the MBS in balance when measured at market values. This result is counterintuitive and contrary to what is generally reported in the mainstream media, but its validity is established by the experience of the 1970s, the last period of rising interest rates. Gold rose throughout that decade along with climbing interest rates.

The 261.5 million ounces of Gold Certificates held by the Federal Reserve are valued at gold's year-end exchange rate of $1,519.50 per ounce. So as of that date, 1.97% of the currency recorded in M3 derives its value from gold. The other 98.03% derives its value from debts that have been alchemised – turned into currency – by the Federal Reserve and the nation's banks.

The Fear Index

> Basically gold is a way of going along on fear, and it's been a pretty good way of going along on fear from time to time.
>
> Warren Buffett on CNBC, March 2, 2011

Readers of my work may recognise that the ratio resulting from the market value of the gold on the MBS divided by M3 is my principal gold valuation model, dubbed the Fear Index. The Fear Index is the same calculation as the ratio Sir Isaac Newton established to manage fractional reserve banking in the Bank of England.

The Fear Index is an objective method to determine the value of gold, whether it is over, under or fairly valued. It is explained in *The Money Bubble*[64], along with two other objective methodologies I use to determine gold's valuation in terms of national currencies, so I will only provide here a brief overview of the Fear Index.

In Figure 11, it is applied to the U.S. banking system, but the Fear Index can be calculated for any national currency or the aggregate of all national currencies globally applied to the total weight of gold in central banks. The Fear Index calculation for the U.S. dollar as of 31 December 2020 is:

Figure 11 – Fear Index as of December 2020

$$\frac{U.S.\,Gold\ Reserve * Gold's\ Market\ Price}{M3} = Fear\ Index$$

$$\frac{261.5\ million\ ounces * \$1{,}892.70\ per\ ounce}{\$25{,}186\ billion} = 1.97\%$$

The Fear Index measures the risk to which holders of national currency are exposed to bank credit. In other words, $1.97 of every $100 of currency has value because of gold in the U.S. reserve. The value of the other $98.03 of bank liabilities circulating as currency is dependent on debts owed by countless borrowers. These calculations assume that the U.S. Gold Reserve actually contains the physical metal it is supposed to contain. Since the massive dishoarding that occurred in the 1960s, questions have been raised as to whether much of the reserve has been surreptitiously removed from Fort Knox and the other U.S. Treasury vaults in Colorado and New York.[65]

The logic of the Fear Index is based on the recognition that the value of ledger currency and gold correlate. The dollar and gold are competitors, and success is measured in terms of the relative quantity of purchasing power held by either alternative. That outcome is determined by the interaction of supply and demand for gold in relation to the supply and demand for dollars, and the Fear Index measures whether gold or the dollar is winning the competition.

When people are fearful about the safety of their purchasing power, they move it from dollars into gold. Conversely, when people have confidence in the dollar and the U.S. financial system, the quantity of their purchasing power that they hold in dollars grows in relation to the purchasing power held in gold. Hence the name Fear Index is deliberately chosen. Rising or falling fear about the safety of one's purchasing power determines whether they choose to hold their purchasing power in gold or dollars.

Figure 1 shows that gold preserves purchasing power over prolonged periods of time. Its short-term fluctuations do pose a risk, but those changes are ephemeral because debasement is the consistent outcome in the history of national currencies. While purchasing power is of course an important consideration when choosing to hold dollars or gold, it is not the only one.

Purchasing power does not provide an assessment whether gold is over, under or fairly valued. Nor are inflation and deflation important in determining whether gold's exchange rate is appropriate or not. Or whether to buy gold or sell or spend it. What is important is no different for gold than any other asset. It is whether gold is undervalued, fairly valued or overvalued, which is how the Fear Index can be useful. Its current level can be compared to historic results, with a relatively low Fear Index indicating undervaluation and a high Fear Index the opposite.

People's perceptions are constantly changing, including their assessment of dollar currency. Fear about the safety of one's purchasing power held as dollars will increase during periods of inflation or in a financial crisis. At other times, there will be growing confidence that the purchasing power stored in the dollar will be there when it is needed. These changes in sentiment result in fluctuations in demand for the currency and are visible in the following chart drawn to a log scale, which begins with the creation of the Federal Reserve in 1913.

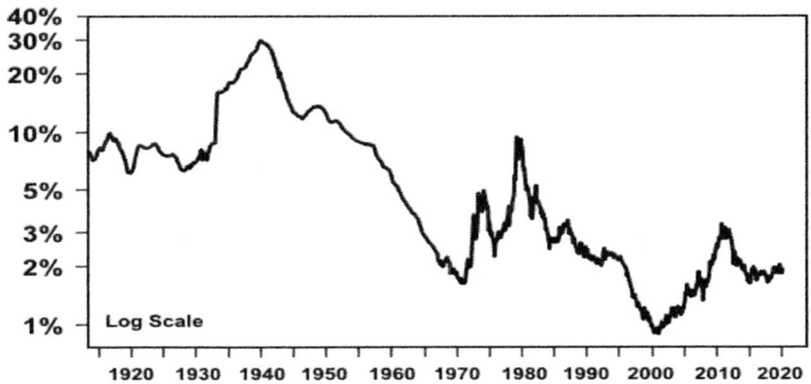

Figure 12 – Fear Index, January 1913 to December 2020

When the Fear Index is rising, it is a reflection of the market assessment that the risk of holding dollars is rising. Note how the Fear Index rose during the Great Depression, the inflationary 1970s, and in the early part of this century after the collapse of the internet bubble, the 911 attack, and the 2008 financial crisis. In these periods, demand for the dollar declines, and demand for gold rises. As a result, the purchasing power of gold increases relative to that of the dollar. It is the natural outcome that occurs when the interaction of the four forces of supply and demand of gold and the dollar favour gold in preference to the dollar. Conversely, when the Fear Index is falling, it means the demand for the dollar is gaining relative to gold.

Bank failures and uncertainty from the prevailing political and economic turmoil during the Great Depression and the start of the Second World War caused the Fear Index to rise toward 40%. It is not surprising that this high level was reached and then began turning lower in the early 1940s. Economic activity was improving, and the tide of the war was turning in favour of the Allies. These factors helped restore the badly shaken confidence. None of the other spikes in the Fear Index resulted in the degree of fear that permeated during the Great Depression and the early years of the Second World War.

The chart of the Fear Index clearly shows that to assess gold's value in terms of the dollar, it is irrelevant whether the dollar is on a formal gold standard. As natural money, gold is always the money by which currencies are assessed, which is the reason the Fear Index is so useful to measure gold's value in relation to the dollar or any other national currency. Two points stand out; these are the relative level and the trend.

When the Fear Index is low, gold is undervalued, but the level considered to be low has generally declined as governments and banks took steps aimed at marginalising gold to increase the reliance on ledger currency. Doing so enabled banks to make greater profits by extending more credit, while governments increase their power with greater control over the national currency. In Newton's time when the lessons of the 1696 panic remained in living memory, a low Fear Index was anything under 40%. Thereafter, the Bank of England worked at reducing that level throughout the nineteenth century. In 1929, 6% was low, but low was 1% at the beginning of the twenty-first century. So even though the Fear Index is an objective measure, some subjective judgement needs to be made as to what may be considered a low level in the period in which the Fear Index is being assessed, which leads to the second point.

The trend in the Fear Index is as important as the actual level. These trends can last for years, or even decades. The uptrend beginning in 1929 lasted for thirteen years, which then began a 29-year downtrend ending in 1971. It is a basic principle of portfolio management to follow the trend to accumulate assets that are undervalued and then sell them when they are overvalued, using the proceeds to buy undervalued assets. This principle also applies to money and currency.

In the twentieth century, gold reached its maximum demand in 1942, when the outcome of the war was still uncertain and the prevailing expectation was for another Great Depression when the economic activity boosted by the war ended. That moment was the time to spend your gold and/or invest it in undervalued dollar denominated assets. The question now is what happens next?

The future is unpredictable, but the Fear Index chart provides some guidance. It is unlikely that the 0.9% low in 2001 will ever be seen again. The undervaluation of gold was just too stark. That extreme undervaluation marks the end of centuries of efforts by governments and banks to marginalise gold.

It is perhaps symbolic of their efforts that this record low was in part the result of the announcement in 1999 by Gordon Brown, then the Chancellor of the Exchequer, that the Bank of England would be dishoarding half of its gold reserves. Both then and now it can clearly be seen as bald propaganda to disparage gold. It nevertheless led to gold's historic undervaluation and a multi-decade low price, dubbed by wags as the 'Brown bottom'.

Currently the 1.97% level of the Fear Index is low by historical results, indicating that gold remains undervalued. Also, as seen in Figure 12, the downtrend in the Fear Index from 2013 ended in 2015, and since then has been in an uptrend, albeit modest so far.

The Quality of Currency

There are two sides to a currency's MBS, but only the left side reflects the quality of the currency. In other words, bank liabilities circulate as currency only because the holders of the currency believe that bank assets have value.

All the debts on the MBS have been lumped into one category because banks do not disclose their loan data. So it is impossible to determine the precise valuation of each and every debt, but the precision of an item-by-item tally is not necessary. The MBS aims to illustrate the fundamental differences between debts and gold, of which three are noteworthy.

1. Face value

An ounce or gram of gold may equal any varying number of dollars, so its face value may change. In contrast, debts cannot be more than face value. A $1 million loan made by a bank to a borrower will never be worth more than $1 million. However, it can be worth less than $1 million if the borrower is unable to repay or if interest rates rise, causing the market value of long-term fixed rate debt to decline. This result contrasts with gold because one gram of gold will always be nothing more or less than one gram of gold.

2. Dollars differ

Aggregating bank assets and liabilities in the MBS can perpetuate the widespread mistaken belief that all dollars are the same, but they are not. A dollar on deposit in JP Morgan Chase is that bank's liability and backed by its assets, while a dollar on deposit in Bank of America is its liability backed by its assets. Dollars are believed to be homogeneous and therefore are generally interchangeable, but they are not identical. Their difference is of particular importance during a banking crisis, which is another corollary of Gresham's Law. Purchasing power moves from bad banks to banks considered to be safe. In contrast, gold is fungible. One gram of gold today is identical to one gram of gold in Roman times or any other period of history.

3. Asset certainty

A gram of gold stands for certainty. If the gold is stored in a safe and secure vault, there is the certainty that the gold's value can be realised when it is needed, which is not true for debts. Not all debts are equal. Some debts will be repaid in a timely fashion. Others will never be repaid because they are owed by borrowers without the financial capacity or willingness to repay their debt. A debt can only be realised if it is repaid. This need to repay a debt to realise the purchasing power it conveys creates a degree of uncertainty, which is of course higher in borrowers with a weak financial capacity than in borrowers that have a strong financial capacity. Though the uncertainty varies, it nevertheless always exists, in contrast to gold. The implications of this uncertainty are enormous when a substantial number of the debts cannot be repaid, as occurs with a day of reckoning in an economic bust.

When taken together, the above three factors impact the quality of any national currency. When viewed in dollars, it is therefore reasonable to assume that the $25,175 billion of debts on the MBS are not worth this amount. Imprudent loans to real estate developers, companies engaged in highly leveraged takeovers, and many Third World countries represent just three areas in which some debtors do not have the financial capacity to repay their obligations. As a result, many of the loans that are owed to banks will never be repaid, which is reflected in the dollar value of gold and the resulting discount to the market valuation of the debt in the MBS. It is therefore reasonable to accept that $484 billion of loans on the MBS are not worth that amount, but there is more to gaining an understanding of the quality of currency.

Every time we begin an exchange to purchase a product with currency there is a reckoning. We test whether the currency we are spending can be converted into the thing we need or want to buy. Normally the currency is accepted by the seller without question, but not necessarily in an economic bust.

A reckoning occurs the moment banks learn whether they have the financial capacity to meet their liabilities, which depends ultimately on the loans extended to their borrowing customers. Bank deposit customers also have a reckoning, which determines whether the deposit can be spent to purchase useful goods and services or converted into gold or a viable currency. These reckonings appear throughout history, most recently in 2008. As bad as that crisis was, it was not as earth-shaking as what occurred in 1933. Banks had made too many loans. Consequently, the book value they reported in their periodic disclosures overstated their true value, and many banks were bankrupt and closed because their liabilities were greater than the market value of their assets.

Periodically throughout monetary history, a panic inducing a bank-run has inevitably ensued when the liabilities of a bank exceeded the nominal value of its assets. After the reckless credit excesses in the Roaring Twenties, many loans in the early 1930s were non-performing with little or no hope for repayment. It created a black hole in the left side of the MBS, resulting in liabilities greater than the value of assets. Wealth cannot be created out of thin air; assets have to be produced, purchased or confiscated.

There are two alternative solutions to eliminating the black hole and bringing an MBS back into balance. Either the quantity of liabilities is reduced, and/or the aggregate value of the assets is increased. The Great Depression was deflationary because the first alternative was pursued. Over 3,000 banks failed and went into bankruptcy, reducing the liabilities in the MBS, and the purchasing power they represented. That is to say, the quantity of dollar currency declined by 27%. The net result of having fewer dollars circulating in commerce was a substantial increase in the purchasing power of the dollar, provided of course they were banknotes redeemable into gold or dollars on deposit in a bank that did not fail. The deflationary pressure was exacerbated by the economic downturn, which caused many creditworthy borrowers to repay their loans, further contributing to the decline in assets and liabilities in the MBS.

There was at the same time an effort to increase the assets in the MBS. President Franklin Roosevelt confiscated gold held by U.S. citizens adding it to the U.S. gold reserve, but he also devalued the dollar. After the devaluation, $35 was needed to exchange for one ounce of gold instead of the previous $20.67 rate. With the stroke of a pen, the dollar value of the gold reserve increased by 69%. Then the mendacious propaganda began, aimed at perpetuating the myth that the dollar was still as good as gold. But a promise to deliver a tangible asset is never as good as owning the tangible asset itself.

Just days after the President's Executive Order the U.S. Treasury Secretary said, 'We are definitely on the gold standard. Gold merely cannot be obtained for several days.' Claiming the dollar was on a gold standard was a figment of the Treasury Secretary's imagination. For U.S. citizens, those several days turned out to be 40 years and 9 months. Alan Greenspan provided the reason the gold standard had been abandoned in his 1962 essay entitled 'Gold and Economic Freedom': 'The abandonment of the gold standard made it possible for the welfare statists to use the banking system as a means to an unlimited expansion of credit.'

Mr Greenspan's conclusion indicates that the federal government had another aim, different from what was announced to the people. Gold was confiscated by Roosevelt in the United States for the same reason it was confiscated in Russia by Lenin, in Italy by Mussolini, and in Germany by Hitler, namely, to get it out of the hands of the people.

It was claimed then and now by statists and their apologists that the confiscation was necessary to increase the U.S. gold reserve, but that claim is disproved by the maths. Had the dollar been devalued to $35.33 per ounce, slightly more than the $35 rate chosen by Mr Roosevelt, the same valuation of the U.S. gold reserve necessary to re-establish confidence in the dollar would have been achieved, but without any confiscation.[66]

Relatively little gold was actually confiscated. Few people turned in their gold, recognising that the order to do so was not only theft, but unconstitutional. So, to confiscate as much gold as possible, the federal government had to rely on what it could get from gold being vaulted in banks. The nation's banks were ordered to turn over to the federal government the gold owned by their customers and stored with them for safekeeping, in exchange for $20.67 of currency. The devaluation occurred after the confiscation.

The devaluation of ledger currency has the same result as the debasement of precious metal coins, which is a decline in both purchasing power and the quality of the currency. Debasement occurs, as we saw with Henry VIII, when base metal is mixed in a coin so that the weight of precious metal stamped on the coin is less than the actual weight of metal content in the coin. The same principle applies to ledger currency. Its debasement occurs when reducing its share of the monetary balance sheet as a percentage of total assets.

There is another way in which banks lower the quality of their assets. The saying describing this result is that 'banks lend long and borrow short', which creates an asset/liability mismatch in a bank balance sheet. Banks do not only make demand loans, which the bank can call for repayment at any time. To earn a higher interest rate and generate greater profit, banks also extend loans which do not require repayment for one or more years. The risk arises because these long-term loans are often funded with short-term deposits, which impairs liquidity and the ability of a bank to meet its liabilities, particularly in a banking crisis.

The quality of a country's currency broadcasts for everyone the state of that government's creditworthiness. If the currency is losing purchasing power – and national currencies have been on a downhill ride for decades – the government's financial position is deteriorating.

The creditworthiness of any borrower is first and foremost dependent on cash flow. For governments around the world cash flow is constrained. Annual increases in national debts are becoming larger and will start accelerating as interest rates rise. The financial repression being used by central banks to keep interest rates at artificially low levels cannot continue indefinitely, with untold consequences when the reckoning arrives.[67]

People who hold national currencies learn from the loss of their purchasing power from inflation and banking crises that trust in the currency is not reliable when based on hollow promises of politicians and bankers. Their aim is to perpetuate a system favourable to their vested interests.

Bad assets in the MBS mean bad currency. Debt-backed ledger currency that has value based on alchemised debts is today the lifeblood of the global economy, which warrants caution. Ledger currency can become toxic, as we remember from the events in 2008 or as we can read from history books what happened in the Great Depression.

The Quantity of Currency

Having looked at the left side of the MBS, the right side also needs analysing. It is a measure of the quantity of currency in circulation.

There are opposing points of view about how much currency is needed in the economy, and whether increases in the quantity of currency can spur economic activity. This latter point is very much in vogue with governments and central bankers. They have pumped huge amounts of currency into circulation in their expectation that their intervention can stimulate economic activity that was sent reeling by the Covid-19 pandemic.

Sometimes their currency creation may work, but as is typical in economics, sometimes it does not. Occasionally too much currency creation has the same effect as too much gasoline pumped into an engine that prevents it from starting. The impact of currency creation can be overridden by other factors such as too high a tax rate or too heavy regulatory burdens that impede economic activity and thereby thwart central bank intervention aimed at pumping up the economy.

The amount of currency for a given level of economic activity is illustrated with a simple formula.

Figure 13 – The Quantity of Currency Equation

$$MV = PT \text{ and } PT = GDP \text{ so:}$$
$$MV = GDP$$

Where:
M is the quantity of currency,
V is the velocity of circulation,
P is the price level, and
T is the volume of transactions.

This formula has limitations and is often misused. For example, it purports to measure GDP, which is then brandished as an indication of a country's wealth and the well-being of its citizens. GDP includes government spending, so this formula could be used to conclude that more currency creation given to the government to increase its spending makes a country wealthier and its citizens better off, but the dire circumstances in Venezuela disprove that notion.

Government spending should not be part of GDP because it is a tax that reduces wealth in people's hands. GDP should only measure private sector activity - true wealth creation. It is wealth creation that raises the standard of living, not government spending.

Another limitation arises when the formula attempts to explain the velocity of currency, which is how quickly it is spent. Because the formula is a tautology, velocity is included as a variable only to make the equation balance. So this formula cannot explain why velocity varies, which of course is the result of decisions by individuals to spend or save the currency they hold.

Nevertheless, despite these limitations, the Quantity of Currency Equation is useful in one respect. Because the quantity of currency and GDP can be measured to a reasonable degree of accuracy, the velocity of currency can be calculated. When viewed over a long time, the calculations of velocity provide an indication whether there is too much, too little, or the right amount of currency in circulation. This outcome is illustrated in the following chart measuring U.S. dollar velocity.

From 1960 to the early 1990s, velocity fluctuated on either side of 1.8, with this lengthy stability in the ratio ($V = GDP/M$) suggesting the right amount of currency was in circulation. Velocity then began to rise reaching nearly 2.2, which implies that more currency was needed given the level of economic activity at that time.

Figure 14 – Velocity of U.S. Dollar M3

Source: Federal Reserve Bank of St. Louis

After peaking in 1997, velocity has been in prolonged downtrend. It declined to what was a record low after the Great Financial Crisis from central bank currency creation and then kept declining. This protracted decline indicates that too much currency is being created and forced into circulation. There is more currency in existence than is needed to sustain the level of economic activity being generated. The world is awash in dollar liquidity no one needs or wants. The supply of new currency is outstripping the demand for it, which is a typical pre-condition for inflationary price increases.

There is one prevailing reason for the decline in velocity caused by the excessive currency creation by the Federal Reserve and the nation's banks since the Great Financial Crisis. The spending of the U.S. federal government is out of control, causing huge annual deficits. It is therefore issuing unprecedented amounts of debt that are being turned into currency by Federal Reserve and commercial bank alchemy. The likely consequence for the dollar is an acceleration in the loss of its purchasing power.

Measuring Currency Debasement

The MBS and the Fear Index are useful in another way, namely, comparing currency used in the past to currency today. A dollar at any time in the past is different from a dollar today. The dollar has been debased in two respects. Its purchasing power and its quality have both declined.

Falling purchasing power has become the expected course based on historical observation for any currency not linked to gold. National currency loses purchasing power over time when increases in its quantity are greater than an increase in demand for that currency. The currency can be eroded in this way even when it consists solely of precious metal coins as occurred, for example, in Spain in the sixteenth century with gold and silver plunder flowing into the country from the Americas. The disruption in Spain was short-lived because the plunder was limited.

Central banks ignore this reality about the quantity of currency by thinking that no amount of currency can be too much. The Federal Reserve is wedded to this misguided thinking as illustrated by Figure 14.

The decline in purchasing power is only part of the change national currencies incur over time. Their quality erodes too. The quality is decreased when, for example, base metal is added to a precious metal coin. The quality of ledger currency falls as its reliance on gold is decreased, which can be seen in the MBS and measured by declines in the Fear Index.

To compare a unit of currency over time, changes in the quantity of currency are measured in terms of purchasing power, which then also requires an adjustment reflecting the change in quality to arrive at a meaningful analysis of the changes in a currency over time. For example, Jane Austen describes people's financial situations throughout her novel, *Pride and Prejudice*, which I have chosen because many people are familiar with it. Mr Darcy's annual income is reported to be £10,000, which obviously had a greater purchasing power in 1813 when the novel was published than that amount has today.

Using the gold sovereign as an approximate measure of the pound at that time, Mr Darcy's annual income was 2,435 ounces. That amount equals £3 million at the current £1,252 exchange rate. With this adjustment, we can now easily understand in present day terms how comfortably Mr Darcy was able to live, but the quality of the pound has also changed over this period of time.

M3 in the United Kingdom today is £2,842 billion, and its gold reserve is reported as 9.97 million ounces. At the current exchange rate of £1,252 per ounce, the market value of the gold reserve is £12.5 billion, so the Fear Index is 0.44%. In 1813 it was 32%, 73 times greater. Given that the value of the pound in 1813 had significantly more backing than presently, it had less risk, which is another way of stating that it was of higher quality.

The 1813 data for the U.S. dollar is not available, precluding a direct comparison. It is nevertheless reasonable to conclude that given the decreasing reliance on gold in today's currency systems, as illustrated by Figure 12, there has been a significant deterioration in the quality of the U.S. dollar.

For example, when the dollar's Fear Index is 10%, the quality of the dollar is twice as high than it is when the Fear Index is 5%. At 10%, every $10 of $100 of circulating currency derives its value from gold, which is twice the value derived when the Fear Index is 5%. The quality of the currency is higher as the Fear Index increases because gold does not default, making it fundamentally different from debts on the MBS, all of which are based on promises. When less gold supports a ledger currency's value, it perforce is of lower quality and higher risk. While most focus today is directed to the quantity of currency, the quality of currency as measured by the Fear Index is also important, particularly so in a currency crisis.

The Stable Price Ruse

In her book, *A Mountain of Crumbs*, Elena Gorokhova describes life in the former Soviet Union. 'The rules are simple: they lie to us, we know they're lying, they know we know they're lying but they keep lying anyway, and we keep pretending to believe them.' This quote is relevant today when the lie is related to a currency foisted on the public.

Central banks and their government sponsors claim that one of their tasks is to maintain stable prices. As an example, the Federal Reserve contends that along with full employment, its primary mission is to achieve stable prices measured in U.S. dollars. This aim is regularly and routinely offered to the public and Congressional committees as justification for the Federal Reserve's existence to perpetuate its exclusive position of power and privilege.

Stable prices exist when the average consumer price for goods and services is constant over time because the currency being used to measure them retains its purchasing power. As the chart of crude oil prices in Figure 1 makes clear, central banks have not been successful in this stated endeavour. In fact, price stability is far beyond any central bank's reach.

Price stability is an impossible task because in the real world, which is different from the world of academics and their clever but unworkable theories, things are not static. People change their mind, and their demand preferences vary. Any change in demand alters the price of a good or service. People's wants and needs change constantly, so their demand for goods and services is constantly changing as a result.

Similarly, the supply of goods and services is constantly changing too. Production depends on the ability of the producer to deliver, which in turn depends on everything from acts of God to the myriad factors impacting the producer's production capabilities. So the supply of goods is not static. As a result of this interaction between changing supply and demand, prices fluctuate, but the factors determining prices are actually a bit more complicated than that. The supply and demand of money changes as well.

There are four forces at work that discover the price of any product. They are the supply of the good being purchased, the demand for that good, the supply of the currency being used to discover the market price of the good, and finally, the demand for that currency.

How can a central bank be expected to achieve price stability by managing only the quantity of currency? It is just one of these four forces, and even then, only one type of many different currencies that are available for use to discover prices when considering the dozens of national currencies in existence.

Even if central banks were trying to achieve price stability for a basket of goods and services, what services should be included? One service important to some people may be completely non-essential to others. 'The Consumer Price Index is an artificial statistical creation from an arithmetic adding, summing and averaging of thousands of individual prices, a statistical composite that only exists in the statistician's calculations.'[68] This reality describes just one of the limitations of indexes, like the Consumer Price Index or the Producer Price Index (PPI), but there are others.

What would the PPI have been if the government in 1970 had decided to include computer chips in its compilation of this index because these were becoming ever more important to the way we work and live? The cost of chips has declined in dollar terms to a minuscule fraction of their cost fifty years ago. Its inclusion in the index would have disguised much of the inflation suffered over this period by offsetting in the PPI much of the price rises of the other goods and services in the basket. This loss of purchasing power in the dollar would have been hidden by the technological achievements that have significantly reduced the price of computer chips, just like recent declines in dollar purchasing power have been mitigated by cheaper imported goods replacing American made products.

Technology lowers prices while creating excessive currency raises them, so there is a need to measure these two counterbalancing forces to better understand changes in the price of goods and services. Expansion of the quantity of currency in circulation puts upward pressure on prices. The full impact on prices from this expansion might not be felt if there is simultaneous downward pressure on prices from the latest technologies. Many products needed for everyday life over time become less expensive from technological advancements and enhanced efficiencies in production, improving the standard of living for many. Governments use this circumstance to their advantage to understate cost of living indices in contrast to the outcome during the gold standard.

For example, wages remained relatively fixed during the era of the Industrial Revolution, while prices fell because of technological improvements to the necessities of life like cloth manufacturing and farming. This deflation meant that individuals could achieve a greater surplus between their income and their living costs even though wages remained the same. Regardless of whether the net increase in their surplus was spent immediately or saved for the future, the net result was greater wealth that meant an improvement in their standard of living.

In a sound monetary system, prices will normally decline over time because of technology. Technology improves the quality of life and lowers costs, which enables workers to get more from their purchasing power. That is the way it is used to be, namely, the consumer benefits, but today government benefits from technological advances because they hide currency debasement.

There have been powerful disinflationary forces embedded in the massive technological innovation that has so far defined the internet era. Governments are using these technological achievements to make inflation look lower than it really is, and debased currency is preventing individuals benefitting from the lower prices resulting from new technology. Price stability is an invented goal concocted by central bankers in the twentieth century to hoodwink the public because the natural decrease expected in cost of living indices has disappeared along with the reliance on gold.

In fact, not only is price stability impossible, we do not want to achieve it. Assume a severe drought were to destroy a substantial portion of the grain crop in the United States, causing prices to soar and the CPI to rise. To achieve its goal of price stability, should the Federal Reserve raise interest rates to decrease the quantity of dollars in circulation to fight this crop price inflation?

When viewed in this light, the so-called goal of price stability clearly does not make any sense. It actually looks pretty silly. It is impossible to predict the future, so no one - including central banks - can adjust the supply of currency to create a stable, unchanging price. Any interventions attempting to do so will have unintended consequences, as explained by Alan Greenspan to the *Wall Street Journal:*

> Government actions almost inevitably have unintended consequences, he said. 'There were unintended consequences to almost every action I was involved in' as Fed chairman, said Mr. Greenspan, who himself cut interest rates to help stave off a bond- market crisis in 1998, and later was accused of helping inflate the stock bubble of the late 1990s. 'If we anticipated the unintended consequences that were going to happen we might have changed the policy,' he said, but he added that it is impossible to forecast all the consequences of government action.[69]

Mr Greenspan makes clear that the unintended consequences were undesirable outcomes. Had they been favourable, he would not have stated that he would change the policy if he knew in advance what those unintended consequences would be. Although he may not have been trying to make the point, he is broadly arguing that any policy intervention is harmful, which is a logical conclusion.

Jean Claude Trichet, former President of the European Central Bank, described market intervention as a 'weapon'.[70] Only harm comes from weapons, and financial harm can be hurtful too. This frank admission in an unguarded moment by a leading central banker indicates how central banks view themselves in relation to people whose actions make up the market. As Ludwig von Mises advises: 'It is necessary to restrict the power of those in office lest they become absolute despots. Society cannot exist without an apparatus of violent coercion. But neither can it exist if the office holders are irresponsible tyrants free to inflict harm upon those they dislike', or in my view, inflict harm on those markets trying to reflect free market forces but are impeded by central bank intervention.

There is another reason for ending government intervention. Human nature can make it difficult to just say 'no'. Few have the fortitude, honesty and willingness to be in the tough and unpleasant position of a central banker taking away the so-called 'punch bowl' from which new currency flows endlessly. With the exception of the Bundesbank when managing the Dmark, central bankers have proven they cannot do it. Therefore, money should be left to natural forces, which is a basic premise of the Theory of Natural Money.

Governments undertake interventions in order to achieve an outcome they desire, regardless as to whether the population agrees with the outcome. Individuals will seek the outcome they desire in their pursuit of happiness whether or not the government agrees, which gives rise to 'black markets'.

They are so named because they operate in the shadows outside of government scrutiny, but it is a disparaging misnomer. In reality, they are unfettered markets operating without government involvement. A scholarly analysis detailing and examining all the harmful effects of government intervention in the economy is beyond the scope of this book but is of merit and warrants consideration.

As it relates to currency, government intervention results in the currency's insidious debasement. Any debasement is harmful because it distorts economic calculation, which then disrupts commerce. It also interferes with the sound analysis required before making an investment, which leads to bad decisions and the misallocation of capital.

Debasement is theft and, because it is hidden from view, the theft is easy to do, which explains why currency debasement has become so pervasive. Governments can get away with it, but like everything in our world, there are limits.

The Outlook for the U.S. Dollar

Since the 1944 Bretton Woods conference, the U.S. dollar has been the world's reserve currency. This term is still used today to describe the international role of the dollar, but it is meaningless to speak of a reserve currency when it is not redeemable in gold. In fact, that is what the term 'reserve' means. It is the supply of gold held for safety in a fractional reserve system that is not needed at the moment but is available if required, for example, to settle a payment obligation in money instead of currency. But like the definition of other words relating to money and currency, apologists for what now serves as the international monetary system have twisted the word 'reserve' to give it a new definition that fits what exists today.

These word games are intended to delay the end of the U.S. dollar's role as the world's reserve currency. While the timing of events is always problematic, monetary history shows that reserve currencies have a limited life. The reserve currency role is lost when the currency eventually becomes too abused and debased by government mismanagement to continue serving internationally, as clearly illustrated in Figure 15.

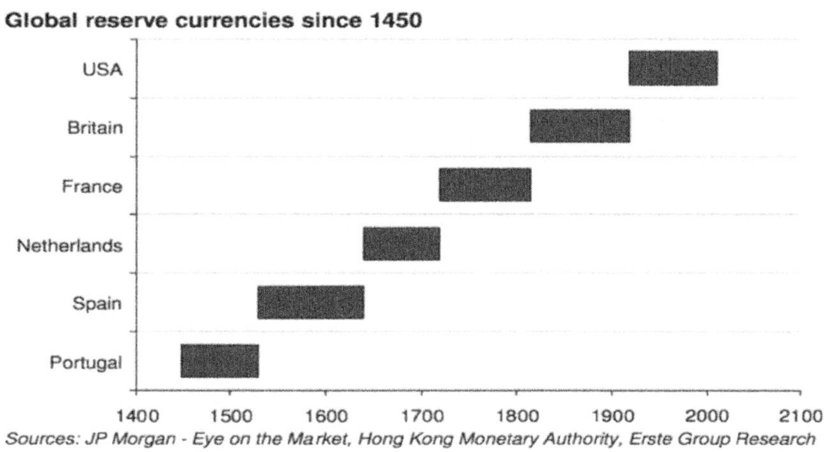

Figure 15 – Global Reserve Currency Status

Government can force currency to circulate domestically through fiat, regulations, and penalty for non-compliance, but those weapons applied domestically do not work internationally, as evidenced by an announcement in the *Jakarta Post* on 28 June 2021 that should be of concern to the dollar's managers. 'Indonesia and China are closer to reducing their reliance on the U.S. dollar as they plan to start using their own currencies for bilateral trade and investment within weeks.' The head of financial market development of Indonesia's central bank briefing the news media about the decision said the step was taken 'so we do not depend 100 percent on the U.S. dollar anymore.'

Forcing a national currency to circulate internationally requires gunboat diplomacy, which the U.S. government has applied in recent decades when countries attempted to challenge the dollar's supremacy.[71] While gunboat diplomacy can be effective to a certain extent, it has limitations too. Pulitzer Prize-winning journalist, Chris Hedges, recently wrote:

> In 2015, the dollar accounted for 90 percent of bilateral transactions between China and Russia, a percentage that has since fallen to about 50 percent. The use of sanctions as a weapon against China and Russia pushes these countries to replace the dollar with their own national currencies.[72]

Countries that are powerful enough to challenge the U.S. government can keep U.S. gunboats at bay. These countries can freely choose whether to use the reserve currency, and like China and Russia are doing, decrease their reliance on the dollar by developing alternative payment systems. It is the opposite outcome that one would expect from Gresham's Law. While bad currency drives out good money domestically, internationally there is a choice. The dollar is being driven out of international circulation in recognition that it has moved from being a neutral tool in commerce to become a geopolitical weapon.[73]

The dollar's position is eroding because central banks outside the U.S. orbit are accumulating gold to prepare for whatever is coming next, which cannot be predicted given that we never know how the future will unfold. Nevertheless, it is reasonably certain that given gold's track record and unique attributes, it will eventually return to its rightful role at the centre of global commerce, even though we cannot predict when that will happen.

The ongoing debate about the prospects for the dollar has been intense ever since its formal link to gold was broken in 1971. This debate has rested upon the widespread belief and expectation derived from objective observation of monetary history that the U.S. government's currency policy will eventually fail, and that the dollar, like all other fiat currencies before it, will ultimately collapse.

That the dollar has lost 98% of its purchasing power since 1971 when measured in terms of gold is sufficient proof that this expectation for the dollar is indeed well founded. Even though the dollar has not collapsed – at least not yet anyway – and still circulates as currency domestically and internationally, albeit in a diminishing role, there is much deserved trepidation about what lies ahead, and not just for the dollar.

All national currencies are based on central bank management and not linked to gold or the discipline it provides. National currencies are being continuously debased, making the cost of living to rise globally. The Federal

Reserve and other major central banks even declare openly their inflation policy aimed at lessening the purchasing power of the currency they are supposed to be prudently managing. What is worse, this currency debasement is lauded by a fawning mainstream media.

Share prices, stock market indices, and other assets are being measured with a currency that is being inflated, causing distortions in economic calculation that lead to the misallocation of capital. As a result, entrepreneurs are misled into investing in projects that are uneconomic, and in some cases environmentally destructive, which would be clear to them when evaluated properly with natural money. These errors in turn lead to a misallocation of resources.

Empirical evidence is provided, for example, by the real estate boom related to the euphoria for second homes to be used for holidays in Spain prior to the 2008 financial crisis and the overbuilding of homes at that time in Florida and California. Spurred by central bank policies facilitating easy to obtain loans, borrowers directed resources into buildings that should never have been built. When the 2008 financial crisis hit, empty hulks of buildings were left half-built because tools were laid down and workers were fired. Those buildings that remain unfinished or unoccupied to this day were not and will probably never be economic. Resources were spent on them because of the flawed analysis undertaken before construction started that evaluated an investment's merits using fiat currency and central bank manipulated interest rates.

It was a typical build-and-they-will-buy attitude that has marked the peak of previous booms arising from easy credit. All the labour, time, and capital spent on those derelict hulks was wasted, but there was another cost. It is the destruction to the environment from the resources used during construction, not to mention the half-built eyesores that remain on formerly pristine land.

When currencies are debased, capital is invested in things that never would have been started if the project was properly evaluated with natural money instead of a national currency. These buildings in the boom were started on the back of cheap credit, and the skeletons of half-built buildings are just one obvious example of the environmental destruction that has occurred from the misallocation of capital by abandoning money and substituting national currencies in economic calculation, but the outlook promises to worsen.

Ominous Parallels to the Currency of the German Empire

Reviewing what happened to the currency of the German Empire is instructive to appreciating the risks arising from the direction in which the

U.S. dollar is headed. The collapse of the Reichsmark, the German mark, is the quintessential currency collapse, and the stark parallels to the U.S. dollar are ominous.

German speaking people were historically organised as a loose confederation of independent states. After Prussia's success in the Franco Prussian War in 1871, a unification of these states emerged under Otto von Bismarck as Chancellor of the German Empire, with the king of Prussia being given the title of German Emperor. To cement a centralised power and further diminish that held by the states, a central bank, the Reichsbank, was formed in 1876 to issue banknotes redeemable into gold, for which the 'mark' was the numeraire and designated unit of account.

As a unified force, the German Empire became the dominant power in continental Europe. It was a wealthy country and achieved one of the world's highest standards of living. The goldmark remained the currency until the outbreak of the First World War, when it was replaced by the papierenmark, the 'paper mark', an irredeemable banknote. It was fiat currency that circulated by law and was accepted in commerce on the belief that the government of the German Empire stood behind it. The eerie parallels from that time to today's U.S. dollar and the blind faith people are placing in the financial capability of the U.S. government are unmissable.

After the war and the emperor's abdication, Germany reorganised as the Weimar Republic, named after the town where the new government formed a national assembly. Rudolf von Havenstein remained the head of the German central bank, the Reichsbank, a position he held since 1908. He was given the responsibility for replacing the wartime papierenmark and managing the new currency, irredeemable banknotes called the Reichsmark. These two currencies were essentially the same. Only the name changed, but the Reichsmark was now circulating in a time of peace.

The war was of course costly to Germany, but not in the same way as after the Second World War. The country's infrastructure remained largely intact because the war was fought on foreign soil. It was therefore envisioned that resources previously directed to the war effort would again be employed usefully to return the high standard of living Germans enjoyed before the war. It did not work out that way.

After being trained as a lawyer and receiving a doctorate in law, Dr Havenstein spent his entire career in government. So, like many Federal Reserve officials, he never created wealth with private sector employment, but in contrast to them, Havenstein benefitted from his experience with sound currency redeemable into gold, the pre-war goldmark. Nevertheless, Havenstein strayed from those factors that enabled the goldmark to circulate successfully. In 1923, the Reichsmark became worthless in a spectacular hyperinflationary collapse. The reason for the collapse is instructive and makes clear the ominous parallels to the U.S. dollar.

Dr Havenstein believed that his duty was to serve the State, not the people. His unequivocal allegiance to the State is the duty of all central bankers, except as previously explained, those who worked in the Bundesbank and managed the Dmark until it was superseded by the euro. This overriding duty to the State is the funding of a government's perennial budget deficits that lead to excessive currency creation, which is the toxicant that killed the Reichsmark.

The fledgling Weimar government faced a number of problems, one of which was a lack of money. Another was fulfilling the promises of politicians, which far exceeded the government's financial capacity. So instead of operating within its limited resources and reducing expenditures, the government began borrowing currency. The amounts quickly became so large that its debt instruments were not being purchased by those who had Reichsmarks, or who had other currencies that could be exchanged for Reichsmarks and wanted to lend them to the Weimar government.

Unable to receive from borrowing and tax revenue the funds it wanted to spend, it was left two alternatives. The government could reduce its expenditures, or it could turn to the Reichsbank. It chose the line of least resistance, which is of course the second alternative.

Government officials explained to Dr Havenstein that funds were needed to meet its spending plans. He was told that the government did not have enough funds to spend in supporting the economy, paying pensions that were promised, and funding other commitments. As the head of the Reichsbank, he reached the point where a decision was required, what I call a 'Havenstein moment'.

It is the point in time that an independent central bank says 'yes' or 'no' to the government. The bank either decides to force the government to live within its means by not buying its debt instruments, or alternatively, it accommodates the government by relying on alchemy to purchase government debt paid for with newly created currency.

The Reichsbank was created as an independent central bank, so it was within Dr Havenstein's power to reject his government's request, but he instead put the Reichsmark on a path that ultimately led to hyperinflation and its collapse. It was his duty to serve the State, which as a first priority meant perpetuating its existence. To achieve that goal, the government needed more purchasing power, and its requests for funding were never-ending. The Reichsbank under Dr Havenstein's management kept buying the government's debt with newly printed Reichsmarks, causing a hyperinflationary death spiral for the currency.

Increases in the quantity of currency caused prices and interest rates to rise, which resulted in higher government expenses. Higher spending meant bigger government deficits, increasing its reliance on the Reichsbank for the currency it needed to spend. That meant more currency creation, and so it went on and on until the Reichsmark's spectacular collapse in November 1923, the same month Dr Havenstein reportedly died of a heart attack.

The German economy lay in ruins. The middle class that accumulated Reichsmarks for savings and relied on government promises was devastated, many of them becoming destitute. Law and order began to disintegrate as countless people struggled to survive.

The Federal Reserve and other central banks are today unfortunately following the same path taken by Mr Havenstein. It is alchemy on steroids given the enormous amounts of government debt instruments being alchemised into their national currency. It leads to the question whether national currencies, and particularly the U.S. dollar, are about to hyperinflate, and if not, what is going to prevent that outcome?

Potential Hyperinflation of the U.S. Dollar

Monetary history clearly shows that the over issuance of currency has never solved economic problems. Never. But that is what central banks are trying to do. They are trying to disprove history while ignoring the wisdom of Ludwig von Mises:

> There is no means of avoiding the final collapse of a boom brought about by credit expansion [currency creation]. The alternative is only whether the crisis should come sooner as the result of voluntary abandonment of further credit expansion, or later as a final and total catastrophe of the currency system involved.

The Federal Reserve is doing what the Reichsbank did under Dr Havenstein. The similarity though is masked because the dollar's currency system is different from that which prevailed in Germany. Hyperinflation manifests itself in two different ways, which depend upon the nature of a country's currency system.

In Germany in the 1920s and in Zimbabwe two decades ago, the central bank printed paper currency, which it then used to purchase newly issued government debt instruments. These banknotes were then spent by the government. In these two countries few people had bank accounts, so the preponderance of commerce was therefore conducted in cash transactions using banknotes printed by the central bank. A Google search for images of the Reichsmark hyperinflation reveals pictures of stacks upon stacks of banknotes needed to conduct even small value transactions.

The hyperinflation that more recently wrought havoc in many

countries in Latin America manifested differently. Cash currency was relatively unimportant in Latin America. Each banking system in Brazil, Argentina and to some extent in Venezuela is well developed, so most people had bank accounts. Therefore, deposit currency was being used for the preponderance of commerce in these countries. Instead of moving banknotes by hand to complete transactions, deposit currency was moved by cheques, plastic cards, and wire transfers.

Unlike Germany, where the Reichsbank used its newly printed banknotes to purchase its government's debt instruments, Latin American central banks bought their government's debt instruments with deposit currency. Simple bookkeeping entries added assets to their balance sheet and correlative liabilities from the deposit currency added to the government's current account. Central bank balance sheets expanded with these bookkeeping entries to create more deposit currency, which describes what is happening to the dollar.

Over the past two years the Federal Reserve's balance sheet has roughly doubled, but this alchemy of transmuting debt into currency is not only happening at the Federal Reserve. Figure 16 shows that federal government debt instruments owned by banks have trebled since 2008 and increased over fivefold since 1995.

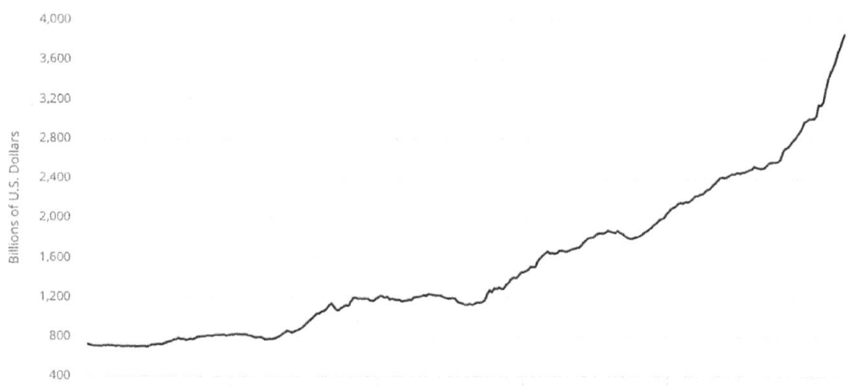

Figure 16 – Treasury and Agency Securities, All Commercial Banks

Source: Federal Reserve Bank of St. Louis

This rapid increase in currency far exceeds any increase in economic activity during this time period. It explains why the velocity of the dollar illustrated in Figure 14 is rapidly declining. There is too much dollar currency.

Hyperinflation does not arise from banks making too many loans to private sector companies. It invariably occurs for one reason – too much government spending. Ever increasing amounts of purchasing power are needed to meet this spending, which inevitably comes from currency creation by the government's captive central bank.

The dollar and other national currencies have long passed their 'Havenstein moment'. Despite Federal Reserve governors' longstanding promises, it can never normalise. The financial system is bankrupt. Its near zero-interest rate and permanent intervention policies are not implemented to normalise, but to keep the dollar currency system from collapsing. As a greater number of people start catching on, more financial repression and propaganda can be expected to maintain demand for the dollar, but the inevitable hyperinflation will eventually occur, which I expect is not too far in the future.

The perceived need to 'pump up the economy' after the Covid-19 pandemic is being widely misinterpreted as a fight against deflation, which is exactly what people thought was happening shortly before the Reichsmark was swooped up in its hyperinflationary whirlwind. Recent commodity price increases suggest that inflation is accelerating. But it is not only supply and price of these products that portend more inflation.

The biggest change in a currency's purchasing power can come from a drop in demand for the currency, which can be volatile. A poorly managed national currency can see the demand for it drop precipitously, resulting in a flight from the currency. Because national currencies are being debased, demand for them can be fleeting as purchasing power moves from the inferior currency to a better one or out of currency altogether into alternatives like real estate or the stock market. Equities provide an indirect ownership to real assets, which explains why stock markets soar in price during hyperinflation.

When confronted by his own 'Havenstein moment', Dr Havenstein directed the Reichsbank to take the easy alternative. Instead of forcing the government to tighten its belt by restricting spending, he chose alchemy and currency creation. Unfortunately, around the globe governments and central bank policymakers today are taking the same path.

There is no hyperinflation of prices yet, which authorities use as a rationale to explain why banks can continue to alchemise more currency out of debt, but there is no misreading the fact that the dollar and other national currencies are on a hyperinflationary course. Worryingly, there are signs that hyperinflation is getting much closer, and the U.S. dollar may even be on the cusp of hyperinflation, given the signs already evident.[74]

1) US dollar's declining foreign exchange rate

The U.S. Dollar Index, which measures its rate of exchange compared to a basket of six other national currencies, peaked in January 2017. It is not that these other currencies are better, but rather, none of them are the world's reserve currency. The dollar is widely held just for that reason. Thus, these other currencies are not subject to a major risk held by the dollar, namely, a dramatic drop in demand from the decline or complete loss of its position as the world's reserve currency.

2) Gold's rising exchange rate

Since December 2015, gold's exchange rate has been rising against all the world's currencies, and last year reached a record high. Although it may be that gold is being purchased because of its traditional role as a safe haven without counterparty risk, it is not unreasonable to conclude that gold is also rising because its purchasing power reflects a decline in the purchasing power of national currencies.

3) Rising commodity prices

Commodity prices appear to have reached a major low in 2020. The S&P GSCI Commodity Index has nearly doubled over the past year. While demand for commodities have no doubt increased because of post-pandemic economic recovery, the unusually rapid increase in the index with its 12-month near doubling in price suggests that currency debasement is also a factor.

4) Rising stock market

The stock market is not climbing because of good economic conditions. The economy will not improve until the number of people employed actually increases above the pre-pandemic level, and that is not yet happening. While the unemployment rate is falling, there are 6 million fewer people working now than before the pandemic, which does not include another estimated 4 million people who dropped out of the work force and are not counted in the unemployment numbers. Stock markets are rising because one's purchasing power invested in well-chosen equities is safer than being placed in dollar denominated assets like bonds and bank deposits.

5) Negative interest rates

Nominal and real interest rates when adjusted for the true rate of inflation are negative. For this reason, a bank deposit loses purchasing power over time because the interest rate is not high enough to compensate for rising prices, even when excluding the tax consequences from the interest income. In hyperinflation, interest rates never rise rapidly enough to offset the loss of a currency's purchasing power. What is more, the Federal Reserve and most other central banks are pursuing a zero-interest rate policy, suggesting that negative real interest rates will remain for the foreseeable future, further weakening the demand for currencies and increasing the likelihood of a flight from currency that manifests as hyperinflation.

6) Contrary opinion

Few today are prepared for or even expect hyperinflation. More to the point, the prevailing psychology today is based on blind faith expectations that governments and central bankers will get things right. A similar outlook prevailed in the Soviet Union before the collapse of the rouble, such was the heavy reliance on the belief in government pronouncements in that country at the time.

7) Rising yields on U.S. Treasury bonds

T-bond yields always provide an important leading indicator. During the inflationary 1980s, the term 'bond vigilantes' was coined. These investors and traders would sell their bonds on the slightest whiff of inflation, forcing up interest rates, which in turn would stop the inflationary pressures that were building. The bond vigilantes are back, but less visible because central banks' purchases have largely dulled the impact of bond vigilante sales. Nevertheless, bond yields are rising.

8) Global adherence to harmful economic dogma

Governments around the world have embarked on a course of runaway spending based on two misguided beliefs, namely, that it spurs economic activity and that there is no limit to what they can borrow. These suppositions are the foundational plank of a supposedly new economic insight called Modern Money Theory. Dr Havenstein's experiment at the Reichsbank proves that this economic dogma is not new. It leads to hyperinflation, which is worrying given its enthusiastic embrace by statist political leaders and the shallow academic analysis of their sycophants.

Runaway government spending causes runaway inflation, which raises prices and interest rates that worsen the government's annual deficit. That in turn causes more borrowing and puts the currency on a hyperinflationary death spiral, just like occurred with the Reichsmark, with its far-reaching consequences on German society that were the prelude to the Second World War.[75]

Governments have absorbed the world's savings, yet they want to borrow more. So with newly created currency, unaccountable central banks recklessly conjure up phantom purchasing power out of thin air. What Murray N. Rothbard observed for the United States applies throughout the world: 'The Federal Reserve, virtually in total control of the nation's vital monetary system, is accountable to nobody, and this strange situation, if acknowledged at all, is invariably trumpeted as a virtue.'

Protecting Your Wealth from Hyperinflation

Good management of one's personal portfolio comes from focusing on risk and value as well as employing purposeful action to accumulate undervalued assets and sell those that are overvalued. This clear strategy does not only apply to equities and other investments. It is also the right strategy for money, namely, your purchasing power and the liquidity in your portfolio.

Money is the bedrock asset of anyone's portfolio. Gold plays an essential monetary role. Owning gold enables you to postpone your spending and investment decisions, while preserving your purchasing power for some future date.

Given its importance, do not take risks with your gold. Thoughtful diversification can mitigate the risks. Gold should be stored in vaults in different countries so that this bedrock asset is held in different geographic locations and political environments using different vaulting companies.

Because value is subjective, some assets may have no price in the eye of those people who decide that their purchasing power can be held more usefully in other ways for use in the future. This observation explains why some people lacking knowledge or who are otherwise ill-informed consider gold to be a 'pet rock.'[76] Yet different levels of knowledge and understanding is a market reality that creates opportunity for those who understand gold's attributes and usefulness and recognise when it is undervalued.

One has to be patient when it comes to value. Patience is needed as a result of our inability to predict the future with certainty. So the only approach that makes sense when it comes to portfolio management is to focus on value. Accumulate undervalued assets and sell overvalued ones and assess their value regularly. Ongoing events will change the market's overall perceptions of the relative value of assets.

Even gold can become overvalued or undervalued when viewed in terms of national currencies, other money-substitutes like silver, and in fact, against any asset. The Fear Index illustrates that gold at present is undervalued.[77] History shows that a fair value for gold will be achieved eventually as will periods of overvaluation. Whether that fair value for gold is achieved with a higher or lower price from current levels depends on whether central banks expand or contract the quantity of national currencies.

Things do indeed change because of central banks.

It is not a reasonable proposition that gold's 5,000-year history as money ends here. Even a cursory reading of monetary history shows that gold always becomes the money of choice eventually. It happens when common sense returns to political leaders and the polity electing them. Until that happens, the risk of ever greater currency debasement from inflation and potentially even hyperinflation is growing.

In hyperinflation, the basic principle is to own things instead of promises. As the risk of inflation increases, own tangible assets, not financial assets, as illustrated by the categories of wealth in Figure 2. It does not make financial sense to hold currency in a bank account or in any kind of currency denominated asset like bonds when you cannot earn enough interest income to offset the loss of purchasing power. So look for tangible alternatives.

One of the first alternatives to consider is your liquidity. Everyone needs purchasing power and it needs to be unconditional so that it is available when you need to spend or invest it. Gold of course provides this liquidity. Silver is a gold-substitute that also provides liquidity and may enhance your purchasing power if the gold/silver ratio returns to lower levels.

Presently about 68 ounces of silver equal one ounce of gold. Historically the ratio has been 16 ounces, which some geologists say approximates the amount of silver in the earth's crust relative to gold. If the ratio declines, silver outperforms gold and your purchasing power increases, but the opposite occurs if their ratio rises.

Land and buildings are obvious examples of tangible wealth, but they typically are not liquid assets. When correctly chosen, equities can provide an escape from hyperinflation with some safety. For example, if an investor in Germany owned Mercedes Benz shares during the Reichsmark hyperinflation, the investor still owned those shares after the currency collapsed because this car manufacturing company managed to survive by navigating the hyperinflation. This outcome contrasts with anyone that lost wealth by owning Reichsmarks or assets denominated in Reichsmarks, like banknotes, bank deposits, insurance policies, annuities, and bonds.

The key to understanding hyperinflation involves both the supply and demand for currency. Rapid increases in the quantity of currency matter of course, but so does any change in the demand for the currency. If people start using their dollars to spend and invest them in non-dollar denominated assets, it is another way of saying that the demand for dollars is decreasing. A rapid decrease in demand is possible at any time, which would mean that hyperinflation could occur very quickly particularly given today's means of near instantaneous communication, including social media. It would be a flight from currency into real things.

The United States and most industrialised countries were almost at a complete financial standstill in 2008. A worst outcome was avoided because government and central banks did everything they could to keep the system from total collapse. As a result, no banks, other than Northern Rock in the United Kingdom and Lehman Brothers in the United States, failed. When facing their 'Havenstein moment', government authorities and managers of national currency led by the United States took the line of least resistance, which has triggered an accelerated growth in the quantity of U.S. dollars and other national currencies. Their decision prevented the derivative markets from blowing up and all the trillions of dollars of those promises from disappearing in a massive liquidation. Instead, they have kicked the can down the road, as the saying goes, by unleashing an inflationary, and I think, eventually, a hyperinflationary course.

When is it going to happen? No one can predict that. But looking at the worrying things that are happening at present, one can intuitively sense that currencies are heading in the wrong direction toward a cliff edge. Going over that cliff would be a currency collapse, just like dozens of those in recent decades caused by central banks that have taken a step too far from prudent management and instead chose to keep shovelling phantom purchasing power to their government.

It is clear from monetary history that printing currency has never solved economic problems, but that is what government and central banks are trying to do. They are trying to disprove history, and the mainstream media agrees with them. The mainstream media in Weimar Germany also agreed with Dr Havenstein, who thought he was doing the right thing because he was following what had become conventional economic thought. Like today, economists back then encouraged Havenstein to continue putting more currency into circulation to keep the economy from collapsing and to keep unemployment from rising. It may have worked for a short while, but eventually, it had the exact reverse effect from what the new academic theories about State control of currency had predicted. Governments and central banks are trying these same theories again, and we can see that they are leading to trouble.

The present system is unsustainable. Something must give because there are limits to everything in our world, including the mountain of global debt that has been built, and the alchemising of an increasing amount of this debt into national currencies by the Federal Reserve and other central banks. There will be growing amounts of wealth destruction from a loss of purchasing power of the dollar and other national currencies because of artificially low interest rates and inflation. The Covid-19 shock highlights the fragility in today's financial and currency system, for which the consequences are still unfolding.

Will governments change direction before reaching the cliff edge?

Will the cliff edge be reached soon, or could it still be years away? What can be done to prevent a hyperinflationary outcome?

The balance of this book provides answers. It is not a prediction, but an explanation of what has worked in the past. The focus is on the United States. Not only did it mend its currency system after the hyperinflation of its first national currency, but the direction taken after that event set the country on a course that would preclude any future monetary problems. Unfortunately, it veered off course.

9. Money and Currency in America

The choice before us is simple. Shall we have gold and political freedom, or shall we have paper [currency] and political tyranny.

Ron Paul, former U.S. Congressman

The monetary history of the United States is a study of the centralisation of power and privilege. Some historical background is needed to put money and currency in America within a proper context.

The American War for Independence was truly revolutionary when considering its profound consequences for money and liberty, the twin pillars of a free society founded on natural law. Political leaders in the American colonies wholeheartedly embraced the intellectual propositions on natural rights being espoused by John Locke and other luminaries of the Age of Enlightenment, and those fundamental principles of freedom were popularised throughout the colonies by firebrands like Thomas Paine and Patrick Henry.

Representative government in Virginia began in 1619, just a few years after the first settlers arrived and established a permanent base. The British government applied a policy of salutary neglect to its American colonies but began asserting greater control after the conclusion of the Seven Years' War in 1763. The American colonists found those measures to be harmful to their liberty and prosperity and waged war against the greatest military superpower of their day to protect their natural rights.

America and the Law

Within society, there are objective standards, the most noteworthy of which are the inalienable rights of life, liberty, and the pursuit of happiness, against which all human action must be evaluated. Human action need not be codified in man-made law for it conform to the basic principles that govern society.

To Americans fighting for their independence in 1776, law came from nature, and secondarily and only to the extent that it was accepted by them, from laws imposed by Britain, of which those related to taxation were eventually deemed onerous and unfair when they became excessive. The rallying cry of the day, 'No taxation without representation', is more than a political slogan encapsulating the grievances of the American colonists against Britain. These freedom fighters first and foremost chose to 'mutually pledge to each other our Lives, our Fortunes and our sacred Honor' for the unrestricted right to live their life in accordance with natural law and without interference from the State. They also understood that taxation of one's labour is theft, and as such, a violation of natural law. As Thomas Jefferson expressed it in his first Inaugural Address it is 'a wise and& frugal government, which shall restrain men from injuring one another, shall leave them otherwise free to regulate their own pursuits of industry and improvement, and shall not take from the mouth of labor the bread it has earned.' Consequently, any part of one's labour could only be taken by government with that person's consent.

By reassessing the role of the State, disparate colonists came together to rally around a common cause. The core element was, even to those who remained loyal to the monarchy, the profound questioning about the legitimacy of the authority of the State over the individual. In their view, natural law establishes an ethical framework for human interaction in society because each individual possesses, as an inherent feature of being human, certain values that govern reason and behaviour. The rules defining what is right and wrong are not created by monarchs or promulgated by legislatures. There are natural governors that civilised people intuitively understand and accept, the most basic of which in all human action is to do no harm. The British government's interventions were harming the colonists and impeding their freedom and pursuit of happiness.

America's War for Independence began after years of growing tension that led to increasing hostility, and eventually war. It was justified for cause, as penned in 1776 in the Declaration of Independence: 'The history of the present King of Great Britain is a history of repeated injuries and usurpations, all having in direct object the establishment of an absolute

Tyranny' of the 'thirteen united (sic) States of America.'

I noted 'united' purposefully to point out that it was not capitalised.[78] It is meaningful to acknowledge that Thomas Jefferson wrote it that way. It reflects how the colonists viewed themselves after declaring their independence. It was not an emergent single nation, but a confederation of states that are equally sovereign, which is re-confirmed in the concluding paragraph.

> We, therefore, the Representatives of the united(sic) States of America, in General Congress, Assembled, appealing to the Supreme Judge of the world for the rectitude of our intentions, do, in the Name, and by Authority of the good People of these Colonies, solemnly publish and declare, That these United Colonies are, and of Right ought to be Free and Independent States; that they are Absolved from all Allegiance to the British Crown, and that all political connection between them and the State of Great Britain, is and ought to be totally dissolved; and that as Free and Independent States, they have full Power to levy War, conclude Peace, contract Alliances, establish Commerce, and to do all other Acts and Things which Independent States may of right do. And for the support of this Declaration, with a firm reliance on the protection of divine Providence, we mutually pledge to each other our Lives, our Fortunes and our sacred Honor.

The colonies became thirteen 'united States of America'. By declaring their status as states, they were no different from their former master. Each of the former thirteen colonies became 'as Free and Independent' as the 'State of Great Britain'.

In one key respect, each colony was already acting an independent sovereign state, having established their own constitution and assembly. For example, once the settlers in Jamestown had established a viable community, the Virginia General Assembly was formally established in 1619, which set the precedent for the other colonies that would follow. The difference after the revolution was that these state bodies became responsible solely to the people in the state and not a British governor.

As tensions with Britain increased, the colonies in 1774 formalised a federal political structure with a national assembly called the Continental Congress to address matters that were a common concern of all the states. In 1776 it pronounced the Declaration of Independence, which was agreed to by all thirteen states, and a year later established the Articles of Confederation. Its governing provisions did not extend to the Congress any meaningful power, so its requests to the States were often ignored. The sovereign power to govern was retained by each individual state.

Early American Currency

The British pound was the numeraire prior to the revolution, but the colonies did not have a common currency, which consisted of various foreign coins. The most plentiful coins were Spanish pieces of eight, called dollars, composed of silver, and it became the currency of choice. To emphasise the break from Britain once independence was declared, the silver dollar became the numeraire during the revolution and remained in that role after independence was gained.

In addition to this silver coin, there was also paper currency issued by the government of each colony. Each colonial government printed its own paper currency, called bills of credit, that were spent into circulation. For example, a state would typically purchase goods on credit, with the seller receiving a paper promissory note from the state, namely, the bill of credit. Once issued, these bills would circulate in commerce like a banknote.

With banks only recently having been established in London, there were no banks in the colonies. Americans extended credit to each other or relied on credit from merchants and banks in Great Britain.

The Continental Congress also issued its own paper currency as bills of credit. Though denominated in dollars, they were not redeemable into silver coin. In day-to-day use they were called 'continental dollars' to distinguish them from silver dollars.

Though the term was not used in colonial America, the continental was in essence a fiat currency, just like the dollar today. The continental bills of credit circulated in commerce because they were backed by the full faith and credit of the Continental Congress. They were initially accepted in commerce in anticipation of future tax receipts to be collected by the government. There was the belief when these bills of credit were first issued that the Continental Congress would eventually redeem them for silver or gold. That belief was misplaced for anyone who accepted the promise of future redeemability.

Over time, reliance on that belief declined as too many continentals were being issued, so their discount to the silver dollar began to widen. In other words, soon after they were first issued, it was taking an ever-greater amount of continentals to exchange for coin. Because colonial Americans understood that gold and silver were money, they did not say the silver 'price' was rising. Rather, their transactions were expressed to reflect the fact that the purchasing power of the continental was falling in relation to the numeraire, which is the proper way to express as well as measure currency debasement.

Despite the growing discount, continentals continued to be issued because the Continental Congress claimed the need to meet its expenses, even though the states and many individuals were contributing to the war effort. The continental eventually hyperinflated in a total collapse. Because it had become worthless, the continental had stopped circulating as currency six months before fighting ended with the surrender of Lord Cornwallis in Yorktown in October 1781. It was disparaged by the saying of the day, 'Not worth a continental'. No amount of continental dollars was worth one silver dollar.

The collapse of the continental created a period of monetary and economic uncertainty, which continued after the War for Independence was won. Because of this disorder and the worry that the British Empire with its bases in Canada and the Caribbean posed a military threat to the newly independent thirteen sovereign states, the leading political figures of the day met in Philadelphia in May 1787 to discuss the prevailing circumstances and to plan for the future.

With the collapse of the continental fresh in everyone's memory, money was one of the key topics of discussion. This lament by John Adams during the Constitutional Convention is similar to the quote attributed to Henry Ford at the beginning of Chapter 1: 'All the perplexities, confusion and distress in America arises not from deficits in the Constitution [being drafted] or [its predecessor, the Articles of] Confederation, nor from want of honour and virtue, so much as downright ignorance of the nature of coin, credit, and circulation.'

The outcome of the meeting in Philadelphia four months after it began was the written Constitution, which expanded the confederation into a common market with a common currency and unified defence. Its Preamble explains the reasons behind its creation and the expectation for the future:

> We the People of the United States, in Order to form a more perfect Union, establish Justice, insure domestic Tranquility, provide for the common defence, promote the general Welfare, and secure the Blessings of Liberty to ourselves and our Posterity, do ordain and establish this Constitution for the United States of America.

The framers understood money, credit, currency, and their differences. They knew that money is gold, that paper currency even when redeemable into gold introduces counterparty risk, and that deposits in banks are the most dangerous currency of all. They wrote into the Constitution basic monetary principles that served the people and the states reasonably well until the regime taking power in 1933 began totalitarian steps that uprooted core principles enshrined in the Constitution that changed money and liberty in America.[79] Those changes are explored in Chapter 10.

A Common Market and a Common Currency

When the framers of the Constitution spoke of the loss of power from the American states to a federal authority, they called it 'consolidation', and they were adamantly opposed to it. Yet they saw the need to form 'to form a more perfect Union', as stated in the Preamble.

To do that they aimed to achieve what Europe established after the Second World War, namely, the creation of a common market without barriers to trade at each state's border which was a logical step to take given that the states already shared a common currency, the silver dollar. But the framers went one step further. They sought a shared defence should any state be invaded, much like Europe's common market was protected by NATO. Even though peace in North America was established with the Treaty of Paris, there were concerns by many in the thirteen states about their future security given that Britain remained the supreme military power of the day, which continued to be perceived as a threat. Switzerland provides an elucidatory example of what the framers aimed to achieve:

> The Swiss Confederation –then 500 years old– helped inspire the birth of the American Republic, particularly regarding the interrelated concepts of resistance to oppression, independence from foreign states, neutrality, a people's militia, and federalism.[80]

Each Swiss canton had its own constitution, parliament, police, and courts and was independent within the Confederation of Helvetica (Switzerland) common market and unified defence. Having survived many European wars and two world wars, the country is famed for the defence of its territory and its global neutrality. To consider how far America has moved away from that peaceful political structure the framers intended, ask yourself how many people around the world can name the president of Switzerland?[81]

The importance of establishing a common market is clear from George Washington's Farewell Address to the Nation in 1796. Upon leaving office after serving as the country's first president, he spoke of the 'powerful and obvious motives to union [a common market] affecting all parts of our country.'[82] Benjamin Franklin also advocated a common market, and more to the point, a common currency. His printing business produced currency for the colonies and the Continental Congress. From this experience he understood the advantages of a common currency and implored the delegates at the convention preparing the new constitution to 'make such general Ordinances...to those that may relate to our general Commerce; or general Currency.'[83]

To achieve a common market, the framers understood the need to create other basic elements upon which a common market would flourish. The states already shared a common language and legal framework. Missing was a means for commerce conducted with a common currency to extend cross state borders without impediments. The Articles of Confederation were lacking in this regard, but are addressed in Article I, Section 8 of the Constitution, which lists the seventeen powers granted by the states to the federal government.

One of these powers is the Commerce Clause, which prohibits internal barriers to commerce at any state border. Another Article I, Section 8 power could be called the Numeraire Clause, which gives Congress the power 'to coin Money, regulate the Value thereof, and of foreign Coin, and fix the Standard of Weights and Measures.'

Since Biblical times exact, honest weights and measures have been an important principle for achieving a harmonious society. The framers were well versed on passages in the Old Testament that exact weights and measurements are essential to honest, ethical, and legal commerce. As John Adams made clear: 'Our Constitution was made only for a religious and moral people. It is wholly inadequate for the government of any other.' Given the aim to establish a common market and a common currency, it is understandable that the power in the Numeraire Clause was delegated from the states to the federal government for inclusion in the Constitution.

Though the purpose and intent of this Numeraire Clause was clear to the framers, it is today generally misunderstood and usually misinterpreted, often purposely, by those who see it as a barrier to their control of the currency. The clause adheres to Newton's monetary principles that money is a measurement tool. Gold is money based on weight and earned purchasing power, not promises.

Note that the states give Congress the power to 'coin money', not to print paper currency. There obviously is a fundamental difference between these two distinct processes. Like the British parliamentarians in 1694 who argued against giving the power to create currency to the Bank of England, the framers understood the link between money and liberty. The collapse of the continental currency and the havoc it wrought was fresh in their minds. They recognised that a sound currency was one of the reasons to form a 'more perfect Union'. To provide the legal basis for a sound monetary system as well as to avoid a repeat of their experience with the continental, the framer's written words in the Constitution were purposeful and meant to ensure that the power to print currency would never again be given to the government or placed in the hands of politicians.

The Numeraire Clause also gave Congress the power 'regulate the Value thereof, and of foreign Coin,' which is another key phrase that is frequently misunderstood. America was bimetallic; both gold and silver coins circulated. So to 'regulate the Value thereof', namely the gold and silver coins conveying purchasing power that the federal government had the power to mint, the Constitution gave it the power to define and then regulate the gold/silver ratio at which the gold and silver coins were to be exchanged in relation to each other.

This provision to 'regulate' is necessary from a practical point of view. If, for example, the ratio valued silver too low in terms of gold when compared to the market rate, silver could be exported to take advantage of those countries where its higher, true value could be realised, leaving Americans with insufficient amounts of silver to mint coins and conduct commerce.

Proof that this interpretation of 'regulate' is the framers' original intent comes from a similar provision appearing in Britain not too many years later. The long title of its Coinage Act of 1816 reads as follows: 'An Act to provide for a New Silver Coinage, and to regulate the Currency of the Gold and Silver Coin of this Realm.' [my emphasis]

There is another monetary provision in the Constitution. Article 1, Section 10 lists those things that a state cannot do. Included is the provision that 'no State shall...emit Bills of Credit; make any Thing but gold and silver Coin a Tender in Payment of Debts.' This clause makes clear that the states cannot interfere with the power they have delegated to the federal government to coin precious metals. It also makes clear that the states cannot print paper currency, namely, to 'emit Bills of Credit' or accept them in payment. Speaking to the limited monetary power within the Constitution granted by the states to the federal government, Thomas Jefferson could not be clearer on this point: 'I deny the power of the general government to making paper money, or anything else a legal tender.'

These monetary provisions of the Constitution are not complicated. The states have power granted to them by the People under each state constitution. The states then delegated to the federal government the power to coin money and agreed not to print paper currency. Yet America now has a paper currency system, with most Americans not recognising that the dollar bill in their pocket is a 'dollar bill of credit'. It is evidence that there are many Americans, including politicians taking an oath to support and defend the Constitution, who need to read and learn the Constitution.

Power has become 'consolidated' in the federal government, to use the framers' term. It happened over time and how it happened is beyond this book's scope, but one simple test will illustrate how pervasive the thinking has become to make the notion of consolidation appear normal. Look at any modern schoolbook that publishes the Constitution of (sic) the United States. Then look at the original signed document, which actually says that it is the 'Constitution for (sic) the United States of America'. The word 'of' in the title makes the USA appear as one entity, disguising the fifty united states, with each American state a sovereign power.

That one small word significantly alters the framer's intent that the country is comprised of sovereign states of equal status. Their intent is made clear if you think of the federal government as a service provider to the original thirteen, and now fifty states, and it has been given seventeen powers to complete these assigned service provider tasks. The states are only united to the extent of the seventeen powers they delegated to the federal government to carry out on their behalf. Other than these seventeen powers, all consolidation of power assumed by the federal government is antithetical to the original intent of the framers of the Constitution.

It must be noted that the Federal Reserve strengthens this consolidation. With the power to print currency and the other powers it subsequently usurped, like controlling interest rates and bailing out banks, the Federal Reserve now controls the American economy and every individual's purchasing power held in dollars.

The framers established the framework for an economically sound and politically honest money. Subsequently, politicians dismantled what was created so that the federal government defies not only the spirit of the monetary provisions in the Constitution, but also the letter of the law. For example, the federal government cannot issue bills of credit, and the states cannot allow the use of bills of credit in payment. Yet there are dollar bills of credit in everyone's pocket circulating as currency.

The money of the united sovereign states of America is gold and silver coin. To get around the constraints of the Constitution, politicians began a process starting with the creation of the Federal Reserve in 1913. Despite the repeated pronouncements to the contrary, the present Federal Reserve dollar is not constitutional money.

With this recognition, it follows that the Federal Reserve system is unconstitutional. The letter of the law and the original intent of the framers are clear. The federal government has no authority to extend to an entity a power not given to it by the states. The federal government does not have the legal authority to authorise the exclusive powers it has given to the Federal Reserve.

It is telling that the constitutionality of the Federal Reserve's creation has never been tested in the Supreme Court. It has sidestepped the matter by refusing to hear or rule on cases brought before it by contriving arguments that defy logic. By doing so, the Supreme Court has avoided a confrontation with those seeking an all-powerful central, consolidated government in defiance of the Constitution.

The dollar used in commerce today is not the dollar intended by the framers. A captive central bank now provides the U.S. government with all the currency it needs to meet its spending aspirations, no matter how broad they are or how flagrantly they enable the federal government to violate the limits imposed on it by the Constitution. How it happened is brilliantly explained in *Pieces of Eight: The Monetary Powers and Disabilities of the United States Constitution* by Edwin Vieira, a 2-volume 1600-page masterpiece of outstanding scholarship.

Transforming the Dollar from Silver Coin to Fiat Currency

Once the Constitution was formally adopted, the federal government set out to fulfil its responsibilities. One of its first pieces of legislation was the Mint Act passed by Congress and signed into law by George Washington in 1792 for 'regulating the Coins' to be produced by the mint being authorised by this act. It defined the dollar as 371.25 grains of pure silver, and $10 could be exchanged for one gold eagle containing 247.5 grains of pure gold, thereby defining the gold/silver ratio at 16.67.

The U.S. Mint began operating in October 1792, and there were privately owned mints coining money at that time as well. The success of the mints depended on the quality of the service they provided, and Gresham's Law prevailed. The coins of some private mints were of higher quality and in some cases contained a slightly higher weight of metal than the dollar's definition. So these coins were saved, and the U.S. Mint's coins were used in commerce. There is nothing in the Constitution that prevents coining by private enterprise.

Congress had the responsibility to adjust the gold/silver ratio as required by market realities so that there was always sufficient metal available for coinage. The first adjustment occurred in 1837 by raising the content of the eagle to 258 grains of gold, which lowered the ratio to 16. The next change was made in 1900 with the Gold Standard Act, but it did not adjust the ratio. It changed the numeraire from silver to gold. The double eagle of 23.222 grains of pure gold became the numeraire, putting the dollar on a gold standard at $20.67 per ounce.

Soon thereafter began the degeneration of the dollar. Recall that it was a time that the British pound had already begun degenerating as Newton's Rule was already being insidiously eroded. American bankers were learning from their British counterparts how they could expand their profits and mitigate their losses from fractional reserves by gaining greater control of the currency and banking system.

In particular, the bailout of Barings Bank in 1890 was informative to them. Even though Barings had extended imprudent loans to speculate on investments in South America, the bank's managers and shareholders were saved by the bailout led by the Bank of England. American bankers saw that they too could be protected from loss and their mismanagement by relying on bailouts organised by a central bank. They did not have to wait long for their opportunity.

The Panic of 1907 began with the failure of the Knickerbocker Trust Company, the third largest in New York City. Fractional reserve banking had enabled it to overextend its financial capacity by making highly risky loans related to an attempt to speculatively corner the shares of United Copper Company. The corner failed, and the share price collapsed, which set off a run on the bank to withdraw deposits. The purchasing power being held as deposit currency at the top of the Exter pyramid in Figure 8 began to move down the pyramid to safer levels.

The interconnectivity of deposit currency within the banking system sent ripple effects felt by other banks. Customers of those banks also moved their purchasing power from deposit currency to banknotes, and just like in the Barings collapse, some chose to redeem their banknotes for gold coin to ensure that their purchasing power was held in a currency that provided the highest degree of safety. But the Barings financial panic was managed by the Bank of England, and America did not have a central bank to bailout Knickerbocker, its managers, and shareholders.

More than a century had passed since crafting the monetary provisions of the Constitution. It had been seven decades since President Andrew Jackson had defeated the attempts by bankers to erect a central bank. Even though those events were no longer in living memory, the most respected political leaders understood the link between money and liberty, and, because of numerous bank failures, Americans recognised the inherent fragility and risks of fractional reserve banking. Caution therefore prevailed, and many individual Americans took extra care in protecting their purchasing power and their liberty. However, political winds were changing in both Britain and America.

By the beginning of the twentieth century, the radical tracts of Karl Marx were having an impact on politics and economics. The classical liberalism of John Locke, Adam Smith, other writers of the Age of Enlightenment as well as Ludwig von Mises and many others that honoured a moral society based on individual freedom with an unfeigned protection of property rights was being turned on its head by regressive socialist theory.

> Where Marx envisioned classes of people locked in a struggle, Mises described comparative advantage. What Marx viewed as exploitation, Mises saw a flourishing network of mutually beneficial exchanges and ever more productive capital accumulation. Where Marx saw conflict, Mises saw cooperation.[84]

Because Marx's ideas involved the suppression of individual rights and subordinate an individual's pursuit of happiness to attain a collectivist ideal, they could not be sold to the polity on their merit. Nevertheless, they were a godsend to demagogues seeking power for themselves through supremacy for the State. It is therefore not surprising that experience has demonstrated that welfare programmes inevitably lead to authoritarian political regimes to 'make socialism work'. By claiming to 'help people', socialist progressives and autocrats purported to claim the moral high ground. By appealing to the ignoble instincts of human nature, the immorality of theft of private property through taxes and corruption became acceptable, with the proceeds being used to gain popularity or win elections. To the extent that programmes had a humanitarian purpose, it was incidental.

An example is the socialist programme begun in Germany in 1883 by Bismarck. It was the world's first step toward a socialist State that in the 1920s morphed into national socialism. Bismarck's aim of seeking control is clear when he claimed that 'Whoever has pensions for his old age is far more easier to handle...because he has a pension to look forward to.'[85] (my emphasis)

The difference between a bribe and humanitarian care became even less clear when Britain's welfare state began in 1906. The Liberal Party used the promise of welfare payments from state funds to achieve electoral popularity. Not surprisingly, they won a landslide victory and gained control of Parliament. Until the outbreak of the First World War, they passed numerous legislative acts that took funds from taxpayers to make payments to tax-eaters.

Just like American bankers were learning from their British counterparts, it was not long before American progressives were doing the same in politics. Their impact on the change in the mindset of society can be seen in movies about the Wild West. The role of the nineteenth-century sheriff was to keep the peace in accordance with natural law. He maintained order and arrested the 'bad guys' while armed with his 1873 Colt 45 pistol called the 'Peacemaker'. Keeping the peace became secondary to the role of twentieth-century police. The progressives in government began to focus instead on the enforcement of man-made law. The concise statement of 'Law Enforcement', now often seen emblazoned on the side of police patrol cars, led to oppression and subjugation. An individual's pursuit of happiness became subject to man-made law, with individuals going to jail for victimless crimes.

The progressives were not only adversely impacting societal relationships. Those being elected to the federal government took aim at America's legal structure, including the Constitution. They began chipping away at fundamental provisions like the prohibition on direct taxes and state appointment of senators. The checks and balances so carefully crafted and stated in the document to protect individual rights and to prevent a ruling elite were being gradually eroded. Political control was becoming increasingly centralised within the federal government.

It was in this evolving environment in 1910 that a cabal of plotters representing various banking interests met secretly at Jekyll Island, Georgia.[86] The dust from the Knickerbocker collapse had just settled, but the inherent instability of fractional reserve banking remained. Their scheming led to the creation of the Federal Reserve system and a new type of dollar currency issued by Federal Reserve Banks and imposed on the states, even though the federal government did not have the legal power under the Constitution to grant a power to others that it did not itself possess.

The bankers' narrative was that a central bank could provide an 'elastic currency' to address the fractional reserve problem. As bank depositors moved their purchasing power down the Exter Inverted Pyramid, new currency would be created by the central bank to keep the Monetary Balance Sheet illustrated in Figure 10 in balance. If the right side of the balance sheet declined because purchasing power was removed from the banking system, new currency would be created by the Federal Reserve, thereby preventing a decline in prices that would occur if the quantity of currency were to otherwise contract. It did not work out that way.

As noted by Milton Friedman in *A Monetary History of the United States, 1867-1960*, the Federal Reserve did not provide an elastic currency during the Great Depression. Instead, it allowed the fractional reserve system to work in reverse. The quantity of currency declined for two reasons.

Customers withdrew their purchasing power from banks to place it in safer alternatives. Second, many banks failed, which destroyed the purchasing power of customer deposits in those banks. The result was the greatest economic disaster America had ever seen, but the scope was more far-reaching. It was worldwide because of a global reliance on the British banking model.

The resulting chaos provided the opportunity for the newly elected President Roosevelt to usher in a radically progressive agenda that undermined the gold standard and individual liberty. The economic and banking crisis was used as the deceitful excuse[87] in 1933 to confiscate gold owned by U.S. citizens. Further, the Federal Reserve dollar was no longer redeemable into gold, moving it even further away from the Constitution.

The Gold Reserve Act of 1934 created a new monetary world. Its purpose in the words of Mr Roosevelt announcing this new law is 'to regulate dealings in gold and...bring gold transactions permanently under the supervision of the federal government.' The previous free market in gold 'seriously hampered the government's control of its (sic) monetary system.'

His words reveal the absolute statist he was. Money is power, and power is enhanced with complete control and ownership of the system by which currency circulates. It is this ownership that Roosevelt sought, as highlighted by the possessive 'its' in the quote above, but his actions struck at the very essence of liberty, namely, the right to contract.

Roosevelt declared that the federal government's obligation to repay its debts in gold as it had promised was null and void. This default of its obligations led to various lawsuits regarding the gold clause in these debts that required they be repaid in gold, rather than dollars. By inequitably settling these cases, the Supreme Court in effect declared that the federal government had the right to break not only its own contracts, but that the power of the federal government was greater than the right of contract between two individuals, thus disrupting what had always been the foundation stone of voluntary cooperation upon which western civilisation was built. It was an audacious grab for absolute power.

Roosevelt's confiscation of gold from U.S. citizens and the prohibitions from using gold as currency gave the federal government control over currency. Usurping the right to contract, to which the Supreme Court acquiesced, gave it control of all aspects of the economy and private enterprise. The country, like parts of Europe in the 1930s, was becoming fascist, with private ownership of assets and many aspects of life itself subject to federal government control.

Self-reliance and the pioneering spirit of individuals interacting in society under the principles of natural law had made America great, and the country became the beacon of freedom. The new societal order, however, put the interests of an all-powerful dominant State ahead of the individual, even to the extent that Americans no longer owned their own money. It was confiscated, and the banknotes that they were now required to use were under the control of the Federal Reserve in an unconstitutional currency system. The deposits customers had placed in banks were now redeemable in Federal Reserve banknotes, without access to gold. The risks of fractional reserve banking remained.

The federal government's control of dollar currency came initially from the National Bank Act in 1863 and was then expanded with the Federal Reserve Act. Those provisions were strengthened under Roosevelt to enhance and expand federal government control. Its control of the dollar and the system by which dollars circulate is indirect, as these are managed by national banks that own the Federal Reserve system. The federal government's indirect 'ownership' derives from control over national banks that are chartered and supervised by the federal government. These banks must follow federal government dictates or risk losing their licence to operate.

Unbridled by the Roosevelt administration and then awakened by the world war to the powers of borrowing, spending, and taxing, the State began to grow. The dollar began suffering from the effects of policies that debased its purchasing power.

The final coup de grâce to the dollar came in 1971 with a so-called Executive Order by President Richard Nixon. It happened without an act of Congress even though in the Constitution the executive branch of the federal government has no monetary authority. By his Executive Order, a presumed power that itself is not provided in the Constitution, President Nixon broke the last remaining formal link between the Federal Reserve dollar and gold. That one action meant that the State would continue to grow because the banking system would ensure that it received whatever dollar currency it needed to meet whatever amount of dollars politicians chose to spend. It removed the last vestige of any monetary discipline. It is a direct consequence of this usurpation of power that the federal government's debt obligations and other financial promises have reached astronomical proportions.

The federal government's control over the dollar is indirect, but also absolute. What is today called the 'U.S. dollar' is neither a constitutional dollar nor even a United States dollar, despite its name. The dollar today is a Federal Reserve dollar, which is fascistically organised by being issued by privately owned banks that are under government control. Every dollar bill records on its face that it is a 'Federal Reserve Note', the term 'note' harking back to the days when these promissory notes owed either gold or silver to the bearer. As fiat currency, they now do not owe anything.

The Federal Reserve these days contends that its primary mission is to achieve price stability for the dollar and to adopt policies geared toward full employment. These aims are regularly and routinely offered to the public and Congressional committees as justification not only for its existence, but also to enhance and bolster its exclusive position of power and privilege.

The Federal Reserve has had many goals in its history. It no longer mentions the elastic currency it was supposed to provide when first established. Having failed miserably in that task during the Great Depression, one would have hoped that America's experiment with central banking would have ended then and there. There have been other failures too, such as regulation. Banks are heavily regulated, but they fail, except the large banks bailed out by the federal government because they are deemed 'too big to fail'.

There is an even bigger problem that regulatory overview by the Treasury and the Federal Reserve has not addressed. They allowed a credit boom to spin out of control leading to the 2008 financial crisis, and then arranged for taxpayers to bail out the banks. Their regulatory efforts failed, despite decades of practice and tightening controls. Regulations are not a practical way to exert discipline on bankers and the currency process, so regulations will always fail in this task.

Any regulatory framework will always be skirted by those bank managers who are unscrupulous or dishonest. In a level 'playing field' without favour to any one group, the free market is the best regulator. In Joseph Schumpeter's 'creative destruction' description of the dynamics of a market economy, things improve when allowing the bad banks, their bad managers, and bad systems – such as fractional reserve banking – to fail and be replaced by alternatives.

Unfortunately, once the power to create currency is in the hands of the government or its agents, it remains. Politicians become very protective of their control of currency. They do everything within their power to guard it, even imposing Draconian capital controls because the ruling elite understands that their power rests on their control of the currency and banking system. So as has occurred in America, new excuses have been developed and offered to justify the existence of the central bank and to further enhance its power.

The Federal Reserve has at different times been described as 'essential' because it was needed to create an elastic currency, regulate the banks, act as a lender of last resort, keep interest rates stable or move them higher or lower, provide a national cheque clearing system, et cetera. Perhaps this would be tolerable if the Federal Reserve was successful in any stated endeavour. It has never done any of these things efficiently – and some of them not at all – but the Federal Reserve carries on nonetheless.

Its endurance of course is not a mystery. We never hear from the Federal Reserve's apologists the real reason for its longevity. The Federal Reserve and the protector and sponsor of its monopoly privilege, the federal government, are in cahoots. The federal government contends that the Federal Reserve acts independently without political influence. The Federal Reserve pretends it is seeking price stability and full employment for the country, while its true mission is to make everybody believe the federal government is solvent. The Fed does this by buying federal government debt instruments, controlling interest rates, and otherwise taking whatever steps it believes are necessary to provide all the Federal Reserve dollars that politicians in the federal government need to meet their collective spending aspirations.

What is worse, the dollar is now circulating on the same basis as its predecessor, the continental. Both are irredeemable into precious metal. Both rest on the full faith and credit of the government. Even though the dollar is constantly losing purchasing power and is a mere shadow of its former self, it has not yet totally collapsed like the continental, but that anomaly can be explained by one key difference between them.

To the extent that the continental circulated, it was by choice of the people using it in their transactions, many of whom chose to use the various foreign coins circulating in the former thirteen colonies. There was no law forcing the continental's circulation to the exclusion of other currencies, which explains how the dollar is different. It has a monopoly position and is fiat currency. The dollar has been declared 'legal tender' and circulates by force of law and penalty, again in defiance of constitutional principles.

> Most unquestionably there is no legal tender, and there can be no legal tender, in this country, under the authority of this government or any other, but gold and silver, either the coinage of our own mints, or foreign coins, at rates regulated by Congress. This is a constitutional principle, perfectly plain, and of the very highest importance.
>
> Senator Daniel Webster, 1836

Gold does not need a government imprimatur to be accepted as tender in payment. Further, gold will circulate as currency because of its usefulness as money, provided governments do not issue any currency. Gresham's Law then applies because government issued currency is by nature inferior to gold, which explains why legal tender laws are used to force government issued currency to circulate. Without that use of force, government currency would collapse like the continental. A common currency achieved by force of law is inferior and abusive to individual rights, in contrast to a natural common currency, gold, that is accepted voluntarily.

Money and Liberty in America

The Federal Reserve dollar circulates because of the force of law and the threat of penalty, which is to be expected in a fascistic system. Therefore, people keep using the dollar and will continue to use it until it too collapses, but to delay that collapse for as long as possible, liberty will continue to be eroded. Only regimentation and control can keep a fiat currency in circulation, and the worse the currency becomes, the great the regimentation and control.

> It is impossible to grasp the meaning of the idea of sound money if one does not realize that it was devised as an instrument for the protection of civil liberties against despotic inroads on the part of governments. Ideologically it belongs in the same class with political

> constitutions and bills of rights. The demand for constitutional guarantees and for bills of rights was a reaction against arbitrary rule and the nonobservance of old customs by kings. The postulate of sound money was first brought up as a response to the princely practice of debasing the coinage. It was later carefully elaborated and perfected in the age which – through the experience of the American continental currency, the paper money of the French Revolution and the British restriction period – had learned what a government can do to a nation's currency system.
>
> Ludwig von Mises, *The Theory of Money and Credit*, 1952

The framers of the Constitution understood from experience, in Mises's words, 'what a government can do to a nation's currency system'. It is therefore understandable that the monetary provisions in the Constitution are clear, as are those of the Mint Act of 1792.

The Constitution identifies only three federal crimes, one of which is 'to provide for the Punishment of counterfeiting the Securities and current Coin of the United States.' Counterfeiting a coin is done the same way as counterfeiting a U.S. T-bill or any other debt instrument. It is done by imitating something valuable with an inferior copy of less value with the intention to deceive. Logically, therefore, it is counterfeiting for the federal government to contend that a $20 Federal Reserve Note is as valuable as a $20 gold double eagle coin.

The framers viewed counterfeiting and debasement to be crimes against humanity, with serious consequences to the perpetrator of debased coins, fraud, or theft from the Mint. The Mint Act states that the perpetrator of 'the said offences, shall be deemed guilty of felony, and shall suffer death.'

It is only the subsequent, wilful misinterpretations of these monetary provisions and their acceptance by the voting public that has allowed America's monetary system and the dollar to deviate from what Mises describes as an 'instrument for the protection of civil liberties against despotic inroads on the part of governments.'

The American Constitution was purposefully designed to prevent tyranny to protect an individual's inalienable rights. The framers were as concerned about the tyranny of democracy as they were about the tyranny of government. James Madison, the principal author of the Constitution, said the people 'must enable the government to control the governed; and in the next place oblige it to control itself.'

The House of Representatives was designed to represent the people, while the Senate was meant to represent legislatures of the individual states that appointed their two senators to protect each state's interests. The presidency was designed to represent the system as a whole by having executive power to implement lawful legislation, while the Supreme Court determined whether legislation is consistent with the seventeen powers in the Constitution delegated to the federal government by the states and protective of the Bill of Rights. The Electoral College is another component of the framers' vision of a state-governed confederated republic, in contrast to a central government with consolidated power that emerged in the twentieth century from the corruption of a constitutional monetary system. The establishment of the Federal Reserve has helped create and perpetuate a ruling elite, returning to America the political power structure and societal structure the War for Independence was fought to overthrow.

Government intervention in nearly all aspects of economic and human activity is perhaps the salient distinguishing factor of the twentieth century. Nobel Laureate Friedrich Hayek alerted the world to this new reality in 1944 with his insightful and prescient *The Road to Serfdom*, written during the waning years of the Second World War.

Hayek's central theme is that wars expand the power of the modern State because the national planning to fight the war continues even during times of peace. This perennial government planning expands the State over time in other areas like social welfare, with harmful results. Most importantly, economic activity is impeded by the growing State as people and resources become less productive. In other words, because the government does not create consumable goods and services, it is an economic burden to the productive sector of the economy, leading to a divided society of taxpayers and tax-eaters.

As the government grows, interest groups become increasingly numerous and powerful, leading to political corruption. More wars or even foreign policy tensions and economic crises can propel demagogues and dictatorial leaders to expand further state powers to the detriment of each and every one of us. In Hayek's words: 'Emergencies have always been the pretext on which the safeguards of individual liberty have eroded.'

Hayek noted that the subtle damage inflicted upon the productive economy and the visible growth of the State arising from socialism become evident only over time. We have now reached that stage evidenced by the growing wealth disparity and stagnant standard of living. In some countries, more people depend on salary or benefits from the State than those who provide it with the taxing revenue the State needs to meet its promises.

To attain liberty, a level playing field is necessary. In the words of former Congressman Ron Paul: 'Liberty and sound money are the only neutralizing agents to Deep State power.' A sound monetary system with gold as the central core imposes discipline and controls a government's propensity to usurp more and more power. Righting the balance between individuals and the State is essential to overcome the compulsion by politicians to intervene in human action, which reveals their insatiable desire to rule others. With self-assured hubris, politicians use their power to damage free markets long before they ever understand how they work.

Gold's direct correlation to human liberty is its most important attribute. In this regard, in 1976 a friend gave me a copy of a speech that was critically important to my understanding of the link between money and liberty. The speech was delivered in 1948 by Howard Buffett, the father of Wall Street legend Warren Buffett. To our good fortune, his address was published two days later in the *Commercial and Financial Chronicle* and is reprinted in full in the Appendix, but I will comment on excerpts from it.

The senior Buffett was a successful Omaha businessman who chose to contribute to his community by serving four terms in the House of Representatives. Rep Buffett's insightful words had a profound effect and opened my eyes. After all, who better than a Congressman to recognise that the federal government was fundamentally altering its relationship with the American people? And who could possibly have more standing than someone with insight and prescience who speaks to us across decades? Rep Buffet was too far ahead of his time, so sadly, few listened to his concerns and even fewer appreciated his wisdom when he addressed a group of businessmen in 1948.

The passage of time has proven Rep Buffet right, so the ideas of this brilliant Congressman from Nebraska should be re-examined in light of our quest to protect individual liberty. His words speak for themselves, but keep in mind the distinction made in this book between money and currency to get a clearer understanding of his message.

> Is there a connection between human freedom and a gold redeemable money? At first glance it would seem that money belongs to the world of economics and human freedom to the political sphere. But when you recall that one of the first moves by Lenin, Mussolini and Hitler [and Franklin Roosevelt] was to outlaw individual ownership of gold, you begin to sense that there may be some connection between money, redeemable in gold, and the rare prize known as human liberty.
>
> Also, when you find that Lenin declared and demonstrated that a sure way to overturn the existing social order and bring about communism was by printing press paper money, then again you are impressed with the possibility of a relationship between a gold-backed money and human freedom.

Rep Buffett recognised that the federal government had changed. It no longer was the quaint non-interventionist institution it was during his youth. He understood that the ingenious checks and balances so thoughtfully and carefully interwoven in the Constitution to protect individual liberty had been abused and broken.

> Today Congress is constantly besieged by minority groups seeking benefits from the public treasury. Often these groups control enough votes in many Congressional districts to change the outcome of elections. And so Congressmen find it difficult to persuade themselves not to give in to pressure groups. With no bad immediate consequence it becomes expedient to accede to a spending demand. The Treasury is seemingly inexhaustible. Besides the unorganized taxpayers back home may not notice this particular expenditure – and so it goes.

He goes on to say: 'Because [a politician's] continuance in office depends upon pleasing a majority of the pressure groups', there is a natural propensity for overspending. Rep Buffett recognised this reckless tendency to be a political fact, with predictable and discouraging results if left uncontrolled.

> From 1930-1946 your government went into the red every year and the debt steadily mounted. Various plans have been proposed to reverse this spiral of debt...All of these proposals look good. But they are unrealistic under our paper money system. They will not stand against postwar spending pressures.

The demise of the Gramm–Rudman Balanced Budget & Emergency Deficit Control Act of 1985, the Balanced Budget & Emergency Deficit Control Reaffirmation Act of 1987, countless extensions of the federal government's debt limit, and numerous other proposals from Rep Buffett's time to the present to control spending are a testament to his understanding and insight that truly reaches across the decades. But Rep Buffet did not stop with just an accurate statement of the problem. He also provided the solution. He knew what was needed to set things right and to bring unbridled spending under control.

> Before 1933 the people themselves had an effective way to demand economy. Before 1933, whenever the people became disturbed over Federal spending, they could go to the banks, redeem their paper currency in gold, and wait for common sense to return to Washington. That happened on various occasions and conditions sometimes

> became strained, but nothing occurred like the ultimate consequences of paper money inflation.
>
> When the people's right to restrain public spending by demanding gold coin was taken from them, the automatic flow of strength from the grass-roots to enforce economy in Washington was disconnected...The gold standard acted as a silent watchdog to prevent unlimited public spending.

Rep Buffett clearly understood the consequences of his recommendation, which was to re-establish and then protect individual liberty. He also recognised the outcry that would result among those who would criticise the restoration of constitutional money.

> Most opponents of free coinage of gold admit that that restoration is essential, but claim the time is not propitious. Some argue that there would be a scramble for gold and our enormous gold reserves would soon be exhausted.
>
> Actually this argument simply points up the case. If there is so little confidence in our currency that restoration of gold coin would cause our gold stocks to disappear, then we must act promptly.

Unfortunately, the redeemability of the dollar into gold was not restored, and as he predicted, much of the U.S. gold stock disappeared. The 22,100 tonnes held in May 1948 has been drastically reduced to 8,100 tonnes today, with nearly all the dishoarding occurring by 1968. This dissipation happened in a way that Rep Buffett would have found alarming. He understood irredeemable currency posed a threat that would deplete American wealth because at that time, it was illegal for U.S. citizens to own gold bullion and coin. So the 'gold [in the U.S. Gold Reserve] is not subject to demand by American citizens. It could all be shipped out of this country without the people having any chance to prevent it.' And so it was.

This reduction of the gold stock robbed the American people. They created the wealth that built it, but they were helpless to stop its dispersal.

What motivated Rep Buffet? Although it may be hard to understand or accept in today's environment of cynicism and flagrant self-interest, his words reveal him to be a true statesman, whose aim was to serve his country and fellow Americans. According to Wikipedia: 'His wife said he considered only one issue when deciding whether or not to vote for a bill: Will this add to, or subtract from, human liberty?'[88] In one introspective moment, Rep Buffett provides a frank and candid personal assessment and expresses a sincere concern for taxpayers whose votes put him into office.

> Far away from Congress is the real forgotten man, the taxpayer who foots the bill. He is in a different spot from the tax-eater or the business that makes millions from spending schemes. He cannot afford to spend his time trying to oppose Federal expenditures. He has to earn his own living and carry the burden of taxes as well.
>
> Each of you is in business to make profits. If your firm does not make profits, it goes out of business. In politics votes have a similar vital importance to an elected official. That situation is not ideal, but it exists, probably because generally no one gives up power willingly.
>
> Perhaps you are right now saying to yourself: 'That's just what I have always thought. The politicians are thinking of votes when they ought to think about the future of the country. What we need is a Congress with some 'guts.' If we elected a Congress with intestinal fortitude, it would stop the spending all right!
>
> I went to Washington with exactly that hope and belief. But I have had to discard it as unrealistic. Why?
>
> Because an economy Congressman under our printing-press money system is in the position of a fireman running into a burning building with a hose that is not connected with the water plug. His courage may be commendable, but he is not hooked up right at the other end of the line. So it is now with a Congressman working for economy. There is no sustained hookup with the taxpayers to give him strength.
>
> But for most beneficiaries a Federal paycheck soon becomes vital in his life. He usually will spend his full energies if necessary to hang onto this income. The taxpayer is completely outmatched in such an unequal contest. Always heretofore he possessed an equalizer. If government finances weren't run according to his idea of soundness he had an individual right to protect himself by [redeeming his dollars for] gold.'

Here is the nexus of the link between money and liberty. Representative government works when each individual can vote with their money and their pocketbook by demanding gold instead of a money substitute forced into circulation when dictated by law. Rep Buffett's insight explains why the taxpaying middle class has become alienated in recent decades. People are frustrated because they are unable to bring about the political change necessary to improve their lives. The fiat currency system is not 'hooked up' to gold, disconnecting the taxpaying working class from what happens in Washington, D.C.

Rep Buffett championed gold as money because he understood that human freedom is dependent upon it. For that reason, he advocated the principle that currency must be redeemable in gold. By analysing the regimes of dictators, which invariably aimed to control the country's money by confiscating gold as an essential part of the process to secure absolute power, he concludes that the 'connection between money redeemable in gold and a rare prize known as liberty' is irrefutable.

> In a free country the monetary unit rests upon a fixed foundation of gold or gold and silver independent of the ruling politicians. Our dollar was that kind of money before 1933. Under that system paper currency is redeemable for a certain weight of gold, at the free option and choice of the holder of paper money.'

The remedy proposed by this brilliant Congressman from Nebraska is not new. Rather, it is a fundamental principle important in the history of America. It is a safeguard against political mismanagement enshrined in the Constitution, specifically the monetary powers and disabilities of Article 1.

Rep Buffet also accurately understood that federal government 'finances will never be brought into order until Congress is compelled to do so. Making our money redeemable in gold will create this compulsion.' With federal government borrowing nearly one-half of what it spent in fiscal year 2020, we could do well by learning from this insight. There is no single action that could do more to affectively control the federal government, nor do so in a more democratic way than returning to gold, constitutional money.

However, it will not be an easy task. Rep Buffett said with considerable foresight:

> I warn you that politicians of both parties will oppose the restoration of gold...Also those elements here and abroad who are getting rich from the continued American inflation will oppose a return to sound money. You must be prepared to meet their opposition intelligently and vigorously. They have had 15 [now 89] years of unbroken victory.
>
> But, unless you are willing to surrender your children and your country to galloping inflation, war and slavery, then this cause demands your support. For if human liberty is to survive in America, we must win the battle to restore honest money.

> There is no more important challenge facing us than this issue -- the restoration of your freedom to secure gold in exchange for the fruits of your labors.

Rep Buffett's speech is significant for several reasons and highlights matters of timeless importance. When a ruler can call in a national currency on a whim or allow a central bank to debase it as a matter of policy, the citizen of any country is in reality no more than a serf to their ruler. Only years before Buffett spoke, Stalin had done just that in Russia, literally decimating what tiny fraction of wealth his countrymen had left under his oppressive communist regime, by calling in ten old debased roubles and replacing them with one new rouble.

The gold confiscations by Lenin, Mussolini, Hitler, and Franklin Roosevelt left indelible marks on the twentieth century, which was blighted by fascism and authoritarian rule. This observation leads directly to the correlation between gold and human freedom. The possession and use of gold as currency is essential to human freedom. Repeating the insightful observation by Ralph Waldo Emerson: 'The desire of gold is not for gold. It is for the means of freedom and benefit.' Money is power, and the use of gold to define the monetary unit inexorably limits the powers of the State.

Communism and fascism have taken the powers of the State to extremes, but throughout the developed world today, there is a recognition that almost every nation state has become grotesquely bloated, paying hand-outs not only to special interest groups but to a vast clientele that has become beholden to governments on which they rely. They have strapped on a government funded feedbag, and it is very difficult to shift that status quo by rolling back the role of government to those days only decades ago when its role was governed by the limited powers granted to it and limited tasks expected of it. Expect protests and rioting if there are government cutbacks.

In the United States, the phenomena of the Tea Party and the election of Donald Trump are manifestations of growing dissatisfaction with profligate government spending and a bloated state eroding individual liberty, as is the emergence of leaders labelled a 'populist'. It is no accident that political groups recognising that government is on the wrong course come to the fore at a time when reliance on ever growing amounts of fiat currency are created to bail out favoured interests and address every other ailment imagined or real causing disquiet or threatens to weaken federal government power.

However, as Rep Buffett points out, if the currency was again redeemable in gold, governments everywhere would very quickly have to mend their ways because gold is an effective governor that exerts discipline on the currency creation process. Or to put it another way, reckless government spending would provoke a run on the banks which could not be satiated by printing fiat currency – because you cannot print gold.

The results of our actions and our written words live on forever. We are fortunate that Rep Buffett's wisdom was recorded for posterity. Unlike his contemporaries, who did not act on his insight and prescience, there is no reason not to do so. The accuracy of his conclusions is self-evident, now that time has proven him right.

The time has come to re-establish a constitutional federal government by returning to constitutional money. The power to control the politicians in Washington D.C. will then be returned to the people, which is where it rightfully belongs, rather than in the hands of the ruling elite which controls the banks and the currency system of the Federal Reserve dollar.

Because money is the foundation upon which society exists, restoring constitutional money would put America back on the right path to attain true liberty by re-establishing the essential balance between individuals and the State, as would any other country that chose to follow the monetary provisions of the American Constitution. Rep Buffett has provided the blueprint. All Americans need to do is act.

Regimentation or Inflation

In 1943, the Brookings Institute published *The New Philosophy of Public Debt*. It was written by H.G. Moulton, who noted that the 'old' philosophy is the 'great and continuous growth of the public debt imperils the financial stability of the nation and undermines the very foundations of the economy economic system... And that the [US Department of] Treasury must be soundly solvent in order that the nation may prosper and progress.'

That proposition contrasts markedly with the 'new' philosophy that states 'a huge public debt is a national asset rather than a liability and that continuous deficit spending is essential to the economic prosperity of the nation...[and]...The conception of a balanced budget belongs in the category of obsolete economic dogma.' To which philosophy do you adhere?

Mr. Moulton analyses both philosophies, and his observations are particularly relevant to present day circumstances. For example, he concludes that:

> ...exchange [rate] depreciation can be set in motion...[by]...an uncontrolled expansion of the public debt. When investors lose confidence in a government's ability to maintain financial equilibrium, an effort is always made to transfer investments in that country to safer quarters. American Treasury difficulties in the 1890s were largely due to the withdrawal by foreigners of funds invested in the United States.

> There was a flight of capital away from what had come to be regarded as a dangerous spot.
>
> Similarly, there may be a flight of domestically-owned capital to safer havens in foreign countries. An excellent illustration of a capital movement of this type is found in the flight from the [French] franc in the middle of the 1930s, occasioned chiefly by the rapid expansion of the public debt and loss of confidence in the fiscal stability of the government.

Most harrowing is his observation that as 'the French government finances went from bad to worse...[this deterioration]...undermined the very foundations of business enterprise, employment, and social and political stability.' He then concludes with the stark reality that: 'It will be necessary to make a choice. With unlimited debt expansion we cannot prevent inflation without the use of totalitarian methods of control. No compromise or halfway measures can adjust the difficulties. The choice is between regimentation and inflation.'

Mr. Moulton was writing in 1943, and we now know that there is only one viable alternative, namely, gold as money. Regimentation and inflation always end in disaster. The Soviet Union and all the other command economies following the dictates of regimentation collapsed. The present collapse of the Venezuelan economy is a good example that makes clear the inevitable and unavoidable outcome of both regimentation and inflation. The more socialism that is applied, the greater will be the regimentation needed to get compliance with the socialist dictates. Each measure further erodes everyone's liberty, but governments can never control one's free will.

The federal government has been relentlessly moving toward more regimentation of individual behaviour and the American economy. It is a brazen attempt to avoid its default of the U.S. national debt, which has passed the point at which it is repayable. Consequently, the debt is in the process of being repudiated over time by the destruction of the dollar's purchasing power from inflation. Central banks throughout the globe are assisting governments in achieving this outcome through their financial repression that is forcing interest rates to remain at artificially low levels.

The regimentation is being employed to hide an ongoing repudiation of the debt in the false hope that it goes unnoticed through a relatively slow pace of inflation. The question remains how long this ruse can continue before the U.S. federal government faces the same fate as the character Mike Campbell in Ernest Hemingway's 1926 novel *The Sun Also Rises*. When was asked about his money troubles and how he became bankrupt, Campbell replies: 'Two ways. Gradually and then suddenly.' After decades of growing perennial deficits, the federal government's financial picture is no longer deteriorating gradually.

As economically sound and politically honest money, gold encourages and facilitates harmonious interactions among individuals. All interactions increase knowledge and commerce, and the growth of these two fundamental pillars that mark advances in civilisation result in higher standards of living to the benefit of humankind.

Time to Restore the Monetary Checks and Balances

Monetary debasement is an age-old practice, just the method changes. The Romans mixed copper into gold coins and lead into silver ones. With the introduction of ledger currency by the Bank of England, debasement now takes place on bank balance sheets. The result is that people throughout the world have needed to confront ever-worsening monetary problems and recurring banking crises. These troubles are not insoluble. They result from two principal causes.

First, today's currency and banking system is based on a seventeenth-century mercantilist model that is not fit for purpose in our modern economy. Second, public officials fail to acknowledge that the only economically sound and politically honest money is gold.

It is a sign of the times that people only think in terms of responses from the State to solve problems; they do not look for solutions from the free market. It is a sad situation, but one that is to be expected from generations of public-school indoctrination and a corporativist media serving State interests.

Monetary reform needs to be based on the original intent of the Constitution and the first legislation of the newly formed government, the Mint Act of 1792, not what judges may subsequently interpret for political expediency. In fact, the rule of law has been insidiously eroded over decades by the general acceptance of political expediency.

If we look back at what made America great, it was not reliance on government. It was self-reliance and individual achievement, or in other words, human action in the pursuit of happiness unfettered by mindless government red tape and the ill-conceived notion of political correctness. The autocrats who stress a politically correct scheme imply that they are taking the moral high road, when in fact, they are doing the exact opposite with their selfish aim to impose their will on others who do not agree with them. It is natural for people to have differing viewpoints and opinions, and there is no harm to this reality provided everyone respects everyone else's inalienable rights of life, liberty, and the pursuit of happiness, including the right of absolute privacy.

History shows that governments and the demagogues who lead them are the source of problems, so it is ironic that they relentlessly promote and see themselves as solutions. Demagogues use symbols, like a national flag, to appeal to a wide audience by conjuring up an emotional response to past glories as a way to overlook present realities. The monetary problems faced today are a direct result of government actions, or more to the point, not following the Constitution. We have abandoned the monetary wisdom of the framers. We must remember that they lived through the collapse of America's first national currency and did not want future generations to suffer the same fate.

Efforts in Congress and state legislatures seeking change are noble but have been ill-fated and will remain so until there is a change in thinking and a return to America's legal roots and principles. Fortunately, millions of thinking Americans are being educated on the most important subject, which is gold's use as money because a society of free people can only exist and prosper if the monetary system is honest.

The federal government is content with the growing power it wields and is so misguided from its constitutional role that it offers little hope for meaningful change. The best possibility for well-reasoned change is at the state level, given the monetary powers they hold as so clearly stated in the Constitution. The states must stop accepting dollar bills of credit, whether as banknotes or deposit currency. The alternatives are precious metal coin circulated the old way moving hand to hand, and the new way, with weights of metal ownership being transferred digitally by private enterprise, as implemented by Goldmoney. Nothing in the Constitution prohibits private initiatives from investing their own time and capital to improve the circulation of currency, including cryptocurrency. Unleashing the free market to create currency solutions is the logical and only way to proceed to attain the best possible outcome.

Thus, the key to true monetary reform is re-establishing the rule of law and removing government altogether from the business of creating currency, except the minting of precious metal coin as allowed by the Constitution. The way to achieve this objective is through education, and ultimately by creating a level playing field to enable competition in currencies. In this way, individuals are free to choose which currency to use. That currency will come from private entrepreneurs and their initiatives, not from dictates of the federal government or its politicians and the vested interests that control them.

People are the all-important monetary authority, which tragically is a power that has been usurped from us. It has already led to dreadful consequences, but as bad as the effects of decades of inflation have been, worse is yet to come. A terrible outcome awaits us when the mountain of debt now being piled up by ongoing budget deficits of the federal government eventually comes crashing down. It need not be this way, but a critical 'check and balance' has been dismantled. By changing the essence of the dollar from a unit of account defined as a weight of precious metal to a bookkeeping entry of no precise measurement or definition, the people's authority over the federal government was undermined and then ended.

Alchemising the U.S. National Debt

Many concerned Americans are aware of the monetary and fiscal problems facing the nation. Enemies of the federal government's red ink repeatedly muster their forces to do battle. Unfortunately, even if the proponents of sound federal government finance win a battle, they will still lose the war to re-establish fiscal prudence, as made clear by various attempts to control federal spending since the 1930s. These well-intentioned but misguided attempts have failed to rein in the unconscionable aspirations of spendthrift Congresses, and they have they also failed to put a backbone in presidents who are always willing to disperse congressional largesse.

The proponents of fiscal prudence are fighting the wrong enemy. Rather than attacking the spending that results from the federal government's present business as usual stance, they should focus their sights instead on the underlying cause of that spending, a monetary system – and an unconstitutional one at that – gone awry. To do battle they must unsheathe their most formidable weapon, Article 1, Sections 8 and 10 of the Constitution, which impose meaningful conditions on the country's monetary system. These important provisions state that the money of the United States – the monetary unit of account to be used in finance and commerce called the dollar, the eagle, double eagle or whatever name is chosen as the numeraire – shall be a defined weight of gold or silver.

The framers understood money and currency, and they understood the political process. More importantly, they understood that money and politics do not mix in a healthy way. They learned that reality from their experience with the currency issued by state governments before the War for Independence, and they learned it again from the currency of the Continental Congress issued under the Articles of Confederation that was the law of the union of the thirteen sovereign American states created after the War for Independence.

With the Constitution, the states changed the nature of the confederation by creating a 'more perfect union'. They did not dispose of the confederation by adopting one consolidated government for the whole country. They only relinquished to the federal government seventeen defined powers, and each state remained sovereign in all other respects.

The framers carefully crafted the Constitution to prevent the federal government from having the authority to turn its own debt instruments into currency, 'bills of credit', in their terminology. Regrettably, it did not work out that way. Once the turmoil of the hyperinflationary collapse of the continental currency was no longer in living memory, political leaders seeking greater power began to tinker with the monetary provisions of the Constitution, with the consequence that today the pockets of Americans carry dollar 'bills of credit'. The important monetary constraints on governmental power have been unshackled. Debt, including those of the U.S. government, is being alchemised into currency.

Before the creation of the Federal Reserve, there was a limit to the federal government's propensity to spend dollars. Spending was controlled by the number of dollars received as revenue or available from new borrowing. There was a rigorous discipline imposed by the Constitutional restraints because the quantity of dollars that could be created was indirectly tied to the weight of gold stockpiled in bank vaults.

If too many dollars were created, the quantity of dollars relative to the weight of gold became inordinately imbalanced. People would respond as they did in the Panic of 1907 by redeeming their dollars into gold. The bad banks caught up in the panic would fail, raising the Fear Index. The resulting reduction in the quantity of dollar currency was brought back toward a workable level compared to the weight of gold in reserve, just like occurred when the run on the Bank of England ended in 1696.

Today there are no constraints on the creation of dollars. If the federal government does not receive enough dollars from revenue, it borrows them. Those debts are then alchemised into dollar bills and dollar bank deposits.

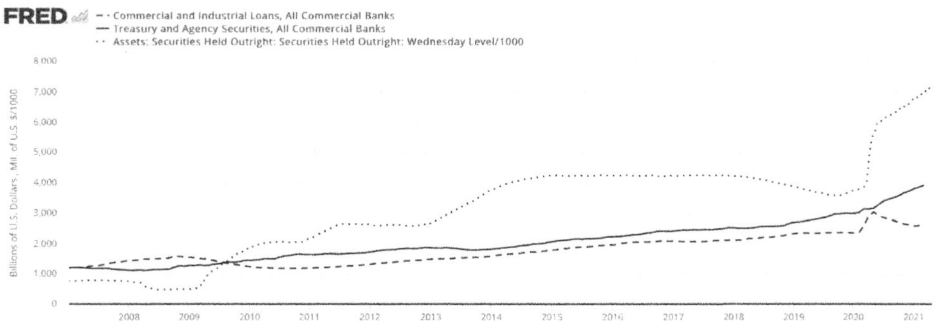

Figure 17 – Bank Assets

Source: Federal Reserve Bank of St. Louis

This chart shows that bank loans are declining while their ownership of U.S.

government debt instruments is growing. Additionally, the quantity of U.S. government debt instruments held outright by the Federal Reserve and alchemised by it is surging weekly to record highs. The $2.6 trillion of bank loans is dwarfed by the $3.9 trillion of U.S. government debt instruments banks own and the $7.2 trillion owned by the Federal Reserve.

President Calvin Coolidge once famously said: 'The chief business of the American people is business. They are profoundly concerned with producing, buying, selling, investing and prospering in the world.' While his comment is still true for the vast majority of the American people, the chief business of the banking system is now alchemising U.S. government debt instruments into dollar currency, not making loans to American enterprises for producing, investing, and prospering.

The banking system exists to bring together depositors and borrowers. Today, however, it has been commandeered to make governments look solvent by providing them with currency. Again referring to Macaulay: 'Money must be had, and could in no other way be had so easily.' But did the Constitution need to be trampled in the twentieth century to provide those dollars created 'out of thin air'? Did the right of each individual need to be trampled by a government unshackled from the Constitution and Bill of Rights whose principal objective was to protect individual liberty?

The monetary system is what it is, but I am focused on what it was, which according to the law of the land as clearly stated in the Constitution is what it should be once again. The choices before the American people are clear. The alternatives are cogently made former Congressman Ron Paul, a true advocate of liberty. They are: 'Individual liberty, peace, and prosperity or big government, war, and dependency.'

10. The Role of Government

The care of human life and happiness, and not their destruction, is the first and only object of good government.

Thomas Jefferson[89]

Every reasonable person will no doubt agree with these sentiments expressed by Thomas Jefferson in 1809 having just completed eight years of service as the third President of the young American republic. Where people differ is the definition of good government.

Most people want to live their lives without government interrupting their pursuit of happiness. This group would share the sentiments of Henry David Thoreau, who opened his pamphlet, *Resistance to Civil Government, or Civil Disobedience*, with the memorable portrayal 'That government is best which governs least.'

At the opposite end of the spectrum are the progressives and autocrats. They see government as a tool that can be used as an all-powerful force to direct individual behaviour. They view markets as the means to impose their interventions and manipulation of prices to force artificial, unnatural outcomes suiting their aims. They see control over a nation's currency as an essential ingredient to command the economy and steer it in whatever direction those choose, even putting it on a war footing coupled with forced conscription. From that coercion, these misguided, and in many instances, malevolent if not downright evil political leaders can shape society in the image they selfishly aim to achieve.

The American War for Independence was fought to overthrow the remnants of European feudalism and the concept of an all-powerful ruling nobility. American victory in that seven-year war meant that a new relationship between people and government was forged for the thirteen former colonies. A revolutionary yet auspicious outcome was achieved by the framers of the Constitution by relying on the fundamental concepts then being developed in the Age of Enlightenment. They changed humanity's social contract by implementing a political structure based on the supremacy of the individual over the State.

The Political Structure of the American Constitution

Winston Churchill warned: 'A nation that forgets its past has no future.' That stark admonition can also apply to a nation that misinterprets its past, which is particularly tragic for America, long deemed the world's beacon of liberty.

Independence for America was formalised by the Treaty of Paris that the warring parties signed in September 1783. Quoting from the Treaty, 'His Britannic Majesty acknowledges' that the thirteen colonial territories, each of which is named, 'to be free sovereign & Independent States; that he Treats with them as such, and for himself his Heirs & Successors relinquishes all Claims to the Government Propriety and Territorial Rights of the same & every Part thereof.'

This monumental declaration by George III ended feudalism in America, which though fading by the eighteenth century had been the dominant social structure in Europe since medieval times. From that moment, no American landowner owed any allegiance or duty to the monarch or any British noble, nor was any American obliged to live and work on land that could be claimed by the monarch or nobles.

With allodial land titles now available as a result of ending feudalism, land ownership was absolute. Each American could live on the land an individual owned without being subject to a higher authority. It meant that provided they adhered to the precepts of natural law, within their property's boundary Americans were free of government interference in their life and property. This newly attained freedom gained from the War for Independence was far reaching as the humanist and physiocratic principles of the Age of Enlightenment came to splendid fruition in the thirteen newly freed sovereign states.

There were no taxes on land or personal property because in contrast to a feudal serf, a free person does not pay money to the State for the inalienable right to live on their own land and use their possessions. There was no direct tax on one's labour because it takes from that person their time, which is theft and immoral. Genuine morality came into tax policy in another way.

A person might not agree on how a tax collected by the federal government was spent, for example, to fight a war or to defend the indefensible practice of slavery. The intent as written in the Constitution[90] was for the federal government to exist only on income from indirect taxes imposed upon a transaction, for example, duties on imports from abroad so that the tax only fell on the well-off able to afford imported luxury items. In this way, a free person who opposed the practice of slavery could avoid paying any tax to the federal government by simply foregoing imports or other transactions on which federal indirect taxes were levied. Following this principle, Thoreau refused in 1846 to pay a poll tax to protest slavery and the war with Mexico, which was a war he explained three years later in his famous aforementioned essay was 'the work of comparatively a few individuals using the standing government as their tool'.

There was no forced conscription because there was no federal military nor any requirement to pay feudal homage to the State. There were no regulations nor anything else to stop a free person from their pursuit of happiness, except the ethical framework of natural law and inherent human values that govern reason and behaviour. These new Americans enjoyed the basic natural rights of a free people earned for them and their posterity from their suffering and ultimate success in the War for Independence. There was no higher authority to impede their pursuit of happiness.

It was an ordered liberty under natural law that governed society and life in the new republic. American citizens were free in the truest, most fundamental, and wide-reaching sense of that word. Their freedoms stated in the Bill of Rights were protected by each state's constitution and the federal government's adherence to the seventeen powers in the Constitution delegated to it by the states limiting its authority to act. It was the zenith of the Age of Enlightenment.

Years ago in London I was watching a popular TV programme called *Antiques Road Show*. Its experts travel throughout the United Kingdom to explain items given to them to evaluate, with the owners then being able to find out whether they own a valuable antique or just an interesting curio. One offering was particularly intriguing, and I remember it well. It was a set of crystal toasting glasses used to celebrate a major event, typically a family wedding or perhaps the birth of a child. The expert dated them to the 1780s and advised that they were probably made for export to the American market. What caught my attention was the engraving on the side of the glass, 'Property and Liberty'. From those words it was easy to envision the owners of those glasses toasting not the birth of a child, but a new era arising from an experiment in government and individual sovereignty never before seen. Not only were Americans free, they now also had the power to control their future. What is clear is that America has strayed far from its hard-fought heritage and the liberty once achieved and enjoyed.

The preamble to the Constitution begins with 'We the People' to convey where the power to govern originates in America. It rests with the people, not a king, a national assembly, a president, nor any man-made law without the consent of the person to be governed by that law. People acting in accordance with natural law can then choose to delegate their power to others, which is the key to understanding the significance of the American revolution. No longer would America have a monarch dictating law to it. No longer would Americans be subjects to monarchical rule. By ousting an outdated and unloved European order, Americans now became citizens, unlike the British people who remained subjects of their king.

The political structure between the states and the federal government as prescribed by the Constitution and flowing from organic American law can be visually compared to a waterfall with 'the People' at the top. They in turn delegate to elected representatives in the state where they live certain powers to form a state government further down the waterfall to protect their life, liberty, and pursuit of happiness. Next comes the federal government, which is at the bottom of the waterfall. The states delegated seventeen specific powers to the federal government that are carefully enumerated in the Constitution and reconfirmed in the Bill of Rights. To make clear the limitations of federal government power, the Tenth Amendment specifically notes that any powers not delegated to the federal government by the Constitution are reserved by the states or the people.

The lower the level of the waterfall, the less the power to govern, and only with those powers delegated by the level immediately above. In this legal and societal structure, the federal government cannot exercise powers that were not delegated to it. Similarly, a state cannot exercise power not delegated to it by its citizens.

Unfortunately, that waterfall has been turned upside down in the twentieth century because of power grabs by progressives and autocrats in the federal government, which have led to the present system of unconstitutional dollar currency and voluminous man-made law and regulations. These barriers to liberty and the pursuit of happiness are far distant from what the framers of the Constitution established and intended for their progeny.

They found the concept of a single sovereign power to be abhorrent. That structure with a single monarch was a cause of the revolution, so they were not going to reimpose on Americans the yoke they had just discarded. They went to great lengths in the Constitution to delegate a small number of carefully defined powers to the federal government. They purposefully wanted the powers of the federal government to be few and limited, which would avoid the creation of a ruling elite that would be harmful to individual liberty and an American's pursuit of happiness.

The federal government was created by the states when they adopted the Constitution. The federal government is the creation of the thirteen original sovereign states and the other thirty-seven territories which became states by the rules and procedures provided in the Constitution. The role of the federal government is to function as a unified entity in carrying out on behalf of the states the seventeen powers delegated to it by the states. It acts from federal territory known as the District of Columbia, the popular name of the new world in the seventeenth and eighteenth centuries, latinised like Britannia and Germania. The name itself highlights the separation of state and federal power; it was not named the District of the United States.

The American Constitution is built upon a fundamental concept of 'checks and balances' between the legislature, judiciary, and executive branches comprising the federal government. The framers crafted the document to prevent any one branch from becoming too powerful relative to the other two branches, and more importantly, preventing the government itself from usurping authority from the People or the states, or for that matter, from the states usurping authority from the federal government. There are various provisions in the Constitution listing powers that the states agree to forgo, particularly in relation to money and currency.

America has strayed far from what the framers created. There is a need for serious introspection by each American to evaluate the present structure of government in comparison to what previously existed. They need to look at what was once achieved and the freedom Americans once enjoyed by understanding what the Constitution and the Bill of Rights provide. This quote by Johann von Goethe should give pause to most everyone: 'None are more hopelessly enslaved than those who falsely believe they are free.'

Many people do not understand how to experience, or even comprehend, the freedom of the colonists who fought for and won their independence. Freedom is not achieved by being reliant on any person or dependent upon a cheque from an employer or government. With self-reliance anyone can choose how to live their life and be free to benefit from everything life has to offer. With basic principles from the Age of Enlightenment, the framers crafted the American Constitution and built a system of natural liberty upon which a culture of freedom set America apart from the rest of the world.

Government and Society

Society is the result of a mutually beneficial interdependency among individuals, and the role of government – indeed its sole purpose – is to ensure the protection of each individual's pursuit of happiness as is his or her right, as derived from the laws of nature. In *The Law* Frederic Bastiat wrote in 1850: 'Life, liberty, and property do not exist because men have made laws. On the contrary, it was the fact that life, liberty, and property existed beforehand that caused men to make laws in the first place.' Thus, government acts should be formulated and implemented to enhance purposeful human interaction spurring rational self-interest, thereby encouraging the 'invisible hand' of Adam Smith.

The level of hypocrisy today is appalling. Nowhere it is more hurtful than the elected leaders who swear to uphold the Constitution and then abuse its fundamental provisions established to protect individual freedom. To repeat the cautionary advice of John Adams: 'Our Constitution was made only for a religious and moral people. It is wholly inadequate for the government of any other.'

Money and liberty are fundamental building blocks that are essential for channelling everyone's invisible hand equitably. Money and liberty are essential constituents of a well-ordered society of free people that enable each individual to pursue happiness by seeking to fulfil their needs and wants. They do this as they live their life, during which there are countless interactions with others pursuing their own unique goals to achieve what each of them believe to be their own desired happiness, all of which in the new American republic took place within a societal structure governed by natural law.

The sole purpose of government is to enable everyone's pursuit of happiness by protecting their life, liberty, and property from aggression. John Galt in Ayn Rand's classic, *Atlas Shrugged,* precisely describes its role: 'The only proper functions of a government are: the police, to protect you from criminals; the army, to protect you from foreign invaders; and the courts, to protect your property and contracts.'

Government acts should not be implemented to solve a problem for one group of people singled out from others. Staunch advocate of Adam Smith's natural liberty, Nobel Laureate James M. Buchanan, quotes Smith to make this point:

> To hurt in any degree the interest of any one order of citizens for no other purpose but to promote that of some other, is evidently contrary to that justice and equality of treatment which the sovereign owes to all different orders of his subjects.[91]

Any act of government must be designed to build a meritorious society that provides equal opportunity without favour. To govern a nation and attain a harmonious society, all government activity must be achievable through non-aggressive action that ensures gold's use as money and promotes maximal liberty.

Seeking Social and Economic Harmony

> The Party told you to reject the evidence of your eyes and ears. It was their final, most essential command.
>
> George Orwell, 1984

Economic harmony goes hand-in-hand with a harmonious society. The recurring financial crises and currency debasements that blight monetary history not only affect our well-being, they also impact our wealth and personal freedom.

It is important to recognise the dramatic changes that have been taking place in the United States for more than a century. Only then can one begin to comprehend what is happening to the country. The political and economic framework designed and put into the Constitution is being insidiously dismantled. Americans are losing – and many will forcefully argue have already lost – what these wise and extraordinary men and women of colonial America so unselfishly fought for, achieved, and left for posterity. Their wisdom and guidance are being abandoned.

America used to be viewed as a melting pot of immigrants in the pursuit of happiness who arrived in the country seeking new opportunities. Individuals of varied and different backgrounds and cultures would learn a new language and heritage to recast themselves as Americans to share a common touchstone that set the country apart from the rest of the world. This shared and valued principle they embraced was each individual's acknowledgment and healthy respect for everyone else's rights. You and your neighbour might have diametrically opposed views on lifestyle, religion, and other topics and disagree on many judgements of value. But all was well, provided no one's rights were violated, which is the defining feature of a free society. The inalienable rights of life, liberty, and the pursuit of happiness, in which I include property and privacy, are sacrosanct and to be protected from interference, whether by individuals acting alone, as a mob, organised as a government, or any other armed force.

Everyone was free to hold their own opinions. You did not have to agree with your neighbour, nor did most care what their neighbour said or thought. Nor was there any government dictate outlining what was permissible to say or even think or how to live one's life or any attempt to control what an individual chose to do to their body, which is the only tangible thing over which each human being has absolute control and undeniable ownership. There was no concept of political correctness, nor should there be in a society of free people.

If no one's basic rights are violated, there is harmony, but that ideal situation is rapidly disappearing. It is being destroyed by the goal shared by all progressives and autocrats, which is to bend others to enforce on them whatever fanciful goal or whim the autocrat fancies.

The United States has changed from the Republic of confederated sovereign states which it once was, to what the framers of the Constitution abhorred, an overreaching monarchical-like consolidated national power. In the Republic they left, the federal government established a single monetary unit of account and a unified defence. The Constitution was designed to protect a common market between the states and the rule of law in relation to individual liberty and property rights. That was it. Nothing more and nothing less, and this limit on federal government power was the beauty of the framers' genius.

They understood the conflicts that arise when one group has the ability to impose its will on another group, which is known as the tyranny of the majority. They understood the animosity and alienation people sense when 50.1% of the voters impose their will on the 49.9% minority, so the Constitution has a carefully crafted political structure that mitigated this harmful outcome from an uncontrollable democracy.

The framers understood that the only thing upon which everyone throughout the sovereign states would agree is a common defence because there is strength in numbers, a rule of law maintained by an honest judiciary system, and that gold and silver are money. Only these three things are of benefit to everyone. Anything else provided by government or any restriction imposed by government can only benefit one group to the detriment of others, which is a divisive outcome that the framers took pains to avoid.

From Feudalism to Freedom to Fascism

> If America ever does seek Empire, and most nations do, then planned reforms in our domestic life will be abandoned, States Rights will be abolished – in order to impose a centralized government upon us for the purpose of internal repudiation of freedom, and adventures abroad. The American Dream will then die – on battlefields all over the world – and a nation conceived in liberty will destroy liberty for Americans and impose tyranny on subject nations.
>
> Attributed to American statesman George S. Boutwell (1818-1905).[92]

Thomas Jefferson observed that: 'A free people claim their rights, as derived from the laws of nature, and not as the gift of their chief magistrate.' This exceptional political leader also provided this clear message: 'Rightful liberty is unobstructed action according to our will within limits drawn around us by the equal rights of others. I do not add 'within the limits of the law' because law is often but the tyrant's will, and always so when it violates the rights of the individual.'

In other words, man-made law can be used harmfully as a mechanism by a tyrannical power, whether exercised by one person or a group of people banded together and organised as a government to control other people. As Martin Luther King, Jr. put it bluntly but clearly: 'We can never forget that everything Hitler did in Germany was "legal" and everything the Hungarian freedom fighters did in Hungary [in the 1956 revolution against Soviet Union supported tyranny] was "illegal".'

The tyrannical power of man-made law can control not only what you do, but also what you own. What one may possess is not necessarily what he or she thinks they own.

For example, today there is little ownership of land as the former colonists understood it. Few today have allodial title to the land they occupy. Nearly all land in America today is owned by the state in which the land is located, unless the land was purchased by the federal government as provided in the Constitution with 'the Consent of the Legislature of the State in which the Same shall be, for the Erection of Forts, Magazines, Arsenals, dock-Yards, and other needful Buildings.'

As an aside, it is important to note that a precise interpretation of the Constitution means that national parks are unconstitutional because the power to create parks was not specifically granted to the federal government. That may seem harsh, yet it is not because states are better placed to manage parkland in their territory, rather than some distant federal government, or alternatively, parks can be privatised. The important point is that rules are not made to be broken, and powers to act that are not delegated to the federal government are not to be assumed or taken. The Constitution contains the means by which it can be amended, if the states were to decide the federal government should own parks in their territory.

As victors over European feudalism in the War for Independence, Americans enjoyed absolute title of tax-free, unregulated land. With their allodial title to the land they owned, they were 'kings of their domain', in contrast to the serfs of Europe who occupied and worked a plot of land for the lord of the manor or the monarch who owned that land.

After obtaining freedom from their revolution, the rights of property owners in America were equal, whether the humblest log cabin or the most opulent mansion. With allodial title, owners of property could do whatever they chose, provided they adhered to natural law. For example, even with allodial title, an owner could not pollute a water course running through their property because it would harm those property owners downstream.

Today the occupiers of land and any buildings on it pay property taxes as tribute to the State for the 'privilege' granted to them by the State allowing them to live on the land and in the buildings on it. But it is not neo-feudalism.

It is fascism, a repugnant political ideology that only allows the pretence of ownership. The State allows you to occupy land provided you follow what it as the sole arbiter deems and proclaims to be the law. This observation is particularly relevant to money. The underlying truth to the matter is beautifully crafted in this observation by nineteenth century author Lysander Spooner:

> If any man's money can be taken by a so-called government, without his own personal consent, all his other rights are taken with it; for with his money the government can, and will, hire soldiers to stand over him, compel him to submit to its arbitrary will, and kill him if he resists.

Imagine the abuse of individual rights that is possible when government has the power to create currency through a central bank and then force the circulation of that currency through law it enforces with the threat of penalties or imprisonment. Actually, there is no need to imagine it because this abuse is manifest today in dozens of countries.

The District of Columbia is where big banks, corporations, and global elites exchange cash for influence and privilege at the expense of the public. It did not used to be that way. When President Andrew Jackson in 1832 vetoed the proposed recharter of the Second [Central] Bank of the United States, he said, 'It is to be regretted that the rich and powerful too often bend the acts of government to their own selfish purposes.' His veto honoured not only the spirit of the Constitution, but the letter of the law.

In his farewell speech to the nation in 1960 after serving two terms, President Dwight Eisenhower warned that 'we must guard against the acquisition of unwarranted influence, whether sought or unsought, by the military-industrial complex. The potential for the disastrous rise of misplaced power exists and will persist.' Given the decimation of the country's industrial base over the past six decades, excepting the arms industry, his warning should be redirected to the military/financial complex.

As has happened throughout history and is occurring often today, governments act with impunity and relentlessly attack any challenge to their power. From the all-powerful position it has usurped controlling the currency and the economy through its central bank, the State promulgates and enforces its man-made law to the benefit or detriment of individuals or groups of its choosing. The immoral State invariably uses its man-made law and countless regulations to repress, by force if necessary, the rights of any individual deemed by the State to be detrimental to it. In the words of Ayn Rand: 'There are two potential violators of man's rights: the criminals and the government.' She also argued: 'We are fast approaching the stage of the ultimate inversion: the stage where the government is free to do anything it pleases, while the citizens may act only by permission, which is the stage of the darkest periods of human history, the stage of rule by brute force.'

It is worth noting that Ayn Rand passed away in 1982, which leads to the question whether the inversion she envisioned has occurred. Many will claim that it has, particularly now in reaction to the restrictive Covid-19 public policy decisions by countries around the globe that have stripped basic rights from individuals. These include a person's right to work, the forced closure of privately owned businesses, and more recently, imposing a policy violating the right of assembly that some are calling 'medical apartheid' because it separates people by whether they have received Covid jabs or not. What is worse, with forced jabs statists are now attempting to control a person's body, which could reasonably be viewed as a violation of the sixth Nuremberg Principle, the moral code resulting from the trials of Nazi party members following the Second World War. The pandemic has been so successful to the nefarious agenda of statists, it can be expected they will continue using it to promulgate more man-made law to obtain greater control and erode or eliminate civil liberties.

Actions taken in the United States regarding the enforcement of man-made law are the continuation of a deliberate policy that can be traced back to the infamous Gold Clause Cases in the 1930s. Their outcome has led to centralized autocratic government that only allows the pretence of private property. It is, in other words, the political structure called fascism.

After the federal government under President Roosevelt confiscated the gold of U.S. citizens in 1933, there were several legal challenges in the courts claiming that the government acted unlawfully and contrary to the provisions of the Constitution, which is a view you may share with me and many others who have read what the Constitution says and understand its original intent. When these cases eventually reached the Supreme Court, it sided with the government. It was a huge victory for the progressives and autocrats of the Roosevelt administration, and it accelerated the changes already occurring from the beginning of the twentieth century that were insidiously altering a citizen's relationship to the federal government.

The matter upon which the Gold Clause Cases rested was the obligatory character of contracts entered into by the United States federal government. The basic principle was established soon after the federal government began operating, namely, that it was subject to the obligations written in the contract. It could not subsequently use government authority to alter the obligations it had agreed to in the contract. Writing to the Senate,

Alexander Hamilton, then Secretary of the U.S. Treasury in the administration of George Washington said:

> When a government enters into a contract with an individual, it deposes, as to the matter of the contract, its constitutional authority, and exchanges the character of legislator for that of a moral agent, with the same rights and obligations as an individual. Its promises may be justly considered as excepted out of its power to legislate unless in aid of them. It is in theory impossible to reconcile the idea of a promise which obliges, with the power to make a law which can vary the effect of it.

Hamilton's view was reconfirmed in the Sinking-Fund Cases in 1879, in which the Court unequivocally stated that the federal government must adhere to a contract's obligations:

> The United States are as much bound by their contracts as are individuals. If they repudiate their obligations, it is as much repudiation, with all the wrong and reproach that term implies, as it would be if the repudiator had been a State or a municipality or a citizen.

This legal precedence and moral guidance remained the law until the majority of the Supreme Court in 1935 claimed the exact opposite, so a vociferous opposition by the dissenting justices is understandable. Because of this case's importance, I quote here the opening paragraphs of the dissenters' brief to the Court's 5-to-4 decision but recommend reading the arguments of each party.[93]

> The enactments here challenged will bring about confiscation of property rights and repudiation of national obligations. Acquiescence in the decisions just announced is impossible; the circumstances demand statement of our views. 'To let oneself slide down the easy slope offered by the course of events and to dull one's mind against the extent of the danger, that is precisely to fail in one's obligation of responsibility.'
>
> Just men regard repudiation and spoliation of citizens by their sovereign with abhorrence; but we are asked to affirm that the Constitution has granted power to accomplish both. No definite delegation of such a power exists; and we cannot believe the farseeing framers, who labored with hope of establishing justice and securing the

> blessings of liberty, intended that the expected government should have authority to annihilate its own obligations and destroy the very rights which they were endeavoring to protect. Not only is there no permission for such actions; they are inhibited. And no plenitude of words can conform them to our charter.
>
> The Federal government is one of delegated and limited powers which derive from the Constitution. It can exercise only the powers granted to it. Powers claimed must be denied unless granted; and, as with other writings, the whole of the Constitution is for consideration when one seeks to ascertain the meaning of any part.'

The four dissenting justices could not be clearer. This Supreme Court decision was far-reaching because it overturned law based on centuries of Anglo-Saxon legal precedent and condoned the blatant dishonesty of government action. As occurred in 1694 with the acceptance of fractional reserve banking in the formation of the Bank of England, a government once again, when presented with two different courses of action, took the self-serving path by choosing expediency instead of honesty.

Going forward from the 1935 decision, any private right established by contract must give way to whatever the federal government deems to be public policy, and national security is always the excuse it gives. So to be consistent with this misguided Supreme Court decision, the federal government justifies its initiatives with the word 'war' as a preface, whether the War on Poverty, the War on Drugs, War on Terror, etc., all of which are supposedly undertaken in the name of national security. What goes unsaid is its war on the Bill of Rights and individual freedom.

To avoid doing harm and to act honestly, an individual, entity and even a government must fulfil the obligations of a contract. The words of Supreme Court justice Louis D. Brandeis provide a warning: 'Crime is contagious. If the government becomes a law-breaker, it breeds contempt for the law.' Yet, ironically, he sided with the majority of the Court that condoned the gold theft by the federal government, providing a prime example of influential leaders in the District of Columbia being detached from the polity and talking out of both sides of their mouth. In the aftermath of the Gold Clause Cases, Justice James McReynolds with his dissent to the Court's 5-to-4 decision declared that 'the Constitution as many of have understood it has gone.' The boundary within which federal power was to be limited had been pierced, and the Constitution is still gone today.

The Constitution is to an alarming extent a dead letter even though every political leader in the federal government takes an oath to support and defend it. They then hypocritically ignore or are oblivious to the wisdom of its framers and misinterpret both the spirit and the letter of what is written and what was intended, and generally what prevailed up to the 1930s.

Society is dependent upon the fulfilment of promises, but the federal government unfortunately broke its promise by confiscating private property, namely, gold, and then organised the justification of its reprehensible action with the outcome of the Gold Clause Cases. An honest and moral government does not revoke its contractual obligations and then claim it to be an acceptable action, much less one to be lauded by claiming justification in the name of national security and contending it acted in everyone's best interests. Instead, the moral alternative is that a government goes bankrupt and, like every other overleveraged debtor unable to settle its obligations, works out a scheme with its creditors.

What is even more reprehensible, the Gold Clause Cases disrupted the inalienable right of every individual to contract with another person or entity without government interference. But there is more.

The Gold Clause Cases not only disrupted the intended outcome of the contracting parties, they also turned asymmetrical relations between individuals and the federal government into a dictatorial, hierarchical one. They upended the principle in the previously described 'waterfall' of power flowing from the people to lower levels of authority, namely, to the states and then to the federal government. By defying logic, common law principles, the written word of the Constitution, and the framers' original intent, these Gold Clause Cases were used to strengthen the new legal system that began being built at the turn of the twentieth century by progressives and autocrats to ensure the federal government reigned supreme with the unbridled power of an absolute monarch.

The inalienable right to private contract is a basic principle of a lawful society. It is not specifically stated in the Bill of Rights. It obviously did not need to be included because it is a fundamental right that is well understood and accepted as a precept of law. It is on the same standing as 'innocent until proven guilty', which also does not appear in the Bill of Rights.

It is clear that the right of contract is sacrosanct from the fourth amendment that prevents the seizure of property and the seventh amendment that disputes are to be resolved 'according to the rules of the common law' for which there are several centuries of precedent. Only autocratic governments attempt to deny an individual's inalienable rights, fascistically seize private property, and ignore centuries of legal precedent.

Natural Law Principles

The fundamental building block of a free society is natural law. It is the basis of Anglo-Saxon common law that evolved over centuries. Natural law was the focal point of the Age of Enlightenment, and it rests on two fundamental principles:

- If you use it, you must pay for it, and
- Do no harm.

Both points are far-reaching. Together they are the underlying legal principles for an honest and moral society. Each point is worth examining.

The first is straightforward, which explains why so many toll bridges existed in the early days of the American Republic. Infrastructure was built by private enterprise, and the investors were compensated by the tolls charged. Before investing their capital, they would carefully examine the market to measure the potential for a new bridge, for example, and then decide whether its construction would be a wise investment. The government was not involved in the decision nor was any tax money used in the bridge construction or maintenance. The use of tax money to build and operate a toll-free bridge would be unfair to taxpaying people who had no need for the bridge and no intention of ever using it.

A modern example today would be a person living in a city centre with no car or even a driver's licence. It is not fair to use tax money paid by that person for, as an example, the interstate highway system. Nevertheless, the automobile industry encouraged the Eisenhower administration to build it. Auto manufacturers advised tongue in cheek that it needed to be built, not for their benefit, but rather, it was needed because of that old chestnut, national security.

Another example is free national health care, by which opinionated do-gooders and other 'world improvers' undermine society in two ways with their socialistic ideas imposed by government intervention. They belittle the individual by assuming that no one as they become an adult and set out in life is capable of deciding whether to pay for medical needs out of their pocket as they occur or by purchasing medical insurance from privately owned companies. Second, free national health care is not fair for people who live a healthy life and are expected to pay through taxes for the treatment of those people who make bad decisions and lead an unhealthy life. Government intervention, particularly when aimed at achieving socialistic ends, is harmful to society, which leads to the second principle of natural law.

The second principle of 'do no harm' is more profound than the first. It does not just apply to doctors and their Hippocratic oath. It relates to every possible human action, all of which have consequences. To act ethically by doing no harm, a person must do everything to which they have agreed, which is the basis of contract law. Further, they must not aggress against another person or their property because doing so would cause harm.

Harm is not always caused directly. It may be an indirect result that goes unseen and can occur even when there are good intentions. In other words, even a well-meaning do-gooder with the best of intentions can inadvertently cause harm.

I have always highly valued the timeless adage of Lao Tzu, the sixth-century BCE contemporary of Confucius: 'Give a man a fish and you feed him for a day. Teach him how to fish and you feed him for a lifetime.' Even a kind act of charity has consequences that can be harmful if the individual receiving the handout becomes dependent on it as has occurred with many healthy people receiving State aid, rather than working and contributing to society. Recent events in the United States provide an example. A labour shortage has developed because unemployment benefits are higher than wage rates.[94]

Freedom and liberty come from self-reliance. People dependent upon a government cheque are not free. The same holds true for people in a corporation, no matter how financially strong the company may be. A change of management could bring sweeping changes, including the loss of employment for many.

An honest analysis will reveal that government intervention of all sorts inevitably causes more harm than good because government interventionists cannot possibly know what is in the best interests of any individual, let alone the mass of a country's citizenry, which is the topic of Friedrich Hayek's famous speech when accepting the Nobel Prize, 'The Pretence of Knowledge'. Despite their claims to the contrary, governments are not as smart as the combined wisdom of the market, which means that government intervention and its socialistic aims are impractical, unworkable, and therefore harmful.

The Volstead Act, which banned alcoholic beverages in the United States, is illustrative here. The attempt to ban alcoholic beverages led to the formation of organised criminal syndicates to give consumers what they wanted, but what is worse, caused everyone who wanted a beer to become a lawbreaker.

Not only does government intervention operate contrary to basic principles of the market process, socialism is an abnormal, twisted ideology that ignores the reality of human nature. It is therefore logical as well as a matter of principle that every individual has a right to opt out of any nanny-state programme on the basis of informed consent and accept the consequences of their decision. Even government regulation intending to protect the consumer does not override the right of the consumer using informed consent to knowingly choose to opt out of any government scheme and thereby ignore government regulators of man-made law.

People will do what they want to do, and as long as they act consistently with natural law, there is no reason to make anyone a lawbreaker of unneeded man-made law and stop them in their pursuit of happiness. If a government or any wealthy individual or entity wants to change behaviour, it should be done through education, not prohibition. For example, as people learned about the ill effects of cigarettes, there has been a reduction in smoking. 'The overall lung cancer incidence is decreasing by approximately 2.2% to 2.3% per year.'[95]

The pursuit of happiness is a strong motivation in human nature. As occurred with the ban on alcohol, its prohibition bred contempt for the law, which diminishes social order. This occurs because if there is a demand, entrepreneurs will seek ways to fulfil it, even if sociopaths break all concepts of natural law to do it. Gangsterism flourished in the 1920s as a direct consequence of depriving people of alcohol.

The policy of 'No child left behind' is another example of the misguided nanny-state. It is not necessarily aimed at changing behaviour, but increasing government's involvement in child education, which is harmful. The parents of children, and not the State, should make all decisions about a child's well-being. 'No child left behind' is a slick slogan that appeals to the heart but is harmful if misinterpreted to imply that all children are equal. No two people are alike, but everyone should have equal opportunity.

Governments are tyrannical by nature, and the levers of tyranny being pulled by nationalist, socialist do-gooders and self-righteous world improvers are the worst. In the words of famed author and lay theologian C.S. Lewis:[96]

> Of all tyrannies, a tyranny sincerely exercised for the good of its victims may be the most oppressive. It would be better to live under robber barons than under omnipotent moral busybodies. The robber baron's cruelty may sometimes sleep, his cupidity may at some point be satiated; but those who torment us for our own good will torment us without end for they do so with the approval of their own conscience.

The role of a proper government is simply to make sure that in a just and peaceful way everyone's rights are equal and protected on a level playing field of equal opportunity, which more often than not is better served by private enterprise than any government. Even the judicial system could be privatised if the parties to a contract agree to use private courts, and many do. Private mediation and arbitration services are used frequently to settle disputes, and their success depends as it does just like any other business providing a service, on its track record and the resulting reputation of the mediator.

Success or failure of government is rarely measured, with the result that there is little accountability. Good or bad, governments remain in power. Even where they obviously fail when their national currency collapses, they usually start over with a new fiat currency replacing the one that failed. In that regard, America's experience is rare. After the collapse of the continental, the framers of the Constitution led the country in the correct direction with their decision to embed gold and silver coin as money in the Constitution. That outcome stands in marked contrast to the fascist path taken by Weimar Germany after the collapse of the Reichsmark.

Winston Churchill is credited with first saying 'Never let a good crisis go to waste.' While he may have said it with good intentions, it is now seen as an exploitive statement to advance a political agenda or reward the vested interests of those in control of the political process. The crisis of the Great Depression had a direct bearing to the Gold Clause Cases. That crisis was not wasted by statists and those with vested financial interests in the banking system.

The economic crisis was a direct result of the banking crisis caused by excessive debts from their overextension of loans made possible by the fraudulent practice of fractional reserves. Yet it was the gold standard that was given the blame for the economic crisis, and gold itself, which is constitutional money, was taken from the hands of U.S. citizens, just like Lenin had already done in the Soviet Union and Hitler and Mussolini were doing in Europe. Fascism was taking hold and gaining ground on both sides of the Atlantic. Those unknowledgeable about the true cause of the 1930s crisis blindly accepted what they were told by political leaders.

It is revealing that the Gold Clause Cases that eroded liberty rested on money, but not surprising given the inextricable link between money and liberty. These cases put the right to private contract under de facto control of the federal government, as is every other inalienable right. Government today has the power to declare illegal anything you want to do.

With that sobering observation, I return to these provocative words of Ayn Rand and the worrisome inversion of law and justice contemplated by her over four decades ago.

> When you see that in order to produce, you need to obtain permission from men who produce nothing; when you see that money is flowing to those who deal not in goods, but in favors; when you see that men get rich more easily by graft than by work, and your laws no longer protect you against them, but protect them against you... you may know that your society is doomed.

I am not so pessimistic and would express her conclusion differently by saying, 'Our society needs change.' The insight of investment manager and gold advocate Lawrence Lepard is appropriate here: 'Fix the money, fix the world.' Change needs to begin with the monetary system.

The American dream of ever-rising prosperity that enables each generation to live better than its predecessor has ended. That dream depended on gold's use as money, limited government, and a wholehearted respect for private property. To make this goal possible again, I would start by removing all the gold from central banks and distribute it by weight equally to the country's citizens, restoring gold to its rightful and historical role as money and currency upon which global commerce is based. I would then close every central bank and ban them, fractional reserve banking, and phantom purchasing power from civilised society forever.

Central Banking is a Barbarous Relic

> It is a sobering fact that the prominence of central banks in this century has coincided with a general tendency towards more inflation, not less. By and large, if the overriding objective is price stability, we did better with the nineteenth-century gold standard and passive central banks, with currency boards or even 'free banking'. The truly unique power of a central bank, after all, is the power to create money, and ultimately the power to create is the power to destroy.
>
> Paul Volcker[97]

In his *A Tract on Monetary Reform* in 1923, Keynes used the term 'barbarous relic' to disparage the gold standard, not gold itself, although since then gold has often been called a barbarous relic by voices unfriendly to it. It has been my long-held view that central banking is the real barbarous relic.[98] Given the dominant position of the United States since the end of the Second World War and the central role of the U.S. dollar in international trade and finance, my comments focus on the Federal Reserve, but apply to all central banks. To some extent they all impair individual liberty because of the essential nature of central banking and how these sycophantic arms of the government operate.

Central bankers meet behind closed doors that are a veritable iron-curtain that shield hidden secrets. When they emerge from a meeting, they tell you - sometimes weeks after the event - what they want you to hear. These half-truths are as destructive as a lie. Is there a place for such contempt of the polity in a society of free people?

Their defiance of the principle that free people should be in control of their government clearly illustrates why central banking is a barbaric relic. Money is power, and the egregious allocation of monetary power to central banks through their ability to conjure phantom purchasing power allows the undemocratic usurpation of political power to favour the anointed few. Rigging market prices and interest rates through their intervention has become the principal task of central banks. This market intervention is one of the reasons governments allow central banks to operate; it serves the aims of the all-powerful State. But central bankers cannot predict the future.

> In an interview, former Fed Chairman Alan Greenspan said government intervention can create moral hazard. 'Oh, I think so,' he said. While he declined to comment on current monetary policy, he mentioned 'too big to fail' as an example. Government actions almost inevitably have unintended consequences, he said. 'There were unintended consequences to almost every action I was involved in' as Fed chairman, said Mr. Greenspan, who himself cut interest rates to help stave off a bond- market crisis in 1998, and later was accused of helping inflate the stock bubble of the late 1990s. 'If we anticipated the unintended consequences that were going to happen we might have changed the policy,' he said, but he added that it is impossible to forecast all the consequences of government action. [99]

No one can predict the future, not even the chairman of the Federal Reserve, and it is inevitable that the things we do have unintended consequences. These are immutable laws of human existence. It therefore logically follows, why do we give central bankers any power to take action that affects economic activity? We instead need to rely on what guided humanity for millennia, individual free will and the spontaneity of free markets.

For more than 300 years, we have been using money substitutes, and the widespread and intense reliance upon them and phantom purchasing power is unprecedented. The resulting problems are readily apparent. National currencies often become worthless when banks fail, or when governments and their captive central banks pursue reckless policies that erode, and in some cases destroy, the value of the currency. What is more, money substitutes are costly to society because they are based upon promises and credit, which by their nature can be unreliable. Borrowers do default, which is a cost initially borne by banks and when it is beyond a bank's financial capacity, by the taxpayers who bail them out.

When left unrestricted to create an unlimited amount of currency through a central bank and then forcing its circulation through laws and penalties, a government is humankind's deadliest enemy. In the words of gold advocate Peter Schiff: 'Printing money is merely taxation in another form. Rather than robbing citizens of their money, government robs their money of its purchasing power.' Debasement of the currency is the vilest theft and evillest violation of property rights. By taking the purchasing power a person accumulates from his or her labour, governments and central banks are stealing the labourer's time on earth, which is the most precious asset of every living being.

Today, central banks pursue theft of purchasing power as public policy by targeting minimum inflation rates, and then propagandise that this theft of one's time through currency debasement is a beneficial practice. When government was moral, debasement of money was considered a crime against humanity. That explains why the U.S. Mint Act of 1792 required the perpetrator of debasement to 'be deemed guilty of felony, and shall suffer death.' That a minimum inflation rate has become public policy illustrates how far U.S. federal government has degenerated from the moral stance it once held and pursued.

Can the system be regulated so that it works well? History has the answer. Banks are the most heavily regulated institutions in the world, yet they continue to fail. So one can reasonably ask, does regulation ever work? Can we really expect government to control human behaviour and correct recurring excesses? Or is the present system that perpetuates fractional reserve banking and conjures up phantom purchasing power at will hopelessly flawed and should it be jettisoned and replaced?

Regulation is not the answer. It is an example of the widespread misunderstanding of how capitalism works, as well as the lack of recognition that purposeful capitalist activity of individuals restrained only by natural law is critical to the advancement of humanity by improving living standards. Regulation is just another example of the disappearance of self-reliance and the growing expectation of government to keep people safe and solve all problems. This unquestioning belief in government has become a substitute religion for many who seek dependency rather than confronting the challenges and opportunities of life.

Society advances from work, not government handouts nor pandering to the lowest common denominator and increasing the burden of the State. As Frederic Bastiat long ago observed: 'Government is the great fiction, through which everybody endeavours to live at the expense of everybody else.' Society advances from the accumulation of wealth, not from redistributing wealth from taxpayers to taxeaters. Yet as J.P. Morgan warned in 1907: 'There's nothing in this world, which will so violently distort a man's judgment more than the sight of his neighbour getting rich.' People who are not successful in a free society or just have an obstinate nature blame their situation on the freedom that is available to everyone and which others enjoy.

Capitalism is not inherently unstable, as some contend. It is fractional reserve banking that is unstable, and central bank control of a fiat currency that is far distanced from gold increases economic instability. It is therefore reasonable at this point to ask, why does the Federal Reserve or any central bank exist?

It is not for any of the stated reasons. The perennial inflation of the dollar and other fiat currencies make clear that the central banks do not control inflation. Nor do they create employment because capitalism and private industry does that, not central banks.

Every central bank in the world exists for one reason. It is to make sure that government deficits are funded so that politicians get all of the phantom purchasing power they want to spend. Writing in the *Financial Times*, the global strategist for Morgan Stanley, Ruchir Sharma, noted: 'It is also difficult to maintain the fiction that central banks are not part of big government. They are joined at the hip. Governments cannot run up deficits and debt so sharply without central bank support.'[100]

In the absence of any external discipline imposed on the central bank as existed naturally under the gold standard, the central bank will debase the currency by conjuring up of phantom purchasing power until the currency is no longer accepted in commerce and collapses. It then gets buried in the fiat currency graveyard alongside countless other fiat currencies already buried there, which is where today's fiat currencies are headed.

We often hear the adage: 'Don't fight city hall,' with city hall usually meant to be the Federal Reserve, but the concept is apposite to all central banks. When applied to financial markets, it is another way of saying swim with the tide. So when a central bank takes action to achieve some outcome it deems useful, investment decisions taken contrary to that outcome may not work out as you expect, or so the thinking goes.

While following the adage might be reasonable advice in the short-term, do not necessarily use it to make decisions for your portfolio that require a long-term horizon, and by long-term I do not mean multigenerational financial planning. There are any number of factors that limit the power of a central bank taking actions toward its goal with their market interventions, the result of which means the central bank may be unsuccessful in its pursuit. So long-term might be months, not necessarily years.

Fortunes have been made throughout history by betting against central banks. Alasdair Macleod has written extensively on the Banque Royale, established in France in 1717 by mountebank John Law, who before becoming a central banker escaped from London's Newgate Prison to avoid being hanged for murder. Anyone who owned the currency, the livre, issued by the bank he founded were wiped out when the purchasing power of the currency fell to zero.

This event had a profound effect on those who lived through the collapse, including Voltaire, who famously warned: 'Paper money eventually returns to its intrinsic value - zero.' Presumably Voltaire followed his own advice because he reportedly died a rich man.

More recently, George Soros made a fortune in 1992 by betting against the British pound. Headlines at the time of his success proclaimed that he broke the Bank of England. Like most positions taken against a central bank, it was a one-way bet, with little downside risk of loss against the enormous potential for upside gain. How is that possible?

The answer is based on two simple factors. The first is that the market is bigger than any central bank or even a cartel of them working in concert, so the market always wins - eventually. It has been that way throughout monetary history and will not change in the foreseeable future, unless the markets are closed by government decree to institute a totalitarian command economy.

The second reason is that central banks serve their own interests, which is to force some result contrary to normal market forces. They use their power to intervene in the market process in an attempt to force the market to bend to their will, normally to serve some political purpose. So central banks take positions that are on the wrong side of the trade by going against market forces, making a position taken contrary to central banks a one-way bet.

An example is the collapse of the central bank cartel known as the London Gold Pool, mentioned in Chapter 3, when foolhardy central banks followed the instruction of irrational politicians with gold substantially undervalued at $35 per ounce and the dollar grossly overvalued. A more recent example is the ongoing purchase of U.S. Treasury debt instruments by the Federal Reserve with newly created ledger currency that is keeping U.S. dollar interest rates artificially low. Its aim is to maintain the illusion that the U.S. federal government is solvent even though time is running out on that ongoing deception because of growing annual deficits, the $28 trillion national debt, and its contingent liabilities that total well in excess of $100 trillion.

Central banks no longer serve society; they serve themselves and their government handlers first and foremost and take whatever risks they deem necessary to achieve whatever goal they set for themselves. Their rhetoric hides their true intent in an attempt to cloak their actions. They are not custodians tasked to carefully manage and preserve a nation's currency. Their sole purpose is to enhance government power by usurping ever greater control over the economy. Central bankers understand that they have a uniquely privileged position, and they do whatever is required to protect it.

There is a quote attributed to Mayer Amschel Rothschild (1743-1812) that succinctly makes this point. Whether he actually said it or not is irrelevant to the truth of the underlying fundamental concept within the statement: 'Give me control of a nation's currency and I care not who makes its laws.' Because central banks have been granted the privilege of controlling currency and creating phantom purchasing power, they can command politicians.

So when you hear the adage to not fight city hall, think twice before acting. It is propaganda designed like all central bank propaganda to enhance their power. They receive that power by people acquiescing to the propaganda rather than accepting reality, namely, that central banks are not omnipotent nor are they serving your best interests.

Yet despite their obvious self-serving track record, central banks are esteemed and lauded by the mainstream media, which financially benefit from the immense revenues received from bank advertisements. For that reason, ignore those media reports that spoon out the opinions of the central banking elite because they are not serving your interests.

In contrast to the ongoing support and favourable treatment given to banks, gold has few defenders in the media, academia and government. Why is that? It is because gold is unfriendly to the aspirations for power sought by political leaders and their toadies in institutions receiving government grants.

Central banks operate without the constraint applied to every other legal entity. The liabilities of central banks, which are principally the currency they print, are not redeemable. Their profit and loss statement is hardly relevant because they can simply print currency to cover any loss, which is a feature that deems profit to be imaginary. Having little to constrain them, central banks ensure that governments need not compete with anyone for scarce resources.

There is a pressing need to re-balance the relationship between individuals and government. Doing so will provide the opportunity for everyone to live and act within a well-ordered society based on the spontaneity of individual free will rather than ham-fisted government edicts and controls put in place to keep inferior government issued fiat currency circulating in commerce. Put currency into hands of private sector, and let entrepreneurs compete to deliver the best product directly to the people without the favouritism regularly granted by government to special interests.

The Bank of England remained privately owned until it was nationalised in 1946 along with much of British industry by the socialist Labour government elected after the end of the Second World War. The Bank's raison d'être became totally directed to serving the interests of the government. Not surprisingly, the British pound collapsed in 1949 and began a long downtrend of debasement.

The debasement of the U.S. dollar began with the creation of the Federal Reserve in 1913. The loss of the dollar's purchasing power is apparent when comparing its present rate of exchange of an ounce of gold to the $20.67 per ounce rate prevailing back then. Gold has not become more expensive by becoming more useful or rarer today than a century ago. Rather, the dollar is just a mere shadow of its previous constitutional self. Central banking - and the Federal Reserve in particular - made that hollowing out of the dollar possible.

Central banking is a barbarous relic. It is a practice that has outlived its usefulness and become abusive. Central banks are harmful to society because their market interventions and debasement of currency erode social relationships by disrupting economic calculation. They steal the time labourers spend working to acquire earned purchasing power and discourage the savings that are essential to advancing standards of living in our capitalist economy. These conclusions are clear lessons from history, as are the implications for liberty.

There is too much power in the hands of government when it has control over the issuance of currency. It overthrows the existing order in our society as Lenin warned, which is what he sought to achieve from this overriding and unavoidable result. Central banking is more than a threat to liberty; it has become a real and present danger.

11. The Theory of Natural Money

Although gold and silver are not by nature money,
money is by nature gold and silver.

Karl Marx

It is ironic that I quote Marx to begin this submission on a Theory of Natural Money. Few have done as much as him to damage society and obstruct liberty. His writings provided an excuse for autocrats to usurp power from people being misled by spurious ideas and lured by unrealistic promises.

Marx may not have intended that outcome, but his misguided thinking provided the theoretical foundation for cunning statists using his guileful ideas to claim the moral high ground by asserting they will 'improve' society. In reality, all these misconceived ideas in the hands of autocrats have done is impede the pursuit of happiness for countless millions. It is well to remember famed newspaper editor H.L. Mencken's warning about do-gooders and the demagogic autocrats that cling to unnatural reforms that are unrealistic and incompatible with a free society: 'The urge to save humanity is almost always only a false-face for the urge to rule it. Power is what all messiahs really seek: not the chance to serve.'

Marx either did not understand or deceitfully chose to ignore human nature and the spontaneous interaction of people upon which civilisation advances, what we call a free market. It is comprised of people with an innate ability to choose and an inalienable right to possess private property, with each individual acting in their own pursuit of happiness while being led by an invisible hand that achieves mutually beneficial outcomes of the transactions in a free market, assuming no force and fraud. All parties to a completed transaction are better off, which explains why each chose voluntarily to enter into and complete it. The completed transaction improves each individual's situation. Marx failed to grasp these basic concepts that underpin civilisation as well as this time-honoured advice of great consequence by Ludwig von Mises: 'If history could teach us anything, it would be that private property is inextricably linked with civilization.'

There is, however, some meaningful insight in Marx's observation about money, which explains why I reference it. The insight is not by him, but by Ferdinando Galiani, who wrote *On Money* in 1751 and other similar works that have come down through the ages. Marx was simply drawing on what was at the time universally understood, that the natural elements of gold and silver became money by human choice.

This widespread acceptance of what had been intuitively obvious probably explains why a Theory of Natural Money as expounded herein has not, to my knowledge, been previously developed. Everyone knew and willingly accepted that money is by nature gold or silver as J.P. Morgan told Congress and anyone else willing to listen in 1912. 'Money is gold, and nothing else.' No one doubted or questioned his statement.

Sadly, that knowledge about the true nature of money was eroded during the twentieth century. It has now in the main been lost as statism propagandists gained adherents by disseminating through the media, academia, and school textbooks a message that defies natural money principles. 'The younger generations have never been taught how to think. Instead, they are taught what to think.'[101] Few today understand money, and that by nature and logic money is gold.

The Media That Convey Purchasing Power

People work to earn the purchasing power that enables them to buy what they need or want. To use their purchasing power in the market process, it must be conveyed by a medium.

At present, purchasing power can be conveyed by three different media, namely, ledger currency, cryptocurrencies, and a tangible asset, namely, money itself circulating as currency. They are the means of payment used to satisfy the obligation to the worker who earned purchasing power from his or her labour. The worker can accept ledger currency, cryptos in some cases, and in theory if not in practice, the preferred form of money, gold.

Because purchasing power can be conveyed in different ways, people should be able to choose which of the three media to accept in payment. If one does not have a choice of currency to receive in compensation for their labour, one is not free, which is presently the situation in most of the world. Statists disagree. Their argument is that one can take the ledger currency received in payment and use it to buy gold or cryptos, but that misses the important point about whether one is free to choose. This intermediate step to receive gold through ledger currency is not the same as receiving gold directly, even when ignoring the costs and payment risks associated with exchanging ledger currency into gold.

Referring to the United States Gold Reserve Act of 1934 and other countries with similar legislation, no one is free where the purpose of the law is 'to regulate dealings in gold and...bring gold transactions permanently under the supervision of the federal government.' Not only does government supervision stifle freedom, this man-made law is also a violation of the inalienable right to privacy, which is a moral entitlement that some cryptos aim to protect through the confidentiality they offer.

A high degree of protection of one's privacy is possible with gold. A gold coin in storage or circulating from hand-to-hand in commerce is private. Privacy is not available with ledger currencies, which is the currency of autocrats because it enables the control over people that autocrats and other sociopaths seek.

The privacy one can or cannot attain from these three media is not their only stark difference. These three media that convey purchasing power have contrasting essential natures, resulting in varying risks to the reliability and safety of the purchasing power that each store. They also come into existence differently, but all three rely on one fundamental criterion to succeed – trustworthiness.

Artificially Expanding Purchasing Power

The quantity of purchasing power in the present currency and banking system expands in two ways, honestly or fraudulently. It can be increased by honest work with the application of labour, capital and time, adding value to create a marketable good or service, the result of which is earned purchasing power (EPP) created in a natural and beneficial way. An owner of EPP can spend or save it for the future.

If the owner chooses to save their EPP and then lend it or deposit it in a bank, they can earn interest income. Someone can then borrow the EPP lent or deposited in a bank, and the owner of that EPP is compensated for deferring their consumption to the future.

The fraudulent alternative occurs when a bank conjures 'out of thin air' units of phantom purchasing power (PPP). Assume that the bank has loaned all the EPP deposited with it, but a customer still wants to borrow.

The bank has a dilemma with two honest options or a third dishonest possibility.

The first of the honest alternatives is seeking more EPP by borrowing it from other banks who have it, or the bank can try attracting more customers to deposit EPP with it by offering higher interest rates than its competitors. If the bank successfully obtains EPP either way, the bank can lend the EPP to its customer who wishes to borrow.

The second honest alternative is what banks did before the formation of the Bank of England and the institutionalisation of fractional reserves and PPP. It said 'no' to its customer who wished to borrow, telling them that the bank did not have any money available to lend at that moment.

Then there is the third alternative, which is dishonest. Governments have made it legal, but it is fraudulent. The bank can go 'naked' and lend what it does not have. The fraud occurs because of deception, namely, a unit of PPP looks like a unit of EPP when conveyed by the same currency. It is fraud because the bank seeks financial gain from the deception by making the loan instead of advising the borrower that it has no money to lend. It is deceitful because the bookkeeping that gives rise to PPP is essentially and fundamentally different from the way EPP is created. PPP is the result of skilful deception, whereas EPP is created by work, namely, the application of capital, labour, and time.

Given the risk and deceit it entails, is there a net benefit to the economy and society from fractional reserves? More to the point, is fractional reserve banking necessary?

Loans made by banks can increase sound economic activity if used wisely for investment, and not consumption, but a positive result that bolsters economic activity is difficult to achieve when the conjuring of PPP is allowed because of the distortion to economic calculation that occurs. This debasement of purchasing power from fractional reserve banking makes the cost of capital appear cheap. What is more, this debasement negatively impacts the entire M3 of the national currency and therefore every individual who holds it, which outweighs any possible benefit that could arise from loans made with PPP. An even worse outcome is banks issuing the PPP to the government, which uses it to enhance its power and impair individual liberty.

The benefit from loans used for sound purposes to enhance economic activity can be generated without fractional reserve banking. EPP that is saved can be loaned, which is the way it used to work before the Bank of England was created.

More importantly, without fractional reserve banking the cost of borrowing will once again reflect the true cost of capital, which is an essential component to achieving environmental, social and governance (ESG) goals and the natural order. Only a free market and natural money produce the true cost of capital that can wisely govern humankind's use of nature's limited resources to prevent reckless overconsumption and environmental degradation. The use of natural money provides the means to achieve a pristine natural environment.

Components of the Exter Inverted Pyramid

Civilisation began and continues to develop with purposeful human action, namely, the work undertaken to improve one's situation. A worker expects compensation for their effort, and to receive purchasing power when their work is expended for others. Purchasing power is transferred from the payer the moment the worker accepts a payment in exchange for their labour, regardless of whether that worker's effort was expended manually or mentally. Today the labourer's payment is typically measured in units of national currency, but gold and cryptocurrency can also be used to store and transfer purchasing power.

The Exter Inverted Pyramid in Figure 18 illustrates the purchasing power that is its core component. The pyramid itself is a visual representation that encompasses all the purchasing power that exists, both earned and phantom purchasing power. Their aggregated purchasing power is represented by the different currencies being used to convey it as well as the different components upon which the trust in them is based - gold, maths, and debt.

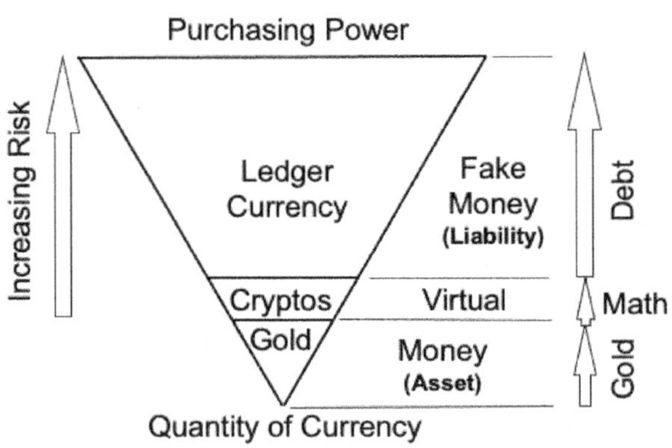

Figure 18 – Money & Fake Money

Each area on the pyramid is not meant to portray the exact amount of purchasing power conveyed by each currency. Rather, the three areas are drawn only for illustrative purposes to provide an indication of relative amounts, namely, that the quantity of purchasing power being stored as ledger currency far exceeds the quantity of that being stored by either gold or cryptos.

Figure 18 also shows the source from where the value of the currency derives, namely, mined gold, complex maths, and, for ledger currencies, the debt of borrowers on bank balance sheets. These three types of currency are drawn within the Exter Inverted Pyramid to reflect the increased risk to the holders of the currencies that are higher up the pyramid. The further away from gold, the higher the risk.

The term 'fiduciary currency' is often used to emphasise that the value of ledger currency relies solely on trust, which is because the currency has no inherent value. Apologists for the banking system like to use this term, thinking that it gives ledger currency a cachet to convey some semblance of respectability in the hope of making ledger currency and the phantom purchasing power it engenders appear and sound acceptable. Let us instead call it what it really is, fake money, which is its label in Figure 18.

The pyramid represents the total quantity of purchasing power that exists and is available for spending by the global workforce. Changing the size of the currency unit being used to measure purchasing power or increasing the number of units does not change the accumulated quantity of purchasing power. They do not increase the size of the pyramid.

As an example, when gold's exchange rate against the dollar rises, purchasing power simply moves from dollars to gold, with no new purchasing power being created. The gold owner has more purchasing power, and the dollar owner has less than before. The purchasing power has simply moved from one currency to another. The size of the pyramid only increases when new purchasing power is created.

The total amount of earned purchasing power derives from labour purposefully employed in the production of a marketable product, not from central banks increasing the quantity of currency through their 'quantitative easing' programmes. The larger the labour force as world population grows, the larger will be the quantity of EPP being stored and held ready for spending or investing.

The amount of purchasing power in the pyramid grows over time with increases in output from the labour force, but also when phantom purchasing power is conjured up by banks. It is therefore useful to calculate the amount of earned and phantom purchasing power, which can then be used to measure the vulnerability to the financial system from inferior ledger currency. These two different amounts also illustrate the cumulative impact of the Cantillon Effect and the extent to which PPP has caused gold to become undervalued.

Global Purchasing Power

Using the U.S. dollar as the standard of measure, Figure 19 is my estimate of total global purchasing power as of June 30, 2021. The aggregation of M3 for each of the three currency media is $121 trillion.

Figure 19 - Global Purchasing Power

June 30, 2021 (trillions of U.S. dollars)		
Gold	$ 10.47	8.6%
Cryptocurrencies	$ 1.30	1.1%
Ledger Currencies	$ 109.41	90.3%
Total	**$ 121.18**	**100.0%**

The M3 calculations are as follows:

- Gold - 182,200 tonnes in Appendix B as of December 2020, plus 1,600 tonnes estimated production for six months in 2021 is 183,800 tonnes of M3, times $1,771 per ounce, which is gold's rate of exchange to the dollar on June 30, 2021.
- Cryptos - There are hundreds of cryptos, but most of them are irrelevant. I aggregated the market cap of the largest fifty cryptos as of June 30, 2021, as reported by CoinMarketCap.com.
- Ledger currencies - M3 is not available for all national currencies. As of June 30, 2021, M3 for the U.S. dollar is $26.4 trillion, and the euro is $22.1 trillion. China M2 is $35.8 trillion, and I have estimated M3 for the rest of the world as $25 trillion, for a total of $109.4 trillion.

From these estimates, there is 10.5 times ($109.41/$10.47 trillion) more purchasing power in ledger currencies than gold. I also estimate that there is 84.2 times ($109.41/$1.30 trillion) more purchasing power in ledger currencies than cryptos. Both estimates highlight the relative extent to which ledger currency dominates our modern economy.

From these estimates of each type of currency, it is possible to put together a subjective measure of earned and phantom purchasing power. The latter comes from banks and their ledger currency. For this analysis, I include cryptos in the phantom purchasing power category because they are not a tangible asset, which means they do not have any inherent value even though they have economic value for use as a currency.

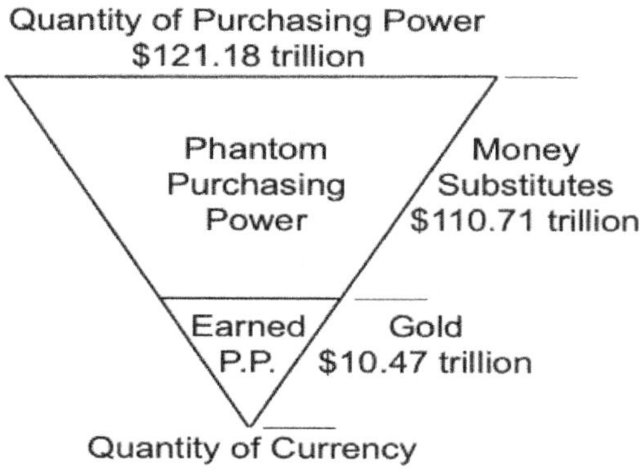

Figure 20 – Exter Inverted Pyramid of Global Purchasing Power

The total quantity of phantom purchasing power is $110.71 trillion ($109.41 plus $1.3 trillion). Therefore, 91.4% of the total $121.18 trillion of global purchasing power is based on the debt of borrowers recorded in bank balance sheets or based on complex maths. This phantom purchasing power circulating as money substitutes is vulnerable because neither ledger currencies nor cryptos have inherent value to fall back on if their economic value as currency were to disappear because of government action, debt repudiation, breaking the crypto math formula, or other disruptive events, including those that cannot today be imagined.

In a banking, economic, or currency crisis, gold's rate of exchange rises. Demand for physical gold increases as people seek safety and flee currencies conveying phantom purchasing power. In some countries, Weimar Germany being the quintessential example, phantom purchasing power completely disappears as the currency collapses. Crises in other countries occurred with a partial destruction of phantom purchasing power. Assuming a twenty percent decline in Figure 20, phantom purchasing power declines to $87.5 trillion. Further assuming total purchasing power remains unchanged at $121 trillion, the amount of purchasing power conveyed by gold increases to $33.7 trillion, which mathematically leads to more than a trebling in gold's rate of exchange to $5,695 per ounce with gold conveying 27.8% of total global purchasing power.

In a crisis total purchasing power typically declines, as occurred in the Great Depression. When banks collapsed back then, a bankrupt bank's depositors lost much, and in some cases all, of their purchasing power. The phantom purchasing power the bank had created returned to from where it came – 'thin air'.

As an example, assume in a crisis total purchasing power declines by twenty percent to $96.9 trillion. Further assume that because of a flight to safety causing a drop in demand for ledger currency, the demand for gold increases, resulting in a $3,000 rate of exchange.[102] Therefore, the value of gold M3 increases to $17.7 trillion, which is 18.3% of the new total global purchasing power. This example mathematically illustrates how gold's rate of exchange rises in a deflationary collapse of global purchasing power.

There is one more example worth pondering. It is the outcome that governments and central banks dread but cannot prevent from happening. It is the Weimar Germany scenario in which fiat currencies around the world collapse, and global purchasing power is conveyed only by gold and cryptocurrencies. Ledger currencies are totally discredited, ending the Bank of England currency model that has prevailed for over three centuries. It is jettisoned, just like other societal models have been jettisoned when they became abusive.

In Figure 19, gold and cryptos are 9.7% of global purchasing power, which will increase about 10-fold if ledger currencies totally collapse. In this scenario, gold and cryptos no longer have a rate of exchange to national currencies, which will cease to exist. Gold and cryptos will have a rate of exchange to each other, unless at some future point cryptos are no longer needed and gold becomes everyone's money and currency.

The future is unknowable, so these hypothetical examples should not be taken as forecasts. Rather, they simply offer the means to calculate possible outcomes for global purchasing power when the next financial crisis occurs, which is an inevitable outcome from reliance on fractional reserve banking and phantom purchasing power.

Saving or Investing Purchasing Power

Some individuals choose to build financial capital by accumulating purchasing power. They generate a surplus by producing more than they need for their immediate spending needs and accumulate the residual purchasing power. This capital is initially stored as savings for use in the future when its owner is ready to spend it to buy a good or service or to make an investment.

Capital is built over time by forgoing consumption now to have the ability to consume at a later date, but as already noted, possessing something in the future is less valuable than possessing it today. Therefore, to forgo present consumption and to accept the risks concomitant with saving or investing accumulated capital, it is reasonable to expect compensation.

To earn the income that potentially can be generated by one's capital, the two alternatives of saving or investing are fundamentally different. One uses money to make an investment, whereas saving is the process of accumulating money itself.

They are also different in another way. An investment is considered to be a riskier way of generating income on one's capital than placing it in a bank as savings. While that idea is generally true historically, it is not true where a national currency is being severely debased. Purchasing power used wisely to acquire tangible assets can be a safer alternative than saving a national currency being debased.

Today, artificially low interest rates make savings of fiat currency a losing proposition. The saver incurs the loss of purchasing power from currency debasement and is not being sufficiently compensated for deferring their consumption to the future. Additionally, many banks are no longer the safe institutions they once were, particularly those with exposure to derivatives and other risky assets. These banks put one's capital at risk.

Prior to the fiat currency era in which we live, saving money was the principle means by which people prudently accumulated capital for retirement, to purchase an expensive item beyond one's immediate resources, or just to be ready for a 'rainy day'. The time-honoured practice of preparing for an uncertain future by accumulating savings in a national currency has been disrupted by increasing government control over the currency creation process, the global adoption of fiat currency, and several decades of ongoing currency debasement. Savers of national currency have learned that perennial rises in the cost of living exceed the interest income earned on their fiat currency savings, particularly in the current environment of near-zero interest rates forced by central banks.

So to prepare for the future, savers have been forced to adjust their ways. The only practical alternative to save purchasing power in a fiat currency world is to accumulate gold. While gold may not generate any income unless loaned to earn interest income, which introduces counterparty risk, Figure 1 shows that gold preserves purchasing power. Saving gold provides a saver with assurance that their purchasing power in the future will be similar to what it is the moment it is saved, which leads to another important point. As illustrated in Figure 18, gold is only one of the three media in which purchasing power is stored and conveyed, and their quality and reliability vary.

Quality and Reliability of Purchasing Power Media

Even though earned purchasing power (EPP) is fundamentally different from phantom purchasing power (PPP), they appear identical by the media that convey them. Nevertheless, they are not identical for two reasons relating to each purchasing power's quality and reliability.

First, the media in which it is stored are inherently different, as illustrated in Figure 18. Each medium has different levels of risk, with tangible assets, like a gold or silver coin in one's hand being the only medium that avoids counterparty risk. These differing levels of risk mean that purchasing power also varies in reliability, the latter of which is usually called its liquidity. In other words, liquidity measures whether the purchasing power is available when you need it, or whether its availability is contingent because it is dependent on factors outside the owner's control that could prevent its use.

Second, compare how the different media come into existence. Gold is produced by the application of labour and capital over time, the ingredients that create wealth. Gold requires work to discover an economically viable ore body, then more work to design and build a mine, and still more work to begin mining, refining, fabricating, and distributing the gold it produces.

Mined gold is a result of the same factors of production as other finished goods and services. One or more entrepreneurs invest time, effort, and capital into exploring for and then extracting gold. The capital of an artisanal miner in Zimbabwe may only be a shovel to move dirt or a pan to sluice gold from a streambed, while the invested capital of a multinational corporation with thousands of workers may amount to many millions. Regardless of their size, all miners spend time, effort, and capital in anticipation of finding and then creating EPP by extracting from the earth this economic good called 'money', of which gold is the preferred form. It is honest work for the lone artisan and the many thousands employed in the same endeavour by a multi-national mining company.

In contrast to gold, PPP does not arise from the three factors that govern the production of money and all other goods and services. Instead of being created by honest work, it is based on debt promising in effect to deliver purchasing power in the future. Any repayment intended for the future introduces risks not found in gold and cryptocurrencies.

PPP does not emanate from the creation of wealth. A person, company or government borrows an amount of currency by signing a promissory note. The bank then increases its assets and liabilities simultaneously by entering a credit to the borrower's account and a debit to its loan portfolio. The bank has created PPP 'out of thin air' that is conveyed by ledger currency. There is some time, effort, and capital involved, but the amount expended is much less than that of an artisanal gold miner and inconsequential when compared to a multi-national gold miner.

A banker making a loan requires more thought than a central banker alchemising government debt instruments to create PPP by printing banknotes, but the amount of work expended is again minimal compared to actual gold mining. The promise on which ledger currency is based is made by the borrower for work yet to be expended from which it is hoped that value will be created, which then in the future will - if all goes well - be sufficient to repay the debt. The promise of a government borrower is based on how much tax can be taken in the future from producers of goods and services.

PPP is just a promise entered into a balance sheet, with minimal labour and a questionable future about repayment of the debts on which it is based. There is a stark difference between the promise of work not yet undertaken by the borrower and the promise of taxes not yet taken by the government when compared to the completed work that produced mined gold. This difference is important to the safety of one's purchasing power but also introduces an issue of fairness beyond that of the Cantillon Effect, which readers will recall highlights the advantage one gains by spending newly created currency before prices of goods and services in that currency rise from the currency's debasement.

An individual who works to earn purchasing power is at an unfair disadvantage to the government that borrows PPP created 'out of thin air' without labour. Purchasing power earned by honest work is different than purchasing power created by bank alchemy. What is worse, by debasing the purchasing power one earns from work, bank alchemy, fractional reserve banking, and fake money are stealing that worker's most precious and limited resource, his or her time spent to produce their EPP.

It is true that gold miners get to spend the newly mined gold first at maximum purchasing power, but it is EPP. There are no adverse effects or an unfair impact because the growth of gold M3 approximates population growth so supply and demand for gold remain close to a natural balance, which explains why gold preserves purchasing power as illustrated in Figure 1. For that reason, existing holders of gold do not incur any disadvantage from new mine production. Any fluctuations in EPP arise from normal supply/demand changes to be expected in a world where nothing is static.

Because ledger currency is a liability of a bank, either banknotes issued by a central bank or deposits held within the banking network, all ledger currency is owned by banks and owed to its depositors and holders of banknotes. It has value because the loans owed to the bank by borrowing customers purportedly have value. Given that banks have different borrowing customers, it therefore follows that dollars on deposit in Bank A have different risks from dollars on deposit in Bank B. Dollars are fundamentally different because the assets that back them and the banks that hold them as ledger currency are different.

Uncertainties about the value of bank assets, which in turn impact the liquidity of a bank's ledger currency and its availability for spending by the bank's customers when needed, highlights a major risk of ledger currency. Ledger currency has risks that one does not have with gold or cryptocurrencies. Additionally, ledger currency does not meet all four functions required for something to be considered as money, nor do cryptos, given that they are not a tangible asset.

Additionally, the essential nature of these media of storing and conveying purchasing power are fundamentally different. If a bank's borrower defaults, the question becomes whether the bank has sufficient capital to repay its debt by returning your deposit to you, which directly impacts the liquidity of your purchasing power. Gold does not default.

Purchasing power held in a bank is contingent upon factors outside of your control, and these risks diminish the reliability of your purchasing power. It may not be available for your use when you need it. The bank must have the financial capacity to repay its debt to you when you ask to spend that purchasing power. There must also be a willingness by the bank and the government that licenses its operation to make available your purchasing power when you choose to spend it.

There have been numerous 'bank holidays' which prevented customers from accessing their purchasing power. Even without a forced bank closure, customers today in many countries have a difficult time converting their bank deposit into banknotes. ATM machines have daily withdrawal limits, and large withdrawals of banknotes at a teller window may require advance notification to the bank and/or the completion of documents requested by the bank, including what you intend to do with their banknotes if they give them to you.

This ability to convert from bank deposits into banknotes highlights a vulnerability of ledger currency, which raises questions about the true motivation of the so-called 'war on cash' that governments are waging. Is the war intended to stop drug trafficking? Prevent individuals from transacting in private with banknotes? Quash privacy on commercial activity for which sales taxes are levied to ensure collection by the government with access to the deposit currency of the payer and payee and the details of their transaction? Stop bank depositors from asking for banknotes during a run on a bank?

These and other questions relate to the core issue being addressed. Namely, that no one is free when their purchasing power is under the control of government or banks, which are licenced government agents. Banks will always comply with government requests so that their licence to operate is not revoked, regardless of whether those requests trample one's rights.

There is a related risk that is often overlooked. The dollar circulating as currency is a liability of the Federal Reserve, which is owned by banks. It is therefore a 'Federal Reserve dollar', or F$, to distinguish it from a constitutional dollar, or C$, which is 11.368 grains of fine gold. These two types of dollars are fundamentally different and distinguishing between them helps to further delineate money from fake money.

The F$ is not an obligation of the U.S. Treasury. Therefore, the references in this book to the dollar are the F$, not the U.S. Treasury dollar, which legally is the C$ coined in gold. If the U.S. government in a future crisis allows the F$ to collapse to zero like its predecessor currency, the continental, the U.S. government's promise to pay purchasing power equal to $28 trillion of debt and over $100 trillion of other contingent liabilities drops to zero, which is a possible outcome that needs to be considered by anyone reliant upon F$ purchasing power now or in the future.

In other words, the ultimate bank bailout – the bailout of the Federal Reserve – may not occur. To save itself and remain solvent in a future currency, economic, or financial crisis, the federal government as the F$'s biggest debtor may decide not to bailout its central bank. It would be following the policy it established in the 1930s to change the law and its contracted obligations to suit its own ends, regardless of whether there exists at the time a genuine national security threat from a foreign power.

One remaining point requires explanation so readers know that I am not opposed to debt, which can be beneficial when properly used to enhance wealth creation through new production. My criticism is directed solely toward a banking and currency system based upon the dishonest practices of PPP, fake money, and fractional reserve banking, for which I have already provided more than a brief glimmer of their ignominious history since their adoption by the Bank of England at its founding and subsequent global institutionalisation. They are dishonest practices that violate natural law. PPP, fake money, and fractional reserve banking have become weapons used by governments and their central banks to suppress individual liberty and impede the pursuit of happiness of countless millions.

The Quantity of Currency

Although Figure 18 does not present an exact representation of the quantity of each currency, it does illustrate that the quantity of purchasing power conveyed by ledger currency dwarfs the quantity conveyed by gold. The extent of this imbalance, looking just at Federal Reserve dollars for example, can be measured using the Monetary Balance Sheet in Chapter 8 and the Fear Index of the F$, which is calculated at 1.97%. The present Fear Index means that the quantity of F$ ledger currency is 50.8 times larger than the F$ quantity of gold at their exchange rate prevailing on 31 December 2020, compared to the 2.5 times guideline recommended by Newton.

Figure 21 shows that F$ M2[108] recently increased at 25% per annum, which is a record high and nearly double the 13% highest annual growth rate set during the inflationary 1970s. A harmful reality of fractional reserve banking is that ledger currency and the PPP it generates can increase at abnormal rates, as is presently occurring with F$s.

Figure 21 – F$ M2 Annual Growth Rate (Monthly)

Source: Federal Reserve Bank of St. Louis

These abnormal increases distort the natural supply/demand relationships of the market process and make accurate economic calculation difficult. There is also the Cantillon Effect to consider. Whoever gets the PPP first benefits the most, and an inferior currency itself puts honest work at a disadvantage when purchasing power is created by bank alchemy. Meanwhile dishonest elected representatives ask themselves why tax people today and potentially hurt their own election prospects when they can force the central bank to create ledger currency?

The Federal Reserve prints F$ banknotes and facilitates the creation of F$ deposit currency within the banking system. The banks conjure up F$s when making loans to its borrowing customers. The federal government and other borrowers benefit the most from the maximum purchasing power of the newly created PPP to spend for consumption or buy assets before their price rises. An example is the large firms buying real estate. On 10 June 2021, Bloomberg headlined that 'Real Estate Prices Are Soaring' followed two days later by a report on Fox News that 'investment firms [are] "killing the dream" of home ownership', given their aim to spend their accumulated F$s and those they may be borrowing to purchase tangible assets.

Companies with access to bank loans are in effect stealing purchasing power from those people who earned it through their labour and do not have access to bank lending or who deliberately choose not to borrow. It takes time for the market to sense that purchasing power is being debased by inflating the currency, but this time lag shortens as people's perceptions about rising prices changes.

The debasement of ledger currency arising from abnormal increases in its quantity made possible by fractional reserve banking can be illustrated with an example. Assume that the quantity of F$s doubles overnight. While this change is occurring, there is no increase in real wealth. In other words, in the instant that the quantity of F$s doubles, there is no simultaneous increase in the quantity of goods and services available for purchase. As a result, there is now twice the quantity of F$s to purchase the same goods and services available for purchase before doubling the quantity of F$ currency. This increase in the quantity of F$ currency is inflationary, and it does not take too long for the price of goods and services to rise rapidly in response to all the newly issued PPP. But a borrower of F$s can spend that PPP before market prices adjust to the debasement that has occurred.

One could argue that the quantity of F$ currency is not doubling at present, and they would be correct. But without discipline being imposed on bank alchemy, the quantity of F$ currency could double and has more than doubled in the dozens of countries where their ledger currency collapsed, including the American continental. Worryingly, current F$ M2 growth is likely to increase given the growth in the quantity of federal government debt being alchemised into F$ fake money by the U.S. banking system, as illustrated in Figure 16.

These F$ statistics, the adverse impact from the Cantillon Effect, and purchasing power created from debt instead of honest work lead to the crucial question: are people better off because of this growth in fake money? Here is how one writer answered it in 1839 when the circulating ledger currency was predominately banknotes.

> A general rise takes place from the expansion of the currency, owing to the abundance of the paper which has been thrown amongst the community by the original borrowers from the banks. This rise goes on with every new emission of paper, and appearing to the public, which is not acquainted with the internal operations of banks, like an increase in value, the spirit of speculation is excited amongst all classes of the community, and purchases are made for no other reason than that the buyers suppose they can sell the next day at a profit. Industrious persons abandon productive employments to pursue speculation, which, however profitable it may be to the successful operator, does not at all add to the wealth of the community, seeing that what is gained by one man is lost by another.

Condy Raguet, *A Treatise on Banking and Currency*, 1839

When the Bank of England was founded in 1694, mercantilism was considered to be wise economic policy. It has since been discredited by countless writers, including for example Murray Rothbard who defined it as 'a system of statism which employed economic fallacy to build up a structure of imperial state power, as well as special subsidy and monopolistic privilege to individuals or groups favored by the state.'[104]

One of those economic fallacies is that a nation becomes wealthier by accumulating more money and currency, whereas goods and services available for consumption and the quality and extent of the nation's infrastructure are the true sources of its measurable wealth. A corollary mercantilist fallacy states that ledger currency is as good as gold, and that increasing amounts of ledger currency increase the nation's wealth and/or is good because the increase stimulates the economy. Though mercantilism has been dispatched to the rubbish bin, for more than three centuries humankind has been subject to the erroneous thinking that more currency is a good thing by mistakenly believing it to be a measure indicating greater wealth and further, that EPP arising from labour producing wealth is the same as PPP, which is simply an accounting entry on the balance sheet of banks. It is time for these mercantilist fallacies to be discarded along with the practice of fractional reserve banking that makes the abnormal expansion of ledger currency possible, which leads to another question. What is a normal increase in the quantity of money?

Milton Friedman proposed to answer this question in his book *A Program for Monetary Stability* published in 1960. He recommended that central banks adopt a rule to manage growth in the quantity of currency, dubbed by him as the K-Percent Rule. He said the growth rate chosen should remain unchanged from year-to-year and further added in 1991, 'I would like to have money controlled by a computer.'[105]

Friedman's K-Percent Rule has often been criticised because it does not allow any discretion in the framing of monetary policy, but that is its strength. Friedman correctly believed that discretion is counterproductive. 'The stock of money [should be] increased at a fixed rate year-in and year-out without any variation in the rate of increase to meet cyclical needs.'[106] He argued against countercyclical currency policy, which was the foundation underlying the creation of the Federal Reserve Act. It was believed that an 'elastic currency' created by the Federal Reserve could be used to dampen the boom-bust cycle that results from fractional reserve banking, but all the Federal Reserve has done is debase the dollars it issues while increasing the power of the federal government, disrupting the careful monetary checks and balances in the Constitution.

Friedman's proposal to control the quantity of currency was a step in the right direction, much like the step taken by Newton. Both recognised the human element that brings into the currency creation process the unintentional error, purposeful dishonesty, and other human frailties. It is necessary to control the quantity of currency, but Friedman did not realise that one could rely on the natural growth rate of gold M3 instead of a computer. Nevertheless, his point is clear. The quantity of currency needs to increase at a controlled growth rate over time.

Like nearly all modern-day economists, Freidman did not recognise the fourth definition of money as a means of final payment to extinguish an exchange. Consequently, he did not distinguish between money and currency, between EPP and PPP. With these omissions, by implication he tacitly accepted the fragility of fractional reserve banking as a given framework upon which to build his model.

There is another shortcoming to his K-Percent Rule. It provides only part of the information needed. It confirms that the supply of currency should grow at the same annual rate but leaves unanswered what that annual growth rate in the quantity of currency should be. With gold, one does not need to choose the growth rate, which history has shown is consistently about 1.8% per annum, approximately the same as world population growth.

The K-Percent Rule also ignores the demand for money, but like any other good or service, money is subject to supply and demand. Economists tend to ignore demand because, in contrast to the supply of money, the demand for it cannot be measured. So some economists assume that demand is constant, but experience has shown that is not the case. Not only does demand change, at times the change can be rapid and violent.

For example, during the banking crisis in the early 1930s, the demand for gold soared as people moved their purchasing power down the Exter Pyramid from unsafe ledger currency into gold redeemable banknotes and eventually into gold coin. Their reaction to protect their purchasing power is understandable. Ledger currency comes with a lot of risk.

As a result of the numerous banking failures in that crisis, different ideas were floated to restore the public's confidence in the banking system. Prominent economist Irving Fischer and several of his colleagues at University of Chicago proposed in March 1933 at the height of the banking crisis to eliminate fractional reserve banking. Dubbed the Chicago Plan, it was rejected, resulting in a forced increase in the demand for ledger currency because gold had been confiscated and became illegal to own. Soon thereafter the Glass Steagall Act and other similar palliatives like federal deposit insurance that unconstitutionally increased State control of the banking and currency system were implemented but did nothing to eliminate the cause of the crisis, which is fractional reserve banking.

The 1930s banking crisis caused people to recognise the inherent fragility of fractional reserve banking. It is a message being relearned by each generation since the first crisis in 1696 that exposed the Bank of England's insolvency.

The ideal aim is to achieve an unchanging purchasing power, which would be the result if supply and demand for currency grew at the same rate. While laudable, that goal is unrealistic. Neither supply nor demand are static; nothing in our world is static. Gold's track record comes closest to achieving the ideal outcome, and its performance is far better than national currencies, as illustrated in Figure 1.

Supply changes as banks increase or decrease the currency they issue, and people's preferences change too, affecting demand for the currency. Another factor affecting currency supply and demand is technology. More efficient ways of spending purchasing power mean that less currency is needed, not more. Advancements in payment systems are speeding up transactions, so less currency moved more quickly can complete the same number of transactions as a currency moved more slowly. So the best possible outcome is to aim for relatively stable purchasing power, which can be achieved by stopping fractional reserve banking and relying solely on gold for money and using it as currency.

A fundamental building block of the Theory of Natural Money is that gold M3 and population growth are closely in sync, which is supported by a comparison of their growth rates. From 1492 through to 2020, gold M3 grew by 1.1% per annum on average, compared to 0.5% for the world's population over this period. The world's population current growth rate is 1.05%, which is nearly identical to gold's long-term average growth rate.[107]

Reviewing recent growth rates is more relevant. During the gold discovery boom years from 1849 in California to 1896 in the Klondike and up until the outbreak of the First World War, gold M3 grew on average by 2.1%, during which time world population grew by 2.3%. From the end of the Second World War to 2015, the latest year for which data is available, world population grew by 1.6% per annum, very close to the 1.8% per annum gold M3 growth during this same period. What is more, gold achieves these consistent growth rates yearly and without the wild swings occurring in F$ growth rates. Therefore, gold achieves the ideal objective that many economists have been seeking. Gold provides a relatively stable purchasing power, as illustrated in Figure 1, without the risks inherent to ledger currency.

It is worth noting that the gold M3 rate of growth is substantially less than the recent 25% rate of growth in F$ M2. This rapid increase is debasing the F$. What is more, F$ M2 growth is volatile. As illustrated in Figure 21, the annual growth rate of F$ M2 at each month end is inconsistent. The swings up and down are frequent and at times violent in that they occur over a relatively short period of time.

Figure 22 illustrates the annual growth rate of F$ M2 and the United States population. The volatility in F$s is clear even when viewing the M2 growth rates for a calendar year instead of rolling 12-month periods, which also highlights another point.

Figure 22 – Annual Growth of F$ M2 & U.S. Population

Source: Federal Reserve Bank of St. Louis

The average annual growth rate for F$ M2 over this period is 7.0%, compared to the 1.0% growth rate of the U.S. population. Even when allowing for demand for F$s from outside the United States, the quantity of F$s is growing much faster than the source of demand. When the supply of anything grows faster than the demand for it, the product is cheapened, which for currency means that its purchasing power is diminished.

In contrast to the F$, gold M3 annual growth over this period ranged between 1.4% and 2.2%, averaging 1.8% per annum. Gold M3 grows consistently and without the huge swings seen in the F$ and other national currency growth rates. It also grows closely in line with world population growth.

Consequently, the supply and demand for gold are similar year after year. For this reason, gold's purchasing power is consistent over long periods of time, as illustrated in Figure 1. The decline in the F$ rate of exchange to gold from F$ 20.67 per ounce in 1913 when the Federal Reserve was created to $1,850 at present results from the excessive expansion of F$ made possible by fractional reserve banking and the foisting of PPP on an unsuspecting public. To the extent that demand for gold rises or falls in the short-term, the cause is a banking or financial panic or loss of confidence in the national currency causing a flight from that currency to the safety of gold, as occurred for example, in the 1930s and the 2008 financial crisis.

Therefore, rises and falls in gold's rate of exchange to national currencies is not a function of the supply of gold, as it would be for example, with a commodity like corn, the supply of which could drop considerably from a severe drought. It is the rising or falling demand for national currencies that causes gold's rate of exchange to fall or rise. In times of fear for the safety of their purchasing power held in national currencies, people wisely opt for gold, which is the logic underlying the Fear Index.

Because demand for national currencies can be fleeting, central bankers act as government spokespersons to propagandise for the national currency as well as to disparage and manipulate the gold market to artificially bolster the demand for the national currency. There is a limited amount of purchasing power in the world, though governments and central bankers try to push this limit to extremes by conjuring up PPP. Regardless of the limit of global purchasing power, which is reached at the peak of an economic and financial bubble, it is a concern to politicians and central bankers when the demand for gold increases because the demand for the national currency decreases. If left unchecked, falling demand will lead to the collapse of a national currency.

The collapse in demand of the Russian rouble is illustrative. Most Russians in 1991 did not believe the rouble was going to collapse, even though the signs were long apparent. They had become so accustomed to the status quo and placing blind faith in the power of the State their view was that the Soviet Union government would never let it happen, even though no government has the power to stop a flight from currency. Today probably nine of ten Americans will tell you the same thing, such is their blind faith in the federal apparatus. The same is true for people in every country with grossly misplaced blind faith belief in government promises, which is widespread notwithstanding decades of examples that would logically lead to the opposite conclusion. Many are blind to central banks going wild with their currency creation, which is most everywhere on the planet.

Gold production is governed by three factors. These are geology, which is the dominant factor, technology, and the expected return on capital employed to mine gold. The world's easy to find and mine gold, typically placer nuggets in streambeds, have over centuries been discovered and removed. Those nuggets ended up in streambeds when eroded away from veins in rock, and these outcrops led to underground mining as miners followed the veins into the earth.

Gold is becoming harder to find and, importantly, mine profitably where it has been found, but technology helps. As an example, in the early 1900s in South Africa, mine shafts were sunk to a depth of 300 metres, which pushed the boundary of shaft building technology to its limits. Advancements in technology today enable the construction of a three kilometre deep vertical shaft for essentially the same weight of gold, when adjusting for gold's smaller percent of global purchasing power.

Technology has also revolutionised mining with a process developed in the 1980s called heap leaching. Previously, gold dispersed over a wide area near the surface was uneconomical to mine. With heap leaching, this disseminated gold became profitable. Instead of drilling into rock to follow veins underground, soil containing the gold was dug from open pits and placed nearby in a large mound, on to which leaching material was sprayed. Over time the leach would concentrate the gold, which would then be refined, and the soil with the gold now removed would be returned to refill the pit, returning the rehabilitated land to its former natural state. Gold mined today by professionals working in principled mining companies is environmentally friendly.

More recently, technology has been helping to discover gold. Ground penetrating radar and other new techniques have proven useful in locating gold ore bodies covered by overburden, which hide near surface veins.

Gold exploration and mining are beyond the scope of this book, but they do relate to a core principle of the Theory of Natural Money. As gold becomes more difficult to find and then mine, new technologies enable gold mining to grow resulting in consistent annual growth in gold M3, meaning that geology (nature) and technology (humankind) are in harmony. It has been that way for more than five centuries, so it is not unreasonable to assume that these unique features will continue making gold the world's natural money for the foreseeable future.

The third factor governing gold production is the cost of capital. Money is invested in projects that make economic sense, which is determined by the cash flow the project generates relative to the risks of the investment. Investors will expect to earn more cash flow by investing capital to explore for gold and building a mine in a high-risk country than they would for a country considered to have lower risk. Consequently, the cost of capital varies, which is to be expected. Nevertheless, the cost of capital is also a governor on new gold production as it is driven by the economics of gold mining. Gold is only mined when a detailed analysis of the project determines that the risk/return criteria make the investment a reasonable undertaking.

So when taken together, geology, technology and the cost of capital govern gold production with the result that gold M3 continues to grow each year fairly consistently, currently about 1.8%. It is the ideal K-Percent Rule money, which explains why gold's annual production was mimicked by Satoshi Nakamoto in his creation of bitcoin. But instead of the mathematical model governing cryptos, gold production is determined by nature and the cost of capital, the latter entailing the same human calculation that has built our capitalist civilisation that has raised humankind's standard of living. The growth of gold M3 at a rate consistent with the growth of world population is a key component of the Theory of Natural Money.

The Misallocation of Capital

While the debasement and inflationary impact of fractional reserves is visible, there is a less visible but pernicious outcome from expanding the quantity of purchasing power through bank alchemy. Unnatural increases in purchasing power cheapen capital, which for the past decade has been made worse by the financial repression currently being imposed by central banks that is forcing interest rates to artificially low levels.

Government intervention to manipulate interest rates misprices risk, which in turn alters economic calculation. Capital flows into projects that otherwise would not be funded, meaning that capital becomes misallocated from where it would be most usefully employed. This misallocation becomes clear at the end of the business cycle. The economic, environmental, and human costs are the consequences of pursuing alternatives other than natural money in an unfettered free market.

Although rarely considered, this cheapening of capital is destructive to the environment. It distorts sound economic calculation, which causes malinvestment and, tragically, the misuse and waste of natural resources. One result is environmental degradation.

There is a natural rate of growth in wealth that arises from the limitations of the resources in our natural world. Excessive rates of growth beyond natural limits will result in environmental degradation. It is a postulate of the Theory of Natural Money that sustainability of the world's resources will not be achieved if economic activity is unnaturally boosted through central bank manipulation or artificial currency creation. In other words, fractional reserve banking and PPP conflict with ESG, the prudent environmental, social and governance goals receiving increasing attention around the world.

Natural money is essential to achieve ESG goals and to live in harmony with nature, accepting the scarcity it imposes. Although resources are limited, their use does not necessarily lead to their exhaustion and a subsequent global catastrophe as argued by Paul Ehrlich in his 1968 polemic, *The Population Bomb.* His resurrection of the Malthusian contention that the world is running out of resources because of population growth was refuted by an insightful academic study establishing that what appears to be an obvious conclusion is not necessarily the correct one. Published by the Cato Institute, it concludes that as the 'ultimate resource', people make other resources more plentiful. Their analysis shows that notwithstanding the population growth between 1980 and 2017 'the planet's resources became 379.6 percent more abundant.'[108]

The earth provides what is needed to fulfil humanity's destiny, but we must live within a natural order of sustainability that ESG aims to achieve. The sound economic calculation that capitalism makes possible in an unfettered market manages competing demands so well that it becomes easy to forget that resources are limited. The average person in an industrialised country lives better today than most anyone in the nineteenth century could have imagined. Nevertheless, companies need to begin their ESG analysis by recognising that today's banking and currency system abuses the environment by perverting economic calculation and reducing the true cost of capital.

Capitalism depends on sound decisions for the investment of capital, which requires careful decisions. To achieve that goal, a capitalist system needs gold because its features act to make it a natural financial navigator. Natural money, like capital itself, is precious and spent or invested wisely after thoughtful consideration about the probability of achieving the expected outcome.

A natural cost of capital results in quality products. A cheapened cost of capital from debased currency results in lower quality products because dishonesty has a profound impact on society, even diminishing one's pride in workmanship.

The prevailing short-term orientation of business is antithetical to the success and advancement of capitalism, which itself determines the standard of living humanity is able to enjoy. Shareholder value maximisation is the holy grail of companies, but not when it is misinterpreted and applied erroneously in the short-term, leading to value and natural resource destruction at some indeterminable future date.

Chapter 8 provided the example of second homes built in the south of Spain prior to the 2008 financial crisis, many of which would never have been built if the cost of capital had been priced correctly. Another example is the depletion of fishing stocks by trawlers built with cheap credit that would not have been built if capital were priced properly by market forces and not central banks.

If the cost of capital is really zero as central banks contend by forcing interest rates to that level, one wag with tongue in cheek proposed removing the Rocky Mountains and using the dirt to landfill the Gulf of Mexico. The scale of that project makes that proposal nonsensical, but it does make clear the important point. The real absurdity is central bank manipulation of interest rates to make people believe that the cost of capital is zero, or even negative in some national currencies.

The lowering of interest rates to artificial levels by central bank financial repression distorts consumption and investment patterns. Accurate economic calculation is not achievable because of these distortions, and malinvestment occurs. The inevitable result is overconsumption of natural resources. Increased borrowing of under-priced purchasing power leads to consumption in the present and environmental degradation, distorting humankind's balance with nature. A detailed analysis of this proposition is beyond the scope of this book, but it is warranted to determine and identify the true destruction to the environment arising from the malicious central bank practice of controlling interest rates, the institutionalisation of fractional reserve banking, and the conjuring of PPP.

A critical point, always worth repeating, is that there is no free lunch in our world. There is a cost to everything, and capital too has a cost. There are different points of view as to what the fair and honest rate of return should be for the use of one's capital, but there is no doubt that it is not free. And here is where fake money has a harmful impact.

By expanding the quantity of ledger currency through PPP, capital can appear to be plentiful, which by implication makes it appear to be cheap. It is not. Capital is as precious as gold itself. Like gold, capital is accumulated over time through hard work. It must be nurtured to grow through savings and sound investments in which property rights are protected and then managed carefully to ensure it is used to achieve the best possible result, which is measured by its rate of return and manifested by rising standards of living.

When capital is properly priced in a market unfettered by government and central bank intervention, it will be employed effectively, in harmony with the environment and natural resources to achieve ESG goals of sustainability. Under those conditions, capital is of greater benefit to society compared to those periods of time when capital is made to appear under-priced, which disrupts the natural order.

Roy Sebag, Chief Executive Officer of Goldmoney Inc., clearly explains regenerative sustainability and the natural order of economic activity in his 2021 annual letter to shareholders.

> This real economy, which is found in every peaceful society, is predicated on the natural mystery of generation; that nature renews itself and provides us with the privilege of prospering with her seasons. In the real economy, man explores nature, comes to learn her limits, and respectfully works within those limits. By consequence, his notion of good or bad work, success and failure, all seem to be tethered to the judgement of the natural order. This common-sense notion of learning from nature which actions are practical and which are impractical introduces a set of ideals which empower our collective knowledge of how best to prosper with nature. These ideals include:

producing more than we consume (saving), consuming only what we need, eschewing debt, and preserving the land and its resources for the benefit of our children.

The actual, true cost of capital is simply hidden, not changed, with the use of national currencies in economic calculation instead of gold. It is hidden by fractional reserve banking, PPP, and interest rates are artificially forced by government and central bank intervention. The resulting distortions to the true cost of capital lead to its misallocation, which disrupts the equilibrium that is needed between humankind and nature. Intervention always has harmful repercussions because it pushes human activity against the natural order and outside the regenerative limits of nature with untold ecological and environmental costs.

Relying on Nature

Naturalism is a philosophical concept built on the premise that thoughtful observation and logical deduction are the bases needed to understand the structure of our world and human nature. From this knowledge flows natural law and the universal, moral principles that govern all human conduct. I contend that happiness is achieved and society flourishes when individuals pursue happiness by acting ethically in harmony with natural law – doing no harm while living life fully.

The origins of naturalism date to the ancient Greeks as well as Confucian thinking in Asia. It developed throughout the ages, and during the Age of Enlightenment took centre stage in France in the works of the physiocrats. François Quesnay (1694-1774), considered to be the intellectual source of physiocracy, predated Adam Smith, who was influenced to an extent by the physiocrats and their focus upon nature, natural law, and free trade.

Quesnay opposed the then dominant French mercantilists and their high tax and stringent regulatory policies shackling the economy and grinding much of the population into the widespread, abject poverty that would soon lead to the country's revolution. Because the State had become too big and dominant, Quesnay aimed to cut regulations and taxes. He envisioned an equitable society reliant upon nature with man-made law operating in harmony with natural law. An advocate of competition and free trade among nations, he coined the term 'laissez faire, laissez passer' (let it be, let it pass/go), which has become the guiding principle to achieve an economy unfettered by government intervention, which was also the aim of Smith.

It is an obvious anthropological observation that the immense natural resources with which the earth has been endowed have been purposefully employed when using sound economic calculation to raise humankind's standard of living, which is the welcomed outcome of our civilisation. Whether by a serendipitous occurrence of nature or the intelligent design of a creator, everything that humankind needs to live and to advance is provided by nature, including money.

Natural Money

Gold is natural money. A natural element beyond human control and the frailty of human nature is needed to serve as money by being a neutral tool in the market process. Natural money that cannot be controlled by government promotes cooperation and harmony among people, which are essential components for humankind to progress as each individual pursues happiness. Because of banking practices, society has moved far from that ideal. Banks have promoted the use of fake money from deceitful fractional reserve banking to conjure up PPP. The subsequent institutionalisation of these fraudulent practices has disrupted the spontaneous process by which civilisation advances in harmony with nature.

Figure 23 illustrates the components of a monetary system operating in conformity with nature. It illustrates a world without PPP. In that world, money is gold, which circulates as currency along with cryptos, and all purchasing power has been earned.

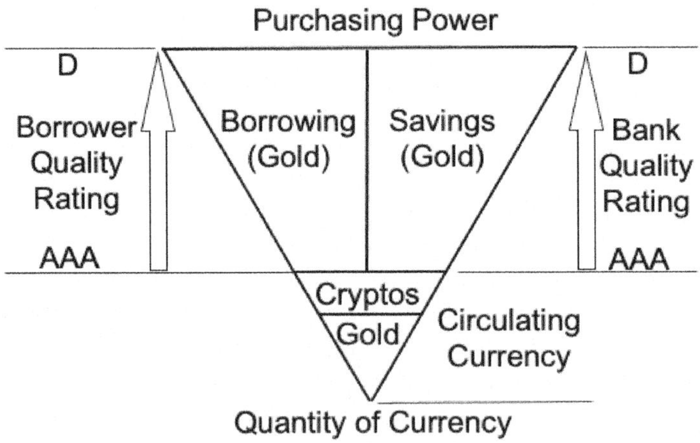

Figure 23 – Exter Pyramid for a System of Natural Money

People who choose to accumulate gold to save their EPP and earn a fee for deferring their consumption to the future have deposited their gold in a bank, which then loans the deposited money to its borrowing customers.

The quantity of gold saved approximates the quantity of gold loaned, and the tenor of each bank's loans matches that of its customers' deposits. Interest rates rise and fall in response to the supply and demand for borrowed money.

In a system of natural money, interest rates are determined by supply and demand for lending and borrowing, not government or central bank intervention. When the supply of gold available for lending is tight and demand for borrowed money is high, interest rates rise, throttling demand by borrowers and enticing owners of gold to deposit their money in a bank. Conversely, interest rates fall when the supply of lendable gold is high and demand for borrowed money is low. Falling interest rates may entice new borrowers or cause depositors to withdraw their gold, if they conclude that interest rates are not high enough to compensate them for the counterparty risk. Unfettered interest rates are the point of convergence that bring the supply and demand of borrowed money into equilibrium in a self-regulating credit system of natural money.

The Exter Inverted Pyramid exists in this natural monetary system for the simple reason that there still are different degrees of risk. A gold coin in hand has less risk than gold deposited in a bank, particularly one with a low-quality 'D' credit rating that loaned its customers' gold to borrowers also carrying a 'D' credit rating. The risk to a unit of purchasing power increases the higher it appears in the pyramid. The higher the risk, the greater the possibility of losing one's purchasing power. The Exter pyramid applies to all monetary systems because there always is risk, which itself varies and changes over time in response to unfolding circumstances.

There are organic circumstances that enable sufficient production of gold to fulfil the need of society to serve as money by providing a consistent means for economic calculation and a method to exchange items of value throughout time. Gold's usefulness arises from a set of natural rules of the physical world. Because of them, it has been said that an ounce of gold bought a toga for a Roman senator and today buys a businessman's suit. How is that possible?

It is possible because gold is natural money. This conclusion is not based on complex mathematical formulas, but rather, careful observation and logical deduction about the physical world. The aboveground stock of gold, its M3, grows at approximately the same rate as the world's population, so the supply and demand for gold are in synch. Technology also has an impact.

A businessman's suit, even though more complex to make than a toga, can be made with fewer hours labour than a Roman toga because of technological advancements, for example, sewing by machine instead of by hand, and more recently, cutting and sewing by computer directed machines.

The price of commodities is also affected by technology. Even though more crude oil is being consumed as world population grows and is becoming more difficult to discover, its price measured in gold remains basically unchanged, as illustrated in Figure 1. This result occurs from technology, or more to the point, the ultimate resource which is human ingenuity and the motivation of individuals to improve their situation in their pursuit of happiness.

It is intuitive that humans either live in harmony with natural law, or in violation of it with adverse consequences to society and the environment. Money and currency, which are gold by nature, are essential to achieve that harmony.

Newton's gold standard was designed to control the managers of national currencies. His mechanism and the discipline it exacted no longer exist, but as illustrated in Figure 1, gold is still the standard. What is more, a goldgram is the world's numeraire.

A goldgram is an unchanging and reliable unit, just like a foot, metre, gallon, litre or pint. It is exceedingly difficult if not impossible to accurately measure prices or the value of the item being measured if the unit of account is changing too. It is difficult to properly assess value when EPP is being debased by PPP.

The fact that a global numeraire is needed to expand and grow commerce cannot be denied. Only an unalterable money unit can provide the sound economic calculation that is needed as the foundation for ethical human interaction.

12. The Future of Money and Currency

The first requisite of a sound monetary system is
that it put the least possible power over the
quantity of money in the hands of politicians.

Henry Hazlitt

It is clear from monetary history that government control over the circulating currency inevitably leads to economic upheaval that often ends in hyperinflation and social chaos. It happened in Weimar Germany in the 1920s, which was a direct conduit into National Socialism. It happened more recently in two countries endowed with immense natural resources, in Zimbabwe, leading to a calamitous breakdown of social order in that country, once one of the richest in Africa. It is happening today in Venezuela, which is endowed with immense natural resources and was once one of the richest countries in South America, but whose inhabitants are now among the poorest in the world. While it is easy to claim that nothing similar could happen in the more advanced societies of the world, one needs to think logically, rather than emotionally hoping that a currency crisis will not happen where you live.

The ramifications of the 2008 financial crisis and other momentous financial events of recent decades continue to reverberate throughout the world, particularly the financial repression and increasing control being exercised by central banks, their expansion of the quantity of fiat currency worldwide, and more recently the Covid-19 induced collapse of the global economy. Again, history is clear. Reversion to the mean is a recurring result of fiddling with money and currency. Unsound currency leads to chaos – financial, economic, and social – that eventually leads to the inexorable return to gold, the world's natural money upon which civilisation has been built over the millennia.

We can return to gold in an orderly way or let chaos reign as the debasement of fiat currencies accelerates into their inevitable collapse. As Edmund Burke observed in his *Reflections on the Revolution in France*, when gold is driven from the economy by a policy that depends on ledger currency:

> The truly melancholy part of the [monetary] policy of systematically making a nation of gamesters is this; that tho' all are forced to play, few can understand the game; and fewer still are in a condition to avail themselves of the knowledge. The many must be the dupes of the few who conduct the machine of these speculations.

In other words, avoid ledger currency in a rigged system. Wealth concentration and income inequality are not a circumstance unique to the present time. Similar episodes have occurred throughout history for the same reason as today – when society moves away from natural money.

Time to Rethink Money and Currency

> In the 1830s, William Leggett, the antislavery Jacksonian editorial writer in New York, proposed the lovely phrase 'separation of money and state.' He was on to something.
>
> Llewellyn H. Rockwell Jr.[109]

Money and gold were synonymous to Mr Leggett, who indeed was on to something. Gold is the pivot upon which a society turns – to order or chaos, to liberty or fascism, to the advancement of humanity's standard of living or economic stagnation. Change is needed, but it goes beyond returning to gold.

While the separation of money and State is an essential ingredient to achieving liberty, so too is the separation of the State and banks, which leads to Thomas Jefferson's assertion that banking establishments are more dangerous than standing armies. Banks work hand-in-glove with government. To put it bluntly, governments cannot produce bullets out of thin air, so governments direct banks to produce phantom purchasing power out of thin air that governments then borrow to buy bullets – 'bullets' being a euphemism for government power to enforce their dictate. It has been that way since the Bank of England was founded to help pay for the Nine Year's

War.

The control system designed and implemented by Sir Isaac Newton was self-regulating, provided the voluntary rules were followed, which they were for a time because there was a sense of honour and morality in the Bank of England and the British government. Also, the leaders of these institutions recognised that the rules governed a monetary system that was mutually beneficial to those countries adhering to them. This financial structure became the backbone of the British Empire. Honour and morality was manifest through the resumption of the pound's redeemability to gold in 1821 after the Napoleonic Wars and up to the Banking Act of 1844, which was the last attempt to control the evils of fractional reserve banking and phantom purchasing power. Thereafter, honour and morality began to fade as banks were supressing Newton's Rule with government consent, if not active encouragement. The resulting unholy alliance that developed has become progressively abusive to individual liberty as banks evolved to become an arm of the State, disrupting the social structure.

The enhanced centralised government power prevalent today facilitated by the removal of gold's role as money in the twentieth century, and particularly the events since 1971, are an aberration in the course of civilisation. History shows that these aberrations to the structure of society continue until they become abusive and therefore unsustainable, after which they soon end. Medieval feudalism is an example. Initially the feudal structure was mutually beneficial to all participants within an ordered, fair community, with the lord of the manor having access to the labour of serfs, who in turn benefitted from the protection offered by the lord's castle. But eventually the structure outlived its usefulness, and after a few hundred years was jettisoned. It led to a new societal structure, the divine right of kings, which also eventually came to an end when it no longer equitably served humankind.

I contend that central banking, government control over currency, the creation of phantom purchasing power, and more generally, the centralisation of power within unaccountable government are in their denouement. This inequitable fascistic structure has outlived its usefulness by becoming authoritarian, abusive, and costly to society and the environment.

A trend toward decentralisation began with the creation of the United Nations. Its charter marks the peak of nationalism by stating that nations have a right to exist, but nations are a legal concept without natural rights. Only individuals have natural rights, and they have become subservient to government power sustained by phantom purchasing power created by banks.

Obvious examples of decentralisation are the collapse of the Soviet Union, and, more recently, the United Kingdom leaving the European

Union. The Brexiteer rallying cry of 'take back control' is an emotive and powerful political slogan. It will be used repeatedly as impatient individuals turn against faceless, costly, and harmful distant bureaucracies and banks feeding the many arms of government with phantom purchasing power.

The world is moving toward decentralisation, and the internet has accelerated its advance. Further acceleration can be expected from the internet's tremendous, untapped potential, particularly in the nascent area of DeFi, decentralised finance. With peer-to-peer finance, cryptocurrencies, and other new developments chipping away at the banking cartel, it is not unreasonable to conclude that 'peak banking' has occurred, in which the maximum rate of extraction of profits by banks has been reached. What follows now is a long-term decline in bank profitability and erosion of their position of privilege and power. Another indication of their peak is the goal to establish central bank digital currency, which might result in less credit creation by commercial banks. More broadly, it likely marks a top in the excesses of the financial services industry, meaning employment in financial services will drop in the years ahead, just like it did in Weimar Germany after that country's flawed currency collapsed. Bad currency requires more employees to deal with its flaws, and the number of employees increases as the currency worsens.

The fiat money system created by central bank and government intervention to displace natural money is artificial and only serves the interests of the ruling elite, the pretentious so-called 'masters of the universe' and their controllers. The economic system built upon central banking has evolved in a way that has allowed the relationship between individuals and government to become excessively unbalanced, reaching the tipping-point that history tells us will lead in time to a new societal structure, like the fate that befell feudalism. Banking initially worked to society's benefit but has degenerated to the extent that it is now abusive, which is clear from the contemptuous central bank policy forcing interest rates to an artificially low level and debasing currency with an inflation goal that raises everyone's cost of living by 2% or more every year.

On March 8, 2021, the *Financial Times* published an article entitled 'Are markets really rigged? The fairness of the US financial system has gone on trial in the wake of the GameStop saga.' It includes a quote from Dennis Kelleher, president of Better Markets, a financial reform advocacy group. Though he is responding to the stock market, his comment could equally apply to the broader financial system: 'Anyone who says this system isn't rigged isn't being honest. We have an incredibly fragmented market system with layers of created complexity that serves no purpose other than to conceal the wealth extraction that the system now serves.'

Central banks and governments are destroying the free market with their interventions to rig and manipulate what is rapidly becoming a centrally commanded economy. Price discovery, unfettered interest rates, capital markets, and capitalist-based economic activity are rapidly disappearing under government controls, regulations, and Marxist-like dictates. The picture of a socialist United States with a ruling elite divided from the polity is complete with the proposal being floated to build a permanent fence around the Capitol. In the words of Alasdair Macleod:[110]

> Governments will always try to persuade us that it is markets and not them at fault. They have been doing this to varying degrees for a hundred years, ever since the abandonment of the gold standard. We are now on the last lap of this delusion. We face the economic calculation problem identified by von Mises. It was the eventual undoing of the Soviet Union, and we have fallen into the same trap.'

Some people still naively believe that the government exists to serve their interests. The reality today is that government serves its own interests, as defined by the politicians and bureaucrats who run it. A command economy is not and can never be a substitute for market-based allocation of the world's limited resources in an equitable and sound ecological manner. Nor can it ever provide the money needed for our capitalist society to operate efficiently so that humanity's standard of living continues to improve without environmental degradation.

Figure 1 illustrates that over the past seven decades gold alone has managed to preserve purchasing power, an essential function required of money. Central banks claim that the preservation of purchasing power of national currencies is their aim, yet they have inflation targets that each year lessen a currency's purchasing power.

This erosion of purchasing power that debases national currencies makes reliable economic calculation exceedingly difficult, muddling the process by which an individual uses prices to make decisions to spend, save or invest their accumulated capital. It deprives low-income and middle classes from accumulating capital by saving money and causes despair among those unable to keep up with inflation and currency debasement to maintain their standard of living. As Margaret Thatcher pointedly warned the British people in September 1974 when her country was suffering from severe currency and economic turmoil: 'Inflation is threatening to destroy our society.'

That outcome is the unfortunate result because currency turmoil leads to wealth concentration among those who understand what is happening to cause the erosion in the standards of living from inflation and other currency and banking ills. With their knowledge they are better able to respond to currency debasement, to protect and enhance their wealth accumulation. For example, in the United States, it has been reported that: 'the best survey data show that the share of wealth held by the top 1 percent rose from just under 30 percent in 1989 to nearly 39 percent in 2016, while the share held by the bottom 90 percent fell from just over 33 percent to less than 23 percent over the same period.'[111] Wealth concentration and income inequality have become topical.

The glaring mismanagement of national currency by governments and their central bank in recent decades has been harmful as class and generation divisions are manifest. On January 15, 2019, Glenn Harlan Reynolds stated in *USA Today* that 'Donald Trump is a symptom of a new kind of class warfare raging at home and abroad', and soon thereafter on May 6, 2019, Niall Ferguson and Eyck Freymann wrote in 'The Coming Generation War' published by *The Atlantic*: 'In short, America's political future will be determined by the outcome of the generation war.'

Lenin's dictum about debased currency overthrowing the existing order of society is proving accurate. That outcome is to be expected because money is central to society and to the 'invisible hand' of capitalism that has built our civilisation by motivating the noble features of human nature. We act to improve our situation, whether with a glass of water to quench our thirst, the satisfaction received from making a charitable donation, saving money to help prepare for an uncertain future, and every other act. We do this because we choose the outcome that we prefer in our pursuit of happiness, as we make decisions to improve our situation.

The Failure of Socialism

> Communism is not the victory of socialist law, but the victory of socialism over any law.
>
> Peter Stuchka, 1920s Soviet jurist

The neglect of key provisions of the American Constitution gives substance to the accuracy of the above quote. This esteemed document was purposefully designed to limit federal power, but clever wordsmiths now interpret it to enhance federal power, which is then broadcast through a compliant mainstream media and readily accepted by a complacent public or imposed on them by force through threats of punishment under various man-made laws that create the opportunity for tyrants and sociopaths to achieve their goal of displaying power.

The pernicious twisting of the Constitution's general welfare clause by the courts in the 1930s is one example.[112] The general welfare of the People is advanced by following the precepts of natural law, not as is now widely believed by pursuing anti-capitalist, pro-socialist actions of a powerful so-called 'nanny state'. Programmes like Social Security are a Ponzi scheme that depend on an increasing number of taxpayers funding a growing number of Americans receiving benefits.[113] As the population ages, the ratio of working-age people supporting old people receiving benefits is decreasing, putting an increasing financial burden on the young, with solvency of the programme in doubt due the multi-decade decline in birth rates and government mismanagement of the programme's annual revenues.

A more egregious example is the abandonment of constitutional money with the forced substitution of fiat currency. This flagrant disregard of the Constitution has along with the acceptance of fractional reserve banking caused America to retrogress to the conditions that led to the collapse of its first national currency and the total destruction of the phantom purchasing power it conveyed.

Focus today typically is in the same direction – towards government. This focus is not a surprise because it is simply a sign of the times in which we live. Most people look to government for solutions to everyday problems. Their focus is misdirected because government creates problems, not solutions, when it expands beyond its reason for being, which is ensuring there is a rule of law that protects each individual's rights so that everyone in society, including the government itself, can interact on a level playing field in which the rules are known and justly applied.

Product shortages and inflation are a distinctive feature of socialist economies because of constraints on private property, government command over the economy, and handouts that discourage labour and production. It must also be remembered that government does not create wealth. It just redistributes wealth created by productive members of society. Alternatively, government destroys wealth, and socialist governments pillory the economy's wealth producers, which are actions that create conflict instead of peace. Answers to problems as well as the creation of wealth come from the free market, not today's misguided fixation toward the State.

Government mismanagement of just about everything it does is well known. This mismanagement arises because government does not have any bottom-line accountability. In contrast to private companies, governments do not go out of business when the market does not like their product. A comparison of public or private enterprises can be made by the perennial losses incurred by the U.S. Postal Service against the profitability of the delivery services provided by Federal Express or UPS. Tech entrepreneurs provide another clear example: 'Elon Musk's SpaceX did in 6 years and for less than $1 billion, what the U.S. government commission concluded 11 years ago would take 12 years and cost $26 billion."[114]

Hong Kong offers another irrefutable example of the superiority of unfettered private enterprise over government policy. Named the 'barren island' because it lacked natural resources, Hong Kong was devastated after the Second World War, with income per capita less than a quarter that of Britain. Fortunately, the governors of the Crown Colony chose to follow a policy of salutary neglect, allowing individuals to pursue their own goals with minimum government interference. This policy defied the recommendations emanating from the island's higher authority in London, which was pursuing interventionist, socialist policies and nationalising industry, actions that disparaged private property and thwarted capitalism. For decades Hong Kong followed its own path, and by 1997 and the handover to China, income per capita in Hong Kong was 40% higher than in Britain.[115]

Governments survive because they live by coercion, including the inferior currency they force on society through self-serving laws. Therefore, the most fundamental premise for any monetary reform is that it should be built upon solutions that come from the free market and unfettered competition because that is where the beneficial changes will emanate.

It is alarming that so many of the ten planks from Marx's 1848 *Communist Manifesto* have been fully or nearly implemented in the United States and many other countries around the world. What is worse, they continue to be advocated and tried notwithstanding clear examples of countless, predictable failures of these policies. Nobel Laureate Friedrich Hayek observed that 'If socialists understood economics, they wouldn't be socialists.' I will paraphrase his insight to add that socialists also need to understand human nature and the process that makes possible the development of civilisation.

Society has taken the wrong path. Capitalism makes people happy. Socialism makes people anti-happy. As Thomas Sowell accurately observes: 'The history of the 20th century is full of examples of countries that set out to redistribute wealth and ended up redistributing poverty.'

A dominating feature of the twentieth century is the failure of socialism. It is marked by immoral government disrupting the equitable social contract that once enabled citizens to control the government they formed under natural law. The result is evident from the erosion of liberty and the undermining of private property. Socialistic government has been hindering the pursuit of happiness for countless millions. Humankind has been enduring and suffering through more than a century of nationalistic social fascism, with socialistic governments acting like the monarchs of old before the Age of Enlightenment.

Ray Dalio, the successful money manager who built of one of the world's largest hedge funds, made the following observation about the 'widening income/wealth/opportunity gaps that pose existential threats to the

United States because these gaps are bringing about damaging domestic and international conflicts and weakening America's condition.'[116] Though he directed his comments to the United States, I believe they apply to many countries also experiencing the same conflicts, the source of which is the incompatibility of capitalism and socialism that he identifies in his article. He then concludes that 'we are now at a juncture in which either a) people of different ideological inclinations will work together to skilfully re-engineer the system so that the [wealth] pie is both divided and grown well or b) we will have great conflict and some form of revolution that will hurt most everyone and will shrink the pie.'

All sane people want to avoid a 'revolution'. In my view the way to do that is to again put into practice what worked well enough up to 1933, which means accepting the wisdom and intent of the framers of the Constitution and following the monetary provisions of that venerable document.

Maximal Liberty

> A man's natural rights are his own, against the whole world; and any infringement of them is equally a crime, whether committed by one man, or by millions; whether committed by one man, calling himself a robber, (or by any other name indicating his true character,) or by millions, calling themselves a government.
>
> Lysander Spooner, nineteenth-century American abolitionist

The predominant lesson from the fall of the Iron Curtain is that command economies do not work. They eventually collapse because society is too utterly complex and human action too splendidly diverse to be ruled by the dictates of a ruling class, which invariably directs activity to serve itself instead of the best interests of the mass of citizens. The rulers achieve this goal through their control over the creation of currency with the use of money substitutes to circulate in commerce, rather than using money itself. Instead, resources need to be allocated by market prices based on economic calculation using the goldgram as the unit of account, and not by dictates that sooner or later hamper the boundless potential of an unfettered economy.

Government actions – however well intentioned – must be frictionless to create a society that gives everyone, whatever their background, a real opportunity to live life in harmony with natural law. That means the man-made law is devoid of impediments that thwart human action, but there is more required to achieve the ideal framework.

The law must be unvaryingly and consistently applied to everyone to safeguard the ownership of 'private property that is an essential foundation of a genuinely free society.'[117] When misused, man-made law, regulations and taxation can be forces that harm an individual's property, their natural rights, and/or stifle personal initiative and their pursuit of happiness to the detriment of society as a whole. The most fundamental principle of natural law - do no harm - prohibits force or aggression against another person or their property while ensuring that everyone has the freedom to act to achieve their own personal goals in their own unique pursuit of happiness.

An effective rule of law requires a legal system based on the principles of natural law. Accordingly, a distinction needs to be made between the crime of aggression against another person or their property and an infraction of man-made law of the State. Writing during the Age of Enlightenment in 1753, Sir William Blackstone in his *Commentaries on the Laws of England* stated: 'This law of nature, being coeval with mankind, and dictated by God himself, is of course superior in obligation to any other. It is binding over all the globe in all countries, and at all times: no human laws are of any validity, if contrary to this.'

In other words, natural law prevails and trumps any man-made law. There is no better explanation as to why this is so than the 'Letter from Birmingham Jail' written by Martin Luther King, Jr. in 1963, to which I have already quoted but is worth quoting again: 'We can never forget that everything Hitler did in Germany was "legal", and everything the Hungarian freedom fighters did in Hungary was "illegal".' Man-made law in those countries made possible a perverted social order of inhuman brutality. In a society in which freedom prevails, a government itself participates under the same natural law principles imposed upon individuals.

Only by meeting these requirements can government policy balance equitably and harmoniously the naturally competing aims of individuals in a world bound by limited resources. Capitalism efficiently sorts out these competing aims, and an essential element to protect our capitalist society is competition in currencies.

Currency should not be monopolised by government, nor should government outlaw any attempts by the private sector to create a better currency. After the adoption of the Constitution, the U.S. Mint faced competition from private mints. They minted coins denominated in U.S. dollars with a precious metal content slightly higher than stated in the Mint Act. This better currency was minted deliberately to protect their name, brand, and reputation by allowing for the imprecision of refining two hundred years ago. Private enterprise always creates a better product than any government undertaking, but as is often the case, those private mints were eventually forced out of business by the inferior currency imposed by government control.

The Case for Private Currencies

> All recorded hyperinflations have been with state currencies. No politician can resist the temptations of the printing press.
>
> Alasdair Macleod[118]

There is a keen insight to Alasdair Macleod's observation. These hyperinflations occur because there is a fundamental difference between national currencies and private currencies.

All national currency today is based on government fiat and circulates by force of law. Private currencies are voluntary; they circulate on merit. In other words, if they are useful, people use them voluntarily. If they are no longer useful, people stop using the private currency long before it could ever hyperinflate. It is the way the market works, but choice is not available in many countries.

In the United States, the Federal Reserve and the banking system are creating endless trillions of dollars to provide the federal government with phantom purchasing power to continue the charade that the federal government is solvent. Central banks will alchemise into currency anything available 'to save the system' built upon discredited seventeenth-century mercantilist thinking that is no longer appropriate and suitable. There exists today communication technology that has fundamentally improved the ability of people to engage in commerce by interacting with each other regardless of where they are in the world.

Thus, domestic and international commerce can advance to a new level with the emergence of a global currency made available through the internet by private payment providers. Their success and longevity will not depend on political objectives and power-plays of government, but rather on whether these new companies are providing a useful product to the market that enables these private companies to make a profit and stay in business.

It is this vision that was behind the creation of Goldmoney that my son and I launched in 2001 as the product of my three decades of analysis, study and thinking about the future of money and currency. It and more recently, cryptocurrencies, are built on the premise that advances in technology improve currency, which makes commerce more efficient. The inherent flaws and costs within the present system by which national currency is issued and then used to purchase goods and services, particularly in cross-border payments, provide a tremendous commercial opportunity by developing a better product. It is understandable that there are numerous companies proposing unique solutions, lower costs, and new products to overcome existing inefficiencies.

It is logical to expect that there will be battles, with government fighting to protect what it sees as a sovereign right to control a nation's currency, which unfortunately many governments are doing increasingly without any kind of restraint or responsibility for their actions. Governments do not have this right nor any exclusivity over monetary matters because money and currency are products of the free market, but even when ignoring this point for the moment, a reasonable conclusion is that electronic, digital currency made available by privately owned payment providers is an idea whose time has come. This observation is particularly true for those electronic currencies that aim to target cross-border commerce that is beyond the scope of any one country and any one sovereign power.

National currencies have become disruptive to economic activity and therefore harmful to society. The financial imbalances that occur today throughout the international monetary system result from fractional reserve banking and phantom purchasing power. These excesses have been heightened by first removing gold from the monetary system and then breaking the direct link to gold in 1971, ending the essential discipline needed in the currency creation process. In the absence of that discipline, credit expansion has become uncontrollable. Monetary history clearly demonstrates that excessive credit creates a 'bubble' that always has an inevitable adverse impact on national currencies and society, as is clear from the many countries where the national currency has collapsed.

Governments claim that their interventions in the market process are protecting people, like their recent clamour advising to avoid cryptocurrencies. But that propaganda is keeping people tied to the current inferior system and ignorant about new possibilities while imposing hurdles on innovation.

The reality is that national currencies are subject to political dictates and are thus controlled by vested interests that influence and dominate the political process. In contrast, private currencies circulate through private enterprises driven by the bottom line, which incentivises these companies to deliver the best possible product to their customers. If it does not achieve that goal, the private company goes out of business, which contrasts with central bankers. They never go out of business and have no bottom-line accountability. Central banks do not have bottom-line accountability to deliver the best possible product, so national currencies do not serve the peoples' needs.

In America there is a battle to be fought for the restoration of constitutional money. We are told that gold is irrelevant. This book explains why those voices are wrong. Those voices serve those benefitting from a corrupt financial system, not the people.

Gold is natural money that preserves purchasing power. Because of its usefulness, people voluntarily choose to hold gold in preference to the artificial money substitutes circulating by force under legal tender laws. 'Depriving the state of this exclusive power would force accountability first and foremost. If the threat of violence and imprisonment were stripped away, the public could freely evaluate the quality of different currencies and act accordingly.'[119]

Central bankers know that today's national currencies are inferior to gold, but their system and their livelihood depends on them, so they will do 'whatever it takes', to use the banal dictum of the former head of the European Central Bank, Mario Draghi, to defend a system of seventeenth-century origin that favours the State over the individual. Until gold once again circulates as currency, instead of the people controlling their government, the government will control the people.

A perfect world does not need police, gold, and other restraints in response to human nature and unprincipled behaviour, but it is not a perfect world. Gold is needed to provide discipline in the money creation process, which is now absent. By the Federal Reserve's own calculation, since its establishment in 1913, the dollar has lost 96.13% of its purchasing power.[120] Yet Figure 1 shows how gold preserves purchasing power. Its history as money is unassailable.

Is it not somewhat arrogant for governments to pronounce that gold is no longer money? After 5,000 years of usefulness, is it reasonable to conclude that gold will stop being money? Has it not been clear over the past fifty years since President Nixon's unconstitutional act in 1971 that gold is essential to the monetary process and therefore crucial to society?

Governments do not make gold money; people do. Nor can governments stop gold from being money. They have only hindered its circulation as currency.

The Illusions of Prosperity

> If the rise in the prices of stocks and real estate is considered as a gain, the illusion is no less manifest. What makes people believe that inflation results in general prosperity is precisely such illusory gains.
>
> Ludwig von Mises

Our world does not allow for a so-called free lunch. It is readily and widely understood that it is impossible to get something for nothing, as Milton Friedman explained in his book, *There's No Such Thing as a Free Lunch.* This immutable law of nature applies to money.

Currency creation by banks conveying newly contrived phantom purchasing power (PPP) during a period of so-called 'easy money' creates the illusions of prosperity. The PPP engenders an artificial economic boom. The end result is always the immeasurable cost of an economic bust. The deliberate creation of PPP by banks along with a currency to inject it into the economy is unnatural and therefore harmful.

Any stimulus to economic activity from this newly created PPP is also unnatural, so the economy itself becomes riddled with uneconomic projects that waste natural and human resources. These malinvestments occur from using the newly created currency and the PPP it conveys to evaluate the project. Economic miscalculations are the inevitable result. Prosperity and higher standards of living do not come from borrowed money and consumption. They come from savings and purposeful work.

Purchasing power is created naturally when miners produce gold and artificially when a bank lends PPP created through fractional reserves. Borrowing through fractional reserve banking is an artificial expansion of purchasing power, which cheapens the currency and is disadvantageous to savers, but savings are essential to enable investments in our capitalist economy. There is a fundamental difference between money created by work and the PPP conjured up by fractional reserve banking. The illusions of prosperity arise because the PPP appears identical to earned purchasing power created from work. Yet the two are as different as night and day, or more appropriately, as different as fraud and honesty.

The inevitable financial crisis hits when the newly created currency arising from bank alchemy stops flowing freely. Banks always turn off the tap when they eventually focus on their survival by coming to grips with those loans that no longer appear repayable in the changing economic climate of an engineered boom. This reduction of credit in turn takes the froth out of bubbly stock markets and other assets. Over-priced assets literally fall back to earth as wealth destruction arising from the contraction of credit takes hold. PPP disappears by returning to the thin air from which it emerged, like the disappearing Cheshire cat in Alice in Wonderland that fades into the ether with its smirking grin knowing that it got the better of you in believing that there was substance to it. Thomas Paine accurately describes this process:

> Paper notes given and taken between individuals as a promise of payment is one thing, but paper issued by an assembly as money is another thing. It is like putting an apparition in the place of a man; it vanishes with looking at it, and nothing remains but the air.

Creating currency out of thin air does not create wealth. Borrowing does not make one wealthier. Borrowing does not make a country wealthier. We need to shed ourselves of seventeenth-century monetary dogma and the false notions surrounding today's neo-mercantilist practices. We need to recognise that money is simply a tool we use in commerce to improve our situation by working to create wealth. Further, money itself is a product that comes from labour, time, and the application of capital, not from bank alchemy.

Returning Gold to its Historical Role as Currency

> The return to gold does not depend on the fulfilment of some material condition. It is an ideological problem. It pre-supposes only one thing: the abandonment of the illusion that increasing the quantity of money creates prosperity.
>
> Ludwig von Mises

Gold and its use as the world's money are beneficial to commerce. A gram of gold, or goldgram, is not only the world's numeraire, but can once again become its common currency, which is beneficial for the same reason as a common language. The worldwide use of the English language has been and remains a boon to global commerce because it facilitates communication, which is the same outcome achieved by a common currency.

An important aspect of gold is that its value is not just expressed numerically. It is also expressed emotionally in the sense that owning gold provides safety of one's purchasing power. Gold has an established 5,000-year track record as money that is outside the banking system. Gold is tangible, so there is no counterparty risk when owning physical gold. In other words, gold is not money that depends on a bank or a government promise. Nor is it forced to circulate by any man-made law. Gold is money because of its natural features and attributes, so it is chosen voluntarily by people to hold their wealth today just like it was chosen all the way back to prehistory.

Gold was the world's common currency, a rightful distinction it held as international money and the principal currency for millennia until the twentieth century. Its role was diminished after the Second World War, with gold's role as currency ending in 1971 by diktat as the U.S. federal government sought to expand its power and impose its will on the Western world as the Cold War raged. The U.S. federal government was successful in exerting its power as countries prudently sought protection under the U.S. nuclear umbrella, but that bipolar world disappeared with the end of the Cold War three decades ago.

In March 2020 a collapsing global economy produced an historic equity collapse. Repeating its ploy from the 2008 financial crisis, central banks around the world wildly printed unprecedented amounts of national currency in an attempt to make governments appear solvent and to 'save' the financial system by keeping asset prices excessively above their economic or utility value. Only time will tell whether their actions will lead to the outcome that central banks are hoping or the alternative that monetary history and logic suggest will be the result, which is a currency collapse.

We are now in a period of economic and currency and banking uncertainty that is leading to events that inevitably are causing a return to the mean. In this process of rebalancing the social order, gold is waiting in the wings for its moment to emerge centre stage with worldwide recognition as money.

Gold needs to be returned to its rightful role at the centre of global commerce, but it must be done in a way that is long-lasting. An important element of the theory of natural money is that its restoration must be done through private currencies and not central banks, which have proven themselves incapable of maintaining a sound monetary system. The global economy needs to discard the remnants of mercantilism and the shackles of the seventeenth-century practices that created ledger currency. The time has come to rely on private enterprise and competitive currencies.

The new record high rate of exchange gold achieved against the U.S. dollar and other national currencies in August 2020 is an indication of what is yet to come, but there are questions that cannot be answered. Do governments and their central banks realise the destructive path they are pursuing and return to gold voluntarily? How will gold overcome Gresham's Law and once again be used as currency?

Here is where technology can turn gold into a common global currency, which has been the aim of Goldmoney, though it has often been impeded by regulatory hurdles protecting the old order. With its unique digital gold currency, it offers a modern up-to-date form of gold currency using today's technology. Gold remains safely stored in a vault, and ownership of a weight of gold is transferred instantly to the payee when clicked by the payer on a laptop or mobile phone.

The American Constitution sets the ideal monetary model for the world to follow and implement. It was deliberately designed to prevent the U.S. federal government as well as the state governments from abusing the issuance of currency and ensured the best economic prospect for the different states by creating a common currency, the silver dollar, with a common market, much as existed in Europe before the creation of the politicised European Union. The framers achieved their goal, which was protected through carefully crafted checks and balances of political power to establish a system of natural money that ensured natural liberty.

The political structure left people free to do what they wanted with their labour, their property, and possessions. An individual was the ruler of their domain, which was their land owned with allodial title. Natural liberty was achieved because people were no longer subject to any monarch, government, or superior power. By not requiring obedience to the authority of man-made law without their consent, Americans who carefully chose their jurisdiction and governing law were free with only the law of nature for their rule as directed by its guiding principle, do no harm. They protected their status by being careful to sign only those agreements that could be fulfilled and were consistent with their legal and jurisdictional situation, which is a good procedure to follow in any day and age.

Why not respond to nature? Why do humans think we can improve on what nature has provided for us? Our ancestors in prehistory had already figured out what money is. What inexplicable human trait or frailty prevents people from figuring it out again? If we do, commerce will again be governed by the discipline inherent within the laws of nature and the true cost of capital. Gold is money not because of the brute force of law like national currencies. It is money by choice.

Our Future

Money is the barometer of society's virtue.

Ayn Rand

We live in a world in which humankind has the potential to live life fully without government control and with unimpeded liberty in the pursuit of happiness as envisioned during the Age of Enlightenment. It is the political structure implemented in America by the country's Constitution and prevailed until the changes imposed in the twentieth century that disrupted money and liberty. The return to that desired structure begins with a return to gold and adherence to the Constitution's monetary provisions.

I believe there is a consensus that we seek a currency and banking system that facilitates financially prudent behaviour, but there is a need to reach a consensus on how to achieve it. The way to do that is to inform people about the inequities of the present system and propose a new model that prohibits fractional reserve banking, outlaws phantom purchasing power, ends all government intervention, and returns to natural money.

Humanity is in a bubble, a money bubble. Humanity has lost sight of what money is, and governments are headed down the wrong path, with disastrous consequences. What are those consequences?

They include the theft of one's time spent working to attain purchasing power, degradation of the environment, and the erosion of liberty. People in numerous countries have suffered immensely when their currency system collapsed, but worse is on the horizon. Imagine Venezuela on a global scale with people in all countries around the globe trying to cope with a crumbling currency and banking system destroying society as we know it while wreaking havoc on everyone's standard of living. The implications for peace and liberty are ominous.

There is little doubt that the blame for recurring financial catastrophes rests on today's obsolete and flawed system of circulating currency, which itself derives from equally obsolete and flawed seventeenth-century mercantilist thinking and practice that unfortunately still prevails. Fractional reserve banking is a fraudulent scheme that violates a basic monetary principle. Increasing the quantity of currency by creating phantom purchasing power does not mean a nation has become wealthier. This widely believed fallacy is undeniably disproved by the Theory of Natural Money that rests on gold's proven track record as money.

Today's antiquated banking system, introduced when the now discredited theory of mercantilism reigned supreme, is intimately tied into the nation's currency, but the time has come to realise that it is not fit for purpose. What may have worked well enough in the eighteenth and nineteenth centuries began to unravel before the dawn of the twentieth century as demagogic politicians usurped greater power and governments became increasingly unprincipled and unethical. The currency and banking system then continued to morph unabatedly, particularly when autocrats sought increased control of it to provide the means to fund two horrific world wars or more recently, socialist programmes expanding the reach of the State that diminish individual liberty and erode the inalienable right to private property.

As President Roosevelt wrote to Colonel Edward Mandell House on 21 November 1933:

> The real truth of the matter is, as you and I know, that a financial element in the larger centers has owned the Government ever since the days of Andrew Jackson. This country is going through a repetition of Jackson's fight with the Bank of the United States – only on a far bigger and broader basis.

Roosevelt and his ilk were the antithesis of Jacksonian ideals, and unfortunately, they won their fight. It is a regrettable outcome for everyone who cherishes the inalienable rights stated in the American Declaration of Independence and the protections of them as provided in the Constitution and Bill of Rights. What emerged in the 1930s and worsened since then is an oppressive unconstitutional financial and political system created by power-seeking demagogues usurping and controlling the levers of government. People in America and elsewhere are not in control of their government.

The autocrats have been emboldened by those in media who share their statist agenda and egged on by a growing popular voice falling victim to socialist dogma persistently contending that a 'free lunch' is possible, even though history and logic show that no such thing exists. A grievous consequence of this lurch into a currency netherworld is the pernicious too-big-to-fail doctrine applied by governments to large banks, which is a mutual support agreement between government and the big money centre banks aided and abetted by central banks around the globe serving as the keystone to this iniquitous alliance.

As a result, individuals have been forced to use and depend on currency that is backed by nothing but government and bank promises, many – and probably most – of which are hollow because they require financial commitments to deliver purchasing power that are beyond the capacity of these institutions to fulfil. This inferior currency is forced into monopolistic circulation by government fiat, which is an affront to freedom seeking individuals because their inalienable right to choose has been taken away from them. What is more, bank created currency serves the anti-capitalist aims of socialists and autocrats.

Vladimir Lenin knew what he needed to control the polity and impose on it his Marxist agenda. In October 1917 shortly before taking power as a result of the Russian Revolution, he wrote: 'Without big banks socialism would be impossible. The big banks are the "state apparatus" which we need to bring about socialism, and which we take ready-made from capitalism.'

Bad currency interlocked with an antiquated banking system that serves the State rather than society has become an ominous, dominant force. It is insidiously destroying our capitalist society and the inalienable rights upon which individual liberty depends.

Over a century ago the famed British historian, Lord Acton, asserted that 'the issue which has swept down the centuries and which will have to be fought sooner or later is the People versus the Banks'. It is reasonable to assume that the excesses of the government-banking alliance have become so egregious that the inevitable battle he predicted is upon us, given the harmful distortions to economic life from inflation, price controls, market interventions, gold manipulation, negative interest rates, and all the other distortions and abuse resulting from central bank power. That power has made a travesty of what is today called a 'market'.

Acton also said, 'Power tends to corrupt, and absolute power corrupts absolutely', the accuracy of which is demonstrated by central bank financial repression. Confirming that power corrupts, Thomas Jefferson said:

> Whereas it appeareth that however certain forms of government are better calculated than others to protect individuals in the free exercise

> of their natural rights, and are at the same time themselves better guarded against degeneracy, yet experience hath shewn, that even under the best forms, those entrusted with power have, in time, and by slow operations, perverted it into tyranny.

Low approval ratings of government indicate a broad swathe of discontent.[121] The dissatisfaction with one's circumstances arises from being, as the saying goes, caught between the 'millstones of taxation and inflation' while confronting all the other impediments and roadblocks to an individual's pursuit of happiness.

As a currency and banking system becomes more unstable, the impact on politics is undeniable, with traditional coalitions splitting and realigning. The debate is moving from left versus right to totalitarianism versus liberty, to the tax eating parasitic class who live off big government versus the productive, self-sufficient class who just want to be left alone. This political and ideological polarisation is being fuelled by social media platforms and a biased mainstream media that conveys more political ideology than news. It is also fuelled by mendacious politicians across the spectrum.

In September 2000, economist, author, and professor at George Mason University, Walter E. Williams, wrote thoughtfully about the growing polarity of political views in America, which were already apparent two decades ago. In describing this duality, he wrote[122]:

> There's a far more important long-run question we must answer: If one group of people prefers government control and management of people's lives, and another prefers liberty and a desire to be left alone, should they be required to fight, antagonize one another, and risk bloodshed and loss of life in order to impose their preferences, or should they be able to peaceably part company and go their separate ways?
>
> Like a marriage that has gone bad, I believe there are enough irreconcilable differences between those who want to control and those want to be left alone that divorce is the only peaceable alternative. Just as in a marriage, where vows are broken, our human rights protections guaranteed by the U.S. Constitution have been grossly violated by a government instituted to protect them. Americans who are responsible for and support constitutional abrogation have no intention of mending their ways.

His recommendation to resolve the political conflict is peaceful secession, and he offered historical events as a model. 'In 1905, Norway seceded from

Sweden, Panama seceded from Columbia (1903), and West Virginia from Virginia (1863).' He then proffered an example: 'There is no reason why Texiana (Texas and Louisiana) couldn't peaceably secede, be an ally and have strong economic ties with United States.' The sharing of mutual interests is the natural foundation upon which groups form. There is another alternative without waiting for some government to act to serve your interests.

In her novel *Atlas Shrugged,* Ayn Rand suggests that one can be free by choosing not to participate. She described a mystical hideaway called Galt's Gulch where producers gathered to live peacefully and free, while avoiding the moochers using the political process as a tool for lawful plunder to undertake their anti-capitalist actions harmful to society.

When viewed figuratively rather than literally, a liberty seeking individual aiming to enter their own Galt's Gulch can live outside the system that is designed to bind them. To achieve this goal and attain the freedom reasonable people expect when living their life, some individuals move from their country of birth to other parts of the world deemed to be friendly, or at least less restrictive to the way of life being sought. These people are taking to heart the advice of Aleksandr Solzhenitsyn: 'The simple step of a courageous individual is not to take part in the lie.'

Others take their first step by minimising their reliance on national currencies, holding most of their liquidity in gold, silver, and cryptocurrencies. Fortunately, twenty-first-century technology is helping people jettison the oppressive yoke of government control and interference in their lives as they seek for themselves a social structure envisioned by the luminaries of the Age of Enlightenment.

It is time to abandon seventeenth-century monetary theory and practice that promoted State control of ledger currency. It is time to discard the shibboleths of fractional reserve banking and phantom purchasing power to expunge them from commerce. We need to re-assess and fundamentally change current banking practices as well as decide what role, if any, government has in a nation's currency system. I contend, as do many advocates of gold and cryptocurrency and the freedom they make possible, that government has no role if individual liberty is to be preserved, except to coin gold and silver in a fair competition with private enterprises also delivering precious metal currency.

Various monetary theories exist, including the Theory of Natural Money expounded in this book that explains money as an objective reality in terms of nature. It is based on the belief that all things arise from human interaction with natural properties and that money itself is a natural element.

Natural money is the enemy of sociopath authoritarians and the control they seek, who the masses follow by blind faith when beguiled by unrealistic promises. Self-reliance and the freedom it achieves is harder to pursue than the siren song of charismatic leaders and the resulting dependency on government it creates. It is easier to believe and follow than it is to think and stand alone.

Yet logic and history have established that rational self-interest, namely, Adam Smith's 'invisible hand', enables society to advance. When an individual's freedom to act is pursued with natural money and natural law, it leads to the most favourable outcome as measured by the attainment of happiness for the greatest number of people.

Candid observations of recent history indicate a low possibility that any government would be willing to take a proactive stance to adopt gold willingly. It is the nature of the political process that changes are made in reaction to crises rather than prudently designed plans aimed to correct shortcomings or apparent problems, the biggest of which is the currency being used today. Even the American Constitution was written and adopted in reaction to a crisis brought about by the deficiencies of the Confederation and the collapse of the continental currency. And few politicians today could hardly fill the shoes of the framers, so one must remain sceptical that any government will act until the next banking and currency crisis reaches the greatest moment of despair.

The inevitable collapse of fiat currency will disrupt commerce and society. It will be painful, so the sooner we act the better to mitigate the damage and repercussions. To do that it is necessary to change direction and head down the right path, which is constitutional money. To make this change, principled political leaders need to keep foremost in mind the words of John F. Kennedy:

> We are not afraid to entrust the American people with unpleasant facts, foreign ideas, alien philosophies, and competitive values. A nation that is afraid to let its people judge the truth and falsehood in an open market is a nation that is afraid of its people.

Just as meaningful, if less eloquent, are these words of Aldous Huxley: 'Facts do not cease to exist because they are ignored.' It is time for the truth to be told and purposeful actions to be taken to correct the problem.

In the words of Thoreau, 'There are a thousand hacking at the branches of evil to one who is striking at the root.' Environmental damage, wealth disparity, and all of today's other problems are the branches of evil. We need thousands striking at the root of the banking and currency evil foisting a curse on a society that desires to be free.

It is my hope that this book helps address the widespread lack of knowledge about money and currency and the general misunderstanding of their essential nature. With this knowledge the monetary system to be developed in response to a collapse of the U.S. dollar can be guided by the provisions of the Constitution and the re-establishment of natural money, with the rest of the world following America's lead.

Americans who cherish freedom are in a battle for their liberty. It is a war of ideas about government and money. The colonists won the same war for themselves and their posterity and enshrined in the Constitution the principles of liberty that guide all freedom loving Americans.

America, and indeed the world, is in a critical stage of the Prentis Cycle. It is named after an American industrialist, Henning Webb Prentis Jr., who described in his book, *Bulwarks of Freedom*, the recurring transition throughout history of the distinct phases through which societies pass:

> From bondage to spiritual faith; from spiritual faith to courage; from courage to freedom; from freedom to abundance; from abundance to selfishness; from selfishness to complacency; from complacency to apathy; from apathy to fear; from fear to dependency; and from dependency back to bondage once more.

The use of gold as money is indispensable in each and every society built with free markets and protected by the rule of natural law that safeguards everyone's inalienable right to private property and their pursuit of happiness. I am hopeful that the insights in this book will help lead to those actions needed to secure the future of a prosperous and peaceful society in which liberty flourishes.

Epilogue

On March 4, 1837, the seventh president of the United States, Andrew Jackson, gave his Farewell Address to the Nation to conclude eight years in office. Few political leaders anywhere in the world have done as much to protect liberty and in America to support and defend its Constitution. It is fitting to pay tribute to this torchbearer of liberty given his accomplishments as president and to acknowledge the message he provided for posterity in his address that explains the inextricable link between money and liberty.

The entire address is available online at the Miller Center at the University of Virginia.[123] I include here excerpts relating to money and liberty.

His address identifies the important issues explained in this book. Writing at a time before the introduction of deposit currency and when the circulating media were coin and banknotes, he confirms that gold and silver coin are the only Constitutional money. Without mentioning Gresham's Law by name, he notes how paper currency drives good currency – precious metal coin – out of circulation. He vetoed the nascent central bank, the Bank of the United States, because it was unconstitutional. In addition to his warnings about the powers of a central bank, he discusses the boom-and-bust cycle from imprudent credit expansion when banks conjure up phantom purchasing power.

Although he was speaking to his fellow Americans, his comments know no political boundary, and they are timely. It is almost as if his address could have been delivered today because he clearly speaks to the foremost matter that must be confronted and finally resolved to preserve liberty, succinctly labelled by Lord Acton as the People versus the Banks.

We have now lived almost fifty years under the Constitution framed by the sages and patriots of the Revolution...Our Constitution is no longer a doubtful experiment, and at the end of nearly half a century we find that it has preserved unimpaired the liberties of the people, secured the rights of property, and that our country has improved and is flourishing beyond any former example in the history of nations...

The necessity of watching with jealous anxiety for the preservation of the Union was earnestly pressed upon his fellow-citizens by [George Washington] in his Farewell Address. He has there told us that 'while experience shall not have demonstrated its impracticability, there will always be reason to distrust the patriotism of those who in any quarter may endeavor to weaken its bands;' and he has cautioned us in the strongest terms against the formation of parties on geographical discriminations, as one of the means which might disturb our Union and to which designing men would be likely to resort.

The lessons contained in this invaluable legacy of Washington to his countrymen should be cherished in the heart of every citizen to the latest generation; and perhaps at no period of time could they be more usefully remembered than at the present moment; for when we look upon the scenes that are passing around us and dwell upon the pages of his parting address, his paternal counsels would seem to be not merely the offspring of wisdom and foresight, but the voice of prophecy, foretelling events and warning us of the evil to come...

Each state has the unquestionable right to regulate its own internal concerns according to its own pleasure, and while it does not interfere with the rights of the people of other states or the rights of the Union, every state must be the sole judge of the measures proper to secure the safety of its citizens and promote their happiness; and all efforts on the part of people of other states to cast odium upon their institutions, and all measures calculated to disturb their rights of property or to put in jeopardy their peace and internal tranquillity, are in direct opposition to the spirit in which the Union was formed, and must endanger its safety...

It is well known that there have always been those amongst us who wish to enlarge the powers of the federal government and experience would seem to indicate that there is a tendency on the part of this government to overstep the boundaries marked out for it by the Constitution. Its legitimate authority is abundantly sufficient for all the purposes for which it was created, and its powers being expressly enumerated, there can be no justification for claiming anything beyond them. Every attempt to exercise power beyond these limits should be promptly and firmly opposed, for one evil example will lead to other measures still more mischievous; and if the principle of constructive powers or supposed advantages or temporary circumstances shall ever be permitted to justify the assumption of a power not given by the

Constitution, the federal government will before long absorb all the powers of legislation, and you will have in effect but one consolidated government. From the extent of our country, its diversified interests, different pursuits, and different habits, it is too obvious for argument that a single consolidated government would be wholly inadequate to watch over and protect its interests; and every friend of our free institutions should be always prepared to maintain unimpaired and in full vigor the rights and sovereignty of the states and to confine the action of the federal government strictly to the sphere of its appropriate duties...

The result of this decision has been felt in the rapid extinguishment of the public debt and the large accumulation of a surplus in the U.S. Treasury, notwithstanding the tariff was reduced and is now very far below the amount originally contemplated by its advocates. But, rely upon it, the design to collect an extravagant revenue and to burden you with taxes beyond the economical wants of the government is not yet abandoned. The various interests which have combined together to impose a heavy tariff and to produce an overflowing Treasury are too strong and have too much at stake to surrender the contest. The corporations and wealthy individuals who are engaged in large manufacturing establishments desire a high tariff to increase their gains. Designing politicians will support it to conciliate their favor and to obtain the means of profuse expenditure for the purpose of purchasing influence in other quarters; and since the people have decided that the federal government can not be permitted to employ its income in internal improvements, efforts will be made to seduce and mislead the citizens of the several states by holding out to them the deceitful prospect of benefits to be derived from a surplus revenue collected by the general government and annually divided among the states; and if, encouraged by these fallacious hopes, the states should disregard the principles of economy which ought to characterize every republican government, and should indulge in lavish expenditures exceeding their resources, they will before long find themselves oppressed with debts which they are unable to pay, and the temptation will become irresistible to support a high tariff in order to obtain a surplus for distribution. Do not allow yourselves, my fellow-citizens, to be misled on this subject. The federal government can not collect a surplus for such purposes without violating the principles of the Constitution and assuming powers which have not been granted. It is, moreover, a system of injustice, and if persisted in will inevitably lead to corruption, and must end in ruin. The surplus revenue will be drawn from the pockets of the people – from the farmer, the mechanic, and the laboring classes of society; but who will receive it when distributed among the states, where it is to be disposed of by leading state politicians, who have friends to favor and political partisans to gratify? It will certainly not be returned to those who paid it and who have most need of it and are honestly entitled to it. There is but one safe rule, and that is to confine the federal government rigidly within the sphere of its appropriate duties. It has no power to raise a revenue or impose taxes except for the purposes enumerated in the Constitution, and if its income is found to exceed these wants it should be forthwith reduced and the burden of the people so far lightened.

In reviewing the conflicts which have taken place between different interests in the United States and the policy pursued since the adoption of our present form of government, we find nothing that has produced such deep-seated evil as the course of legislation in relation to the currency. The Constitution of the United States unquestionably intended to secure to the people a circulating medium of gold and silver. But the establishment of a national bank by Congress, with the privilege of issuing paper money receivable in the payment of the public dues, and the unfortunate course of legislation in the several States upon the same subject, drove from general circulation the constitutional currency and substituted one of paper in its place.

It was not easy for men engaged in the ordinary pursuits of business, whose attention had not been particularly drawn to the subject, to foresee all the consequences of a currency exclusively of paper, and we ought not on that account to be surprised at the facility with which laws were obtained to carry into effect the paper system. Honest and even enlightened men are sometimes misled by the specious and plausible statements of the designing. But experience has now proved the mischiefs and dangers of a paper currency, and it rests with you to determine whether the proper remedy shall be applied.

The paper system being founded on public confidence and having of itself no intrinsic value, it is liable to great and sudden fluctuations, thereby rendering property insecure and the wages of labor unsteady and uncertain. The corporations which create the paper money can not be relied upon to keep the circulating medium uniform in amount. In times of prosperity, when confidence is high, they are tempted by the prospect of gain or by the influence of those who hope to profit by it to extend their issues of paper beyond the bounds of discretion and the reasonable demands of business; and when these issues have been pushed on from day to day, until public confidence is at length shaken, then a reaction takes place, and they immediately withdraw the credits they have given, suddenly curtail their issues, and produce an unexpected and ruinous contraction of the circulating medium, which is felt by the whole community. The banks by this means save themselves, and the mischievous consequences of their imprudence or cupidity are visited upon the public. Nor does the evil stop here. These ebbs and flows in the currency and these indiscreet extensions of credit naturally engender a spirit of speculation injurious to the habits and character of the people. We have already seen its effects in the wild spirit of speculation in the public lands and various kinds of stock which within the last year or two seized upon such a multitude of our citizens and threatened to pervade all classes of society and to withdraw their attention from the sober pursuits of honest industry. It is not by encouraging this spirit that we shall best preserve public virtue and promote the true interests of our country; but if your currency continues as exclusively paper as it now is, it will foster this eager desire to amass wealth without labor; it will multiply the number of dependents on bank accommodations and bank favors; the temptation to obtain money at any sacrifice will become stronger and stronger, and inevitably lead to corruption, which will find its way into your public councils and destroy at no distant day the purity of your government. Some of the evils which arise from this system of paper press with peculiar hardship upon the class of society least able to bear it. A portion of this currency frequently became depreciated or worthless, and all of it is easily counterfeited in such a manner as to require peculiar skill and much experience to distinguish the counterfeit from the genuine note. These frauds are most generally perpetrated in the smaller notes, which are used in the daily transactions of ordinary business, and the losses occasioned by them are commonly thrown upon the laboring classes of society, whose situation and pursuits put it out of their power to guard themselves from these impositions, and whose daily wages are necessary for their subsistence. It is the duty of every government so to regulate its currency as to protect this numerous class, as far as practicable, from the impositions of avarice and fraud. It is more especially the duty of the United States, where the government is emphatically the government of the people, and where this respectable portion of our citizens are so proudly distinguished from the laboring classes of all other nations by their independent spirit, their love of liberty, their intelligence, and their high tone of moral character. Their industry in peace is the source of our wealth and their bravery in war has covered us with glory; and the government of the United States will but ill discharge its duties if it leaves them a prey to such dishonest impositions. Yet it is evident that their interests can not be effectually protected unless silver and gold are restored to circulation.

These views alone of the paper currency are sufficient to call for immediate reform; but there is another consideration which should still more strongly press it upon your attention.

Recent events have proved that the paper-money system of this country may be used as an engine to undermine your free institutions, and that those who desire to engross all power in the hands of the few and to govern by corruption or force are aware of its power and prepared to employ it. Your banks now furnish your only circulating medium, and money is plenty or scarce according to the quantity of notes issued by them. While they have capitals not greatly disproportioned to each other, they are competitors in business, and no one of them can exercise dominion over the rest; and although in the present state of the currency these banks may and do operate injuriously upon the habits of business, the pecuniary concerns, and the moral tone of society, yet, from their number and dispersed situation, they can not combine for the purposes of political influence, and whatever may be the dispositions of some of them their power of mischief must necessarily be confined to a narrow space and felt only in their immediate neighborhoods.

But when the charter for the Bank of the United States was obtained from Congress it perfected the schemes of the paper system and gave to its advocates the position they have struggled to obtain from the commencement of the federal government to the present hour. The immense capital and peculiar privileges bestowed upon it enabled it to exercise despotic sway over the other banks in every part of the country. From its superior strength it could seriously injure, if not destroy, the business of any one of them which might incur its resentment; and it openly claimed for itself the power of regulating the currency throughout the United States. In other words, it asserted (and it undoubtedly possessed) the power to make money plenty or scarce at its pleasure, at any time and in any quarter of the Union, by controlling the issues of other banks and permitting an expansion or compelling a general contraction of the circulating medium, according to its own will. The other banking institutions were sensible of its strength, and they soon generally became its obedient instruments, ready at all times to execute its mandates; and with the banks necessarily went also that numerous class of persons in our commercial cities who depend altogether on bank credits for their solvency and means of business, and who are therefore obliged, for their own safety, to propitiate the favor of the money power by distinguished zeal and devotion in its service. The result of the ill-advised legislation which established this great monopoly was to concentrate the whole moneyed power of the Union, with its boundless means of corruption and its numerous dependents, under the direction and command of one acknowledged head, thus organizing this particular interest as one body and securing to it unity and concert of action throughout the United States, and enabling it to bring forward upon any occasion its entire and undivided strength to support or defeat any measure of the government. In the hands of this formidable power, thus perfectly organized, was also placed unlimited dominion over the amount of the circulating medium, giving it the power to regulate the value of property and the fruits of labor in every quarter of the Union, and to bestow prosperity or bring ruin upon any city or section of the country as might best comport with its own interest or policy.

We are not left to conjecture how the moneyed power, thus organized and with such a weapon in its hands, would be likely to use it. The distress and alarm which pervaded and agitated the whole country when the Bank of the United States waged war upon the people in order to compel them to submit to its demands can not yet be forgotten. The ruthless and unsparing temper with which whole cities and communities were oppressed, individuals impoverished and ruined, and a scene of cheerful prosperity suddenly changed into one of gloom and despondency ought to be indelibly impressed on the memory of the people of the United States. If such was its power in a time of peace, what would it not have been in a season of war, with an enemy at your doors? No nation but the freemen of the United States could have come out victorious from such a contest; yet, if you had not conquered, the Government would have passed from the hands of the many to the hands of the few, and this organized money power from its secret conclave would have dictated the choice of your highest officers and compelled you to make peace or war, as best suited their own wishes. The forms of your government might for a time have remained, but its living spirit would have departed from it.

The distress and sufferings inflicted on the people by the bank are some of the fruits of that system of policy which is continually striving to enlarge the authority of the federal government beyond the limits fixed by the Constitution. The powers enumerated in that instrument do not confer on Congress the right to establish such a corporation as the Bank of the United States, and the evil consequences which followed may warn us of the danger of departing from the true rule of construction and of permitting temporary circumstances or the hope of better promoting the public welfare to influence in any degree our decisions upon the extent of the authority of the federal government. Let us abide by the Constitution as it is written, or amend it in the constitutional mode if it is found to be defective.

The severe lessons of experience will, I doubt not, be sufficient to prevent Congress from again chartering such a monopoly, even if the Constitution did not present an insuperable objection to it. But you must remember, my fellow-citizens, that eternal vigilance by the people is the price of liberty, and that you must pay the price if you wish to secure the blessing. It behooves you, therefore, to be watchful in your states as well as in the federal government. The power which the moneyed interest can exercise, when concentrated under a single head and with our present system of currency, was sufficiently demonstrated in the struggle made by the Bank of the United States...

It is one of the serious evils of our present system of banking that it enables one class of society – and that by no means a numerous one – by its control over the currency, to act injuriously upon the interests of all the others and to exercise more than its just proportion of influence in political affairs. The agricultural, the mechanical, and the laboring classes have little or no share in the direction of the great moneyed corporations, and from their habits and the nature of their pursuits they are incapable of forming extensive combinations to act together with united force. Such concert of action may sometimes be produced in a single city or in a small district of country by means of personal communications with each other, but they have no regular or active correspondence with those who are engaged in similar pursuits in distant places; they have but little patronage to give to the press, and exercise but a small share of influence over it; they have no crowd of dependents about them who hope to grow rich without labor by their countenance and favor, and who are therefore always ready to execute their wishes. The planter, the farmer, the mechanic, and the laborer all know that their success depends upon their own industry and economy, and that they must not expect to become suddenly rich by the fruits of their toil. Yet these classes of society form the great body of the people of the United States; they are the bone and sinew of the country--men who love liberty and desire nothing but equal rights and equal laws, and who, moreover, hold the great mass of our national wealth, although it is distributed in moderate amounts among the millions of freemen who possess it. But with overwhelming numbers and wealth on their side they are in constant danger of losing their fair influence in the government, and with difficulty maintain their just rights against the incessant efforts daily made to encroach upon them. The mischief springs from the power which the moneyed interest derives from a paper currency which they are able to control, from the multitude of corporations with exclusive privileges which they have succeeded in obtaining in the different states, and which are employed altogether for their benefit; and unless you become more watchful in your states and check this spirit of monopoly and thirst for exclusive privileges you will in the end find that the most important powers of government have been given or bartered away, and the control over your dearest interests has passed into the hands of these corporations.

The paper-money system and its natural associations – monopoly and exclusive privileges – have already struck their roots too deep in the soil, and it will require all your efforts to check its further growth and to eradicate the evil. The men who profit by the abuses and desire to perpetuate them will continue to besiege the halls of legislation in the federal government as well as in the states, and will seek by every artifice to mislead and deceive the public servants. It is to yourselves that you must look for safety and the means of guarding and perpetuating your free institutions. In your hands is rightfully placed the sovereignty of the country, and to you everyone placed in authority is ultimately responsible. It is always in your power to see that the wishes of the people are carried into faithful execution, and their will, when once made known, must sooner or later be obeyed; and while the people remain, as I trust they ever will, uncorrupted and incorruptible, and continue watchful and jealous of their rights, the government is safe, and the cause of freedom will continue to triumph over all its enemies.

But it will require steady and persevering exertions on your part to rid yourselves of the iniquities and mischiefs of the paper system and to check the spirit of monopoly and other abuses which have sprung up with it, and of which it is the main support. So many interests are united to resist all reform on this subject that you must not hope the conflict will be a short one nor success easy. My humble efforts have not been spared during my administration of the government to restore the constitutional currency of gold and silver, and something, I trust, has been done toward the accomplishment of this most desirable object; but enough yet remains to require all your energy and perseverance. The power, however, is in your hands, and the remedy must and will be applied if you determine upon it...

In presenting to you, my fellow-citizens, these parting counsels, I have brought before you the leading principles upon which I endeavored to administer the government in the high office with which you twice honored me. Knowing that the path of freedom is continually beset by enemies who often assume the disguise of friends, I have devoted the last hours of my public life to warn you of the dangers. The progress of the United States under our free and happy institutions has surpassed the most sanguine hopes of the founders of the republic. Our growth has been rapid beyond all former example in numbers, in wealth, in knowledge, and all the useful arts which contribute to the comforts and convenience of man, and from the earliest ages of history to the present day there never have been thirteen millions of people associated in one political body who enjoyed so much freedom and happiness as the people of these United States. You have no longer any cause to fear danger from abroad; your strength and power are well known throughout the civilized world, as well as the high and gallant bearing of your sons...You have the highest of human trusts committed to your care. Providence has showered on this favored land blessings without number, and has chosen you as the guardians of freedom, to preserve it for the benefit of the human race.

Appendix A - Howard Buffett

Human Freedom Rests on Gold Redeemable Money

By Hon. Howard Buffett, Congressman from Nebraska

Reprinted from *The Commercial and Financial Chronicle*, May 6, 1948

Is there a connection between Human Freedom and A Gold Redeemable Money? At first glance it would seem that money belongs to the world of economics and human freedom to the political sphere. But when you recall that one of the first moves by Lenin, Mussolini and Hitler was to outlaw individual ownership of gold, you begin to sense that there may be some connection between money, redeemable in gold, and the rare prize known as human liberty.

Also, when you find that Lenin declared and demonstrated that a sure way to overturn the existing social order and bring about communism was by printing press paper money, then again you are impressed with the possibility of a relationship between a gold-backed money and human freedom.

In that case then certainly you and I as Americans should know the connection. We must find it even if money is a difficult and tricky subject. I suppose that if most people were asked for their views on money the almost universal answer would be that they didn't have enough of it.

In a free country the monetary unit rests upon a fixed foundation of gold or gold and silver independent of the ruling politicians. Our dollar was that kind of money before 1933. Under that system paper currency is redeemable for a certain weight of gold, at the free option and choice of the holder of paper money.

Redemption Right Insures Stability

That redemption right gives money a large degree of stability. The owner of such gold redeemable currency has economic independence. He can move around either within or without his country because his money holdings have accepted value anywhere.

For example, I hold here what is called a $20 gold piece. Before 1933, if you possessed paper money you could exchange it at your option for gold coin. This gold coin had a recognizable and definite value all over the world. It does so today. In most countries of the world this gold piece, if you have enough of them, will give you much independence. But today the ownership of such gold pieces as money in this country, Russia, and all divers other places is outlawed.

The subject of a Hitler or a Stalin is a serf by the mere fact that his money can be called in and depreciated at the whim of his rulers. That actually happened in Russia a few months ago, when the Russian people, holding cash, had to turn it in -- 10 old rubles and receive back one new ruble.

I hold here a small packet of this second kind of money -- printing press paper money -- technically known as fiat money because its value is arbitrarily fixed by rulers or statute. The amount of this money in numerals is very large. This little packet amounts to CNC $680,000. It cost me $5 at regular exchange rates. I understand I got clipped on the deal. I could have gotten $2-1/2 million if I had purchased in the black market. But you can readily see that this Chinese money, which is a fine grade of paper money, gives the individual who owns it no independence, because it has no redemptive value.

Under such conditions the individual citizen is deprived of freedom of movement. He is prevented from laying away purchasing power for the future. He becomes dependent upon the goodwill of the politicians for his daily bread. Unless he lives on land that will sustain him, freedom for him does not exist.

You have heard a lot of oratory on inflation from politicians in both parties. Actually that oratory and the inflation maneuvering around here are mostly sly efforts designed to lay the blame on the other party's doorstep. All our politicians regularly announce their intention to stop inflation. I believe I can show that until they move to restore your right to own gold that talk is hogwash.

Paper Systems End in Collapse

But first let me clear away a bit of underbrush. I will not take time to review the history of paper money experiments. So far as I can discover, paper money systems have always wound up with collapse and economic chaos.

Here somebody might like to interrupt and ask if we are not now on the gold standard. That is true, internationally, but not domestically. Even though there is a lot of gold buried down at Fort Knox, that gold is not subject to demand by American citizens. It could all be shipped out of this country without the people having any chance to prevent it. That is not probable in the near future, for a small trickle of gold is still coming in. But it can happen in the future. This gold is temporarily and theoretically partial security for our paper currency. But in reality it is not.

Also, currently, we are enjoying a large surplus in tax revenues, but this happy condition is only a phenomenon of postwar inflation and our global WPA. It cannot be relied upon as an accurate gauge of our financial condition. So we should disregard the current flush treasury in considering this problem.

From 1930-1946 your government went into the red every year and the debt steadily mounted. Various plans have been proposed to reverse this spiral of debt.

One is that a fixed amount of tax revenue each year would go for debt reduction. nother is that Congress be prohibited by statute from appropriating more than anticipated revenues in peacetime. Still another is that 10% of the taxes be set aside each year for debt reduction.

All of these proposals look good. But they are unrealistic under our paper money system. They will not stand against postwar spending pressures. The accuracy of this conclusion has already been demonstrated.

The Budget and Paper Money

Under the streamlining Act passed by Congress in 1946, the Senate and the House were required to fix a maximum budget each year. In 1947 the Senate and the House could not reach an agreement on this maximum budget so that the law was ignored.

On March 4 this year the House and Senate agreed on a budget of $37-1/2 billion. Appropriations already passed or on the docket will most certainly take expenditures past the $40 billion mark. The statute providing for a maximum budget has fallen by the wayside even in the first two years it has been operating and in a period of prosperity.

There is only one way that these spending pressures can be halted, and that is to restore the final decision on public spending to the producers of the nation. The producers of wealth -- taxpayers -- must regain their right to obtain gold in exchange for the fruits of their labor. This restoration would give the people the final say-so on governmental spending, and would enable wealth producers to control the issuance of paper money and bonds.

I do not ask you to accept this contention outright. But if you look at the political facts of life, I think you will agree that this action is the only genuine cure.

There is a parallel between business and politics which quickly illustrates the weakness in political control of money.

Each of you is in business to make profits. If your firm does not make profits, it goes out of business. If I were to bring a product to you and say, this item is splendid for your customers, but you would have to sell it without profit, or even at a loss that would put you out of business. Well, I would get thrown out of your office, perhaps politely, but certainly quickly. our business must have profits.

In politics votes have a similar vital importance to an elected official. That situation is not ideal, but it exists, probably because generally no one gives up power willingly.

Perhaps you are right now saying to yourself: 'That's just what I have always thought. The politicians are thinking of votes when they ought to think about the future of the country. What we need is a Congress with some 'guts.' If we elected a Congress with intestinal fortitude, it would stop the spending all right!'

I went to Washington with exactly that hope and belief. But I have had to discard it as unrealistic. Why? Because an economy Congressman under our printing-press money system is in the position of a fireman running into a burning building with a hose that is not connected with the water plug. His courage may be commendable, but he is not hooked up right at the other end of the line. So it is now with a Congressman working for economy. There is no sustained hookup with the taxpayers to give him strength.

When the people's right to restrain public spending by demanding gold coin was taken from them, the automatic flow of strength from the grass-roots to enforce economy in Washington was disconnected. I'll come back to this later.

In January you heard the President's message to Congress, or at least you heard about it. It made Harry Hopkins, in memory, look like Old Scrooge himself.

Truman's State of the Union message was 'pie-in-the- sky' for everybody except business. These promises were to be expected under our paper currency system. Why? Because his continuance in office depends upon pleasing a majority of the pressure groups.

Before you judge him too harshly for that performance, let us speculate on his thinking. Certainly he can persuade himself that the Republicans would do the same thing if they were in power. Already he has characterized our talk of economy as 'just conversation.' To date we have been proving him right. Neither the President nor the Republican Congress is under real compulsion to cut Federal spending. And so neither one does so, and the people are largely helpless. But it was not always this way.

Before 1933 the people themselves had an effective way to demand economy. Before 1933, whenever the people became disturbed over Federal spending, they could go to the banks, redeem their paper currency in gold, and wait for common sense to return to Washington.

Raids on Treasury

That happened on various occasions and conditions sometimes became strained, but nothing occurred like the ultimate consequences of paper money inflation.

Today Congress is constantly besieged by minority groups seeking benefits from the public treasury. Often these groups control enough votes in many Congressional districts to change the outcome of elections. And so Congressmen find it difficult to persuade themselves not to give in to pressure groups. With no bad immediate consequence it becomes expedient to accede to a spending demand. The Treasury is seemingly inexhaustible. Besides the unorganized taxpayers back home may not notice this particular expenditure – and so it goes.

Let's take a quick look at just the payroll pressure elements. On June 30, 1932, there were 2,196,151 people receiving regular monthly checks from the Federal Treasury. On June 30, 1947, this number had risen to the fantastic total of 14,416,393 persons.

This 14-1/2 million figure does not include about 2 million receiving either unemployment benefits of soil conservation checks. However, it includes about 2 million GI's getting schooling or on-the-job-training. Excluding them, the total is about 12-1/2 million or 500% more than in 1932. If each beneficiary accounted for four votes (and only half exhibited this payroll allegiance response) this group would account for 25 million votes, almost by itself enough votes to win any national election.

Besides these direct payroll voters, there are a large number of State, county and local employees whose compensation in part comes from Federal subsidies and grants-in-aid.

Then there are many other kinds of pressure groups. There are businesses that are being enriched by national defense spending and foreign handouts. These firms, because of the money they can spend on propaganda, may be the most dangerous of all.

If the Marshall Plan meant $100 million worth of profitable business for your firm, wouldn't you invest a few thousands or so to successfully propagandize for the Marshall Plan? And if you were a foreign government, getting billions, perhaps you could persuade your prospective suppliers here to lend a hand in putting that deal through Congress.

Taxpayer the Forgotten Man

Far away from Congress is the real forgotten man, the taxpayer who foots the bill. He is in a different spot from the tax-eater or the business that makes millions from spending schemes. He cannot afford to spend his time trying to oppose Federal expenditures. He has to earn his own living and carry the burden of taxes as well.

But for most beneficiaries a Federal paycheck soon becomes vital in his life. He usually will spend his full energies if necessary to hang onto this income.

The taxpayer is completely outmatched in such an unequal contest. Always heretofore he possessed an equalizer. If government finances weren't run according to his idea of soundness he had an individual right to protect himself by obtaining gold.

With a restoration of the gold standard, Congress would have to again resist handouts. That would work this way. If Congress seemed receptive to reckless spending schemes, depositors' demands over the country for gold would soon become serious. That alarm in turn would quickly be reflected in the halls of Congress. The legislators would learn from the banks back home and from the Treasury officials that confidence in the Treasury was endangered.

Congress would be forced to confront spending demands with firmness. The gold standard acted as a silent watchdog to prevent unlimited public spending.

I have only briefly outlined the inability of Congress to resist spending pressures during periods of prosperity. What Congress would do when a depression comes is a question I leave to your imagination.

I have not time to portray the end of the road of all paper money experiments. It is worse than just the high prices that you have heard about. Monetary chaos was followed in Germany by a Hitler; in Russia by all-out Bolshevism; and in other nations by more or less tyranny. It can take a nation to communism without external influences.

Suppose the frugal savings of the humble people of America continue to deteriorate in the next 10 years as they have in the past 10 years? Some day the people will almost certainly flock to 'a man on horseback' who says he will stop inflation by price-fixing, wage-fixing, and rationing. When currency loses its exchange value the processes of production and distribution are demoralized. For example, we still have rent-fixing and rental housing remains a desperate situation.

For a long time shrewd people have been quietly hoarding tangibles in one way or another. Eventually, this individual movement into tangibles will become a general stampede unless corrective action comes soon.

Is Time Propitious?

Most opponents of free coinage of gold admit that that restoration is essential, but claim the time is not propitious. Some argue that there would be a scramble for gold and our enormous gold reserves would soon be exhausted.

Actually this argument simply points up the case. If there is so little confidence in our currency that restoration of gold coin would cause our gold stocks to disappear, then we must act promptly. The danger was recently highlighted by Mr. Allan Sproul, President of the Federal Reserve Bank of New York, who said:

> 'Without our support (the Federal Reserve System), under present conditions, almost any sale of government bonds, undertaken for whatever purpose, laudable or otherwise, would be likely to find an almost bottomless market on the first day support was withdrawn.'

Our finances will never be brought into order until Congress is compelled to do so. Making our money redeemable in gold will create this compulsion.

The paper money disease has been a pleasant habit thus far and will not he dropped voluntarily any more than a dope user will without a struggle give up narcotics. But in each case the end of the road is not a desirable prospect.

I can find no evidence to support a hope that our fiat paper money venture will fare better ultimately than such experiments in other lands. Because of our economic strength the paper money disease here may take many years to run its course. But we can be approaching the critical stage. When that day arrives, our political rulers will probably find that foreign war and ruthless regimentation is the cunning alternative to domestic strife. That was the way out for the paper-money economy of Hitler and others.

In these remarks I have only touched the high points of this problem. I hope that I have given you enough information to challenge you to make a serious study of it.

I warn you that politicians of both parties will oppose the restoration of gold, although they may outwardly seemingly favor it. Also those elements here and abroad who are getting rich from the continued American inflation will oppose a return to sound money. You must be prepared to meet their opposition intelligently and vigorously. They have had 15 years of unbroken victory.

But, unless you are willing to surrender your children and your country to galloping inflation, war and slavery, then this cause demands your support. For if human liberty is to survive in America, we must win the battle to restore honest money.

There is no more important challenge facing us than this issue -- the restoration of your freedom to secure gold in exchange for the fruits of your labors.

Appendix B - Gold M3

	Gold M3	Mined	Δ			Gold M3	Mined	Δ			Gold M3	Mined	Δ
1900	15,695	386	2.5%		**1940**	43,337	1310	3.0%		**1980**	86,641	1220	1.4%
1901	16,088	395	2.5%		**1941**	44,591	1080	2.9%		**1981**	87,921	1280	1.5%
1902	16,534	451	2.8%		**1942**	45,656	1120	2.4%		**1982**	89,261	1340	1.5%
1903	17,027	496	3.0%		**1943**	46,480	896	1.8%		**1983**	90,661	1400	1.6%
1904	17,550	526	3.1%		**1944**	47,222	813	1.6%		**1984**	92,121	1460	1.6%
1905	18,122	575	3.3%		**1945**	47,934	762	1.5%		**1985**	93,651	1530	1.7%
1906	18,728	608	3.3%		**1946**	48,657	860	1.5%		**1986**	95,261	1610	1.7%
1907	19,349	623	3.3%		**1947**	49,385	900	1.5%		**1987**	96,921	1660	1.7%
1908	20,016	668	3.4%		**1948**	50,134	932	1.5%		**1988**	98,791	1870	1.9%
1909	20,699	687	3.4%		**1949**	50,905	964	1.5%		**1989**	100,801	2010	2.0%
1910	21,384	689	3.3%		**1950**	51,701	879	1.6%		**1990**	102,981	2180	2.2%
1911	22,081	699	3.3%		**1951**	52,481	883	1.5%		**1991**	105,141	2160	2.1%
1912	22,784	705	3.2%		**1952**	53,283	868	1.5%		**1992**	107,401	2260	2.1%
1913	23,486	694	3.1%		**1953**	54,082	864	1.5%		**1993**	109,681	2280	2.1%
1914	24,159	663	2.9%		**1954**	54,928	965	1.6%		**1994**	111,941	2260	2.1%
1915	24,870	704	2.9%		**1955**	55,814	947	1.6%		**1995**	114,171	2230	2.0%
1916	25,556	685	2.8%		**1956**	56,737	978	1.7%		**1996**	116,461	2290	2.0%
1917	26,188	631	2.5%		**1957**	57,698	1020	1.7%		**1997**	118,911	2450	2.1%
1918	26,767	578	2.2%		**1958**	58,688	1050	1.7%		**1998**	121,411	2500	2.1%
1919	27,306	550	2.0%		**1959**	59,750	1130	1.8%		**1999**	123,981	2570	2.1%
1920	27,808	507	1.8%		**1960**	60,861	1190	1.9%		**2000**	126,571	2590	2.1%
1921	28,306	498	1.8%		**1961**	62,006	1230	1.9%		**2001**	129,171	2600	2.1%
1922	28,788	481	1.7%		**1962**	63,231	1290	2.0%		**2002**	131,721	2550	2.0%
1923	29,343	554	1.9%		**1963**	64,533	1340	2.1%		**2003**	134,261	2540	1.9%
1924	29,922	592	2.0%		**1964**	65,878	1390	2.1%		**2004**	136,681	2420	1.8%
1925	30,500	591	1.9%		**1965**	67,253	1440	2.1%		**2005**	139,151	2470	1.8%
1926	31,095	602	2.0%		**1966**	68,629	1450	2.0%		**2006**	141,521	2370	1.7%
1927	31,688	597	1.9%		**1967**	69,976	1420	2.0%		**2007**	143,881	2350	1.7%
1928	32,275	603	1.9%		**1968**	71,324	1440	1.9%		**2008**	146,171	2300	1.6%
1929	32,873	609	1.9%		**1969**	72,672	1450	1.9%		**2009**	148,621	2490	1.7%
1930	33,523	648	2.0%		**1970**	74,058	1480	1.9%		**2010**	151,361	2600	1.8%
1931	34,216	695	2.1%		**1971**	75,406	1450	1.8%		**2011**	154,180	2680	1.9%

	Gold M3	Mined	Δ			Gold M3	Mined	Δ			Gold M3	Mined	Δ
1932	34,966	754	2.2%		**1972**	76,781	1390	1.8%		**2012**	156,930	2750	1.8%
1933	35,756	793	2.3%		**1973**	78,131	1350	1.8%		**2013**	159,890	2960	1.9%
1934	36,607	841	2.4%		**1974**	79,381	1250	1.6%		**2014**	162,940	3050	1.9%
1935	37,540	924	2.5%		**1975**	80,581	1200	1.5%		**2015**	166,060	3120	1.9%
1936	38,565	1030	2.7%		**1976**	81,791	1210	1.5%		**2016**	169,170	3110	1.9%
1937	39,657	1100	2.8%		**1977**	83,001	1210	1.5%		**2017**	172,400	3230	1.9%
1938	40,830	1170	3.0%		**1978**	84,211	1210	1.5%		**2018**	175,700	3300	1.9%
1939	42,059	1230	3.0%		**1979**	85,421	1210	1.4%		**2019**	179,000	3300	1.9%
										2020	182,200	3200	1.8%

Further Reading

A History of Gold and Money, 1450-1920, Pierre Vilar, Foundations of History Library, 1976.

A History of the Precious Metals, Alexander del Mar, George Bell & Sons, 1880.

A Monetary History of the United States 1867-1960, Milton Friedman and Anna Jacobson Schwartz, Princeton University Press, 1963.

A Treatise on the Coins of the Realm, Charles Jenkinson, Earl of Liverpool, Effingham Wilson, 1880.

Denationalisation of Money, Friedrich A. Hayek, Institute of Economic Affairs, 1978.

Economics and the Public Welfare, Benjamin Anderson, D. Van Nostrand Company, Inc., 1963.

History of The Bank of England, A. Andreades, P.S. King & Son, 1909.

Human Action: A Treatise on Economics, Ludwig von Mises, Contemporary Books, 1963.

Jefferson and the Rights of Man, Dumas Malone, Little Brown and Co., 1951.

Organization of Debt into Currency, Charles Holt Carroll, D. Van Nostrand Co. Inc., 1964.

Richard Cantillon: Entrepreneur and Economist, Antoin E. Murphy, Clarendon Press, 1986.

Socialism, Ludwig von Mises, Liberty Classics, 1981.

The Bank of England: A History, (Two Volumes), Sir John Clapham, Cambridge Press, 1944.

The Case for a 100 Percent Gold Dollar, Murray N. Rothbard, Cobden Press, 1984.

The First Nine Years of the Bank of England, James E. Thorold Rogers, Clarendon Press, 1887.

The Market for Liberty, Morris and Linda Tannehill, Laissez Faire Books, 1984.

The Mystery of Banking, Murray Rothbard, Richardson & Snyder, 1983.

The Pound Sterling, A History of English Money, A.E. Feavearyear, Oxford Press, 1932.

The State and the Monetary System, Kevin Dowd, St Martin's Press, 1989.

The Theory of Money and Credit, Ludwig von Mises, Yale University Press, 1953.

The Ways and Means of Payment, Stephen Colwell, J.B. Lillincott & Co., 1859.

Total War and The Constitution, Edward S. Corwin, Alfred A. Knopf, 1947.

Two Treatises of Government, John Locke, Mentor Books, 1960.

What Has Government Done to Our Money?, Murray N. Rothbard, Mises Institute, 1990.

Endnotes

[1] https://www.pursuit-of-happiness.org/history-of-happiness/aristotle/

[2] Ferguson, Niall, *The Great Degeneration: How Institutions Decay and Economies Die*, Penguin Books Ltd., United Kingdom, 2012.

[3] *Financial Times*, London, May 17, 2021.

[4] Thomas Jefferson letter to John Taylor, May 28, 1816. https://founders.archives.gov/documents/Jefferson/03-10-02-0053

[5] The bullion coins that no longer circulate as currency but remain coins of the realm are exceptions, e.g., the British sovereign.

[6] See *The Introduction of Paper Currency and Banking* in Chapter 6.

[7] *The American Mercury*, October 1957, pp. 79-80

[8] https://memory.loc.gov/service/gdc/scd0001/2006/20060517001te/20060517001te.pdf

[9] 'What's a better bet right now: a house in the UK or gold?', *MoneyWeek*, Dominic Frisby, June 24, 2020.

[10] https://www.marketwatch.com/story/why-buffet-thinks-investing-in-gold-is-stupid-2013-04-18

[11] Bloomberg: 'JP Morgan's Metals Desk Was a Criminal Enterprise, U.S. [Government] Says' https://www.bloomberg.com/news/articles/2019-09-16/jpmorgan-s-metals-desk-was-a-criminal-enterprise-u-s-says

[12] https://founders.archives.gov/documents/Madison/01-12-02-0248

[13] Murray N. Rothbard, *The Mystery of Banking*, Second Edition (Ludwig von Mises Institute, Auburn, Alabama, 2008).

[14] Daniel J. Mitchell, 'Comparing the Economic Growth of East Germany to West Germany: A History Lesson', May 11, 2019.

[15] Adam Michel, 'Data Show Poorest Americans Are Benefiting Most from Strong Economy', May 8, 2019.

[16] 'Our age has to face great economic troubles. But this is not a crisis of capitalism. It is the crisis of interventionism...' Ludwig von Mises, *SOCIALISM An Economic and Sociological Analysis*, (New Haven: Yale University Press, 1951).

[17] John Maynard Keynes, *The Economic Consequences of the Peace*, New York: Harcourt, Brace, and Howe: 1920.

[18] Jean-Baptiste Say, *A Treatise on Political Economy or the Production, Distribution and Consumption of Wealth*, 1803.

[19] 'Our costly dalliance with Lord Keynes', by Alasdair Macleod, *Goldmoney Insights*, August 22, 2019. See also: 'The Origins of Keynesian Economics: How Did It Get So Popular?', by Robert Blumen, *Mises Wire*, June 5, 2021.

[20] For example, the cost of storing gold in the company I founded, Goldmoney, can be as low as 0.12% per annum, which can be less than some banks charge for current account fees.

[21]https://www.goldmoney.com/images/media/Files/Old_GM_WP/theabovegroundgoldstock.pdf

[22] Myra P. Saefong, 'In 20 years, the world may run out of minable gold', MarketWatch, March 31, 2015.

[23] Further analysis of Mr Roosevelt's dollar devaluation and the confiscation of privately owned gold is available in an article I published on November 23, 2011, 'The Myths and Reality of Gold Confiscation' https://www.fgmr.com/myths-and-reality-of-gold-confiscation/

[24] For a detailed discussion on contango, see *The Golden Sextant* by Reginald H. Howe, 1991. http://www.goldensextant.com

[25] https://www.joc.com/drexel-burnhams-victims-included-small-investors-and-big-countries_19920301.html

[26] Reuters: 'JP Morgan to pay $920 million for manipulating precious metals', September 29, 2020, and Bloomberg: 'Inside the JPMorgan Trading Desk the U.S. Called a Crime Ring', September 28, 2020.

[27] 'Gold Policy in the 1930s', Mark Thornton, Richard Timberlake, Jr., Thomas Thompson, Independent Institute, May 1, 1999.

[28] https://wikileaks.org/plusd/cables/09BEIJING1134_a.html

[29] An analysis of the use of taxes to impair precious metals from circulating as currency is beyond the scope of this book, but some readers may find this article in Forbes to be interesting.
https://www.forbes.com/sites/briandomitrovic/2014/09/08/transacting-in-gold-can-shaft-the-irs/

[30] 'Central banks are selling gold, FT reports - or want markets to think so', Chris Powell, GATA.org, October 7, 2020.

[31] https://www.bloomberg.com/opinion/articles/2017-02-17/dole-food-had-too-many-shares

[32] Georg Friedrich Knapp, *The State Theory of Money* (London: Macmillan and Co., 1924).

[33] See *The Introduction of Paper Currency and Banking* in Chapter 6.
[34] Copper coins can trace their origin to 600-BCE. Copper was viewed to be a valuable metal, but not a precious one. The first copper coin in Britain is the penny, which was first minted in 1714 to replace the silver penny.
[35] James Turk and John Rubino, *The Money Bubble: What To Do Before It Pops*, Dollar Collapse Press, 2014.
[36] , Murray N. Rothbard, *The Mystery of Banking* Second Edition (Ludwig von Mises Institute, Auburn, Alabama, 2008).
[37] https://www.goldmoney.com/research/goldmoney-insights/time-to-learn-about-money
[38] https://www.etymonline.com/word/currency
[39] Thomas Babington Macaulay, *The History of England from the Accession of James II,* Chapter XX, London: 1848.
[40] 'The Bank of England Restriction. 1797-1821.' *The North American Review* 105, no. 217 (1867): 393-434.
http://www.jstor.org/stable/25108102
[41] Carpenter, Cecil C. 'The English Specie Resumption of 1821.' *Southern Economic Journal* 5, no. 1 (1938): 45-54.
[42] Horsefield, J. K. 'The Origins of the Bank Charter Act, 1844.' *Economica*, New Series, 11, no. 44 (1944): 180-89.
[43] Adie, Douglas K. 'English Bank Deposits before 1844.' *The Economic History Review* 23, no. 2 (1970): 285-97.
[44] Anthony Daniels: 'Political correctness is communist propaganda writ small. In my study of communist societies, I came to the conclusion that the purpose of communist propaganda was not to persuade or convince, nor to inform, but to humiliate; and therefore, the less it corresponded to reality the better.' https://en.wikiquote.org/wiki/Anthony_Daniels_(psychiatrist)
[45] 'The Sordid Origin of Hate-Speech Laws', Jacob Mchangama, Hoover Institution, December 1, 2011.
[46] https://thenationalpulse.com/commentary/alan-greenspan-big-reveal-secret-recipe/
[47] Marjorie Deane and Robert Pringle, *The Central Banks*, Penguin Books Ltd, Harmondsworth, England, 1994.
[48] https://en.wikiquote.org/wiki/Woodrow_Wilson. See also: 'The unhappiness of Woodrow Wilson', Andrew Leonard, Salon.com, December 21, 2007.
[49] https://www.businessinsider.com/ben-bernanke-explains-why-well-never-see-another-gold-standard-2012-3?r=US&IR=T
[50] Edward Bernays, *Propaganda*, Horace Liveright Inc., New York, 1928.
[51] *The Theory of Money and Credit*, Ludwig von Mises, New Haven,

Connecticut: Yale University Press, 1953.

[52] *Gold Standard,* Michael D. Bordo, The Library of Economics and Liberty https://www.econlib.org/library/Enc/GoldStandard.html

[53] https://home.treasury.gov/system/files/266/CJ_FY09-BPD.pdf

[54] Congressional Record: Proceedings and Debates of the 76th Congress, First Session, Volume 84, Part 11, p639.

[55] Ibid. 'Gold Policy in the 1930s'.

[56] For example, the list of felonies and criminal monetary penalties imposed on JP Morgan Chase Bank is documented here: https://www.corp-research.org/jpmorganchase Also, the former International Monetary Fund head, whose predecessor resigned in 2011 over a sex assault scandal, was found guilty of criminal charges for making a government pay-out when serving as the French finance minister but instead of a career ending event, did not face any punishment and was subsequently appointed head of the European Central Bank.
https://www.independent.co.uk/news/world/europe/christine-lagarde-convicted-imf-head-found-guilty-negligence-fraud-trial-a7484586.html

[57] William Stearns Davis, *The Influence of Wealth in Imperial Rome*, Macmillan Company, New York, 1910.

[58] James Turk and John Rubino, *The Coming Collapse of the Dollar*, Doubleday, New York, 2004.

[59] 'Biden shows he will wield US financial system as foreign policy weapon' by Katrina Manson, *Financial Times*, April 17, 2021.

[60] https://iea.org.uk/wp-content/uploads/2016/07/Denationalisation%20of%20Money.pdf

[61] The Federal Reserve stopped reporting M3 in February 2006. The M3 measure reported here is provided by: www.shadowstats.com

[62] https://en.wikipedia.org/wiki/Reality-based_community

[63] The Federal Reserve stopped reporting M3 in February 2006. The M3 measure reported here is provided by: www.shadowstats.com

[64] Turk and Rubino, ibid.

[65] Is There Really Gold in Ft. Knox? By Joshua Green, *The Atlantic*, June 24, 2011.

[66] https://www.fgmr.com/myths-and-reality-of-gold-confiscation/

[67] 'Heading Toward the Tipping Point', 17 April 2019.
https://www.fgmr.com/heading-toward-the-tipping-point/

[68] Monetary Inflation's Game of Hide-and-Seek, Richard M. Ebeling, American Institute for Economic Research, May 18, 2021.

[69] The *Wall Street Journal*, August 29, 2011.

[70] https://www.centralbanking.com/central-banking/news/1418468/trichet-intervention-central-bank-weapon

[71] 'The Real Reasons for the Upcoming War With Iraq' by W. Clark, Independent Media Center. January 2003.
https://www.cse.unsw.edu.au/~norman/CurrentAffairs/DeeperNew.html

[72] 'The Unraveling of the American Empire', Chris Hedges, Consortium News, April 19, 2021.

[73] 'Sanctions Are Destroying U.S. Dollar's Status as World's Top Currency' by Tom O'Connor, April 5, 2021.
https://www.newsweek.com/sanctions-destroying-us-dollar-status-top-currency-1580619

[74] See also 'The emerging evidence of hyperinflation', Alasdair Macleod, Goldmoney Insights, October 1, 2020.

[75] 'The Weimar Republic, Hyperinflation, and How They Paved the Way for Hitler' by Rabbi Berel Wein, JewishHistory.org, March 5, 2010.

[76] 'Let's Be Honest About Gold: It's a Pet Rock' by Jason Zweig, The *Wall Street Journal*, July 17, 2015.

[77] Using the Fear Index to measure valuation is explained more fully in *The Money Bubble*, Turk and Rubino, 2014.

[78] https://www.archives.gov/founding-docs/declaration-transcript

[79] For an in-depth legal and historical analysis of America's monetary systems before and after the adoption of the Constitution, I recommend: *Pieces of Eight: The Monetary Powers and Disabilities of the United States Constitution* by Edwin Vieira

[80] 'The Swiss Confederation In the Eyes of America's Founders' by Stephen P. Halbrook, J.D., Georgetown University Law Center, 2012.
https://www.stephenhalbrook.com/law_review_articles/swiss_confederation.pdf

[81] Currently Mr Guy Parmelin, since 1 January 2021.

[82] https://millercenter.org/the-presidency/presidential-speeches/september-19-1796-farewell-address

[83] https://www.archives.gov/philadelphia/exhibits/franklin/currency.html

[84] 'Mises on the Myth of Marx' by Carmen Elena Dorobăţ, December 26, 2016.
https://mises.org/wire/mises-myth-marx

[85] A.J.P. Taylor, *Bismarck. The Man and the Statesman*, London: Hamish Hamilton, 1955.
https://en.wikipedia.org/wiki/State_Socialism_(Germany)

[86] G. Edward Griffin, *The Creature from Jekyll Island, A Second Look at the*

Federal Reserve, American Media, West Lake Village, California, 2010.
[87] See: 'The Myths and Reality of Gold Confiscation' https://www.fgmr.com/myths-and-reality-of-gold-confiscation/
[88] https://en.wikipedia.org/wiki/Howard_Buffett
[89] https://founders.archives.gov/documents/Jefferson/03-01-02-0088
[90] The framers wrote the Constitution with provisions so that it could be amended. They addressed the slavery issue, which they regrettably failed to end. Slavery and involuntary servitude were finally ended with the 13th Amendment.
[91] 'The Justice of Natural Liberty', Buchanan, James M., *The Journal of Legal Studies* 5, no. 1 (1976). See also: 'The Essential James Buchanan', Donald J. Boudreaux and Randall G. Holcombe, Fraser Institute, 2021.
[92] *Testimony of Two Men* by Taylor Caldwell, Doubleday & Company, Garden City, New York, 1968.
[93] https://tile.loc.gov/storage services/service/ll/usrep/usrep294/usrep294330/usrep294330.pdf
[94] 'Labor Shortage Draws Attention of U.S. Lawmakers', *Wall Street Journal*, June 3, 2021.
[95] 'Decline in Cancer Death Rate Largely Driven by Decreasing Lung Cancer Mortality', Andrea S. Blevins Primeau, Cancer Therapy Advisor.com, January 28, 2021. https://www.cancertherapyadvisor.com/home/cancer-topics/lung-cancer/lung-cancer-nsclc-mortality-projected-decrease-risk/
[96] C.S. Lewis, *God in the Dock: Essays on Theology and Ethics*, William B Eerdmans Publishing Co, 1970.
[97] Dean and Pringle, 1994
[98]https://www.goldmoney.com/images/media/Files/Old_GM_WP/barbarous_relic100511.pdf
[99] The Wall Street Journal, August 29, 2011
[100] 'The idea the state has been shrinking for 40 years is a myth', Financial Times, Ruchir Sharma, April 25, 2021.
[101] 'Life Within The Matrix Is Our Future', P. C. Roberts, Paul Craig Roberts Institute for Political Economy, October 13, 2020.
[102] An increase in gold's rate of exchange from $1771 to $3000 is the same percentage increase as occurred in 1933, $20.67 to $35.00 per ounce.
[103] F$ M2 is used in Figure 19 and subsequently because the Federal Reserve stopped reporting F$ M3.
[104] https://mises.org/library/mercantilism
[105] https://www.youtube.com/watch?v=b50jply_hFU
[106] Milton Friedman, *A Program for Monetary Stability* (New York: Fordham

University Press, 1960).
https://en.wikipedia.org/wiki/Friedman%27s_k-percent_rule
[107] https://ourworldindata.org/world-population-growth#how-has-world-population-growth-changed-over-time
[108] 'The Simon Abundance Index', Gale L. Pooley and Marian L. Tupy, Cato Institute, December 4, 2018.
[109] https://mises.org/library/speaking-truth-monetary-power
[110] 'The free markets slow death', Alasdair Macleod, Goldmoney Insights, October 10, 2013.
[111] Chad Stone et al., 'A Guide to Statistics on Historical Trends in Income Inequality', Centre on Budget and Policy Priorities, December 11, 2018.
[112] 'The General Welfare Clause: An Exploration of Original Intent and Constitutional Limits Pertaining to the Rapidly Expanding Federal Budget' by Steven T. Voigt
https://dspace2.creighton.edu/xmlubitstream/handle/10504/40671/20_43CreightonLRev543(2009-2010).pdf
[113] *Social Security: Lies, Myths and Reality*, James Turk, Greenfield Books, 1992.
[114] 'Elon Musk's SpaceX', TechStartups, Nickie Louise August 3, 2020.
[115] Neil Monnery, *Architect of Prosperity: Sir John Cowperthwaite & the Making of Hong Kong*; London Publishing Partnership, 2017.
[116] 'Billionaire Hedge-Fund Manager Warns a 'Revolution' Is Coming', Bess Levin, *Vanity Fair*, April 5, 2019.
[117] Eamonn Butler, *Foundations of a Free Society*, The Institute of Economic Affairs, London 2013.
[118] 'In Praise of Hayek's Masterwork', Goldmoney Insights, May 9, 2019.
[119] 'Let's Level the Playing Field between the Dollar and Competing Currencies', Michael Milano, Mises Institute, May 19, 2021.
[120] https://www.minneapolisfed.org/about-us/monetary-policy/inflation-calculator/consumer-price-index-1913-
[121] https://news.gallup.com/poll/1597/confidence-institutions.aspx
[122] http://walterewilliams.com/it%27s-time-to-part-company/
[123] https://millercenter.org/the-presidency/presidential-speeches/march-4-1837-farewell-address For clarity and conformity to current usage, I have changed 'General Government' to 'federal government'.

Index

Printed in Great Britain
by Amazon

16985823R00203